793- 4333

254 5143

*downtown
west end
S. end*

# Building a
# New Boston

# Building a New Boston

## Politics and Urban Renewal 1950–1970

**Thomas H. O'Connor**

Northeastern
University Press

Boston

Northeastern University Press

*Library of Congress Cataloging-in-Publication Data*

O'Connor, Thomas H., 1922–
    Building a new Boston  :  politics and urban renewal, 1950–1970  /
Thomas H. O'Connor.
        p.   cm.
    Includes bibliographical references and index.
    ISBN 1-55553-161-X (alk. paper)—ISBN 1-55553-246-2 (pbk.: alk. paper)
    1. Urban renewal—Massachusetts—Boston—History—20th century.
2. Boston (Mass.)—Social conditions. 3. Boston (Mass.)—Economic
conditions. 4. Boston (Mass.)—Politics and government. I. Title.
HT177.B6O36    1993
307.3'416'0974461—dc20                    92-42258

Designed by Peter Blaiwas

Composed in Sabon by Coghill Composition Co., Richmond,
Virginia. Printed and bound by Thomson-Shore, Dexter, Michigan.
The paper is Glatfelter Offset, an acid-free sheet.

MANUFACTURED IN THE UNITED STATES OF AMERICA
99  98  97  96  95      5  4  3  2

*To* JEANNE *and* MICHAEL
*who have made their parents very proud*

# Contents

*List of Illustrations*   ix

*Introduction*   xi

1. *"A Hopeless Backwater"*   3

2. *Forming a New Coalition*   37

3. *Visions and Designs*   66

4. *"Where's Boston?"*   89

5. *Trial and Error*   113

6. *A New Beginning*   150

7. *"The Stars Were Right"*   182

8. *Progress and Populism*   210

9. *Changing Times*  249

*Conclusion*  284

*Notes*  301

*Bibliography*  331

*Index*  335

# Illustrations

Map of Boston   2
Long Wharf and the Custom House tower, 1915   5
Quincy Market, ca. 1905   16
Curley campaigning for mayor in 1949   27
A triumphant John B. Hynes   33
Mayor Hynes and the planning commission   46
Otto and Muriel Snowden   58
Slum clearing begins in the South End   76
Building the Central Artery   85
Cardinal Cushing helps serve the elderly   95
*Back Bay Train Yards*   99
Boston College Citizen Seminar   103
The West End in 1952   129
The West End during demolition   136
The beginning of West End development   139
Charles River Park   140
Collins political cartoon   159
John F. Collins and John B. Hynes, 1959   162
Ed Logue, Mayor Collins, and waterfront model   174
The Prudential Tower   179
New City Hall   187

Dock Square in the 1920s    198
Faneuil Hall and Government Center    201
"The Rich Get Richer"    222
Devastated residents of Barry's Corner    223
Demolition of Barry's Corner property    223
Kevin White and John F. Collins, 1967    263
Melnea Cass and Mayor White    268
Faneuil Hall Marketplace    278
The Boston skyline of the 1990s    292

# Introduction

As every year goes by, fewer and fewer people can recall the old city of Boston the way it used to be during the 1930s and 1940s, when the Custom House tower was the only high-rise structure visible along a low and undistinguished skyline. Residents under the age of thirty, visitors coming into the city for the first time, tourists arriving to admire the famous historic sites, all look around them and see an urban metropolis similar in most respects to other American cities they know. An impressive skyline, a series of modernistic buildings, a centrally located government center, an active convention site, a bustling market district, an attractive waterfront area, an international airport, a major highway interchange—all the familiar ingredients of a modern, up-to-date city.

There was a time, however, not really that long ago, when Boston was on its way to becoming a ghost town—a run-down, worn-out relic of the past, rapidly discouraging any further investment or any significant interest. It was generally viewed as a city with a historic past, a troubled present, and no discernible future. Boston was a city, declared one issue of the *U.S. News and World Report*, that was "dying on the vine." Gone were its textile mills, and its once-busy harbor was "virtually stagnant." New building of any importance was a rarity, observed the writer, and the nation's highest property tax rate "threatened the city with bankruptcy."[1]

Boston's transformation from a depressed and dilapidated community of the past, badly divided by social conflicts, ethnic rivalries, and religious differences, into a rebuilt and refurbished city of the future—all in less than twenty years—is an absorbing story of faith, courage, skillful politicking, and sheer determination. There was, after all, nothing assured or inevitable about the rebuilding of Boston. Many old cities have disappeared completely, become irrelevant, or declined into lifeless historic monuments, frozen in time and place. The interesting thing about Boston was not only the rebuilding of its physical structure but also its movement back into the ranks of vibrant and livable cities. "At one point, we were like Detroit," remarked former mayor Kevin White in a recent television interview. "Ten years later, we were one of the five most prestigious cities in the country."[2]

The modernization of Boston was not without its critics, however, and certainly not without its problems. Urban renewal changed the face of a charming old city that many residents loved the way it was, with its winding streets, its antiques shops, and its varied clusters of people. Directed by political leaders, real estate developers, and urban planners who believed that only sweeping demolition would cure the cancerous blight that had descended on many parts of the old city, the process brought devastation to the multicultured West End, destruction to the streets of old Scollay Square, and an end to an unimpaired view of Boston Harbor. White ethnic neighborhoods challenged the inroads of large-scale development and organized to prevent what they regarded as the subversion of their cherished family values and their familiar way of life. Boston's black communities, too, organized their own opposition and reacted with equal determination against what they saw as their victimization at the hands of the white political establishment. By the late 1970s the ripple effects of urban renewal had caused damaging racial and economic vibrations throughout the entire city, producing consequences that had never been dreamed of twenty years earlier and that would continue to plague the city for decades.

Urban renewal in Boston, then, provides an absorbing example of how an essentially well-meaning reform movement can produce consequences that were never intended, frequently contradictory, and sometimes tragic. There were many Bostonians, on the one hand, who hailed the "New Boston," a term coined in the 1950s by Mayor John B. Hynes to tout his urban renewal program, as an incredible success story—the metamorphosis of a broken-down old city into an up-to-date metropolis that attracted admiring visitors not only from its own region but from all parts of the world. There were just as many, on the other hand, who looked upon renewal as an unmitigated disaster, with downtown architectural styles that created antiseptic centers devoid of people, with institutionalized housing projects that fostered racism and violence, and with an approach to neighborhood conversion that emphasized real estate values and investment profits at the expense of the working classes and the poor.

Despite the eventful and controversial nature of the subject, however, surprisingly little has been written about the critical two decades in Boston's recent history, the 1950s to the 1970s. For one thing, so many events happened in such a relatively short period of time that it is still difficult to separate fact from fiction, to sort out idle speculation from objective truth—to comprehend the magnitude of it all. For another thing, Boston politics is not only notoriously parochial but also unusually personal, if not downright secretive. Old-time politicians (and quite a few young ones, too) generally follow the well-known dictum of Martin Lomasney, the legendary boss of the West End's Ward 8, to the effect that you never put anything in writing: "Don't write when you can talk; don't talk when you can nod your head." Important decisions are often made in personal discussions, at clubs, at luncheon meetings, during telephone conversations, and on those quiet walks between the State House and City Hall, making it often difficult and time-consuming to trace the origins of motives and decisions. This intimate sense of confidentiality and camaraderie, though commonly associated with Irish politicians, was certainly not limited to them. One member of that exalted group of Brahmin financiers later known collectively as "the Vault" suggested that it was always "a little mysterious" how their decisions came about, considering that no minutes were ever kept of their meetings. "People simply talked on the telephone," he explained.[3]

For generations, in diaries, memoirs, and voluminous correspondence, Bostonians kept careful records of their own lives as well as the events that made their city famous. By the twentieth century, however, the personal anecdote and the verbal expression had replaced the written record as a source of local history. One of the saddest things for the historian of modern Boston is the almost complete absence of official repositories of letters and documents—especially in the case of Mayor

John B. Hynes, one of the central figures in this story.[4] For many years, the city of Boston apparently made no conscious or deliberate efforts to preserve the official papers and correspondence of its mayors or other public officials. As a result, important figures in the city's history such as John F. Fitzgerald, James Michael Curley, Maurice J. Tobin, and John B. Hynes left behind them no official collections of letters, records, papers, or public documents concerning their years in public office. Occasional letters, newspaper scrapbooks, and private correspondence may be found in the hands of relatives, friends, and colleagues, but no organized collections exist that allow the serious historian to trace the course of their various administrations. Fortunately, Mayor John F. Collins and Mayor Kevin H. White have deposited the official records of their administrations with the Boston Public Library. One may hope that Mayor Raymond L. Flynn and successive Boston mayors will continue that welcome tradition.

For now, however, the historian must rely more heavily than usual on personal interviews with participants in the events of Boston history during the 1950s and 1960s, as well as on the various newspapers and magazines of the period for what they had to say about those critical years when Boston was in a state of transition. Unfortunately, in the face of the paucity of written documents, the subjectivity of newspaper sources, and the natural inclination to embellish old memories, the historian is likely to gather information that is not always accurate and often difficult to corroborate. It is my hope that the present account will furnish a reliable basis on which future historians and biographers can either substantiate the existing version or provide another that is more exact.

Each of the many renewal projects, clearance programs, municipal undertakings, corporate enterprises, and private experiments crammed into this twenty-year period deserves a detailed history of its own. Social scientists have already used sophisticated quantitative techniques to compare urban renewal projects in major American cities during the postwar years. Paul Peterson, in *City Limits* (Chicago, 1981), pointed out that the desire for economic growth almost inevitably took precedence over social considerations; John Mollenkopf, in *The Contested City* (Princeton, N.J., 1983), demonstrated the interrelationships between progrowth coalitions in the cities and federal bureaucracies in Washington; and Jon Teaford, in *The Rough Road to Renaissance* (Baltimore, 1990), emphasized the effect of technological and demographic changes on America's aging cities. But in the case of Boston, historians have not yet moved beyond structural hypotheses and economic generalizations to focus on the actual history of the city itself during the postwar decades. The present study is a first attempt to bring together many of the random pieces and see if they fit into a comprehensive mosaic that will offer a meaningful picture of Boston from 1950 to 1970. The primary intent of *Building a New Boston* is to provide a coherent historical narrative, focusing on those political personalities who advocated an extensive program of urban renewal to create a "New Boston" during the 1950s and 1960s, as well as those who opposed the plans of the city administration as destructive of the community and harmful to its people. Studies of architectural designs, additional research into demographic details, and further investigations into the intricacies of urban economics will be left to other scholars who, I hope, will be stimulated by the story set forth here to explore even further this fascinating period in Boston's history.

Among those individuals who have been generous with their valuable time and their invaluable memories, I must single out Richard W. Hynes, the youngest of Mayor Hynes's children, who not only became a good friend and enthusiastic collaborator but was also one of the first to suggest a full-length treatment of his father. John B. ("Jack") Hynes, Jr., and Marie Hynes Gallagher were also helpful with insights and anecdotes regarding their father's life and character. Jerome Rappaport gave generously of his time, discussing real estate developments in the 1950s, and Kane Simonian's views were invaluable concerning the early stages of the Boston Redevelopment Authority. Former mayor John F. Collins was extremely supportive of the project, not only in making available his extensive collection of papers and documents but also in giving so freely of his time for several personal interviews. Edward Logue, too, was a cordial and cooperative source of information concerning the operations of the BRA under his jurisdiction. Former mayor Kevin H. White was always accessible in helping to clarify many significant points in the narrative; and John Galvin, executive director of the Boston College Citizen Seminars for nearly forty years, never failed to provide perceptive views of Boston's life and politics.

My colleagues at Boston College are always sources of scholarly assistance, but I am particularly indebted to Andrew Buni for sharing with me his remarkable knowledge of the neighborhoods and minorities of the city; to Mark I. Gelfand for his unique understanding of federal urban development programs; and to Gary P. Brazier for his professional insights into the workings of city government. Lawrence M. Kennedy, BRA historian, has been especially helpful in providing insights from his own work on institutional planning in Boston, and William P. Marchione has furnished materials from his own studies in the Allston-Brighton area. I am grateful to supervisor Katherine Dibble and her staff in research library services at the Boston Public Library, especially Laura Monti, keeper of rare books and manuscripts, and curator Roberta Zonghi, for providing me with primary source materials essential for this study. Kaethe Maguire, government documents assistant, and the members of her staff at the O'Neill Library at Boston College were consistently friendly in furnishing microfilm materials; and Philip Bergen, librarian at The Bostonian Society, was unfailingly helpful in locating critical historical details large and small.

I would like to express my appreciation to William A. Frohlich, director of the Northeastern University Press, for his personal interest and professional guidance throughout this project. I cannot speak highly enough of the expert assistance I received at every point in the process from Deborah Kops, former editorial director, Ann Twombly, production director, and copy editor Larry Hamberlin. And, finally, I am most grateful for the constant support of my wife, Mary, whose love and understanding has made possible a happy life and a fulfilling career.

*Chestnut Hill, Massachusetts*             THOMAS H. O'CONNOR
*September 1992*

# Building a New Boston

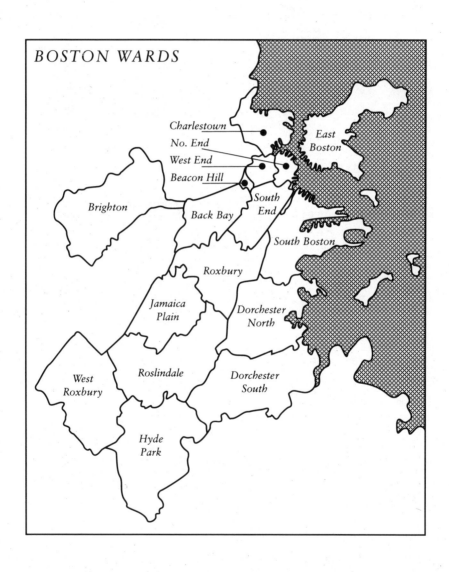

BOSTON WARDS

Charlestown

No. End

West End

Beacon Hill

East Boston

Brighton

Back Bay

South End

South Boston

Roxbury

Jamaica Plain

Dorchester North

West Roxbury

Roslindale

Dorchester South

Hyde Park

# 1.

# "A Hopeless Backwater"

Boston is an old city with a long history. Over the course of three centuries it has suffered difficult trials and has undergone substantial changes. After the disastrous effects of British occupation during the War for Independence, Boston worked hard to recover its political status in the life of the new nation. Later, in the wake of the War of 1812, it made an effective economic transition from shipping and commerce to the manufacture of cotton textiles. During the early 1800s Josiah Quincy, the city's "Great Mayor," implemented a major renovation of the waterfront business area; fifty years later the city had to rebuild its entire retail district after it was wiped out by a devastating fire. Over the years the city adapted to modern ideas, filled in more lands, absorbed waves of alien peoples, and experimented with new ways to live and work.

Perhaps the most serious challenge to Boston's traditional role as a major American city came in the late 1940s and early 1950s, in the aftermath of World War II. At that critical point, its citizens were called upon to assess the damage caused by generations of political feuding, social rivalries, and steady economic decline. Before discussing the ways in which a "New Boston" emerged during the 1950s and 1960s, it is necessary first to recall the distinctive and unique character of the old Boston, which caused city leaders to feel so strongly that significant changes were not only desirable but absolutely imperative if Boston were to survive and prosper during the second half of the twentieth century.

Some older residents can still recall with fondness and nostalgia the city of Boston they knew so well during the 1930s and 1940s. To those Brahmins who still lived on Beacon Hill, or who made their homes in one of the magnificent brownstones in the Back Bay, the city was still "theirs"—no matter how many Irish, Italians, Jews, and other foreign groups had managed to elbow their way in over the years. The ladies might be off to a literary lecture at the Chilton Club or a Friday afternoon concert at Symphony Hall; the gentlemen might stroll across Boston Common to the Somerset Club for lunch after a pleasant morning browsing at the Athenaeum. In either case, they enjoyed the familiar surroundings of a community they thought of as exclusively their own.[1]

Other American cities might choose to have smoothly paved side-walks or modernistic skyscrapers soaring grandly into the sky, but native Bostonians would have none of it. While it is true that in 1914 one architectural firm managed to place a thirty-story tower, nearly five hundred feet high, atop the old Custom House, making it look like what one disgusted critic described as "a vast chimney stack rising from a Roman Temple," over the years leading citizens did their best to see that legislative restraints kept the city skyline down to what they regarded as a civilized level. Don't give over "all wisdom and foresight" to city planners and street commissioners, one concerned Bostonian urged his fellow citizens, warning them that year after year "structures with priceless associations" would inevitably be destroyed by the devotees of "progress."[2]

In 1928 city leaders did agree to modify the local zoning code sufficiently to allow the construction of taller buildings, but insisted they be designed with setbacks, the steplike features that ensure that air and light are not cut off from neighboring buildings. The art deco United Shoe Machine Building, built in 1929, was the first example of this type of construction.[3] The changing of zoning procedures also made possible the construction of other large buildings in the downtown area, such as the State Street Bank Building (1929) on Franklin Street, the New England Telephone Building (1930) at Bowdoin Square, and a new Suffolk County Courthouse (1936). Even though the Federal Post Office and Courthouse that went up in Post Office Square in 1933 rose to a

*In 1915, as the now-familiar tower was being erected atop Boston's Custom House, a view of Long Wharf from Boston Harbor shows how badly the city's waterfront had deteriorated over the years. Later, with municipal funds diverted from the downtown area to the various neighborhoods during the 1930s and 1940s, ocean-going commerce rapidly declined, the docks rotted on their pilings, and the buildings fell into further disrepair. Courtesy of The Bostonian Society.*

height of twenty stories, there was general agreement that the construction of great skyscrapers like New York City's Empire State Building was still decidedly out of the question.[4]

To more average citizens, people whose ancestors more than likely came over to America as impoverished immigrants on the decks of lumber ships or in the stifling holds of third-class steerage, the downtown area in those days was a powerful magnet that never failed to draw them into its fascinating orbit. Although most of these folks had their closest ties with their own ethnic neighborhoods, they had also developed a sort of dual citizenship with the historic inner city. As a result of school lessons, essay contests, bus tours, public lectures, holiday reenactments, patriotic programs, and historical booklets, virtually every resident grew up to become a Bostonian in that term's most catholic and inclusive sense.[5]

For such people, downtown Boston was a marvelous place for themselves and for their families. Taking the subway into the city, neighborhood women did their shopping at R. H. Stearn's, Jordan Marsh, Gilchrist's, and Filene's, rushing off to Filene's famous basement to engage in the exhilarating rough-and-tumble struggle for cut-rate bargains, or walking up to Raymond's, "Where U Bot the Hat," for the sales "Uncle Eph" regularly advertised in the daily newspapers.[6] Along this narrow stretch of Washington Street was located the city's Newspaper Row, home of the *Post*, the *Globe*, the *Herald*, the *Traveler*, and the *Daily Advertiser*, where workers chalked the major headlines of the day on large outdoor blackboards for passersby to read as they went about their daily business.[7]

Just beyond Washington Street was Scollay Square, a colorful area of penny arcades, shooting galleries, and speakeasies spawned by Prohibition. It was here that Sally Keith twirled her celebrated tassels at the Crawford House, while strippers like Anne Corio and Rose La Rose did their bumps and grinds at the Old Howard. On Saturdays, parents made box lunches for their children, took them to a Scollay Square movie for a quarter, and then went to Joe and Nemo's for a nickel hot dog. Right next door was Haymarket Square, where peddlers of all nationalities sold fruits and vegetables from their loaded pushcarts, forming a crowded tangle of handlebars, wheels, and wooden boxes that clogged the narrow streets.[8]

It was into downtown Boston that people went when they wanted to celebrate wedding anniversaries, birthdays, graduations, and other special occasions. The hotels of the city were grand and plentiful, providing not only rooms for permanent residents and transient tourists but also elegant dining rooms, spacious ballrooms, and sumptuous lobbies for local people coming in for an evening on the town. The ornate Vendôme, the sophisticated Copley Plaza, and the elegant Ritz Carlton served a more exclusive clientele from the nearby Back Bay area or distinguished visitors from out of state. The eleven-hundred-room Hotel Statler on Arlington Street offered accommodations at more modest rates for those who wanted to stay in the central part of the city. The Parker House, on the corner of Tremont and School streets, the Hotel Touraine, on the corner of Tremont and Boylston streets, and the

Bradford Hotel, across from the Metropolitan Theater, served an appreciative public.

A succession of exotic art deco theaters along Washington Street—Loew's Orpheum, RKO-Keith's, the Paramount—offered a variety of first-run motion pictures, together with popular vaudeville programs. The Metropolitan Theater, just beyond Stuart Street, always had a special appeal, not only because of its marble statues, huge chandeliers, and impressive staircases, but also because of the huge Wurlitzer pipe organ that rose majestically up out of the orchestra pit. Within the space of a single block along Tremont Street, between Boylston and Stuart, were some of the best playhouses in the country, including the Colonial, the Majestic, the Plymouth, the Shubert, and the Wilbur, where the works of America's leading playwrights could be seen on a regular basis.[9]

For youngsters, too, Boston had special appeal. Schoolchildren regularly made their way on chartered streetcars to visit the State House to gaze up in awe at the expanse of colorful murals in Nurses' Hall, which depicted famous episodes in the Bay State's history, and to look around at the mass of historic banners in the Hall of Flags on either side of Doric Hall. They later wandered among the weathered tombs and headstones in the Old Granary Burying Ground, climbed up and down the marble staircase under the stern, forbidding frowns of the great stone lions in the lobby of the Boston Public Library in Copley Square, or stared goggle-eyed at the rows of ancient Egyptian mummies at the Museum of Fine Arts on Huntington Avenue.

But it was Christmastime, especially, that was the truly magic time to be in Boston. Right after Thanksgiving the city was transformed into a glittering fairyland that attracted people from all parts of the greater Boston area. There was something entrancing about coming up out of the Park Street subway station at dusk and hearing the sounds of Christmas carols echoing across Boston Common from the carillon of the Park Street Church. Night after night the narrow, snow-covered streets were lined with people—young people, old people, entire families—ambling happily along in their galoshes, going from one department store to another, inspecting the toys, marveling at the electric trains, and admiring the sparkling decorations of Christmas trees and colored lights. Invariably these visitors would make their way to the corner of Washington and Summer streets, where the brilliantly lighted windows of the Jordan Marsh department store displayed spectacular tableaus portraying the story of Bethlehem, Santa Claus, scenes from *A Christmas Carol*, and other familiar images of the season. To most people at the time, Boston was as familiar and comfortable as an old shoe—soft, broken in, and well worn, easy to slip on and off.[10] That was in retrospect.

Despite its nostalgic appeal, however, Boston was rapidly slipping into decline. That proverbial old shoe had become cracked, scuffed, and badly run down at the heel. Starting in the early 1920s its economic base had begun to weaken as owners of textile factories had already either liquidated their failing operations or moved out of New England into southern states in search of cheaper labor, lower taxes, fewer union organizers, and more available raw materials.[11] The collapse of the New England textile market, as well as the rapid decline of the boot and shoe industry, caused severe setbacks in employment among the garment workers on Kneeland Street and among the large number of workers in the wool and leather houses along Summer Street.[12] The widespread use of central heating in homes and businesses was killing the market for woolen underwear and heavy wool suits, and young women were showing a decided preference for the new lightweight fabrics made of silk or the new fiber—rayon.[13]

When the Great Depression struck in 1929, it worsened an already failing economy. Along with other communities throughout the nation, Boston suffered the full force of the stock market crash and the resultant bank failures. Working-class families everywhere were devastated by the loss of jobs and the impact of deflation. Small hoards of personal savings, painfully accumulated over the years, quickly disappeared. Mortgages on homes and on small rental properties were foreclosed; husbands and wives were forced to surrender their insurance policies for their cash values; customers pleaded with grocery store owners for further extensions of credit. Stores closed down for lack of customers; hospitals ran short of patients; old theaters went out of business; newer movie houses tried to attract more customers by offering free sets of fancy dishes. By the spring of 1930 at least forty thousand workers were reported to be out of a job, with some estimates putting the figure as high as one hundred thousand. Panhandlers roamed the streets looking for handouts, idle workers waited for boats to come into the Fish Pier with unsalable scraps of codfish, and the jobless curled up on park benches or huddled in the doorways of public buildings. Boston saw its own "Hooverville" go up on the sprawling dump just beyond Columbia Circle off the old Mile Road leading to Dorchester, where destitute vagrants and homeless derelicts tried to find shelter from the cold wintry winds in flimsy cardboard packing crates or in makeshift shanties pieced together out of abandoned sheets of corrugated tin.[14]

As banks failed, businesses collapsed, and the American export trade fell off, the resulting drop in factory production signaled the widespread loss of jobs. From July 1931 to December 1932 unemployment in all trades in Boston averaged 29.72 percent, almost precisely equal to the 30.17 rate reported by twenty-three other large American cities.[15] A few factories were forced to shut down completely; most cut back their hours, spread the work around as much as possible, and tried to stay in operation with skeleton crews and piecework. At the same time, Boston also declined as a major transportation center. The volume of cargo and the value of goods shipped through the port of Boston dropped steadily from 1925 to 1930, and small gains in passenger traffic failed to compensate for those losses. This meant that the usual jobs that had been available to Boston workers at the docks and on the piers disappeared along with the other opportunities for work throughout the city. Railroad traffic, too, both passenger and freight, went into a sharp decline. Even the number of automobiles registered in Boston fell from 111,000 in 1931 to 89,000 in 1933.[16]

Complicating the already dismal economic picture of Boston during the late 1920s and early 1930s was the ever-present personality of James Michael Curley. Wittingly or unwittingly, the city's famous political rogue had a significant influence on the city's changing economic climate. As a bright and ambitious young man who had fought his way up from the rough-and-tumble politics of Roxbury's Ward 17, Curley had already served twice as mayor of the city—once from 1914 to 1917, and again from 1922 to 1926—and was sworn into office for the third time only three months after the stock market crash of October 1929.[17] In his inaugural address on January 6, 1930, before an overflow crowd of jubilant supporters at Symphony Hall, Curley promised to furnish "work and wages" for those in need of "sustenance and employment," and he proposed an ambitious Fifty-Year Plan to develop industry, commerce, and municipal construction.[18]

Despite his grandiose promises, however, Curley was never able to get the amount of money he wanted to fund his plans for extensive public works programs. Many of his proposals died in the Republican-controlled state house, whose financial watchdogs were wary of the growing financial crisis as well as of the mayor's personal political ambitions.[19] Even the emergence of large-scale federal funding in the mid-1930s failed to provide the same degree of opportunity for the Curley administration that it did for so many other big-city bosses. Recent historical studies have shown that Boston never received the amount of federal monies it should have received for a city of its size and relative political importance. Administration leaders in Washington had a deep-seated mistrust of James Michael Curley and other Boston politicians. Whether that mistrust was based on firsthand knowledge or on stereotypical allegations, federal bureaucrats viewed the Curley administration as a big-city machine composed of corrupt political bosses and incompetent rascals who would undoubtedly waste, steal, or thoroughly mismanage whatever federal funds were put into their hands.[20] Depressing reports of local political feuds, neighborhood rivalries, and conflicts among various ethnic groups ("the Yankees look down on the Irish, the Irish look down on the Italians . . .") convinced those who administered federal funding agencies that Boston was simply not the kind of city that could handle large sums of money honestly, equitably, or responsibly.[21]

As a result of these negative perceptions, public funds for emergency projects under various federal relief programs never reached the levels in Boston they did in other American cities during the Great Depression years. Mayor Curley generated some municipal assistance by resorting to stopgap measures—hiring unemployed workers to rake leaves on the Boston Common, offering snow shovelers five dollars a day to clean the streets for the city's 1930 tercentenary celebration, laying miles of curbstones in the public parks—but his long-range plans for major housing and building projects never materialized.[22] In 1931 and 1932 at least ninety thousand of the city's able-bodied workers had lost their jobs (between 25 and 30 percent of the local labor force), while another fifty or sixty thousand were underemployed because of severe cutbacks in factory production. Federal monies were obviously not large enough to substantially alter these gloomy conditions.

In addition to his unintentional role in the breakdown of relations between Boston and Washington during the Great Depression, James Michael Curley had an even more direct influence on the deterioration of the central city's infrastructure during much of the same period. In the course of his four terms as mayor of Boston, extending over the greater part of four decades, Curley developed a consistent pattern of fiscal support and municipal construction that clearly favored the interests of those ethnic neighborhoods from which he drew his political strength, while virtually ignoring the needs of the downtown area of the city, with which he was almost constantly at war.[23]

Curley used whatever public funds were available to him to improve the quality of life of his neighborhood followers. He enlarged the Boston City Hospital to provide better medical facilities for working-class families. At the same time, he established seven new health units in various neighborhoods such as South Boston, East Boston, and the West End, where poor people could receive first-aid treatment for minor injuries and chronic health problems. In communities such as Jamaica Plain, Hyde Park, West Roxbury, and Brighton, Curley built new branch libraries to make available to more people in the outlying areas the marvelous resources of the central Boston Public Library in Copley Square. He developed beaches, roads, and tunnels; he laid out endless miles of roads, highways, parkways, and bridges; he expanded parks, playgrounds, and recreational areas. He extended a number of the streetcar lines and subway systems so that workers could travel into the downtown areas to their jobs and then return to their homes in the neighborhoods. All these projects not only improved living conditions in the neighborhoods but also created the jobs and incomes that the mayor's supporters badly wanted, and that provided the kind of patronage so vital to Curley's base of power.[24]

Although Curley was greatly disappointed that the federal bureaucracy would not give him the unlimited federal funding he wanted in order to pursue more extensive construction projects, he used whatever funds the federal alphabet agencies offered, and made up the difference with what he could extract from local resources. Inevitably Curley's inventive fiscal policies brought him into bitter confrontation with the conservative financial establishment of the city, which had opposed his ambitious rise to political power from the start. Bankers, lawyers, judges, brokers, businessmen, and other members of the downtown elite saw Curley as the antithesis of everything they professed to hold dear—one of the "chief exemplars in Boston of Tammany methods," whose election meant "corruption in politics and business," according to the reform-minded Good Government Association.[25] Political conservatives saw their worst fears realized by the ways in which the mayor's expenditures

were forcing up valuations and taxes to what they regarded as astronomical heights.

Curley, however, blithely brushed aside his opponents' objections.
Tax money was supposed to be used to help people, he insisted, not
hoarded away in bank vaults. Whether the bills were paid, or the budget
balanced, was immaterial to Curley as long as his credit was good and
he was in a position to borrow more money. When he ran out of city
funds to pay bills or cover salaries, he went before the state legislature
to borrow additional money until he could bring in more revenue by
raising the tax rate a notch higher. If there wasn't enough money on
hand to meet current operating expenses until the tax money came in,
he went to the bankers of the city for a loan.[26] Although the Yankee-
controlled banking houses of the city were not at all sympathetic to
Curley and his harebrained schemes, the mayor usually had ways of
"persuading" them to give him the loans he needed. Curley himself took
pleasure in describing how he tried a little "political banditry" on Philip
Stockton, president of the First National Bank, when he balked at
loaning the mayor money. Curley reminded him that a water main's
floodgates were located right under his bank. If Curley didn't get the
money he needed by three o'clock that afternoon, he told the banker, he
would see that the gates were opened and the bank vaults flooded. "He
acceded to my request," Curley wrote in his autobiography, taking
obvious delight in "putting the bankers in their place."[27]

The confrontational relationship that developed between the mayor
and Boston's business community during the 1930s only served to widen
the gap between the "inner city" and the "outer city," between the
Yankee and the Celt, between the Boston of the Protestants and the
Boston of the Catholics. Curley had welded the various ethnic elements
in the neighborhoods—the Irish, the Italians, the Jews, and others—into
a powerful political coalition devoted to him personally and capable of
neutralizing the opposition of the downtown Yankees, who submitted
to his power, but who stubbornly denied him legitimacy. Accepting this
division of power as a political fact of life—indeed, often capitalizing on
it for his own purposes—Curley left the inner city to wallow in its
Puritan self-righteousness while he turned his attention and his municipal favors to those in that "other" Boston who never failed to give him
their loyalty—and their votes. While he showered the various neighborhoods with libraries, health units, parks, playgrounds, and bathhouses,
he neglected the downtown section of Boston and allowed it to fall into

a state of such disrepair that many native Bostonians began to give up all hope of its eventual recovery.[28]

The antagonistic class distinctions and social divisions created by the political and fiscal policies of the Curley administration were reinforced by the approach taken in religious affairs by William Henry Cardinal O'Connell, the leader of Boston's substantial Roman Catholic population. Over the course of the previous century, the general tendency of Boston's Catholic hierarchy had been one of accommodation. The town's first bishop, Jean-Louis Lefebvre de Cheverus, had established cordial relations with the Yankee community, and throughout the nineteenth century prelates such as Bishop John Fitzpatrick and Archbishop John Williams had worked in a quiet, nonaggressive manner to encourage a generally peaceful coexistence between an insecure immigrant people and a hostile native population.[29]

By the time forty-seven-year-old William Henry O'Connell succeeded the aged John Williams in 1907 as archbishop of Boston, the balance of power had finally shifted. Irish Catholics were no longer the oppressed minority that they had been half a century earlier. With the election of a Boston-born Irish Catholic, John F. ("Honey Fitz") Fitzgerald, as mayor of Boston in 1906, and with David I. Walsh becoming the commonwealth's first Irish Catholic governor in 1914, the new prelate recognized that the Irish were moving into positions of considerable political influence. He urged Catholics to adopt a much more independent attitude, one that would have them emphasize their own distinctive culture instead of striving to adapt to the traditions of their host society.[30] From the outset, O'Connell insisted that the old wave of Protestantism was receding and that a new tide of Irish Catholicism was beginning to sweep over the region. "The Puritan has passed; the Catholic remains," he announced bluntly in his sermon on the occasion of the archdiocesan centennial in 1908.[31]

Using the power of his office and the force of his personality, O'Connell, who rose to the exalted rank of cardinal in 1911, established a consistent pattern of separatism throughout the archdiocese of Boston that was designed to free Catholics from all forms of Yankee intimidation. He exerted pressure on pastors and curates, mothers and fathers, to see to it that their children attended parochial schools.[32] Although he himself maintained close and even affectionate relations with many members of the city's Protestant establishment, he warned the faithful of the archdiocese to avoid Protestant churches, and under no circumstance to participate in any non-Catholic ceremonies—even such semi-social events as marriages and funerals. Youngsters were cautioned not to join Boy Scout or Girl Scout troops, not to participate in YMCA or YWCA activities, and not to attend social gatherings at local Neighborhood Clubs.[33] Church leaders organized a parallel series of exclusively Catholic social activities for the young people of the archdiocese. Catholic Boy Scout and Girl Scout troops were created; the Catholic Youth Organization (CYO) was established to provide opportunities for boys and girls to join sports teams, debating clubs, and marching bands. Large numbers of Catholic men were enrolled in the Holy Name Society; Catholic women became members of the Legion of Mary, or of one of the numerous sodalities that existed in every parish.[34] Emphasizing the theme of the "church militant," the cardinal demonstrated to all, in the words of one local journalist, that "the once brow-beaten Irish Catholics have come into possession of Boston."[35]

It is clear that Cardinal O'Connell was making a conscientious effort to preserve the faith and morals of those whose souls had been entrusted to his episcopal care, to help Catholics realize their "full duty to themselves," and to promote in the community at large "a fair attitude toward the Church."[36] He was insistent that Boston Catholics should no longer be pale imitations of Yankee role models, nor passively aspire to the values of the Anglo-Saxon tradition. In the process, however, he unwittingly supplied a substantial socioreligious dimension to those political and fiscal policies of James Michael Curley that divided the city into two separate and often antagonistic armed camps. "The new assertive mood in the church," Curley's biographer Jack Beatty has observed, "closely paralleled the new ethnic politics."[37]

In addition to those internal conflicts and divisions that were plaguing the city, an accumulation of old age, wear and tear, and years of municipal neglect were causing the old town to deteriorate rapidly. Roads, highways, and streets throughout the city were in deplorable condition. By 1930 some ten million dollars in federal money had been assigned to Massachusetts for two hundred different road construction projects, covering as many as seven hundred miles—but none of those funds were earmarked for the city of Boston.[38] To make matters worse, the remarkable increase in automobile traffic was causing terrible congestion in the narrow downtown streets. "There is probably no city in the United States where traffic conditions on the streets of the downtown business section are so near the saturation point as are here in Boston," one city planner complained in the late 1920s.[39] A number of leading citizens were already urging the construction of a six-lane central artery that would make it possible for cars and trucks to bypass the downtown business district completely.[40]

With the falloff of international trade and the decline of shipping during the Depression years, the port of Boston fell into a critical state. Along the bridges that ran from the Commonwealth Pier to Atlantic Avenue the piers were rotting, the pilings crumbling, the timbers warping, and the metal corroding. Local railroad traffic also ground to a halt as serious cutbacks took place in the shipments of raw wool, leather hides, and coffee beans that came in from Latin America, as well as the fruits and vegetables that arrived at United Fruit's terminals. Without imports to ship to other parts of the country, acres of railroad lands belonging to the New York Central off Summer Street, the New Haven yards along Dorchester Avenue, and the Boston and Albany yards off Huntington Avenue all became sprawling graveyards of rusting tracks, empty boxcars, and idle locomotives.

Scollay Square, still one of downtown Boston's more popular recreation areas, was fast becoming a dilapidated collection of run-down movie houses, nondescript barrooms, and sleazy tattoo parlors. Drunks, panhandlers, and derelicts crawled the streets by day and by night, clutching at passersby for nickels and dimes.[41] And only a short distance away, the streets surrounding Josiah Quincy's once-elegant market district had become clogged with motor trucks, horse-drawn wagons, and peddlers' pushcarts. Alexander Parris's handsome Greek Revival market building had become mottled and discolored, the copper-sheathed central dome a dingy green, the granite warehouses on either side blackened with years of dirt, smoke, and pollution.[42]

Closer to the heart of the city, the graceful curve of Tremont Street, across from the Boston Common, had lost its charm. In place of the fashionable shops, where chauffered limousines once came to pick up carefully wrapped packages, there now appeared a motley collection of cut-rate clothing stores, inexpensive cafeterias, and novelty joke shops.[43] The Common itself, now overgrown and untended, no longer offered itself as a delightful oasis in the middle of a modern city. Where once the settlers' cattle grazed contentedly and the gentlemen of the town exercised their horses, the Great Depression had taken its toll. In increasing numbers, the forlorn shapes of unemployed and homeless

*Alexander Parris's magnificent Greek Revival market building, along with flanking rows of granite-faced warehouses, was authorized by Mayor Josiah Quincy in 1825 as a much-needed addition to Boston's discordant market district. By the early twentieth century, however, the once proud buildings were suffering from the effects of age and neglect, while the surrounding streets were congested with delivery trucks, pushcarts, and piles of uncollected garbage. Courtesy of The Bostonian Society.*

men wandered along the winding lanes in oversized shoes, baggy pants, and battered overcoats, begging for food and pleading for handouts. By nightfall most of them were stretched out on wooden benches or curled up on the grass, swigging cheap wine from bottles wrapped in brown paper bags. More and more Bostonians were beginning to steer clear of that historic piece of land, especially after dark, when the absence of effective lighting and adequate police patrols brought the number of robberies to alarming levels.

Even the streets of the exclusive Back Bay were starting to reflect the same shabbiness that was apparent in so many other parts of the downtown area. Many old Boston families had died out; others were no longer able to obtain the kind of hired help necessary to maintain the spacious brownstones. Only a portion of the larger private homes along Commonwealth Avenue and lower Beacon Street were occupied in the fashion for which they were originally intended. Some had been converted into apartments; others transformed into offices for doctors and dentists; still others adapted for preparatory schools and private colleges. The appearance of "To Let" signs in ground-floor windows of familiar old brownstones was a clear signal that many more buildings would soon become rooming houses and tenements. It was a discouraging sign that Boston had already started to lose a great deal of the unique style that had always made it such an outstanding city.

Not even the welcome prosperity of the 1940s, generated by the outbreak of World War II, could provide any permanent remedies for Boston's failing condition. Working-class families in the Boston area, hard-hit by years of depression, benefited from the jobs made available in shipyards, army bases, garment factories, and industrial plants throughout the region. Many small businesses and local industries took on new life with government subsidies and lucrative defense contracts. Hotels, restaurants, movie houses, and barrooms did a flourishing business as visitors, contractors, and military personnel sought out weekend pleasures to relax from the cares of war. But the influx of these wartime profits did little to restore the face of the city or to repair its weakening infrastructure. Boston failed to use the unexpected benefits of this wartime prosperity either to wipe out its deficit or to balance its budget, as many other cities had done during the same period. "City Hall graft is probably no greater than in most cities," conceded the highly respected journalist-commentator Louis Lyons in 1945, "but Boston can afford it less. As the financial capital of New England, Boston has reflected the marked economic decline of the region."[44]

And to many of those who deplored the local financial scene, the continuing intricacies of Boston politics only made future prospects even more depressing. James Michael Curley had gone on to become governor of Massachusetts from 1935 to 1937, but when he tried to win a fourth term as mayor, in 1937, he suffered a disappointing defeat by a young Democrat from Roxbury's Mission Hill district, Maurice J. Tobin.[45] As Curley's successor, Tobin attempted to dramatize the difference between his own brand of "new" politics and that of old-timers like Curley by pursuing a decidedly conservative fiscal policy. These were still the Depression years, however, and Tobin found it an uphill struggle to maintain a tight-money policy in the face of the recession and unemployment that plagued his first term of office, from 1938 to 1941.[46] Tobin's efforts at retrenchment and budget balancing almost proved his undoing, however, when he ran for reelection in 1941. His political rival, Curley, claimed that Tobin's penny-pinching policies may have benefited the city's bankers and businessmen, but had deprived the poor and needy people of Boston of such essential services as hospitals, public restrooms, and public libraries. Although Tobin managed to win reelection, it was by a margin of only a little over nine thousand votes.[47]

The Boston elections were hardly a month old when, on December 7, 1941, the Japanese attacked the American fleet at Pearl Harbor. A big-city mayor in a nation at war, Tobin became involved in the numerous details of civilian defense and home-front activities. Not only did he have to set aside any plans he had for reconstructing the city, but in the face of wartime inflation he also had to modify his program of fiscal controls.[48] He had hardly begun his second administration when James Michael Curley appeared on the scene and announced his intention to run for a post in the United States Congress from the Charlestown-Cambridge Eleventh District, a contest in which he had the satisfaction of defeating Thomas Hopkinton Eliot, who was both the grandson of Harvard's former president, Charles W. Eliot, and a friend of Eleanor Roosevelt.[49]

Halfway through his term of office in Washington, however, the unpredictable Curley suddenly announced that he would be a candidate for the mayor's office in Boston in the next election, despite reports that the wartime Truman Committee was investigating him for improper financial transactions. At the same moment, Maurice Tobin, in the third year of his second four-year term as mayor, issued his own announcement that he intended to enter the 1944 governor's race. He went on to defeat the lackluster Republican candidate, then moved his things from City Hall to the State House, leaving the mayor's office vacant. To fill the awkward gap, the state legislature authorized John E. Kerrigan, president of the city council, to serve as acting mayor until regular elections took place in November 1945.[50]

As World War II came to a victorious close in the intervening months, bewildered political observers could only watch in amazement at the incredible antics of Boston politics. With a growing deficit, an unbalanced budget, a disheartening tax rate, a disorganized city council, an unoccupied executive office, and an interim mayor, even the most optimistic citizen had to concede that the future of Boston did not look promising.

By the time Maurice J. Tobin began his two-year term as governor of Massachusetts, he was turning his attention from the problems of war to the challenges of peace. Once again the New England economy was slipping into recession—in large measure, as one commentator expressed it, because it was essentially "oriented to nineteenth-century conditions."[51] The leather and footwear industries went into decline, and textile plants continued to make their way southward, where lower wages and less unionism attracted capital and management. The Bethlehem shipyards in East Boston and the Fore River shipyards in Quincy were in the process of closing down; the huge army base in South Boston was cutting back operations. Numerous war contracts had been canceled; the machinery and tooling industries were facing substantial layoffs; the housing shortage was growing more serious every day; and inflation kept rising higher and higher.[52]

As they had done more than a century earlier when they sent their capital reserves out to build textile factories at Waltham, Lowell, and Lawrence, Boston entrepreneurs now invested heavily in the region's growing electronics industry, which had taken root in the outlying suburbs along Route 128, the circumferential highway ringing Boston, rather than in the older downtown areas of Boston itself. Charles Coolidge, a partner in the firm of Ropes and Gray and a member of the Harvard Corporation, served as board chairman of the Mitre Corporation, while Charles Francis Adams, son of the former secretary of the navy who came from one of Boston's oldest and most distinguished families, served as chief executive of the Raytheon Corporation. Branches of such firms as AVCO and General Electric were among the sixty-eight new industrial plants that went up along Route 128, and development companies like Cabot, Cabot, and Forbes found the suburban locations preferable to the crowded streets of downtown Boston.[53]

With old businesses drying up, and with new businesses moving out into the suburbs, Bostonians became panicky as they anticipated a return to the disastrous conditions of the Depression era unless the national government came to the rescue with a gigantic infusion of federal monies. Tobin tried his best to forestall such a spirit of defeatism and pleaded for a more positive attitude of local self-reliance, but the general public did not accept the governor's words of reassurance and failed to support him when he ran for reelection in the fall of 1946.[54] Tobin went down to defeat under a nationwide Republican avalanche that swept both houses of Congress for the first time since 1928 and captured a majority of state governorships.[55] Massachusetts Republicans had run an aggressive campaign that featured a Yankee lawyer named Robert Fiske Bradford and revolved around the themes of "Had Enough?" and "It's Time for a Change." In November Tobin not only lost the election but suffered the additional indignity of failing to carry Ward 19, his own home district.[56]

In the meantime, Tobin's decision in 1944 to abandon city politics for the governorship had turned the mayoral election of 1945 into a wide-open contest. As acting mayor, John E. Kerrigan certainly expected to serve a four-year term in his own right. He lost out, however, to James Michael Curley, who blew in from Washington like a cyclone and swept the field.[57] Curley's mayoral victory was all the more remarkable because it took place while he was under indictment by a federal grand jury on charges of using the mails to defraud. Taking office as mayor of Boston in January 1946, Curley took more than a year to exhaust all his judicial appeals; finally, in June 1947, he was sentenced to a term of six to eighteen months in the federal penitentiary at Danbury, Connecticut. "You're sending me to my death," the seventy-two-year-old Curley mournfully intoned to the judge as he walked out the courtroom door.[58]

For the second time in less than three years, the office of mayor was vacant, but this time it could not be filled by bringing back John E. Kerrigan, who was then under indictment by a Boston grand jury. Technically, the city charter provided that a vacancy in the office of mayor be filled by the incumbent president of the Boston City Council. The acting council president at that moment was John B. Kelly, brother of Francis E. (Frankie "Sweepstakes") Kelly, a former lieutenant governor, former attorney general, and perennial campaigner for a state lottery. The prospect of the Kelly brothers running the city of Boston did not at all appeal to the downtown Republicans, and at that point Governor Robert F. Bradford moved into the vacuum and arranged for the state legislature to appoint the Boston city clerk as acting mayor.[59] To impress upon the city clerk, a career bureaucrat named John B. Hynes, that he should not expect to use the opportunity to build up his own political hopes, Hynes was given a raise in pay and a life tenure as city clerk that would cease the moment he became a candidate for the office of mayor. The gesture was to ensure that the political process would be maintained, and that Curley's job as mayor of Boston would still be waiting for him when he got out of prison. Bradford, anxious to maintain orderly political procedures, did not want to convey the impression that the Republicans were trying to steal away the old man's job while he was helpless.[60]

The selection of John B. Hynes to be temporary mayor, however, was by no means as innocent or as haphazard as it first appeared—indeed, according to Hirsh Freed, the whole thing was really quite "incestuous." It seems that Andy Dazzi, a campaigner for Maurice Tobin and for many years something of a legend at the *Boston Globe*, where he served as classified-advertising manager, was a close friend of Johnny Hynes. In the course of his years at the newspaper, Dazzi had become friendly with one of his chief bosses, John I. Taylor, who had also taken a liking to Hynes. Both Taylor and Dazzi were, in turn, friendly with the promotion manager of the *Globe*, Charlie Moore, who later became a public relations consultant for the Eisenhower administration. Moore was also campaign manager for Robert Bradford, and subsequently he became the governor's chief secretary after Bradford's election in 1946. When the question came up of who would be an appropriate and dependable person to fill in for the absent mayor, therefore, it was not at all surprising that in the wonderfully labyrinthine maze of Boston politics, where personal friendships meant so much, the figure of John B. Hynes should quietly and unobtrusively emerge from the shadows of city hall.[61]

A short time later, Governor Bradford sent word that he wanted to see Thomas P. ("Tip") O'Neill, the Democratic minority leader of the state legislature. Telling him it was a "highly personal matter," he asked Tip to come to his office by the side door at seven o'clock that evening, and not tell anyone about the meeting. When they were together, Bradford told O'Neill that Curley was going to jail and that as governor he could either take his office away from him or let him resume his office when he got out of jail. If he stripped him of his office, the Irish would call him a "no-good, bigoted bastard." But if he let Curley keep his job, his Republican friends would never vote for him again. Rather than having people think he was a bigot, he had made up his mind to name John Hynes as acting mayor, and he asked Tip to persuade Hynes to take the job.[62]

As O'Neill tells the story, when he called Hynes to tell him of the governor's offer, Hynes was taken by surprise. Realizing that if he took

Curley's job the members of the Boston City Council might not vote him back in as city clerk, he agreed to accept the offer only if the governor would guarantee him the city clerk's position for life. O'Neill relayed Hynes's request, the governor quickly agreed to write it into legislation, and Boston had an acting mayor for as long as the present incumbent remained in jail.[63]

One day before Thanksgiving 1947, five months after he first set foot in Danbury prison, James Michael Curley's sentence was commuted by President Harry S Truman. Two days later, on Friday, November 28, Mayor Curley, accompanied by his wife, his daughter, and his son, arrived at City Hall, where he was warmly greeted by hundreds of well-wishers, city workers, and newspaper people.[64] Curley breezed into the building, greeted the temporary mayor with a quick "Hello, Johnny, how are you?," and then proceeded to pose for the waiting photographers. When Hynes suggested that they might get together so that he could bring the returning mayor up to date on city business, Curley waved the idea aside. "There isn't occasion for it," he said airily, "I can take up where I left off." What one newspaperman described as Curley's "coolness" to Hynes was further illustrated when someone asked Curley about the presence of so many of Hynes's friends who were old associates of Maurice Tobin at City Hall while he was away. "I understand they were here only as frequent visitors and advisers," he remarked jokingly, and then added in a more menacing tone: "but they won't be here in the future." It was at this point that John B. Kelly, president of the city council, who had been prevented by Governor Bradford from taking over as temporary mayor in Curley's absence, bitterly charged that Hynes had "schemed" to get the post for himself in return for life tenure as city clerk. Asked for his response, Hynes insisted that he had "neither sought nor requested the position"; he had simply complied when asked "to fill in during an emergency in our city government."[65]

Shooing reporters away, Curley entered his office, closed the door, and settled down to work. In the course of the next frantic few hours, he interviewed sixty persons, found jobs for every one of them, and made a series of decisions involving millions of dollars for contracts relating to such things as parking meters, voting machines, and rubbish contracts. When his work was done and he emerged from his office, he boasted expansively to newspaper reporters: "I have accomplished more in one day than has been done in the five months of my absence"—a remark that, he later observed, made Hynes "visibly upset," but that he himself undoubtedly considered typical of the extemporaneous and humorous response the media expected of a man known for his ready wit. He then departed for a four o'clock doctor's appointment; but the morning edition of Saturday's *Globe* carried the headline: "CURLEY RAPS HYNES, PLANS SHIFTS."[66]

As far as John B. Hynes was concerned, Curley's parting shot was a turning point in his life, and that cutting remark about accomplishing more in one day than the temporary mayor had in five months did more political damage than even Curley himself realized. By all accounts, Hynes, with no intention of moving on to higher political position, had expected to return quietly to his comfortable job as city clerk as soon as the mayor returned from Danbury prison. During the summer months of his tenure as acting mayor, Hynes had ridden up to Boston every morning from his summer cottage in Scituate with his brother-in-law Bob Shea and his friends Frank ("Ike") Sheehan, deputy commissioner of school buildings; Bill O'Hare, head of the welfare department; and Bill's brother Jack. Together they would drive along talking about the affairs of the day, listening to Johnny complaining about various problems in city government, and urging him to consider running for the office of mayor in his own right. "Oh, no, never," Hynes would respond with a laugh. "Not me. I'd never want that job in a million years."[67]

That was certainly Hynes's attitude when he spoke with a newspaper reporter on Thanksgiving Day at his Dorchester home. Hynes said he would be "mighty glad" to see Curley return to City Hall the next day, and emphasized that he was "not even slightly interested" in running for mayor "under any circumstances." He said that he would brief the returning mayor on all city business and "pending matters" and then just go "back down the hall" to his old desk in the city clerk's office. Although he acknowledged that his pay would be reduced from the mayor's salary of $20,000 to the city clerk's salary of $7,500, he was not particularly concerned, since keeping up appearances as mayor had actually cost him money. All in all, "being City Clerk is not a bad job," he told the reporter, "and being City Clerk in a big city like Boston has a distinction all its own. I am proud to be City Clerk for the City of Boston."[68]

Curley's contemptuous insult the next day absolutely infuriated him, however, and it was at that moment that Hynes decided to put his own name in nomination for the next mayoral race in November 1949. By the time he returned home to Dorchester late in the afternoon, Johnny

Hynes was hardly able to control his emotions. "I had never seen my father like that before—it was entirely out of character," recalled his oldest son, Jack, who was a teenager at the time. "When Dad came home he was positively livid with rage, and I had no idea what had happened or what it was all about. His face was all flushed, and he stamped from room to room shouting: 'I'll kill him! I'll bury him! I'll get that no-good son of a bitch!' Then he got on the telephone for the rest of the night calling as many friends as he could think of, repeating what Curley had said about him, telling them that he was getting into the race, and asking for their help."[69]

Congressman "Tip" O'Neill was always fond of repeating the old adage that all politics is local, and perhaps nothing demonstrates that more dramatically than Hynes's quixotic decision to run against Curley. Occasionally there is a point in history when great matters turn on some small event, some minor incident that on another occasion might well have gone unnoticed. In the case of John Hynes, that moment came when Curley's offhand joke suggested that Hynes had not carried out his responsibilities as temporary mayor. It is conceivable that Curley might have gone on for one or two more terms in his favorite role as mayor of Boston had it not been for that thoughtless and flippant remark—in which case the history of Boston might well have taken a different turn. But Hynes could not let it go by; it hurt too much. And as far as anyone can tell, it was the single deciding factor that launched this quiet bureaucrat into the boisterous arena of Boston politics.

In response to Hynes's telephone calls, "the gang" came together for the job ahead—longtime pals, cronies, and buddies of Johnny Hynes, all of them filled with that fierce energy and excitement peculiar to the heart of dyed-in-the-wool Boston politicians girding for the fray. Those early days were the "fun days," according to Hirsh Freed, who later recalled some colorful personalities who today seem to have stepped out of Edwin O'Connor's novel *The Last Hurrah*, based on Curley's late years: Senator Elmer Foote (no one could quite recall where he was "senator" from); Sammy Goodwin, the court jester and master of double-talk who kept them all in stitches; "Jabber" Burke, who had once pitched for the Holy Cross baseball team; and "Spider Murphy," a former boxer whose real name was Barney Levenson.[70]

Not only could Hynes call upon his old friends and cronies, but he was also able to draw on the support of a wide range of city employees and local politicians, especially young war veterans, who had come to suspect that the days of the old Curley regime were numbered, and who were looking for a new candidate to support. Former backers of Maurice Tobin saw in John Hynes a political figure with many of the more urbane characteristics of their own former candidate, while a number of aspiring local political figures saw Hynes as an acceptable alternative for the future. James ("Jamie") Kelley, a young veteran from Roxbury, took over as campaign manager, while Phil Chapman from Dorchester, Fred Hailer from Roslindale, Bill Keenan from Dorchester, Mario Umana from East Boston, Charlie Artesani from Cambridge, and many others threw their support to Hynes. Eddie McLaughlin, a World War II navy veteran out of Readville who had served with young Jack Kennedy in the Pacific, also joined the Hynes camp. The son of Curley's fire commissioner, McLaughlin swore that Hynes was "smarter than all the guys around him put together."[71]

Thirty-year-old John F. Collins, who had just been elected to his second term as state representative from the Roxbury–Jamaica Plain district, was another early Hynes supporter. "I was just a young fellow then, fresh out of four years in the service and starting out on a political career, so I didn't know Curley very well. For that matter, I really didn't know John Hynes that well either," Collins later recalled. "But I thought the time had come for Boston to have new leadership. Since he had been city clerk and had had long experience in city hall, I felt that Hynes had an opportunity to restore the relationship between the city and its citizens. Therefore, I decided to support John Hynes."[72]

By and large, it was highly unlikely that the members of the downtown business and financial community would take much of an interest in the coming election. Few of them would lift a finger to help their old nemesis, James Michael Curley, but until they learned a bit more about John B. Hynes there was little reason for the residents of Wards 4 and 5 to see the new candidate as the lesser of two evils. By the time the campaign went into its final stages, however, there was a subtle but perceptible movement of many former downtown supporters of Maurice Tobin—people such as Robert Cutler, Henry Shattuck, Stuart Rand, and Henry Parkman—to throw their not inconsiderable influence behind the challenger.

Capitalizing on a ground swell of dissatisfaction with the prevailing political system, and offering a prospect of a new and more enlightened administration, the Hynes organization drew together a broad-based coalition of reform-minded middle-class Irish, Jewish, and Italian voters, a scattering of downtown Yankee business and financial leaders, and a number of representatives of the black community in the South End–Roxbury district. Dissatisfied with the minor role that blacks played in city affairs, several middle-class blacks saw Hynes's candidacy against Curley as a hopeful sign for the future. That was certainly the attitude of Victor Bynoe, who had served as Tobin's campaign manager in the black community for a number of years, and who now came aboard Hynes's bandwagon. "Victor," he remembers Hynes telling him, "we have a job to do. Your community has been really wrecked because the boys who grab everything have given nothing to the people. And we've got to rebuild the thing somehow."[73]

In addition to attracting established community leaders, however, the Hynes people were also conscious of the necessity of appealing to a whole new generation of younger voters in the city, many of them veterans recently returned from World War II, who were just getting out of college, preparing to marry and settle down, and who would obviously soon become part of the Boston voting bloc. To help them capture as many of these new voters as possible, the Hynes campaign managers—men such as Andy Dazzi, Tom Pappas, and Jim Kelly—brought in a bright young man just out of Harvard Law School, twenty-year-old Jerome L. Rappaport, who had organized the Law School Forum. "I had never met John Hynes, and didn't know much about him at the time," recalled Rappaport, but since the contest appealed to him, and since he could not take the Massachusetts Bar examination until the following year, when he was twenty-one, he agreed to come aboard. He set up a group called Students for Hynes and pulled in college students from such nearby institutions as Boston College, Boston University, Emmanuel College, and Harvard, Suffolk, and Tufts universities, all of them eager, and many of them older veterans with maturity and commitment. Harnessing their energies and talents, Rappaport prepared radio addresses, organized lectures, canvassed voters, and put out a newspaper that supported the candidacy of Hynes.[74]

In working on the campaign, Rappaport learned some valuable political lessons from the old-timers. One was that most of the young people had to be weaned away from some of the long-established legends about the political invincibility of James Michael Curley. The belief that Curley had a "powerful political machine," for example, had to be done away with. Actually, insisted Rappaport, Curley had no machine at all;

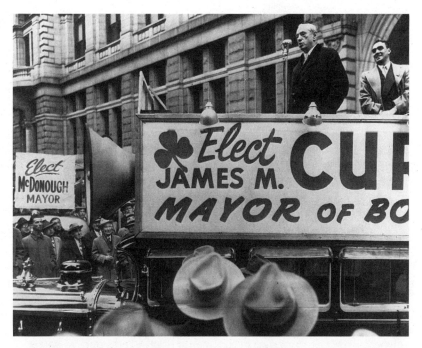

*James Michael Curley was always a colorful campaigner who captivated the Boston voting public with his continuous flair for the unexpected and the dramatic. For the better part of forty years he had served as mayor, governor, and congressman, moving in and out of the political spotlight with amazing regularity. By the 1950s, however, "Young Jim" was in his seventies, and the ravages of old age and bad health had begun to take their toll on his looks, his stamina, and his celebrated speaking voice. Courtesy of the Boston Public Library, Print Department.*

what he had was a highly personalized organization that was, in many ways, rather chaotic. Similarly, the idea that Curley had an absolute lock on the Irish vote in Boston was another myth that had to be dispelled. A close examination of the various elections would reveal serious fractures in the supposedly solid Irish base, just as it would show that Curley won his elections only when a large number of contenders divided the votes.[75]

In putting down these myths and building up the confidence of his young campaigners, however, the old-timers warned Rappaport that his main job was not so much to win the election for Hynes as to keep from losing it to Curley—to avoid making the one costly mistake that would give the wily old politician an opening that would let him "climb all over us." Above all, since Curley still had considerable personal charm and charisma, even among his opponents, the young volunteers were cautioned to avoid appearing to embarrass Curley or treating him publicly in a disrespectful manner. The approach had to be indirect and impersonal, always focusing on issues and avoiding the type of personal confrontation that could boomerang.[76] John Hynes himself followed this advice, conducting an impersonal and dignified campaign in which he never once mentioned James Michael Curley by name—although posters went up throughout the city calling upon the voters of Boston to "Get Rid of Curley Gangsters! VOTE HYNES."

At first Curley expressed genuine surprise at Hynes's decision to run against him; then he displayed obvious amusement at the idea that this unknown and inexperienced bureaucrat would have the temerity to take on one of the most charismatic and powerful big-city bosses in the country. At an impromptu luncheon at City Hall a short time later, Curley raised his glass and offered a good-natured toast that illustrated the comical way in which he viewed the challenge: "Johnny can have my job anytime," he said. "Whenever I quit." This was followed by gales of laughter from the gathering of city hall workers and political hangers-on, who could not possibly take this David-and-Goliath contest seriously.[77]

The 1949 mayoral campaign rolled around—perhaps the last one under the city's old 1909 charter. Once Curley had returned from Danbury prison, his political critics organized to have the city adopt a new "Plan E" form of government, which would introduce a strong council–city manager administration and a system of proportional representation. In part, this was a none-too-subtle attempt to strike a blow at Curley and his type of one-man rule; in part, it was a sincere effort to introduce a more efficient and responsive system of representation. The advocates of Plan E, particularly supported by business, financial, and liberal academic groups in the greater Boston area, sought permission to put the question to the Boston voters at the next mayoral election. The state legislature, however, anxious to avoid taking a public stand on the issue, finally ruled that the first group to file two hundred thousand signatures with the election commission would be allowed to put its referendum on the ballot. Moving with his accustomed skills, Mayor Curley saw to it that it was the proponents of the rival Plan A system—the "strong mayor" type of which he approved—who were the first to file their signatures with the members of an election commission whom he himself had appointed.[78]

In November, therefore, despite the protests of outraged Plan E advocates who were still crying foul, Boston voters not only would choose one out of five mayoral candidates but would also decide whether to select a new charter with a Plan A type of city government. If they voted yes on this question, then they would have a "stronger" mayor for a term of four years; they would also authorize a reorganization of both the city council and the school committee. The city council then had a total of twenty-two members elected on a ward basis—one member representing each of the city's wards. Under Plan A, the council would be reduced to nine members, chosen at large, each member receiving a salary of five thousand dollars a year. At that time, the five members of the school committee served for four years, with three members elected at one time, the other two members elected two years later. Under Plan A, all five members would be elected at the same time and would serve for only two years. Perhaps the most important feature of the Plan A system was that a primary election would be held in September to reduce the number of contestants to two, with a final run-off election in November to determine the winner.[79]

The Plan A proposal generated a great deal of controversy throughout the city. Representatives of the downtown business and financial interests generally supported the change. Henry Shattuck, for example, argued that an at-large council would view municipal problems from a citywide perspective. Councillors elected at large would be subjected to much less pressure from individual neighborhoods, he argued, while the city itself benefit from less logrolling and fewer trade-offs when it came to voting. Representatives from the various neighborhoods, however—places such as Charlestown, East Boston, South Boston, and Roxbury—opposed the new plan, fearing that they would lose whatever power they had accumulated over the years, and that councillors elected at large would be responsible to no particular constituency.

The black community, especially, was split over the ramifications of the plan. Some black leaders vehemently opposed the change, convinced it was designed by the members of the white political establishment to prevent the election of black city councillors. As long as the city followed the old procedure of selecting a councillor from each of the city's twenty-two wards, one or two black councillors were sure to get elected. Once

there were only nine positions, elected on an at-large basis, they contended, black candidates would never have a chance. "Everything was
being done to keep blacks out of office," complained Rev. Michael
Haynes, a well-known Roxbury minister. Other black leaders, however,
supported the new Plan A proposal, convinced that it was at least a first
step in reforming and restructuring the old city government. Victor
Bynoe's brother, John, who looked favorably on the possibility of putting
into effect a "strong mayor" charter, was satisfied with his decision:
"We voted for a new form of government . . . [that] gave much more
administrative responsibility to the mayor. . . . The advantage was to get
rid of them thieves. . . . Everybody was on the take." Controversy over
the Plan A charter, therefore, continued to provide additional excitement
to the mayoral contest as the campaign went into its final stages.[80]

In November 1949 Mayor Curley found himself running against
four political rivals: John B. Hynes, the city clerk; Governor's Councillor
Patrick J. ("Sonny") McDonough; George F. Oakes, a prominent Back
Bay realtor and a registered Republican; and Walter A. O'Brien, a
liberal who the Curley people hoped would draw votes away from any
Republicans who might be tempted to vote for Hynes.[81] Seeing in Hynes
his most dangerous rival, Curley concentrated his attacks on the "little
city clerk," linking him to the downtown business interests and depict-
ing him as "the Republican candidate from the State Street wrecking
crew."[82]

Hynes, in the meantime, campaigned on a pledge to give Boston a
"clean, honest, and efficient administration," and as a result received
generous contributions from a number of conservative Yankee bankers
and downtown business executives, while receiving the endorsement of
the fiercely Republican *Boston Herald* as well as the staunchly Democratic *Boston Post*. Even the sedate *Christian Science Monitor* dropped
its long-standing editorial policy of noninvolvement in municipal politics
and came out in support of John B. Hynes as the only way to finally end
"one-man misrule in Boston."[83]

After weeks of vigorous campaigning, with angry charges and
countercharges flying back and forth, Curley and Hynes were running
neck and neck as the contest drew nearer to what was predicted to be
one of the closest races in generations. Curley told a noontime radio
audience that only his election in 1945 had saved the city of Boston from
disaster. "If I had remained away from the mayor's office in 1946," he
told his listeners, "we would have been a ghost town like many of the

mining towns of the mid-West." He continued to place the blame for Boston's slums on the wealthy landlords who refused to make improvements on the properties they owned in the South End. He promised that he would see to it that the city slowly got rid of "rotten property" and replaced it with modern housing projects. "Skid row," he said in one of his familiar diatribes against old Boston families, "is a heritage of the rumrunners and slave traders."[84]

Hynes, on the other hand, urged his own supporters not to pay any attention to Curley's last-minute appeals. "The present administration is tired and forlorn," he said, playing cleverly on the age factor, which had been a constant element in his campaign. "It has neither the will, the strength, nor the initiative to tackle Boston's problems in the right way." Furthermore, he charged, because the Curley people were "arrogant and defiant of public opinion" and unmindful of their public trust, they must be "eliminated." He encouraged more voters to come over to his side and endorse his candidacy, because he felt that such people supported his belief that attempts to divide the electorate of Boston had ended in "dismal failure." As if underlining that point, on Friday, November 4, Hynes reported that he had received the personal endorsement of Henry Parkman, Jr., a former Republican senator. Sending a cable from Germany, Parkman had written to Hynes: "You have every qualification of character, experience, and ability. Mrs. Parkman and I are voting for you via absentee ballot. Good luck."[85]

The day before the election, the candidates made their final statements as newspapers predicted that a period of fair weather would produce a record turnout of three hundred thousand voters. Curley reminded voters that "Curley Gets Things Done"; Hynes called upon voters to "Restore Boston's Good Name." But the stunning news that day before the elections was a front-page advertisement in which U.S. Secretary of Labor Maurice J. Tobin formally endorsed the candidacy of John B. Hynes and urged voters to "Redeem Boston in the Eyes of America." Although Tobin had remained conspicuously noncommittal throughout the race, a late advertisement by Sonny McDonough, showing a photo of the two of them together and suggesting that Tobin was supporting him, caused Tobin to come out flatly in favor of Hynes.[86] Tobin's endorsement was a shattering blow to Curley and the other candidates, who could only hope that it had come too late to influence those who had already made up their minds. None of them was ready to concede defeat, however, and all of them were determined to fight to the bitter end. All night long, candidates accompanied political rallies as they snaked through the various neighborhoods of the city with long lines of automobiles and packs of roaring motorcycles, horns blowing, sound trucks blaring, and bands playing, red flares blazing, and searchlights sweeping the skies until the early hours of the morning.

As the newspapers had predicted, the turnout was large, the race was close, and the contest fought right down to the wire. When the votes were counted, Hynes had edged out Curley by a margin of only 11,000 votes. The balloting gave Hynes a total of 138,790 votes—the largest ever won by any candidate in the city's history—while Curley came in second with 126,042, the largest vote in the old warrior's long political career. Hynes carried eleven of the city's twenty-two wards; Curley carried the same number. McDonough came through with an unexpectedly poor showing of only 22,360 votes, but they were the critical votes that could have given Curley the election. "I thought he would make a better showing," was all that Curley said to reporters after it was over.[87] Despite the closeness of the outcome and the surprise upset of one of Boston's most famous political figures, many people sensed that something significant had taken place. "The decision rendered yesterday by voters of the city of Boston," commented the editor of the Boston Daily Globe, "marks the end of one era and the beginning of another."[88]

The election of 1949 may have marked the beginning of a new era, but few people had any idea what the new era would be like without James Michael Curley. For nearly forty years he had dominated the political scene in Boston and had established a pattern of ethnic confrontation and social divisiveness that seemed to have become a permanent part of the city's psyche. His reputation for political patronage and municipal cronyism had become so legendary that throughout the country his very name was synonymous with big-city political corruption. The enormity of Boston's tax rate and the chaotic management of its fiscal operations frightened away any significant capital investment in the city's future by private developers, and the reputed venality of its political leaders ruled out significant funding even by members of a supposedly friendly Democratic administration in Washington. The Massachusetts state legislature, still dominated by members of the Republican party, routinely turned a deaf ear to Boston's frequent pleas for financial assistance, and the leaders of the city's hostile business community made

In one of the most remarkable upsets in the city's turbulent political history, in 1949 City Clerk John B. Hynes defeated James Michael Curley to become mayor of Boston. Hynes defeated Curley again in 1951, and a third time in 1955, holding the office of mayor for a total of ten years. A candidate who had never campaigned for elective office, Hynes capitalized on the veterans' vote, the women's vote, and the support of a whole new generation of postwar voters. Courtesy of the Boston Public Library, Print Department.

little effort to associate with a political administration that would not
develop a balanced budget or create a responsible economic structure.

The scandalous fiscal legacy of the Curley years, combined with the
sharp divisions perpetuated between predominantly Irish Catholic politicians and the overwhelmingly Yankee Protestant downtown business
and financial community, produced an economic impasse of gigantic
proportions. Without effective leadership, imaginative coalitions, or
outside assistance of any kind, the aging infrastructure of the city
continued to crumble, and the housing stock deteriorated at a rapid
pace. Boston's once-famous port facilities fell into disuse, its rolling
stock rusted in abandoned railroad yards, and a discouraging number
of businesses left the city every day. No new buildings were being built;
no new housing was being constructed; streets and roads were badly in
need of repairs. Even when more sophisticated industries began to spring
up after World War II, businessmen deliberately avoided the crowded
downtown area by moving to the suburbs.

Running against Curley in 1949, John B. Hynes organized his
campaign around the theme of a reformed and reconstructed "New
Boston." He promised to restore Boston's "good name and reputation
throughout the land" and assured voters that he would do away with the
"arrogance, waste, and inefficiency" that had for so long characterized
operations at city hall. He insisted that he would reduce the tax burdens
that members of the previous administration had placed on working-
class citizens. Noting that women now held the majority of votes in the
city, he appealed directly to female voters to help him "restore Boston's
good name and reputation."[89] By emphasizing the values of honesty and
integrity, Hynes believed he could change the tarnished image of the
city's political system, upgrade the municipality's fiscal operations, and
attract the type of private investment and public funding that would
make substantial reconstruction possible.

The question was, however, whether such a thing as a New Boston
was possible. In the light of the Curley legacy, could the new mayor
carry out his campaign promises? Would he be able to break down
social and religious rivalries that had gone on for generations; form new
alliances between political leaders and business executives; reorganize
the financial structure of the city administration; attract corporate
investments from outside companies; bring in substantial funding from
the federal government; renew the infrastructure of an old and battered

city; and establish the honesty of the mayor of Boston and the integrity of his administration?

Many people felt that while the dream of a New Boston was a lofty ideal, John Hynes would never be able to carry it off. He was an inoffensive bureaucrat who had never before run for public office, had no previous political experience, and who had neither a neighborhood base nor a citywide organization. He would be lucky, they said, if he were elected to a second term, considering Jim Curley's continued popularity and demonstrated political resiliency.

On balance, the odds seemed definitely against Hynes. Not only was he up against a system perpetuated for decades by the Curley regime, but since World War II conditions in the city had changed considerably. In the wake of postwar cutbacks, businesses that had been temporarily stimulated by wartime contracts either shut down or moved out of the state completely. That slowdown would do nothing to buoy Hynes's hopes of attracting outside money and investments for his New Boston, and it would obviously play havoc with the volatile tax rate. Furthermore, within the city itself changes were taking place that could have serious effects on the new mayor's political future. Many of Boston's old-time ethnic neighborhoods, which had supplied such solid support for the city's Irish mayors in the past, were now losing their numbers, their political clout, and their ethnic distinctiveness. Sons and daughters of families that had now been in America for three or four generations had lost touch with their ethnic roots and were all but impervious to old neighborhood appeals. They felt no particular attachments to communities such as Charlestown, Dorchester, East Boston, and South Boston, and when their personal fortunes brightened they left the old three-deckers in which their families had lived for generations and moved out to new split-level ranch houses in the suburbs.

With some notable exceptions, such as the heavily Italian-populated North End, by the late 1940s and early 1950s many of the old neighborhoods of Boston were fast becoming mere geographical expressions. Increasingly transient populations showed little evidence of the ethnic solidarity or the political unity that had once made these districts such a powerful influence in city politics. And with the accelerating movement into the suburbs in search of finer houses and better-paying jobs after World War II, the population of Boston was declining at an alarming rate. In 1950 the population of the city was listed at over eight hundred thousand; over the course of the next ten years it dropped to less than seven hundred thousand, with no sign of leveling off. The Curley era was being ushered out, it is true, but it was by no means clear what would take its place.

# 2

# Forming a New Coalition

Monday, January 2, 1950, was inauguration day in the city of Boston. John B. Hynes, his wife, Marion, and their five children—Jack, the oldest boy, was home from his freshman year at Notre Dame—got up at 5:30 that morning, had a quick breakfast, and attended 6:45 Mass at St. Gregory's Church in Dorchester in preparation for the great occasion. At ten o'clock, before a gathering of more than three thousand persons at Symphony Hall, the fifty-two-year-old Hynes took the oath of office as mayor of Boston in the first of such ceremonies to be televised. Seated on the platform were Secretary of Labor Maurice J. Tobin, representing President Harry Truman; Paul A. Dever, governor of the commonwealth; the retiring mayor, James Michael Curley; and the former mayors Malcolm Peters, Frederick Mansfield, and John Kerrigan. After Archbishop Richard J. Cushing gave the invocation, the incoming mayor delivered a forty-five-minute speech in which he outlined the major goals of his administration.[1]

Touching on a sensitive issue affecting every citizen, he first promised to keep the tax rate below a threatened twelve-dollar rise; then he moved on to the pressing issue of the physical condition of the city. He promised that he would complete the construction of veterans' housing, toward which Boston was entitled to $17.5 million in state funds; that he would present a master plan to obtain federal funding for slum clearance; and that he would untangle the city's snarled traffic patterns by means of such techniques as widening streets and constructing off-street parking, including the construction of a parking garage under Boston Common. Finally, he emphasized the appropriate role of city government in meeting the needs of the elderly, the disabled, and the dependent, especially by improving services at the City Hospital, the Boston Sanitorium, and the Long Island Hospital. Many other things, too, he observed, needed to be done—tightening up contracts, doing away with monopoly and collusion, improving the budget department, cutting back on expenses, "selling" the city of Boston to outsiders, keeping the community free from religious and racial strife—but he indicated that it would take more than the two years of his first administration to bring about all the changes that a new and improved city required. These were relatively modest proposals, generally in keeping with the programs outlined by previous mayors. Although he spoke about seeking federal funding for slum clearance, the new mayor's inaugural address offered little in the way of a broader vision of urban renewal.[2]

Tuesday, January 3, was a working day, and Mayor Hynes pulled up before City Hall in the official limousine at 9:20 A.M., looking more like a downtown businessman than a local politician with his gray hat, a dark gray overcoat over his dark blue double-breasted suit, and conservative red-and-blue striped tie. His driver, friend, and confidant, Bob Curtis, a huge young veteran who had fought in Europe with Patton (and hated him!) and now lived quietly with his mother on River Street, got out and held the car door for the mayor with a broad grin on his beefy face. Greeting well-wishers as he pushed through the wrought-iron gates at the School Street entrance, Hynes strode along the concrete walk flanked on the left by Richard Greenough's 1856 study of Benjamin Franklin and on the right by Thomas Ball's statue of Josiah Quincy, Boston's second mayor. Before him was City Hall, familiar to him after all these years of city service, yet always an impressive sight. A stately building of Concord granite, ornamented with columns and pilasters and topped by a convex mansard roof, it had been built during the Civil War, almost ninety years earlier. Inspired by the Tuileries Palace and the 1850s extension to the Louvre in Paris, designed by Gridley J. F. Bryant and Arthur Gilman, it was among the first of Boston's French Second Empire structures. Walking briskly up the front steps despite the spell of unseasonably warm weather, Hynes went promptly to the mayor's office on the second floor. Moving to one side a huge basket of flowers, and to the other side a large pile of congratulatory letters and telegrams, he settled down at his desk to swear in his department heads and get his administration to work.[3]

At the center of things in the office was his chief aide, Tom McCusker, a former Tobin worker, thin, nervous, excitable, an inveterate chain-smoker, who managed operations, served as appointment secretary, and controlled access to the mayor with an iron hand. "Amby" Griffin, was there too, a quiet and devoted campaign worker from Dorchester, always ready to run errands, get coffee, and do whatever needed to be done. And Harry Fleming was usually in the background somewhere, chewing on a cigar, and giving the general appearance of a holdover from the old Curley days. As things got under way, the new mayor was certainly aware that the *Minneapolis Tribune* had picked Boston as one of eleven "All-American cities" across the country where voters "got mad enough to fight," had turned out the old "big city bosses," and had moved in the direction of improved city government. Boston had been selected because it had rejected Curley, because it had picked Hynes, who promised "progress and integrity," and because it had chosen a new city charter that emphasized reform and accountability.[4]

Although he had worked for a long time in city government and had many personal friends, John B. Hynes was largely unknown to the general public. Even when newspapers carried bits and pieces of his campaign biography, there was little to distinguish the new mayor of Boston from most men his age who had grown up in similar environments. Hynes was born on September 22, 1897, on East Lenox Street in the South End, the son of immigrant parents. His father, Bernard, worked as a car inspector for the Boston & Albany Railroad; his mother, Anna (Healy), passed away when he was only seven years old. John had a difficult early life. There was no money, little food, and not much fun. His father was a dark and taciturn Irishman who sat grimly in his rocking chair and left the family pretty much to look after its own affairs. John and his older brother, Tom, had to work hard to make both ends meet and to help bring up the three younger children by Barney's second marriage. But he never became discouraged, and never lost heart. "If things don't go the right way," his daughter Marie recalled his telling his own children in later years, "don't wallow in it. Pick yourself up and get moving—always look ahead."⁵ That was Hynes's philosophy all through life.

When he was ten, the Hynes family followed the pattern of an increasing number of Irish and moved out of Boston to a home on Rockne Street in the Neponset section of Dorchester, which would eventually become part of Saint Brendan's parish when the new church was built in the early 1930s. As far back as colonial times, Dorchester had been a large, sprawling, rural community lying just beyond the perimeters of Boston, characterized by rich farmlands, lush orchards, and open fields where cattle and sheep grazed contentedly. Although it came to have a successful chocolate factory, a nail factory, and a scattering of paper factories along the Neponset River, the town's population just before the Civil War numbered only a little over eight thousand persons. Even by 1870 its population was still only about twelve thousand, but with its annexation to the city of Boston that year, there began a rapid development. With new waves of immigrants settling into the already overcrowded downtown area after the war, a number of middle-class residents—lawyers, contractors, teachers, salesmen, small businessmen—moved out of the city and made their way to Dorchester, where they built comfortable single-family homes for themselves. As cheaper and more effective streetcar lines began to extend outward from the city during the 1880s and 1890s, members of the lower middle class—machinists, cloth cutters, piano makers, printers, furniture makers—also moved into Dorchester, settling first into less expensive two-family houses and three-deckers, and later moving into the kind of modest, single-family home the Hynes family enjoyed during the early years.⁶

At the age of fourteen, John went to work for the telephone company as an office boy for fourteen dollars a week while attending Dorchester night school, where he learned stenography and other business subjects. After a brief stint in the air corps in World War I, he was appointed by Mayor Andrew J. Peters as a stenographer in the health department. After that, he served in the auditing department, then moved up to become chief clerk in Mayor Curley's office. In 1924 Hynes enrolled in night classes at Suffolk Law School, and was admitted to the Massachusetts Bar in 1927, the year after he married Marion H. Barry from South Boston and began a family that would eventually number three boys, Jack, Barry, and Richard, and two girls, Marie and Nancy. By the time of his marriage he was working in the budget department, and in 1929 he became assistant city clerk under the legendary Wilfred J. Doyle. After service in World War II, where he attained the rank of lieutenant colonel, he became city clerk in 1945, which meant that he also served as clerk of the city council.

In 1936 Hynes had bought a slightly larger single-family house of his own on Druid Street in the Ashmont section of Dorchester, where his last child, Richard, was born the following year, and where he remained for the rest of his life. "My father was a real family man," said his daughter Marie, recalling that he would come home from work every night with the side pocket of his topcoat bulging with a huge candy bar. It became a ritual. He would hang the coat in the closet and then settle down in the easy chair to read his newspaper—and *nobody* was allowed to interfere with his newspaper. Then he would get up, and when the children heard the creak of the closet door they knew he was getting the candy out of his pocket. They would all rush in and gather around, and their father would break up the bar and make sure each one of them got a piece. "He loved to have all the family together, the children and then the grandchildren," said Marie. "I wondered sometimes if he was trying to make up for the lack of warmth and enjoyment he himself never had as a child.

"Daddy was also a real clothes horse," she laughed. "He just loved good clothes and couldn't wait for a chance to go shopping in Filene's basement." He became fond of golf and played it as often as possible, but when the weather was poor or he couldn't get away from work he would stay in town with close friends and play billiards. He fancied himself a good cook, and every Saturday night he had all the members of the family over to the Druid Street home so that he could cook baked beans and frankfurts.[7]

Overall, Hynes was a quiet, gentle, compassionate person who had a love of writing and a gift for composing poetry, who attended Mass every morning, and who telephoned his wife, Marion, regularly at noon every day to see how things were at home. Since he had worked for so long in the vast political bureaucracy of the city, he became friendly with all kinds of people, from janitors and maintenance personnel to the upper levels of civil service professionals and elected officials. Newspaper reporters especially became fond of the new mayor, who usually met with them informally around the glass oval table in his office about four o'clock every afternoon to give out whatever information he had to offer and to pick up stories about what was happening throughout the city.

"John Hynes was what we called a regular guy," wrote the *Globe*'s Joseph Keblinsky, "a fine, kindly gentleman, mild of manner and soft of speech, with a gentle sense of humor and a warm, genuinely non-political smile. He disliked ostentation. He liked poetry, and quite often wrote some rhymes for his own pleasure."[8] Because of his friendly disposition and his approachable personality, all sorts of people came to Hynes for personal advice or career recommendations.

Perhaps because Hynes was little known and his initial organization displayed few differences from city hall assemblages of the past, there was little indication that the new administration was going to be any different from the succession of Irish Catholic administrations that had gone before. It would be difficult to exaggerate the old-time hostilities that still existed as late as the 1950s between the Irish and the Yankees, the Catholics and the Protestants, the inhabitants of downtown Boston and the residents of the neighborhoods. Honed to a fine sharpness by the malicious tactics of James Michael Curley ("God, how the business community hated Curley!" recalled Ephron Catlin, Jr., of the First National Bank), this traditional feuding virtually paralyzed community action, precluded any effective relationships between political leaders and spokesmen of the business community, and prevented the kind of urban progress that was taking place in other American cities. Recalling the long-standing enmity of the Yankees toward Curley, the *Boston Globe* wrote many years later that the "negative attitudes of the Yankee-dominated insurance industry was so fervent that no mortgages on buildings in Irish-dominated Boston were granted."[9] Unable to match the Irish in the multiplication of their numbers, the Yankees had yielded them the political management of the city, but withheld from them the financial resources necessary to change it.

Starting as early as 1884 with the election of Hugh O'Brien, the city's first Irish-born candidate, leaders of the Protestant establishment began deliberately restricting the powers of city government and clipping the wings of its mayor. But it was after the first election of John F. ("Honey Fitz") Fitzgerald in 1905 that the Yankees really got serious. "During these years," wrote one political analyst, "Boston's Yankees had conducted political guerrilla warfare on their Irish adversaries down the hill at City Hall."[10] Using their power in the state legislature, Republicans set limits on the city's ability to borrow funds, and set a maximum on its spending for public schools. They refused to let Boston raise its taxes or increase its assessments without specific permission of the state legislature, and they even insisted on taking the appointment of the city's own police commissioner out of the hands of the mayor. Liquor sales in Boston were regulated by a state licensing board, as were the operations of amusements and dining places. Members of the downtown Good Government Association arranged for the state legislature to appoint a special watchdog agency called the Finance Commission (the "Fin Com"), consisting of seven prominent business and civic leaders, to monitor the municipal administration and investigate "all matters pertaining to the finances of the city." Adding insult to injury, the city of Boston had to foot the bill for the Fin Com, even though its members were appointed by the Republican governor of the Commonwealth.[11]

Although the downtown establishment, having failed to prevent Honey Fitz from defeating the eminent James Jackson Storrow in 1910, had had to watch the Irish upstart become Boston's first four-year mayor, it had succeeded in establishing such a complex of controls and restrictions that it became almost impossible for Boston Democrats to conduct their own affairs or to finance their own needs. Major city expenses had to be borne chiefly by real estate taxes, which rose to such high levels that a comparison made in the 1950s between Boston and twenty other large American cities put the Bay State capital on the top of the charts listing equalized property rates. Even the gradual post–World War II shift in the state legislature from Republican to Democratic control did not particularly work to the city's advantage. Representatives from the outlying suburbs, now basking in the revenues obtained from lucrative postwar real estate and highway deals, assumed a holier-than-thou attitude toward the complicated problems of the big city. They pointed their fingers accusingly at "dirty Boston politics" and refused to support any measures that would help the city solve its complex fiscal problems.[12]

"The old Yankee economic community gave the city to the Irish community, with which it was in conflict in the early days," wrote Joseph F. Slavet, director of the privately funded Municipal Research Bureau, "but it didn't give them the wealth of the city." In setting out to restructure the city in any substantial fashion, Hynes would find that Boston's mayor had both hands tied behind his back. Members of the still Republican-dominated state legislature, to cite one group, would have serious reservations about giving the mayor of Boston and his political supporters the kind of increased funding necessary for making substantial changes in the city's infrastructure. At the same time, members of the generally hostile Yankee business establishment would show little eagerness to sponsor programs put forth by Irish politicians with whom they had been at war for as long as they could remember. The new mayor had yet to establish his credentials.

At first, there seemed no particular reason that Hynes should be any different from his predecessors either in his commitment to the general welfare or in his ability to get things done. Despite his carefully groomed white hair, his good manners, his almost bankerly features, and a general agreement that he was a "nice guy," he was the product of Irish Catholic neighborhoods, he was a career bureaucrat, he had received his job as chief clerk from James Michael Curley, and he was known to be a close friend of Maurice Tobin. Leaders of the downtown business community were already convinced that Boston was in the hands of "supercrooks," according to Ephron Catlin, and had come to believe that all Irish politicians were cut from the same cloth. "Nobody had ever seen an honest Irishman around here," Catlin remarked bluntly, and there was every reason to expect that Hynes was just more of the same.[13] Gradually, however, as the new administration got under way, it began to dawn on people that John B. Hynes might be different from most of the other Boston politicians they had known. He seemed a genuinely honest man, devoted to the principle of public service, who was really interested in performing his duties as mayor to help the city and the people who lived in the city, rather than lining his own pockets and those of his friends and cronies.

Here was a consideration that had a particular appeal to a whole new generation of voters in the city. A great many of these people were recent veterans of World War II, sober and mature, who had returned from their overseas experiences ready to buy a house, get married, raise a family, and take up their civilian responsibilities once again. Most of them came from middle-class families, and a number of them were college graduates. They were less defensive about their ethnic origins, less parochial in their religious beliefs, less insecure about their social status, and more sophisticated in their political idealism than those who had lived through the 1920s and 1930s. Although most of these young men were steeped in the traditions of old-time Democratic politics and thoroughly enjoyed the uproarious anecdotes and stories told by the old-timers, they were beginning to feel that public service was something that demanded more than dirty tricks and practical jokes. While they were still amused at the sight of the typical Boston "pol" walking down School Street in his chesterfield coat with the velvet collar, the pearl gray fedora, the splashy necktie, and the huge cigar sticking out of the corner of his mouth, they were no longer convinced that politics representative of the James Cagney–Pat O'Brien era was any longer relevant to the modern atomic age. They were clearly looking for a new type of political leader.[14]

In many ways, Hynes seemed to fit the mold of this "new" politician—quiet, reserved, competent, respectful, and soft-spoken—indeed, to the point where some people referred to him as "Whispering Johnny." He was a man seemingly without bitterness or rancor; one of his longtime friends once asked him, "Isn't there anyone you hate?," to which he responded after a moment of serious reflection, "Well, yes, there was one fellow who used to steal from the poor boxes." But there were times when Hynes could lose his temper over more serious issues, and his daughter Marie recalled one particular occasion when she saw her father angrier than she had ever seen him before. "One Christmas morning, when Daddy was mayor, we woke up to see a bright new black convertible with a big red bow around it sitting in the middle of our driveway. It was a gift from one of the local automobile dealers who obviously wanted to get a contract for city vehicles without going through the bidding process. Well, when Daddy saw it, he became absolutely furious, picked up the telephone, and hollered at the dealer: 'You get over here and get your car out of my driveway right now or I'm calling the police!' You didn't act that way with my father; that's not the way he did things."[15]

That some forty years later several of the Hynes children could still remember that episode so vividly seems to corroborate assurances that angry outbursts by their father were few and far between. Hynes generally controlled his feelings, worked quietly, and always tried to reduce the level of tensions. He did not try to rekindle old ethnic antagonisms; he avoided setting the needs of the outlying neighborhoods against the interests of the central city; and he refused to employ the old divisive political tactics of pitting Catholics against Protestants. His political appeal was for a new coalition of concerned citizens in which the formerly diverse elements could come together and work for the benefit of the city as a whole. Because of his approach to city politics, many Boston Yankees began to view Hynes as a representative of the Irish much more in the acceptable tradition of the city's first Irish mayors, Hugh O'Brien and Patrick Collins, than in the irreverent mold of "Honey Fitz" or Jim Curley.

There were also more practical reasons, of course, for Republicans to see the new man as a much more acceptable alternative to previous municipal leaders. He did not pose any long-term threat to the establishment. He did not represent any of the ward bosses, nor was he part of any organized Irish Democratic political machine that might move into the power vacuum now that Curley was gone from the scene. While it was true that he was a career bureaucrat who had worked his way up the political ladder eventually to become city clerk, that was not an office usually associated with the direction of a citywide political network.

It took a while for the business community to wake up to the fact

*As mayor of Boston, John B. Hynes (extreme right) decided to launch a series of renovation projects that would clear slums, improve blighted areas, and renew the face of an old and badly scarred city. In forming a special committee to plan renewal projects for the South Station area, Hynes established a new coalition of financial and political leaders by inviting prominent businessmen such as Harold Hodgkinson of Filene's (third from right) to serve on commissions with members of his administration. Courtesy of the Boston Public Library, Print Department.*

that the new mayor was "a decent man," said Ephron Catlin, but slowly the downtown leaders began to appreciate that Hynes was a man they might be able to trust and to work with. Hynes, in turn, quietly and shrewdly moved to establish closer and more familiar ties with downtown Republicans by making some carefully calculated appointments. He put the popular John D. ("Handsome Jack") Brown in the position of city greeter and staff person in charge of distinguished guests. Stuart C. Rand, a well-known downtown attorney who had become an early supporter, was named as a hospital trustee; William F. Keesler, vice president of the First National Bank, was appointed a real estate commissioner; and George Oakes, a former Republican opponent in the 1949 contest, was placed on the city planning board.

"Building bridges with the local business community was one area where Hynes really made a contribution to the city's future development," Kane Simonian, director of the Boston Redevelopment Authority, later reflected. "For years, Jim Curley had fought tooth and nail with the business leaders, and as a result the city had been torn apart— absolutely paralyzed. But now Hynes met with them, talked with them, and listened to them. He would form special committees composed of first-rate people like Bill Keesler of the First National [Bank], Ralph Lowell of the [Boston] Safe Deposit [and Trust Company], Bob Morgan of the Boston Five [Cents Savings Bank], Tom Dignan of Boston Edison, and O. Kelley Anderson of New England Mutual [Life Insurance Company] to give him advice when difficult problems arose. This was a major change in the direction of city government."[16] In future years this would open Hynes to charges that he was "in the pocket" of the downtown bankers, an innocent dupe manipulated by investors and real estate developers. At the time, however, the business community was the only responsible group that could provide the money, the backing, and the leverage he needed to bring about changes in the city.

Hynes had a nostalgic view of the charms of what he called "old Dame Boston," and the question of how to capitalize on the city's impressive historical landmarks and monuments was the subject of frequent conversations with his director of public celebrations, Col. Paul Hines of West Roxbury.[17] Early in March 1951 the chief editorial writer of the *Boston Herald* and the *Boston Traveler*, William Schofield, published an article telling about a conversation he had had with Bob Winn, keeper of the Old North Church, who complained that people came from all over the world to see Boston's famous shrines but ended up seeing only a handful of them. Winn suggested creating a foot path through the city—a "Puritan Path," a "Liberty Loop," a "Freedom's Way," or "whatever you want to call it"—so that visitors would know where to start and what course to follow. A series of signs could guide visitors from one shrine to the next, starting in front of the State House, going down to the Old Granary Burying Ground, along Tremont Street to King's Chapel, then down School Street to the Old South Meeting House. From there, visitors would walk to the Old State House and Faneuil Hall, then on to the Paul Revere House, the Old North Church, and the Copp's Hill Burial Ground. The tourists would end up their "hike" at the North Station, where they could get transportation elsewhere. On a state level, Winn suggested that the same sort of thing could be done with an automobile route taking in such historical sites as Bunker Hill, Old Ironsides, Lexington, Concord, and the Wayside Inn. If Bostonians could develop such a walking tour to keep hapless visitors from "going beserk" trying to follow the complex maze of Boston's streets, Schofield repeated in a follow-up article, they would be recognizing their solemn trusteeship of some of the most "precious of Americana."[18] "I hope Mayor John B. Hynes and [chamber of commerce president] Harry J. Blake are listening today," he wrote, for a public relations idea that would pay back "diamonds for dimes."[19]

Mayor Hynes, already interested in attracting a greater number of tourists to Boston, was indeed listening to Schofield's proposal. Before the month was out he let it be known that he intended to go along with the plan. "It's a good idea, and it won't cost much," he said. "We're all for it." He then turned the project over to his director of celebrations, Paul Hines, for development, and subsequently had the city of Boston give Schofield an appropriate award of recognition.[20] Local business and civic leaders also quickly picked up on the idea. "I'll buy it!" announced Harry Blake, speaking for the Greater Boston Chamber of Commerce; Ralph Eastman of the State Street Trust pronounced the idea a "natural" for Boston; traffic commissioner William Arthur Reilly considered it a "swell idea" and said that he was all for it.

By June it was agreed that the project would be called the Freedom Trail, and a Freedom Trail Foundation was established with Senator Leverett Saltonstall as its first president and Richard A. Berenson as its treasurer. A distinguished wine importer and philanthropist, Berenson provided direction to the new project, and under his guidance the historical route began to take shape, although at first it was little more than a series of painted plywood markers.[21] By 1953 the wooden markers had been replaced with sturdier metal signs, and local businesses saw obvious commercial possibilities in the fact that an estimated forty thousand visitors and tourists were already walking the Freedom Trail each year. In 1958 the Advertising Club's president, Paul Provandie, together with such members as Robert Friedman and Luella Cannam, adopted the Freedom Trail as a permanent community project, as did the Greater Boston Chamber of Commerce. The John Hancock Insurance Company, with the support of its president, Byron Eliot, defrayed the costs of the first brochures; businessmen and bankers made charitable contributions to the project; and the city agreed to lay the paint-and-brick line that led visitors through some of the most important historic sites in Boston. Here was an early example of the way in which Hynes's improved relations with local business interests produced a worthwhile public project that eventually not only publicized the historical importance of Boston but also enhanced the city's commercial attractiveness.[22]

Turning from the downtown area to Boston's surrounding neighborhoods, Hynes sought to build up his own strength among black voters in the South End by bypassing both the local party boss, Dr. Silas F. ("Shag") Taylor, and the old-time Curley Democrats, and by bringing in his own people. He named Victor Bynoe a Boston street commissioner ("Hynes was the first guy that did the right thing," commented Bynoe), and a short time later Hynes appointed Beulah S. Hester to be the first black person on the Board of Overseers of Public Welfare. Mrs. Hester was a social worker and the wife of Rev. William H. Hester, then pastor of the Twelfth Baptist Church, where a young Boston University student named Martin Luther King, Jr., worshiped and occasionally preached.[23] In 1953 Hynes continued to demonstrate his concern with building up a multicultural coalition with four prestigious appointments as trustees to the Boston Public Library: Frank W. Buxton, the editor in chief of the Republican *Boston Herald*; Lee M. Friedman, a prominent Jewish lawyer and noted bibliophile; Richard J. Cushing, the archbishop of the Catholic archdiocese; and Judge Frank J. ("Daisy") Donahue, described by one attorney as "the scourge of the lazy or indifferent lawyer," who was still holding court in his nineties. This was a strategic political coup that could only add strength to Hynes's first years in office and broaden the base of his future political support.

As Hynes settled down to his first term as mayor of Boston, he was not yet ready to involve himself in the broader and more long-range issues he had discussed in his inaugural address. Rather, he concerned himself with the more routine and mundane tasks of city government that were regarded as the appropriate domain of the chief executive. City government during this period was generally viewed as local government, as municipal administration, whose primary function was to deal with largely procedural issues involving departments, boards, and agencies, with water, sewers, and traffic. At the same time, however, a growing number of concerned citizens felt that the time had come for city government to be reformed in its operations and enlarged in its responsibilities. Efforts by respectable civic leaders like Dan Fenn, Frank Moloney, and Dan Ahearn to introduce the Plan E, city-manager type of government was a clear indication of the desire for reform along lines suggested by the National Municipal League.[24]

As a longtime city clerk and professional bureaucrat, Hynes was acutely aware that so many departments, boards, bureaus, and agencies had multiplied over the years, with overlapping functions, conflicting jurisdictions, and bloated personnel rosters, that the operations of city government had become counterproductive and the prospects of hiring any bright young employees practically impossible. Shortly after taking office, therefore, Hynes appointed young Jerome Rappaport as one of his secretaries and assigned him to serve as his liaison to a special commission, composed of the auditor Charles Fox and several other department heads, to suggest ways in which the administrative structure of city government could be reorganized. This was in line with what was going on in Washington at that time, when President Harry Truman asked former president Herbert Hoover to reform the executive departments of the federal government. The so-called Hoover Commission issued a series of reports, recommending some 350 changes designed to eliminate the duplication and overlapping of authority, which were eventually incorporated into the Reorganization Act of 1949.

Adopting a similar approach at the local level, Hynes empowered his commission to have department heads define their roles, explain their missions, provide detailed job descriptions, and offer recommendations for administrative changes and reforms. As a result of their studies and interviews, the members of the Hynes commission came up with an impressive series of printed volumes recommending the consolidation of departments, a streamlining of functions, and a greater and more direct role for the mayor in getting things done. Working from these recommendations during the course of his tenure, Hynes reduced the number of city departments from thirty-eight to twenty-six, reclassified numerous job titles, and reorganized the assessing, fire, library, welfare, and planning departments. He also coordinated inspections among the building, fire, and health departments, as well as being the first executive to install a computer system in the auditing department.

As important as these administrative improvements were, Rappaport complained that there was still no effective mechanism for discussing innovative projects or establishing anything like a long-range master plan for the city.[25] There was a city planning committee, it is true, but it was simply a group of people without an effective director, no perceived function, and no way of getting their ideas or proposals actually into operation. Rappaport was pleased to observe that, in the course of implementing his administrative changes, Hynes also began structuring a different kind of planning board, headed by familiar loyalists like Tom McDonough and Tom McCormack, who not only would continue to focus on routine items of business such as health, safety, zoning, and traffic, but now could also begin to conceptualize the direction in which the city would be headed by the year 2000. For the first time, according to Rappaport, this involved going outside and bringing in some younger people, such as Ralph Taylor, who had received some formal training in urban affairs and city planning, and who could bring their academic expertise to bear on the problems of city government.[26]

In addition to having elected John B. Hynes as mayor in November 1949, the voters of Boston had also chosen to introduce the new Plan A charter, which was scheduled to go into effect in 1951, providing a preliminary election in September and a final run-off election in November. Hynes had been in office only a little over year and a half, therefore, when he had to begin making preparations for reelection. As he laid plans for the 1951 campaign, he found that his opposition consisted of a former police commissioner, Joseph F. Timilty; a retired business consultant, Thomas J. O'Brien; and his old rival, James Michael Curley, who was seeking his fifth term as mayor, hopeful that Hynes's victory two years earlier had been an accident, a fluke, a temporary blip on the local political screen. At the drawing held in the city council chambers on School Street the morning of Tuesday, September 1, it was determined that the name of Hynes would be listed first, Timilty second, O'Brien third, and Curley fourth. Always the optimist, Curley tipped his gray felt hat and quipped to the waiting reporters in his rich, familiar baritone: "The first shall be last and the last shall be first."[27]

But it was by no means a foregone conclusion that the last would be first. As the campaign got under way, it was painfully obvious to Curley that the weight of public opinion as well as the influences of the new citywide coalitions had turned against him. Nevertheless, he struck out at his opponent with all his customary ebullience, accusing Hynes of sitting placidly by while the Republican-dominated state senate killed bills that would have constructed a lagoon in South Boston's City Point section and a new bathhouse in the Orient Heights section of East Boston. Possibly his failure to act on behalf of "the little people," suggested Curley to his listeners with a knowing smile, might be due to the fear of offending "Henry Shattuck and his Republican friends."[28] Curley continued to charge that Hynes was being supported by the downtown "banking clique" composed of such prominent Republicans as Shattuck, Stuart Rand, Henry Parkman, and F. Murray Forbes, whom he likened to the "Bourbons of French Revolution days."[29] He also complained bitterly about the ingratitude of all those successful Irish and Italian contractors "who got their start from Curley" but who had turned against him and were now lining up with the "pressitutes [sic]," downtown bankers, members of the underworld, and the New Boston Committee, "not necessarily in that order."[30] Although he could sneer contemptuously at the young "sunshine patriots" who had formed a liberal political action group called the New Boston Committee under the leadership of a "zealous young barrister" named Jerome Rappaport, young liberals he considered "politically naive" for endorsing Hynes and other "inexperienced candidates," it was obvious that Curley was losing ground.[31]

Hynes generally ignored the personal attacks of his rivals (Timilty kept referring to him as "Sales Tax Johnny") and kept hammering away at the "progress" he had achieved during his two-year term in office. At a succession of house parties, veterans' halls, afternoon teas, television appearances, and radio shows, he demonstrated the way in which political campaigning had changed in the preceding few years as a result of radio and television. Indeed, all the candidates recognized that the old-time outdoor rally was a thing of the past. "People won't come out to rallies," complained Timilty. "They stay at home with their TV and radios."[32] In these smaller but more intimate groups, Hynes spoke of the new facilities he had added to the City Hospital, new traffic lights, new playgrounds for children, a new branch library, the start of a new swimming pool in the North End, plans for one at Franklin Park, $2 million spent on schoolhouse repairs, the completion of a $2.6 million viaduct to the Long Island Hospital, and more public housing than in the entire four years of the previous administration. He reported that over four thousand units of public housing had already been placed under construction, with more to come by the end of the year. Above all, he told his audiences, he had stopped the "tax abatement racket that existed for years" and could now state that "no scandals have occurred since I've been at City Hall, and the name of Boston is now in good repute wherever you may go."[33]

Those were claims that Curley could not let go by unanswered, and he responded to his opponent's list of achievements by recording his own accomplishments in his typically biting fashion. "Why, if Johnny climbed the highest hill and gazed around him in every direction," he quipped to the obvious delight of his listeners, "he would be unable to find a single mole hill, let alone monument, that was erected during his administration. . . . I regret to say that the only monuments Hynes built are a greater debt and a higher tax rate."[34] But Hynes could have his moments too, and occasionally he retaliated with an adeptness that surprised even Curley. On one occasion when both men were together, for example, Curley criticized the Hynes administration for not appropriating seventy-five hundred dollars for an oil painting of George Washington commanding troops at Dorchester Heights during the evacuation of Boston. "Why, when I was mayor," he boasted expansively, "there was always sufficient money for such worthy purposes." "Well," snapped back Hynes with a smile, "if there was any money left in the treasury when I succeeded you, I have never been able to locate it." Even Curley had to admit that he had left himself wide open for that one.[35]

As the preliminary race entered its final days, the candidates stepped up the pace of their campaigning. Hynes spoke to gatherings of women voters at well-attended afternoon teas, emphasizing the "dignified and humane" character of his administration, and on election eve he appeared on local television summarizing his "record of accomplishment" at city hall.[36] At the same time, Curley was speaking to crowds of his own supporters, urging them to take control of the city away from the "banking fraternity" and "non-residents" who had taken over by "chicanery and duplicity." The people of Boston, he declared, were "sick and tired" of having their government run by outsiders who "dictate policy at City Hall."[37] Despite predictions that the cloudy day and rainy weather would keep voters home, more than two hundred thousand Bostonians went to the polls on Tuesday, September 25, to give John B. Hynes a sweeping victory and to endorse the slate of candidates proposed by the New Boston Committee for the city council and the school committee. Hynes received 108,000 votes; Curley followed in second place with 77,000 votes; Timilty came in a poor third with 15,000; and O'Brien was hardly noticed with only 1,400 votes. That meant that under the new Plan A system, Timilty and O'Brien were out of the race; Hynes and Curley would fight it out again at the polls on November 6—only six weeks away. Hynes thanked the voters for their support, promised to continue his progressive administration, and announced he was taking his family up to Maine for a few days' rest and then would be "back on the job." At the Hotel Brunswick, Curley assured his people that the election had gone "just the way we want it. . . . The road is clear, the issues are clear," he declared boldly, "and we start working tomorrow toward victory in November."[38]

In spite of the brave words, however, the road ahead was by no means as clear as Curley said. For one thing, the political omens were not at all bright. Back in 1949 Curley had run up 126,000 votes in his first contest with Hynes; this year he had gathered only 77,000 votes. A drop-off of nearly 50,000 votes in only two years clearly spelled trouble, and Curley was much too shrewd an old campaigner not to spot it right away. Then, too, there was the question of money. Never a wealthy man, Curley's general lack of money sense, his long absences from public office, and his recent tribulations with court cases and lawyers' fees had left him without private income or public funds. Although he continued to leave his name on the ballot, Curley stunned his loyal supporters with the startling announcement that he had decided to make "no contest" for the November run-off since he lacked sufficient funds to finance an "effective campaign."[39] With that, he virtually gave up active campaigning and stopped soliciting votes.

Hynes took no chances, however, always mindful of the clever old politician and his magical bag of tricks, and as election day drew closer he warned his workers at his downtown headquarters at 145 Milk Street not to let their guard down. Curley was "still in the Mayoralty race to win," he cautioned his supporters, and reported that veteran observers were predicting that the ex-mayor would still get about 70,000 votes—his "hard core" strength in any Boston election. Maintaining a vigorous campaign schedule despite a nagging cold that sapped his strength, Hynes went from one neighborhood to another emphasizing what he had already accomplished in his first twenty-two months in office. He spoke about how he had already reduced the tax rate, lowered the city debt, and stabilized the city's finances. As he had done in the preliminary election, he pointed to the building of new roads, new play areas, new additions to the City Hospital, more public libraries, and the largest housing program in any two-year period of Boston's history. He promised a continuation of work under way to ease traffic congestion in the city, to increase traffic safety, and to provide more off-street parking. He appealed to the city's 388,000 voters to "participate in the election," and pledged that he would continue to give them an "honorable, impartial, and dignified government."[40]

At the last moment, on Monday, November 5, the last day before the election, the newspaper headlines announced: "CURLEY SAYS HE IS STILL IN CONTEST FOR MAYOR." Curley obviously could not resist one last effort to inject some excitement into what had become a dull and lackluster campaign, except for the controversy generated by the contests for the city council and the school committee. Pointing out to voters that his name was still on the ballot and that therefore "I'm still a candidate," the old campaigner put on his famous Cheshire smile as he told reporters: "You never can tell what might happen. My opponents are a bit uneasy tonight." But he made no real effort to follow up on his teasing suggestion to move back into the mayor's race once again. Instead, he concentrated on the contests for the city council and the school committee, going on radio to speak out against the pro-Hynes slate of liberal candidates who were being endorsed by the New Boston Committee. After that, he returned to his home on the Jamaicaway, where he later told reporters that he was spending his time "reading up on Aristotle and some of the old boys."[41] Without Curley in the race, it was virtually no contest, and fifty-four-year-old John B. Hynes was reelected for a second term as mayor of Boston by a record margin of 78,000 votes— the biggest lead ever given a mayor of Boston. In this same Plan A election, the slate of liberal candidates backed by the New Boston Committee also won a resounding victory, capturing five of the nine city council seats and taking four of the five seats on the school committee. It was a clean sweep that promised to give Mayor Hynes strong support from the major municipal offices for the next four years.

———

The New Boston Committee, which had been so active in the 1951 campaign, and about which Curley complained so vociferously, had been formed in 1950 by a number of people who had been active in Hynes's first political campaign the year before. Once Hynes was elected, those supporters had been anxious to create a more unified and positive atmosphere in which the new mayor could work during his coming administration. While still serving as an assistant to Mayor Hynes, Jerome Rappaport took the lead in creating an organization he called the New Boston Committee, designed to bring together "men and women from all walks of life—from all religious and racial groups in the city, all neighborhoods, and all spheres of Boston's life."[42] Holding an initial meeting at New England Mutual Hall, the organizers decided to reach into the various neighborhoods, identify four or five widely recognized community leaders in each one, and draw them into a single citywide organization that could initiate programs, promote issues, and support responsible candidates for public office.

"We wanted to create new programs for the New Boston," said Rappaport, "and we wanted to provide a nucleus of political leadership where none existed at that particular moment." According to Rappaport, none of the newspapers—the *Globe*, the *Post*, the *Herald*—served that function, and the unwieldly twenty-two-member city council he considered a "travesty." Curley, at least, had furnished a measure of charisma. Admitting that he was wearing two hats, Rappaport was convinced he could keep his role as head of the NBC separate from his responsibilities as assistant to the mayor—and the mayor seemed to agree. Hynes did not interfere, allowed his young assistant his head, gave the NBC his unofficial blessing, and apparently figured he would deal with any conflicts of interest if and when they arose.[43] Later historians have speculated that this bright and energetic group of civic leaders and social reformers might well have provided the first really effective organization in Boston's political history capable of pulling together the various Democratic factions in the city into a powerful and coherent force, much as the Good Government Association had done for the Republicans.

In some ways, the membership and goals of the NBC were traditional; in other ways they broke new ground. Some people saw the organization as merely a warmed-over version of the old Good Government Association, an early twentieth-century group of downtown bankers, financiers, and businessmen ridiculed by Curley as a bunch of simple-minded "Goo Goo's," whose main objectives were lower taxes, a balanced budget, and a slate of honest and highly qualified candidates. While it is true that rational economic policies and stable political practices figured prominently in the NBC's platform, the organization also urged greater municipal efforts to improve public housing, expand recreational facilities, and upgrade the school system, as part of an overall reform program intended to raise academic standards and eliminate juvenile delinquency.[44]

In a remarkably short period of time, the NBC attracted an impressive group of idealistic people representing a broad range of constituencies throughout the community. Liberal urban reformers such as Dan Ahearn of West Roxbury, Dan Fenn of Cambridge, and Mary Saunders of South Boston joined forced with middle-class Irish Catholics such as Ed McLaughlin, Dr. Albert Murphy, Dr. Charles Kickham, and Jim Flanagan. Well-known Italian-American figures such as Gabriel Piemonte, John Guarino, and Tony Iovino found themselves working for the same political objectives as such Yankees as Francis Gray, Stuart Rand, Henry Shattuck, and Perlie Dyar Chase. Respected members of the black community such as Victor Bynoe; Otto and Muriel Snowden, who had founded Freedom House; Clarence and Harry Elam; Ruth Batson and Melnea Cass, who had been active NAACP members for many years; and Ed Cooper, head of the Urban League, became part of the new effort to change the city, along with an aspiring young Roxbury lawyer named Edward Brooke, who in 1966 would go on to become the first black person elected to the United States Senate since the days of Reconstruction.

In many ways, activities in the black community were directed not only toward enhancing the reputation of the city as a whole but also toward providing the black community itself with a new sense of its own identity and independence. Boston's black population had generally lived a quiet and self-contained existence. For most of the nineteenth century, forming a community of about 1,800 to 2,000 persons, they made their homes along the northwestern slope of Beacon Hill down to Cambridge Street (referred to as "nigger hill"), until 1896, when the Democrats gerrymandered their district, and when the massive influx of new immigrants from southern and eastern Europe persuaded them to move into the lower South End between Washington Street and Columbus Avenue. By the early 1900s, when their numbers were more than 10,000, they were spreading along Columbus Avenue and Tremont

*Otto and Muriel Snowden, longtime residents of Boston's South End, established Freedom House as a biracial effort to reduce barriers to education, employment, and housing opportunities for African Americans. In supporting John Hynes as mayor of Boston, they hoped that large-scale renewal projects would bring long-needed improvements to the neighborhood and eventually provide low-cost housing for a multiracial community. Photograph by Bob Backoff, courtesy of the Boston Public Library, Print Department.*

Street into the upper part of the South End, settling along Northampton and Lenox streets. By the 1930s, with their population having passed the 20,000 mark (still not much more than 3 percent of the city's total population), the black community extended all the way down to Dudley Street in lower Roxbury. "In 1936, this community was almost completely black," recalled Amanda V. Houston of her early years in the South End. "It sustained two weekly newspapers, the *Chronicle* and the *Guardian*, and at least four profitable restaurants, black-owned and operated, that catered to both black and white customers. There were two Slades restaurants across the street from each other, Estelle's and Jobil's. There were four drug stores, a florist shop, an appliance store, barber shops, hairdressing parlors, a tailor, and other black businesses lining Tremont Street."[45]

It was here, in the South End–Lower Roxbury area, that the black community developed its own distinctive political organization by the start of the twentieth century. A handful of local political leaders traded power for patronage, much as the Irish ward bosses had done some fifty years earlier. "Shag" Taylor, a local pharmacist, became boss of Ward 9 with the help of his organization, called the Massachusetts Colored League. During the 1930s and 1940s Shag and his brother Balcom ("Bal") worked with the Curley machine out of their Lincoln Drugstore on Tremont Street, exchanging votes in the black wards for jobs, housing, and occasionally a Thanksgiving turkey.[46] "Shag Taylor could get your street cleaned, fix a pothole, get a vacant lot cleared, garbage collected, an abandoned car removed," recalled Thomas Atkins, a young politician who became the first black Bostonian to win election to the city council. "If you needed someone released from jail, needed a job—whatever. Nobody had any question he was the premier man, he was *the* person, he was the machine's man, and his power came from the Curley machine." While many black residents remained staunch Republicans— loyal to the "party of Lincoln"—the Taylors were among the estimated 65 percent of the black voters in Boston who switched to the Democratic party in 1932, when Roosevelt's New Deal program seemed to offer poor people of every color their only chance for social and economic security. "The community openly supported Franklin Delano Roosevelt and James Michael Curley, men who had promised to help the poor," wrote Amanda Houston. "And while there were no homeless in our streets, and welfare was just a promise, the community saw itself as poor, in need of jobs and financial assistance for housing."[47]

During the 1930s and 1940s the intersection of Massachusetts and Columbus avenues, just one block east of Symphony Hall, became the exciting center of a Boston "Harlem." At the Hi-Hat nightclub, mixed audiences of blacks and whites gathered to enjoy the performances of such celebrated jazz musicians as Fats Waller, Lionel Hampton, Count Basie, and Duke Ellington as they pounded out such famous numbers as "One O'Clock Jump" and "Take the A Train." The Rainbow Room, just up the street on Massachusetts Avenue, attracted more jazz enthusiasts to hear the playing of Lester ("Prez") Young, Buck Clayton, and Cootie Williams. And both the Roseland Ballroom and the Raymor-Playmor Ballroom on Huntington Avenue featured the music of such big bands as those of Benny Goodman, Jimmy Lunceford, Charlie Barnett, and Woodie Herman for all-night dancing. "These sounds were heard for miles around," recalled Reginald Weems, who grew up in the South End, reveled in the music, and frequented the various barbecue restaurants in the area. It was a bright, lively, active community when "the streets were jammed, and so were the clubs."[48] At that time, it was generally assumed that Boston's black population would continue to confine itself to a permanent ghetto in the South End–Roxbury area.

During the critical years of World War II, however, skilled and unskilled laborers came from all parts of the country to New England to work in industrial plants, army posts, armories, and shipyards. Black soldiers and sailors in all branches of the service came to Boston during the war years, and a great many decided to remain once the hostilities were over. As a consequence, Boston's black population nearly doubled in only a decade, rising from some 23,000 in 1940 to over 40,000 in 1950.[49] Since no new construction had taken place in the South End–Roxbury area after 1920, the overcrowded black population was bulging at the seams. When the general prosperity of the postwar years after 1945, bolstered by the G.I. Bill of Rights, stimulated the heavily Jewish population in North Dorchester and upper Roxbury to seek better housing and more challenging schools in the surrounding suburbs, black people began spreading into the former Jewish district with amazing rapidity until, by 1960, they had moved all the way down Blue Hill Avenue to Mattapan Square.

With increasing numbers, with a greater pride in their identity, and with a growing consciousness of their heritage, black citizens displayed increasing resentment against the social and economic injustices that had retarded their progress for so long. They were inspired by the ideals of Rev. Martin Luther King, Jr.; by the 1954 Supreme Court decision in *Brown* v. *Board of Education of Topeka*, which ruled against the old "separate but equal" doctrine and declared segregated schools to be unconstitutional; by civil rights success in such Southern cities as Montgomery, Alabama (1955), and Little Rock, Arkansas (1957); and by the upcoming hundredth anniversary of the Emancipation Proclamation in 1963. The black community in Boston, as in other American cities during the late 1950s and early 1960s, began to organize itself in search of greater recognition for its members and more equal treatment for their neighborhood. The time had come when the South End–Roxbury community should no longer be regarded as a mere sideshow to the city's political campaigns—a tail constantly being wagged by the dog. Social activists began to work even harder to obtain for their community those rights and privileges the rest of the city had long taken for granted. The era of the 1950s in Boston's black community, observed one black historian, was like a "vast pressure cooker" from which the civil rights movement of the 1960s would eventually "explode."[50]

With the addition of a number of black activists, therefore, the New Boston Committee was an entirely different type of coalition for Boston, a new and unlikely amalgam of ethnic and racial groups that ordinarily would never have met together or worked together. "That's how I first met Eddie McCormack, who first ran for city council with the sponsorship of the NBC, as was also true of Gabriel Piemonte," recalled Hirsch Freed, an old Tobin supporter who had gone on to join Hynes. "It was also the way I first met John Collins, who was then in the state legislature but who also used to attend some of the meetings."[51]

When the 1951 municipal elections rolled around, the NBC became a significant factor in Boston politics and gained a remarkable measure of national coverage. Apparently confident that Hynes could handle his mayoralty fight on his own once Curley had announced his withdrawal as an active candidate, the NBC decided to focus its energies on contests for the nine-member city council and the five-member school committee. Since both bodies were to be elected on an at-large basis, and because everything seemed to be up for grabs in this new post-Curley era, a veritable flood of candidates presented themselves to the voters. All in all, at least sixty-five names appeared on the ballot for the city council, with thirty-six offering themselves for the school committee. With candidates running on a nonpartisan basis, with a solid organization of prominent citizens behind them, those who received the NBC's endorsement were the ones best able to reach a citywide audience.

The NBC had been careful to select a well-balanced slate of candidates, and combining this factor with effective grass-roots campaigning, it saw every one of its choices make it through the preliminary balloting in September. Its final list of nine candidates included Gabriel Piemonte, a state representative from the North End; Perlie Dyar Chase, another state representative and a well-known Back Bay attorney; Lee Friedman, a prominent Jewish philanthropist then serving as a trustee of the Boston Public Library; Joseph White of West Roxbury, a former Boston College football star who had served in both the house and the senate; and Patrick Sullivan of Dorchester's Ward 17, who had been in the state legislature for fourteen years. Besides thirty-four-year-old Francis X. Ahearn, a Boston College graduate who had been a strong advocate of the Plan E System, the NBC also endorsed the candidacy of such other young and promising World War II veterans as twenty-eight-year-old Frederick Hailer of Roslindale and thirty-one-year-old Francis Joyce of South Boston. The NBC's slate for the school committee showed a similar attempt to offer a wide diversity of candidates. In addition to a state representative, William Carr of South Boston, a chamber of commerce member, Louis Musco of Boston, and a former school committee member, Isidore Muchnick of Dorchester, two women figured prominently on the list. Alice Lyons of Jamaica Plain, the wife of the headmaster of the Mary E. Curley School, was active in many educational and civic organizations, and Mary K. Fitzgerald of South Boston was also active in Boston social reform movements, an outspoken champion in the fight against racial discrimination.[52]

In the weeks before the final elections in November, the members of the NBC came under fire from a group of old-line Democratic politicians who accused them of being "reds," "pinkos," "commies," "outside agitators," and liberal "do-gooders," and denounced their reform organization as a front for socialist ideals and Marxist goals. On one occasion Curley himself referred to reform candidates as "friends of known supporters of communism."[53]

The critics formed a conservative opposition group called the All-Boston Committee and fielded slates of city council candidates of their own, featuring well-known local politicians whose name recognition, they hoped, would stall the momentum of the NBC drive. William J. Foley, Jr., of South Boston, the son of the Suffolk County district attorney, was certainly a popular favorite; John E. Kerrigan, the former city councillor and temporary mayor of the city after Maurice Tobin had resigned, would be a vote-getter; and Clement ("Clem") Norton, a well-known city councillor and school committee member going back to the Curley days, was also calculated to draw votes. The ABC list also included Michael Ward of Roxbury, who had served many years on both the school committee and the city council; Bill Glynn, a state representative who became well known for sponsoring baseball and football teams of the Billy Glynn Club; and Kathleen Ryan Dacey of the Back Bay, a practicing attorney and public figure active in bar associations and women's groups, who was at that time chairwoman of the school committee. Seeking to offset the efforts of the liberal NBC to take over the school committee, the conservative ABC came up with its own slate of candidates, which included fifty-year-old Joseph Lee, son of the "Father of American Playgrounds," widely known for his own interest in recreational programs; Joseph Tomasello of Brighton; William Hurley of Roxbury; Jerome Troy, an attorney out of Georgetown Law School who served as president of the Young Democrats of Massachusetts; and Timothy McInerney, an attorney from the Mission Hill district who had represented Ward 10 for seven years.[54]

The antiliberal ABC slate received the enthusiastic backing of James Michael Curley, who threw himself into the campaigns for the city council and the school committee and urged all "independent Democrats" to repudiate the NBC.[55] These attacks took their toll on the liberal organization, but the results were still impressive: NBC-endorsed candidates won five seats on the nine-member city council and four of the five seats on the school committee. Although the ABC's Bill Foley proved to be the top vote-getter, NBC candidates Piemonte, White, Ahearn, Joyce, and Hailer took seats in the new city council along with Kerrigan, Ward, and Hurley. In the school committee race, NBC candidates William Carr, Isidore Muchnick, Alice Lyons, and Mary K. Fitzgerald swept the field, with the only other post going to Dr. Patrick Foley, a dentist from South Boston who had run as an independent candidate. One newspaper likened the outcome to a "new Boston Tea Party"; *Readers' Digest* featured Jerome Rappaport as the subject of a highly favorable article; and the National Municipal League cited the NBC as the main reason for Boston's being named an "All-American City."[56]

Like so many other reform organizations, however, the NBC found that it was easier to get their candidates elected than to control them effectively once they got into office. Part of the problem stemmed from the NBC's decision to support candidates whose primary asset was their electability rather than their commitment to the NBC's reform platform. In the months following the election, the public was treated to the spectacle of members of the NBC bickering with their hand-picked city councillors over the way in which they maintained old-time patronage practices. But the NBC's troubles with the city council were comparatively mild compared with its difficulties with the members of the school committee.

The Boston School Committee was the guardian of a long and proud tradition of excellence in public education, but in recent years its members had become much more concerned with using their positions more as a launching pad for higher elective office than as an opportunity to provide a sound education for the children of Boston. Much to its chagrin, the NBC found that it could do little to change that attitude; nor could it cope with the deep divisions created by a plan drawn up by a faculty member at the Harvard School of Education calling for the closing of some neighborhood schools and the consolidation of others in the name of cost efficiency and educational modernization. That proposal caused a serious split within the school committee; several members who supported the plan got into a heated argument with the superintendent of schools, who had come out in opposition to it, and even the members of the NBC itself could not agree about the advisability of the plan. When the organization could get only one of its slate of candidates elected to the school committee in the 1953 elections, the handwriting was on the wall that the NBC was beginning to come apart at the seams. Always small in numbers (never more than three thousand members) and periodically short of cash, the NBC was constantly plagued by the resolute ideas and strong egos of its upper-middle-class membership.[57]

As early as 1952 Jerome Rappaport himself had become disillusioned about the possibility of the NBC's really being able to change things in Boston. He cited efforts by the Sears Roebuck Company to purchase a portion of park land in the Fenway area, to use as a parking space adjacent to its main building, as one example of his growing frustrations. The very nature of the NBC, he said, gave the organization no alternative but to come out in opposition to the idea of taking public park land and using it for private commercial purposes. But it was no contest, he admitted. Because Sears Roebuck advertised heavily in the *Globe*, the *Post*, and the *Herald*, those newspapers came out en masse against the NBC. "Sears got the land," said Rappaport with a slight trace of bitterness, "and the NBC got beat up." Here was clear evidence that nothing had changed and that in the long run the NBC could not really become politically effective, and the young organizer began to reconsider his future in public service. In addition to his own disillusionment with the aims and abilities of the NBC, the young lawyer's appearance in tax-abatement cases seems to have caused "cynical comment and further loss of morale" among the more liberal members of the association.[58]

Rappaport's boss, Mayor Hynes, must have noticed either the changing mood of his young assistant or the disturbing climate in the

NBC, because he called Rappaport into his office one day for an informal chat and suggested that since his specialty was law, perhaps the time had come for him to think about "honing his skills" as an attorney and not be making government service his whole focus—there was, after all, more to life than politics. Rappaport took the mayor's paternal advice to heart—"Hynes," he said, "was underappreciated, even by his closest admirers." He abandoned the NBC and left his city job to pursue the career of law in the private sector.[59]

The demise of the New Boston Committee in the mid-1950s spelled the end to any possibility that liberal Democrats would have an effective, unified organization capable of directing a coherent program of social and political change. Any such agency Hynes might employ in the future to assist him in promoting reform and revitalization in the city of Boston during his first four-year term would clearly have to come from a much different source.

# 3.

# Visions and Designs

It was one thing for Mayor John B. Hynes and his supporters to talk enthusiastically about a New Boston; it was quite another to actually do something about it. Like so many other major cities in the United States, Boston had deteriorated badly over the years. Even before the outbreak of World War II, the federal government had identified the problem of slums as a serious condition that was already retarding the growth and development of cities all over the country. According to the United States Housing Act of 1937, a slum was defined as "any area where dwellings predominate which by reason of dilapidation, over-crowding, faulty arrangement and design, lack of ventilation, light or sanitary facilities, or any combination of these factors, are detrimental to safety, health, or morals." By the time the war was over, there was no question that every major city in the United States had its universally recognized slum area, where the gradual processes of old age, neglect, overcrowding, and faulty construction had produced the corrosive effects described in the government definition. Cincinnati had its Basin Section, Pittsburgh had its Hill District, and Boston had its West End.[1]

The other and more recently categorized phenomenon plaguing America's urban landscape was the process known as blight, which had more to do with the ways in which populations and enterprises had moved—or had not moved—than with the age and condition of the localities themselves. The failure of business enterprises to expand into certain areas where they had been expected to go; the movement of

66

factories and industrial plants into residential areas and fashionable districts; the shift of well-to-do segments of the population into more promising communities; the exodus of racial and ethnic groups out of traditional neighborhoods—all these factors often created pockets of potentially valuable property that were no longer regarded as profitable, productive, or livable. Every city had sections or entire communities that were no longer considered by banks and developers as worthy of further interest or investment because they had been categorized as "blighted." Blighted districts covered almost one-third of the built-up parts of Brooklyn; nearly one-fourth of Birmingham's dwelling units were located in declining areas; more than a quarter of Cleveland's population lived in run-down neighborhoods; and Chicago's Loop was surrounded by a three-mile-wide band of obsolete, wretched buildings.[2]

During the late 1940s and early 1950s local banks had already classified many of Boston's older ethnic neighborhoods, such as South Boston, Charlestown, Dorchester, and Roxbury, as "depressed" or "blighted" areas, and they refused to grant mortgages or assign home improvement loans in those communities. As a result of that policy, known as "redlining," a great many young veterans and their families were forced to go outside the city and use their G.I. loans to purchase single-family homes in suburban areas, where the mortgage rates were lower and the banking policies more liberal. In a short time, as older residents used their welfare payments or their social security checks to keep up payments on their three-decker homes, and as transients moved in and out of housing projects that were now replacing dilapidated buildings, older parts of the neighborhoods began to show signs of the very blight and decay predicted by the banking establishments. The cost of maintenance and repairs became prohibitive, homes fell into serious disrepair, streets were no longer cleaned, garbage piled up in the alleyways, parks and playgrounds were soon neglected, and vandalism became commonplace. Here, indeed, was a classic example of a self-fulfilling prophecy at work.[3]

But in many ways, the whole downtown section of Boston itself could well be considered a blighted area, not only because its age made it one of the oldest municipalities in the United States, but also because its entire inner structure seemed to have collapsed so completely. A prominent Bostonian, the architect William Roger Greeley, made a remarkable statement at a public meeting at Faneuil Hall in late 1944. He lamented that Boston had not shared with London the "advantage" of widespread destruction by aerial bombardment, which would have cleared out the old city and made way for a new one.[4] Although Boston dates its origins as far back as 1630, when John Winthrop came ashore with his Puritan colleagues to build his celebrated "City on a Hill," some sections of the downtown area were of more recent vintage. The Beacon Hill area, for example, was not developed until the early 1800s, after Charles Bulfinch constructed his new State House on the crest of one of the town's three central "mountains."[5] As a growing population demanded more living space, the fashionable Back Bay area began to be filled in around 1858, just before the Civil War, in an ambitious project that continued well into the 1890s with the development of Copley Square. But the downtown section, from the waterfront across Washington and Tremont streets to the Boston Common, was the oldest part of town, and the section most in need of a complete face-lift. From time to time, it is true, serious efforts had been made to rescue the area from the ravages of time and abuse. In the mid-1820s, shortly after Boston exchanged its town meeting form of government for a city charter, its "Great Mayor," Josiah Quincy, carried out an intensive program of urban renewal that cleaned the streets, reduced pollution, and created a brand new market district directly behind historic Faneuil Hall.[6] Some fifty years later, in 1872, a devastating fire wiped out some sixty-five acres of the business section of town, from Washington and Summer streets down Federal and State streets all the way to Atlantic Avenue and the waterfront. So complete was the destruction that a whole new program of urban reconstruction had to be undertaken to replace what had been reduced to a mass of blackened rubble.[7]

Despite these sporadic efforts at rebuilding, however, the downtown area continued to deteriorate as the increasing demands of the various neighborhoods for better housing, lighting, water, sewers, and police and fire protection drew off both money and attention from the needs of the inner city. Local residents recognized the problem, and every now and then they made efforts to stem the tide of decay and turn things around in some dramatic fashion. As early as 1907 the Boston Society of Architects offered a series of what the historian Walter Muir Whitehill called "thoughtful and dramatic suggestions" for creating a New Boston. Complaining that the historic downtown area was in the process of being hemmed in by a series of ethnic neighborhoods made up of "inflammable and dangerous tenements," the architects proposed to rescue the city with a series of elaborate plans involving such innovations as an expansive boulevard along Arlington Street, a monumental civic center at the intersection of Arlington Street and Commonwealth Avenue, an artificial island in the middle of the Charles River, and a new city hall on Beacon Hill. All of this was designed not only to "fill in the gaps in the city plan" and to "avoid congestion by enlarging the business district" but also to retain within the city limits "the prosperous and educated class that now goes to the suburbs."[8]

Although none of these ambitious projections ever got off the drawing board, in June 1907 the commonwealth established a Commission on Metropolitan Improvements to investigate and report on the "advisability of any public works" in the metropolitan district that would work to the convenience of the public, the prosperity of local business, or the general beautification of the district. Two years later, this commission published a brief report, *Public Improvements for the Metropolitan District*, that emphasized the necessity of civic improvement. A mere forty-nine pages, with separate chapters written either by members of the commission or by invited experts, the report focused on the less glamorous but decidedly crucial aspects of the city's underpinnings. Essays on railroads and highways, traffics and terminals, harbors and ports, waterways and canals, sites for civic centers, and recreational facilities along the waterfront all called attention to what had to be done to modernize the old city's aging infrastructure before more ambitious projects could be undertaken.[9]

At about the same time that the Metropolitan Commission's report was being circulated, a group of prominent Boston business and civic leaders, led by the retailer Edward A. Filene and the future Supreme Court justice Louis D. Brandeis, announced what they labeled the Boston-1915 movement. This development took place at a moment in turn-of-the-century American history when a nationwide "progressive" movement was calling for more honest, more professional, and more efficient approaches to city government. In such large cities as Toledo, Detroit, and Milwaukee, reform mayors ousted old-time political bosses, broke up corrupt political machines, fostered municipal ownership of public utilities, and established parks, playgrounds, and recreational facilities for the people. Many felt that Boston, too, could benefit from such progressive ideas, and in 1903 various business and civic groups banded together to form the Good Government Association. Almost entirely Yankee, composed of property owners, bankers, financiers, lawyers, businessmen, and local academics, the members of the GGA supported candidates for public office who possessed background, breeding, education, experience, and integrity—candidates who would presumably work for the interests of the city as a whole, and not for special interests or ethnic constituencies. In Boston, as in other cities, good-government advocates were also caught up in the ideal of the City Beautiful, in which a coalition of high-minded groups could produce not only honest government and humane social reforms, but also a modernized metropolis of which the community could be justifiably proud.

With these ideals in mind, the sponsors of the Boston-1915 program planned to use the six years immediately preceding 1915 as a time to coordinate the individual efforts of local civic, educational, recreational, health, labor, and charitable organizations to develop a comprehensive physical and social plan for the city. The six years of coordinated planning would culminate in a world exposition in Boston in 1915, putting the city on display as a model of progressive government, efficient services, prosperous industries, beautiful public places, enlightened labor policies, and inexpensive housing. In addition to modernizing the physical aspects of the city, the leaders would also put further emphasis on improving public education, achieving public health care, establishing neighborhood centers, promoting the fine arts, increasing the number of branch libraries, and even adopting a "comprehensive system of wage earner's insurance and old-age pensions"—thus combining social reform and municipal planning with civic improvement and business prosperity.[10]

All sorts of meetings, conferences, and workshops took place, a monthly publication called *New Boston-1915* was launched, exhibitions on city planning were put on display in various parts of the city, and efforts were made to galvanize public opinion in support of the project. Unfortunately, the euphoria was short-lived. The steam quickly went out of the movement; participants lost their original enthusiasm; little or no support was forthcoming from the state legislature; suburban communities expressed their opposition to a movement they suspected would be dominated by Boston politicians; and the coalition of supporting institutions and businesses began to crack and fall apart. As early as January 1912 the executive committee reluctantly announced the discontinuance of the Boston-1915 movement, and by the time that the excitement of World War I began to attract the attention of the general public, the movement had disappeared completely.[11] Despite the collapse

of the Boston-1915 movement, however, some mechanisms for municipal planning did continue. In 1913, for example, the Boston Planning
Board was created as an official planning arm for the city, and over the
next quarter of a century that agency provided routine but invaluable
recommendations regarding such things as water supply, sewerage,
parks, playgrounds, traffic, parking, zoning restrictions, and building
codes.

In 1944, the nation's preoccupation with war notwithstanding, the
Society of Architects once again tried to promote architectural reform
in the city, this time by initiating a contest designed to stimulate thoughts
for a workable program to improve the condition of Boston. Administered by Boston University and offering eight thousand dollars in prizes,
the contest was sponsored by Governor Leverett Saltonstall, Mayor
Maurice Tobin, and institutions including the chamber of commerce,
Harvard University, and the Massachusetts Institute of Technology.
Scores of individuals and groups entered the contest, which had a panel
of judges among whom were the industrialist Charles Francis Adams,
the architectural critic Lewis Mumford, and the Boston architect William Roger Greeley. Some idea of the academic and somewhat elitist
approach of the proposals, and perhaps an unsettling preview of things
to come, can be seen in the suggestions of the third-place winners that
the two working-class neighborhoods of the North End and the West
End be transformed into what they called "first-class residential sections."[12] The winning entry was made by a team headed by the Harvard
political scientist Carl Friedrich, who made a "strictly tentative" proposal for a metropolitan solution to Boston's many problems. Arguing
that the whole metropolitan area had "become ill, decaying at the core,
because its vitality has not been a common concern of all those having a
stake in it," Friedrich proposed that all communities within a twenty-
five-mile radius of the city should join in a federation to be called the
Boston Metropolitan Authority, or District. To direct the activities of the
authority, Friedrich suggested a city manager government with a legislative council, possibly based on a proportional-representation system
that would use the existing municipalities as districts.

While the Harvard plan won a first prize of five thousand dollars
and attracted the support of most of Boston's intellectual elite as well as
a great many of its business leaders, the proposal fell flat on its face.[13]
Given the practical political connections of city hall and the long-
established perquisites of the state legislature, the idea of metropolitani-

zation fared no better in 1944 than it had several times in previous years when it had been suggested as a panacea for the ills of the greater Boston area. As a result, the conditions that had plagued the city for so many years continued to eat away at its underpinnings, with few indications of change or improvement.[14] Although there was no lack of plans, programs, suggestions, and ideas to modernize and revitalize the old city, there had not yet appeared either the will or the determination to carry any of those projects into action.

By the time veterans were returning home after World War II, they could see plainly that years of neglect, a decade of depression, and a generation of political feuding between natives and newcomers, Yankees and Celts, Protestants and Catholics, had all taken their toll. The city was in deplorable condition, with no real signs of a future. The *Boston Globe* called Boston "a hopeless backwater, a tumbled-down has-been among cities." John Collins, a future mayor, recalled that "the blight and decay was overwhelming. Seventy percent of the housing stock was substandard. The waterfront was literally falling into the Atlantic Ocean. Scollay Square had half a dozen burlesque houses, honky-tonk places, and tattoo parlors. It was just miserable—and right on the edge of downtown. Nothing new had been built for years. But the people who worked on State Street sat at their rolltop desks and thought everything was all right, because it was the same today as it was yesterday."[15]

City income was going down, city taxes were going up, and established businesses were abandoning Boston every day to relocate in other cities where taxes were lower, labor cheaper, benefits better, and the political climate more congenial. The downtown shopping district along Washington Street was beginning to show the effect of new suburban shopping malls, where access was easy and parking spaces both free and plentiful. Old and familiar department stores were closing every day—Gilchrist's, Houghton and Dutton, Raymond's, and Kresge's had already shut down or were in the process of doing so. Newspapers, too, were fast disappearing: the *Journal*, the *Transcript*, and the *Post* were all gone; the *Herald* and the *Traveler* would merge into a single paper; the *Record-American* would struggle on until 1972; the *Globe* moved out of downtown Boston to Dorchester. Buildings were razed and replaced by parking lots, pizza parlors, or inexpensive discount outlets.[16]

The city was losing people as fast as it was losing businesses. The steady drain of young people out of the central area had been further accelerated as the industries and electronics firms along Route 128 drew an even greater number of educated, middle-class families out into the suburbs.[17] Private homes and buildings in the central city continued to deteriorate at a frightening rate, occupancy rates in downtown office buildings were going down fast, and even many of the handsome brownstone mansions in the fashionable Back Bay section had been transformed into rooming houses and dormitories for local schools and colleges. "Commonwealth Avenue is a beautiful street in many ways," observed the *Back Bay Ledger*, "but it looks like a deserted village in many block lengths, where house after house has been boarded up, and the one-time residents gone." It was obvious that some drastic steps would have to be taken if the inner city were to be saved from the ravages of urban blight. "Given the American devotion to growth and bigness, the common threat of stagnation and decline appeared especially serious," writes Jon Teaford about urban problems in the 1950s. "To be branded a has-been city would be devastating in a nation dedicated to success."[18]

In many American cities that still had some form of effective political machinery, a new breed of urban mayors made their appearance during the late 1940s and early 1950s and began reversing some long-established trends in city government. A number of these new people had college degrees, usually in business or law; some had practical experience in administration and management; many had reached middle age before deciding to go into public service. While they spent considerable time observing the age-old neighborhood amenities—attending wakes and weddings, officiating at graduations and banquets, appearing at community gatherings, and speaking at political rallies—they also made it a point to involve themselves in complicated labor issues and to confer with downtown business leaders at regular intervals. Party bosses found that making alliances with local business and financial interests and supporting downtown redevelopment projects were effective ways not only to reinvigorate the city's economic vitality, but also to capitalize on new sources of state and federal funding that could be used for political patronage.[19] In Chicago, for example, Mayor Richard Daley launched an ambitious program in the early 1950s to revitalize the stagnant downtown area known as the Loop, using a combination of federal urban-renewal funds, the process of eminent domain, and imaginative zoning procedures. The resulting financial growth and real estate expansion produced political dividends as Daley's political machine fashioned a powerful coalition of developers, bankers, and labor union leaders.[20]

The city of Pittsburgh was another example of a large metropolitan area that was in a sharp decline by the mid-1940s, with a downtown area, called the Golden Triangle, in a state of financial collapse. In 1943 Richard King Mellon and a group of corporate heads and wealthy financiers formed the Allegheny Conference to work for the postwar economic development of the city. They found an unlikely ally in the state Democratic boss David L. Lawrence, who ran for mayor in 1945 on a platform stressing the kind of leadership that would bring the city back to life again. He joined forces with the Allegheny group, overwhelmingly Republican, and launched the so-called Pittsburgh Renaissance that eventually rebuilt the downtown area, cleared the slum districts, and attracted major firms to establish corporate headquarters in the inner city. The results of this effort at downtown urban renewal were impressive: Tax revenues, which had been falling in the 1940s, were now on the rise. Property valuations alone grew from $961 million to as much as $1.12 billion in the years between 1947 and 1955.[21]

Other cities followed Pittsburgh's example in linking the political muscle of city hall with the corporate power of downtown boardrooms. Philadelphia, for example, had its counterpart in the Greater Philadelphia Movement organized in 1948; New Haven's Richard Lee put together the Citizens Action Commission in 1954; and Baltimore launched the Greater Baltimore Committee in 1955.[22] And in Albany, New York, GOP Governor Nelson Rockefeller proposed a massive development program in the late 1950s to wipe out the eyesores of blighted neighborhoods that surrounded the state capitol. He launched a ten-year, $2 billion construction project, the Empire State Plaza government office complex, popularly known as the South Mall, as a means of revitalizing the city's decaying South End and enhancing the appearance of Albany as the state's capital.[23]

Unfortunately, no such partnerships, programs, or visionary construction projects materialized in Boston, much to the disgust of an old Yankee entrepreneur like Charles Francis Adams, who complained to a writer from *Fortune* magazine that these days "Bostonians would rather watch the city crumble than rise," and that the old-guard beneficiaries of past enterprises were "protecting the status quo rather than reaching out as in the days of the clippers." Although Adams himself was deeply involved in the expanding electronics activities of the Raytheon Corporation, he had little expectation that any new directions for the improvement of Boston would come from the exalted ranks of the new technocrats, among whom he could detect "no one with enough flair, time, or money to give leadership."[24]

The passage by Congress of Title I of the Housing Act of 1949, appropriating $500 million to aid cities in undertaking urban development projects, did, however, stimulate the city planning board the following year to issue an ambitious and farsighted general plan for Boston. While acknowledging that Boston would continue to have the main responsibility of providing "adequate facilities" for a substantial portion of the "entire metropolitan region," in fact the planning board directed most of its attention to the needs of the downtown area in order to reinforce what it regarded as Boston's central position in the region.

Adopting what it conceded was a rather conservative approach to long-range planning, the board proposed fundamental changes for only 20 percent of the city's land area over a twenty-five year period. Among its more specific recommendations were plans for creating a series of distinctive civic, cultural, and educational districts in the city; redeveloping the dilapidated area along the Atlantic Avenue waterfront; creating a new wholesale produce market area with greater access to highways and truck routes; improving local railroad terminal facilities; and expanding the downtown business district. In suggesting such improvements, the board also emphasized that steps would have to be taken to counteract the increasing use of private motor vehicles by developing better mass transit facilities, and by having the planning board itself coordinate the research activities of the various transportation agencies in the region.

In addition to these specific plans and projects, the planning board also looked to ways of converting unsightly pockets of slum areas and blighted districts—especially those uncomfortably close to the downtown business district—into usable and productive property. Under the terms of the 1949 Housing Act, local public authorities, known as LPAs, would administer federal programs, armed with the power of eminent domain. For Boston, the Boston Housing Authority was named as the LPA, which allowed it to designate strategically located blighted residential districts for redevelopment as business or industrial areas. Operating under the guidelines of the planning board's general plan, the BHA was

*With Congressman John W. McCormack standing at his side, Mayor John B. Hynes poses at the controls of a wrecking crane at Seneca Street as a $4.3 million project to clear a slum section in Boston's South End gets under way. Operating in accordance with federal housing policy that provided up to 30 percent funding from Washington, the plan was designed to convert the so-called New York Streets area into light industrial and commercial use. Courtesy of the Boston Public Library, Print Department.*

empowered to purchase slum property, with the federal government paying two-thirds of the cost, which would then be cleared and sold to a private developer at a price marked down from the prevailing market rate. Overall, the 1950 plan set aside some twenty-seven hundred acres of city land for slum clearance and eventual redevelopment, of which eleven hundred acres received a high-priority status. It was the expressed hope of the board that the city of Boston itself would make additional investments of funds, so that many of these blighted areas could be converted into residential middle-class housing.[25]

As far as the question of low-cost housing was concerned, however, the planning board was decidedly pessimistic. In its view, solving the housing problem was largely a "theoretical hope," not only because of the practical difficulties posed by the prevailing housing shortages in the

Boston area, but also because of the "gross inadequacy of the entire national redevelopment program." In this respect, the board had the support of Mayor Hynes, who insisted that the redevelopment of the downtown business district was his first priority and who had little interest in using renewal monies to bolster the city's deteriorating low-income housing stock. "We have all the low-rental projects we need," said the mayor.[26] Despite these reservations, the board insisted that the low-cost housing issue had to be confronted in some manner—if only to ensure that the disturbing signs of a population flow out of the city into the suburbs be stemmed before it became worse. It suggested giving greater recognition in future planning to such recreational needs as parks and playgrounds, which could be "a major weapon in the fight against blight" by contributing to the happiness of the citizenry as well as in stabilizing property values throughout the city.[27]

It would be several years, however, before many of these ideas concerning urban renewal could be put into practice. Although John Hynes clearly understood the importance of cleaning up slum areas and modernizing the downtown business district, he was not yet in a position to organize new coalitions or to remove the legal and financial obstructions that would make the kind of long-range redevelopment programs that were taking place in other American cities possible in Boston. When it first began back in 1950, the New Boston Committee had shown a great deal of promise as a possible lobbying agency that might have helped pave the way for the fiscal changes Hynes wanted, but its premature collapse during the early 1950s indicated that the mayor would have to look elsewhere for the kind of support he needed for such reforms. Without an effective lobbying agency, for example, Hynes was unable to generate the kind of political leverage necessary to deal with the complicated and apparently insoluble problem of tax assessment in the city. Revising prevailing tax assessments in such a way as to make it more attractive for new companies to move into Boston and for old companies to increase their investments in the city was absolutely essential for any kind of major redevelopment, but it was precisely the kind of issue that proved too elusive for the new mayor at this stage of his administration.

During the Curley years, it had been customary for the city administration to place high assessments on land and real estate property in the downtown business district, typically owned by well-to-do Yankee Republicans. That process had served three major purposes: First, it had

created a constant nuisance and a bothersome headache for the class of
people for whom Curley had an abiding dislike. He had enjoyed their
discomfort immensely. Second, by constantly raising the assessed valuation of business and commercial property, Curley had been able to keep
taxes for working-class homeowners in the neighborhoods to a minimum, although they were still painfully high. And third, whenever some
hard-pressed downtown property owner requested a tax abatement,
Curley had found himself in the self-satisfying position of trading favors
for concessions. That was the way the system had worked year in and
year out, with rumors that the city hall clerks routinely made out the
annual assessment and abatement records in pencil so that it would be
easier for them to make the necessary changes.

Like so many other candidates, Hynes spoke out against the city's
traditional tax abatement system during the 1949 campaign, and he
made promises to end it when he was elected. Once safely in office,
however, he found the practical alternatives both financially difficult and
politically dangerous. If he took the step of bringing down the value of
the commercial property of the city to the true market level, then he
would obviously have to make up the substantial loss in revenue by
jacking up the tax rates on middle-class residential property—something
that would certainly boomerang when angry Boston voters went to the
polls in the next election. The only way Hynes would agree to consider
adopting a more rational method of assessing all property was on the
condition that some alternative source of revenue be found to relieve the
pressure on property. From time to time he talked about such things as
a payroll tax or a sales tax (hence Joe Timilty's taunt of "Sales Tax
Johnny"), but in the absence of support from other Boston politicians,
he did not really pursue the measures or seek the necessary approval
from the state legislature, which would probably have been no kinder to
him than it had been to Maurice Tobin or Robert Bradford when they
had proposed similar fiscal changes.[28] Observing this lack of initiative,
the Yankee bankers and corporate executives demonstrated little faith in
Hynes's ability to make any substantial changes in the city's notoriously
hostile economic climate. In all probability they would still support him
at election time as the lesser of two evils, but they were not yet convinced
that he could inspire the kind of unity and harmony that had led to such
successful enterprises in so many other American cities.[29]

———

The traditional, conservative, business-oriented attitude that prevailed in business and political circles in Boston, as well as in many other major American cities during the mid-1950s, was consistent with what one historian called the "politics of inertia" ushered in by the administration of Dwight D. Eisenhower, which appeared to offer both fulfillment and expectation. As Walter Lippmann expressed it, the likeable former general was a "dream boy" who embodied "all the unsatisfied wishes of all the people who were discontented with things as they are."[30] The troublesome problems of past generations—the economic frustrations of the Great Depression, the material shortages of World War II, the postwar strikes and labor disputes—finally seemed to have resolved. The nation was becoming more prosperous, jobs were plentiful, and never before had Americans seen such a grand array of services for their health, their welfare, and their enjoyment. New light and inexpensive products such as plastics, aluminum, and transistors created whole new industries, as well as mass markets for goods that had once been considered luxury items available only to the wealthy few. With nearly 75 million cars and trucks on the roads by 1956, and a new interstate highway system creating thousands of miles of superhighways across the country, Americans pushed onward beyond the limits of the cities into something called suburbia, where they built new houses, erected new schools, and created new communities.[31]

These were years when Americans appeared to have unbounded confidence that experts—especially when they were working as coordinated teams—would solve the complicated problems of the future. After all, they had seen such specialized groups come up with critical solutions in military affairs (the atomic bomb), in science (television and electronics), in medicine (penicillin and wonder drugs), and now in the initial stages of the nation's space program. There was no reason to suppose that the same interdisciplinary approach that had worked so well in the past could not be used effectively to reshape and reorder America's social and economic structure as well—especially with federal managers playing a quiet but stabilizing role in the process. Everyone seemed to accept that by adjusting the national budget, funding the national debt, and controlling the nation's monetary policies, the Eisenhower administration would gently steer the country in a prosperous direction without at all threatening the free-enterprise spirit of his staunchly conservative supporters.

On the local level, the politics of spending and retrenchment followed many of the same vacillations as the national model. When Robert Bradford succeeded Tobin as governor of Massachusetts in 1947, he made it a point to give close attention to the problems of transportation, especially to the deplorable condition of the state's highways, which had fallen into neglect during World War II. One-third of the state's main routes were more than twenty years old, and owing to a six-year backup in highway construction during the war, less than 5 percent of the roads had been constructed within the previous ten years. Bradford submitted a master highway construction plan in which he requested a start-up bond issue of $100 million, as well as a $13 million bond issue for developing the Boston airport. Since the bond issue required a two-thirds vote of the legislature, the sixteen Democrats in the senate were able to block passage of the measure long enough for Bradford to be defeated by Democrat Paul Dever. During his first term in office, Dever received from the legislature the $100 million bond issue it had refused Governor Bradford one year earlier. The following year, the legislature authorized a second $100 million highway bond issue and provided additional millions for the regular road fund. During this two-year period of 1949 and 1950, the legislature authorized a total of more than $800 million in expenditures, while raising an additional $27 million in taxes.[32]

Just as Dwight D. Eisenhower's victory over Adlai Stevenson in 1952 marked a conservative response to the "big spending" policies of New Deal–Fair Deal Democrats, the victory of Republican Christian Herter over Paul Dever in the Massachusetts gubernatorial race the same year marked a similar response of Bay State voters against Dever's ambitious programs for road building, bridge construction, workmen's compensation, and mental health—and the seemingly endless taxes they demanded. A prevalent "desire for change," along with the undeniable influence of Eisenhower's long coattails, enabled Herter to move into the state house by a very narrow margin. The popular Eisenhower carried the state by a two-to-one vote, as a great many Boston Irish sat on their hands rather than cast a ballot for the likes of Adlai Stevenson and his "egghead" supporters.[33] Along with the rest of the nation, Bostonians were content to bask in the prosperity and "affluence" of the Eisenhower years, confident that a new age had finally come when they could get maximum benefits with a minimum of taxes.

Political leaders had to acknowledge the reality of fiscal retrenchment, but also had to cope with the incredible growth of vehicular traffic that clogged the highways and threatened to strangle the state's economy. In particular, they looked for some way to finance the construction of a major east-west toll road across Massachusetts, from the New York line in West Stockbridge to Route 128 in Weston. Unfortunately, given the wretched condition of the state economy, the low standing of its fiscal reputation, and the angry mood of the voters at any suggestion of a tax increase, there were only so many methods the state government could use to construct such a tollway. The possibility of engaging a private company to undertake the project was not only out of vogue at the time but also fraught with the dangers of patronage and favoritism. The possibility of the state government itself floating a bond issue and raising money on the bond market was also regarded as a futile gesture. Not only would the interest be extremely high, but it was doubtful that investors could be found who would take the chance on backing a cash-starved state that might find more urgent uses for its toll collections than paying off its bondholders. And even if the state did manage to find buyers for its bonds, the exorbitant tolls necessary to pay off the debt would alienate every driver who came through the toll booths. Obviously, some other means would have to be found to build a state highway without actually involving the state.

The state's solution to this perplexing problem was to create the Massachusetts Turnpike Authority in 1952, borrowing the technique from the Boston Transit Commission, the state's first public "authority," created by the state legislature in 1894 in order to construct the nation's first subway tunnel system. Although the members of the boards of authorities are appointed by the governor, the authorities themselves are semiautonomous agencies privately funded by revenue bonds, which are paid for by tolls and other fees. When the bonds are eventually retired, ownership of the authorities' facilities revert to the commonwealth. The objective in setting up an authority was to have its operation, maintenance, and development financed by those who actually use the facilities rather than by taxpayers in general.[34]

As first chairman of the turnpike authority, Governor Dever named William F. Callahan, a man who had gained extensive influence in the General Court by virtue of his intimidating personality as well as his extensive control of public-works patronage. Sometimes compared with Robert Moses, father of New York's system of bridges, expressways, and parkways, Callahan, according to one local writer, was "alternately considered an asphalt-crazed autocrat and a visionary architect of progress." He had been ousted from his job in the Department of Public Works back in 1939 after the Republicans regained the governorship that year, and from that time on he "adroitly manipulated the legal powers of his authority" so that he would never again be at the mercy of any political challengers.[35]

After a few false starts, the turnpike authority managed to float $254 million in bonds in 1954, and in three years Bay State drivers were enjoying the comparative luxury of a 123-mile roadway owned and operated not by the state but by an independent public corporation known as the Massachusetts Turnpike Authority. And when these drivers exited the "Mass Pike," they handed their coins to tax collectors employed not by the state but by the turnpike authority. These quarters, in turn, were deposited with the mutual funds, the pensions funds, the insurance companies, and the numerous other investing bodies that held bonds that had been issued not by the state but by the Massachusetts Turnpike Authority. Here was one way of achieving positive results without going through the standard mechanism of direct state taxes.[36]

While the construction of the Massachusetts Turnpike made it possible for all types of gasoline-powered vehicles—automobiles, taxis, buses, trucks—to crisscross the state at great rates of speed, it only made things worse for traffic conditions in the city of Boston itself. Even before World War II, the question of where to put all the vehicles that came into the city, as well as how to more efficiently transport those vehicles that passed through the city on their way to the North Shore or the South Shore, seemed to occupy the time and attention of planning committees and demand the most immediate solutions. In 1927 the Boston Planning Board conducted an extensive traffic survey, and three years later it produced its *Report on a Thoroughfare Plan for Boston*, which was largely the work of the consultant Robert Whitten, president of the American City Planning Institute. The report offered a series of recommendations calling for a total of ten major and fifty-six lesser transportation projects. The main projects included an East Boston Tunnel under Boston Harbor; a Central Artery cutting through the heart of the city; and a Blue Hills radial highway as an extension of that artery.

Considering the rapid increase in automobile and truck traffic, the proposed Central Artery was considered in 1930 not only an attractive but also an absolutely essential piece of the long-range solution to

Boston's traffic problems. The Whitten plan called for two miles of six lanes, with a capacity of sixty thousand vehicles a day, traveling at an average speed of thirty miles per hour. The thoroughfare, it was believed, would attract 40 percent of the vehicles that were clogging city streets at that time. "The Central Artery, with its upper-level roadway," said the planners, "is a practical way to provide for this through traffic, while at the same time affording enormous relief to the traffic going to and from the Central District itself." Whitten and the planning board argued that it was economically imperative for the Central Artery to be built. The report contended that the people of metropolitan Boston were spending $180 million a year for motor vehicle transportation. Delays reduced efficiency 10–20 percent, so even a 10 percent increase in the efficiency of the traffic flow would be worth $18 million annually. "The proposed express roads and other projects are costly," concluded Whitten, "but they are not nearly as costly as the present condition and delay."[37]

Although the Great Depression caused the construction of the Central Artery to be deferred, subsequent reports of the Boston Planning Board throughout the 1930s continued to urge implementation of the project in much the same terms as the original report. The 1938 report of the board recommended that the city join with metropolitan and state funding sources to construct the project, but at that time the political cooperation and general goodwill necessary for such an undertaking were missing. The Central Artery finally became the key element in Governor Bradford's master highway plan of 1948, but although several contracts were given out during May and June 1951 with a completion date targeted for December 31, 1953, a number of problems associated with the route of the artery through the heart of downtown Boston delayed construction for years and made it the last link in the complex network of highways north and south of the city. It was discovered, for example, that rats infested sections of the old waterfront district as well as many market buildings along Atlantic Avenue, and a special rodent control and extermination program had to be set up to clear the area before work could be started. A major steel strike broke out in April 1952 after the Supreme Court forced President Harry Truman to return plants he had seized to ensure defense needs during the Korean War. This held up critical deliveries of steel to the Boston project for months, while a series of court battles over disputed property rights stopped demolition at several points along the right of way. Meat handlers in the Haymarket Square area complained that they could not move out of

their present locations until their new quarters, complete with complicated refrigerating systems, were fully operational. And residents of the
Chinatown district, as well as proprietors in the nearby shoe and leather
sections, were in an uproar when they learned that the proposed route
of the artery would cut a large swath through their respective areas.

On October 19, 1953, the Boston City Council came out in
opposition to the route that would take the expressway through Chinatown and the leather district, and councillor Gabriel Piemonte moved
that the city of Boston obtain an injunction restraining the commonwealth of Massachusetts from taking any more lands or buildings.[38] A
week later, the acting mayor, Francis X. Ahearn, filling in for Mayor
Hynes, who was in Israel, pleaded with Governor Herter and Public
Works Commissioner John Volpe to halt the work entirely until a better
solution could be found. To destroy the Chinatown district would not
only be a "grave mistake," he wrote, but would also be a "cardinal
sin."[39] Protests became so vigorous that Commissioner Volpe finally
agreed to approve a plan suggested by Frederick C. ("Buck") Dumaine,
president of the New Haven Railroad, to dig a tunnel under Atlantic
Avenue, Dewey Square, and a corner of the South Station, in order to
avoid the disruptive effects of cutting through the leather district and
Chinatown. Even then, however, a large portion of the Chinese Merchants Association building on Oxford Street was torn down as the
Central Artery eventually ate up at least half the land area of Chinatown.[40]

But perhaps the most vehement objections to the proposed Central
Artery came from the residents of the North End, one of Boston's oldest
and most historic neighborhoods, which had been home to a succession
of different immigrant nationalities including Africans, Anglo-Saxons,
Irish, Jews, and finally Italians. Not only was the new expressway
scheduled to destroy more than one hundred dwellings and uproot some
nine hundred businesses, but its projected route would clearly slice off
the historic community from the main part of the downtown area, thus
isolating the North End from the rest of Boston. During the spring of
1950 store owners, restaurateurs, and food wholesalers organized a
"Save Boston Business" committee to protest the coming disaster, while
longtime residents formed a Committee to Save the North End of Boston
to head off what they felt would be the complete obliteration of their
old, colorful, and distinctively Italian neighborhood. But the protests
were too little and too late, and were never sufficiently organized to

*Automobile and truck traffic carefully navigate the construction of the Central Artery as the future Fitzgerald Expressway makes its way through downtown Boston, past High Street, toward Summer Street and the South Station. The distinctive art deco shape of the United Shoe Machinery Building can be seen in the upper right, while the smoke stacks of the Boston Edison electric plant on L Street appear in the left background. Photograph © 1990 by Peter Vanderwarker.*

achieve their desired political effect. Despite the wishful thinking of one resident, who said that he had heard rumors that buildings were going to be torn down but "hoped it wasn't true," in November 1950 the first fifty-four plots of land were taken on Haverhill, Beverly, and Traverse streets in the North Station area. Protests erupted again in October 1951 when North End residents learned that Hanover Street, the main thoroughfare, would be cut off. The old post office, where so many old-time residents had deposited their money, was also threatened with demolition, and local pushcart peddlers on Blackstone Street faced the possibility of eviction. All their protests were ineffective, however, as the central expressway became a reality and slowly began snaking its way through the city.[41]

"In those days, people more or less accepted public improvements," said an engineer, Chandler Rogers, in matter-of-fact tones similar to those used by postwar planners who would soon be involved in redeveloping the West End. "They just accepted them—as opposed to voicing opinions in opposition. I'm not saying that's the way it *should* have been—but that's the way in happened."[42]

Like so many other Bostonians, Mayor Hynes was distressed by the way the expressway was cutting off the North End and the entire waterfront from the rest of the city, but he could find no other practical alternative to the transportation problem. He could only content himself with the prospect that short-term losses would lead to long-term gains. "When the Central Artery is fully completed," he said early in 1955, "it will tremendously accelerate traffic movement in and out of the city, and should, we are extremely hopeful, encourage building improvements and new construction along and in the vicinity of the route."[43] Future generations of Boston motorists who would have to contend daily with incredible traffic jams along an expressway that would already be obsolete before it was completed would certainly take issue with Hynes's bright promises of "acceleration." Nevertheless, it is almost impossible to conceive of any other practical way in which heavy automobile traffic could be shuttled from the North Shore to the South Shore without going through the streets of Boston. Even when it was decided, some forty years later, that the overhead structure should be taken down and replaced by a widened and depressed roadway, the route itself was basically the same as that of the original artery.

As an improved highway system brought more and more vehicles into Boston, the problem of parking in the city became so critical that city leaders began thinking seriously about using the Boston Common. From time to time in the past, as Boston's growing population continually threatened to outstrip the peninsula's meager size, the shrewd glances of real estate developers and land speculators had inevitably fallen upon that invaluable parcel of centrally located property. Even at times when extra land was especially needed, however, the Boston Common was always untouchable and unattainable. That was what the town fathers had originally intended when they purchased the forty-five acres from the Reverend William Blaxton in 1634 and assured "equal Right of Commonage" to every settler of the Shawmut Peninsula. Establishing that not a bit of this common land would ever be released "without consent of the major part of the inhabitants of the town," and forbidding its allocation to any person "for house plotts or garden," they encouraged its use for such acceptable activities as pasturing cattle, grazing cows, exercising horses, and training militia companies.[44] Throughout history, selectmen stubbornly refused to allow the "advocates of trade" to make even the slightest incursion into a public space that over the years had come to assume the lofty status of sacred property, never to be desecrated in any fashion. That attitude helps explain the gasps of horror that greeted the semihumorous proposal made by James Michael Curley in 1915, just after his first election as mayor of Boston. Unable to resist tweaking the aristocratic noses of the Beacon Hill Brahmins, the young politician not only suggested that the Public Garden be sold off so that a series of smaller gardens could be created in the various neighborhoods, but he also proposed that a water-pumping station be constructed under the Boston Common. Although nothing came of this impudent suggestion, the idea of finding some practical and acceptable use for the reserved parcel of land in the heart of downtown Boston was never far away from any developer's imagination. Maurice Tobin proposed a garage underneath the common to the General Court during his term as governor, and his successor, Robert Bradford, made a similar proposal the following year, but most people doubted that such a thing would ever come to pass. "Subways, buildings, and other improvements have now and then threatened to alter the familiar image," wrote David McCord in his delightful series of essays about the sights and sounds of Boston, *About Boston*, published in 1948. "The cry of 'Save the Common' has always prevailed. It will probably prevail against the underground movement for a subterranean municipal garage. I trust so."[45]

Mr. McCord's trust was sadly misplaced, however, for shortly after his election as mayor of Boston in 1946, Curley took up the idea of an underground garage in earnest, supporting his friend and real estate developer William J. McDonald in a private venture to construct such a public facility. Although at first the legislature vetoed the bill, in the spring of 1950 enough members changed their votes—owing to the "application of political heat put on by Governor Dever and Speaker O'Neill," according to the *Herald* columnist William E. Mullins—that the bill leasing out the space under the Boston Common for a period of forty years to McDonald's company, Motor Park, Inc., passed the house and then went on to the senate, where it was "vigorously supported" by Senator John E. Powers.[46] The prospect of a massive fifteen-hundred-car garage being constructed under one of the most sacred and historic sites in the city had residents up in arms. Opponents to the project filed three separate taxpayers' suits seeking (1) to enforce the ancient public trust establishing the common as a recreation area for all time; (2) to enforce the provisions of the $5 million George Francis Parkman trust fund obliging the city to keep the common as a public park; and (3) to restrain the city from incurring alleged illegal obligations. The lower court reviewing the petitions threw its hands up in frustration and passed the issues along to the Supreme Judicial Court, which eventually ruled in Curley's favor. It maintained that neither the original land grant nor the Parkman trust prevented the city from using the land in the public interest. It further ruled that the legislature's act made it lawful for the city to enter into garage contracts.

Year after year went by, however, and no action was taken on the garage. In the course of six years, Motor Park, Inc., was given nine extensions of time to arrange financing of the project, but it failed to meet any of the extensions. By 1955 Mayor Hynes began to show signs of impatience. When the legislature came into session, he filed two bills to allow the garage to be built by an authority. Although the authority plan passed the house, it ran into a storm in the senate, where Powers, looking forward to running against Hynes for mayor himself the coming November, caused the bill to be tabled. At that point, the city announced it was ready to sit down with John Fox, the publisher of the *Boston Post* and one of the many investors, to see whether Motor Park was capable of meeting its obligations. The real test was not only whether Motor Park could raise the estimated $11 million to $15 million it would take to finance construction, but also whether it would be able to get a required completion bond from a bonding company—and at this point the city was decidedly skeptical. "It boils down to a question of dollars and cents," said Hynes's good friend William L. Baxter, a city corporation counsel. "A bonding company must be satisfied that the project is financially sound and practical and feasible. If they aren't they won't give the bond, and the garage won't be built."[47] Hynes would be well into his next term as mayor before the issues of funding and responsibility for the underground garage would finally be resolved. The garage project would be only one of a number of important changes and innovations that Mayor Hynes would attempt to bring about during the course of his administration in order to make his dream of a New Boston a reality.

# 4.

# "Where's Boston?"

The Commonwealth of Massachusetts had available to it a number of creative alternatives, such as semiautonomous "authorities," capable of launching expensive projects to benefit the entire state without going through the taxing process. Mayor John B. Hynes, however, was not so fortunate in carrying out his plans to revitalize and modernize the city. Not only was he limited in his executive powers as mayor, but because of restrictive legislation passed by the General Court some forty years earlier, the city of Boston itself was utterly dependent on the state government for anything of consequence, especially anything involving the expenditure of public funds. Leaving his office at City Hall and walking up to Beacon Hill to meet with state legislative committees, to argue for his programs, and to request necessary funding was a kind of temporal purgatory that the mayor made every effort to avoid. He generally viewed such state legislative bodies as bothersome and obstructionist groups that played political games, engaged in nasty personal vendettas, and generally prevented him from getting the enabling legislation he needed to bring about much-needed changes in the city.

Perhaps because he himself was not a member of "the club," never having served in either the house or the senate, Hynes did not seem to fully appreciate the potential of the state legislature in bringing about the substantial reforms he had in mind. And anyway, he always felt that the personal approach was the best way to advance the legislative process. He made it a practice to telephone the governor and the leaders of the house and the senate and invite them to join him in his office. In his prim and proper manner, like a conservative banker quietly discussing a complicated financial transaction with respectable clients, he would talk with them "man to man—especially the Boston legislators." Basically, Hynes believed it was undignified for him to go to the State House and make a personal appearance before some hostile legislative committee. He regarded the office of the mayor of Boston as an important position; for such a personage to go, hat in hand, before some legislative committee, or even before the members of his own city council (something he routinely avoided), seemed beneath the dignity and prestige of the office. "Curley never went up to the legislature—never. And Tobin—I don't think Maurice Tobin ever went before legislative committees when he was mayor," exclaimed Hynes, who obviously saw no reason for him to go either.[1]

Besides the matter of protocol, the mayor had other and more practical reasons for avoiding legislative committees. Not only did he see himself being continually besieged for jobs and favors, but he especially feared being "sandbagged" by the unexpected or irrelevant questions some hostile legislator might ask that would cause him great embarrassment. "There might be some fellow waiting for him [the mayor] whom he had turned down on some request—and he's waiting, loaded down with all sorts of extraneous questions and charges, and it throws the whole thing out of kilter," he explained. Clearly, he saw the halls of the state legislature or the chambers of the city council as deadly minefields into which he was not about to venture for fear of his political life.[2]

It was, perhaps, because he had such little regard for legislative committees or consultation procedures that the legislative packages Hynes sent up to the hill were so carelessly prepared or so poorly received. A random sampling of the sort of legislation he proposed to the state legislature in 1952 would seem to confirm the opinion of Joseph Slavet, head of the Boston Municipal Bureau, that Hynes's programs were poorly planned. For the most part, they had little sense of priorities—a smorgasbord of inconsequential bills and minor items submitted alongside important issues and substantive proposals. Bills dealing with Dutch elm disease, the location of an incinerator, the fat content of hamburger, and the sale of horsemeat were sent up to Beacon Hill along with bills controlling parking violations, building zones, sprinkler systems, the salaries of court officers, and the custody of neglected children. Over the course of his ten years in office, Hynes had a very low rate of success, ranging from 15 percent to 25 percent of the bills offered. A study of his legislation shows that most of his bills were actually repeaters—old chestnuts filed yearly and routinely defeated— and whatever legislation did pass usually dealt with purely local issues.[3]

According to several observers, the attorney Hynes appointed as lobbyist to plead his case on the hill was of little help in strengthening the city's position. Michael Hourihan was not taken seriously on Beacon Hill, where he was regarded as more of a "court jester" than a responsible advocate of the city's legislative policies. One local representative, Norman Weinberg of Brighton, describe Hourihan's efforts as "clownish" and accused him of spending more time sunning himself at the L Street Bathhouse than putting in time on his job at the State House.[4] The few bills Hourihan did manage to get through the legislature, Joe Slavet observed, were those that private business interests already wanted and were willing to use their own influence to get passed. At the same time, however, Slavet readily conceded that Hourihan was doing his best under conditions made difficult by the long-standing political circumstances and personal rivalries that traditionally confronted all Boston mayors. Sometimes, according to Slavet, many legislative proposals were not brought up for debate or even considered on their own merits because of some deep-seated grudge on the part of a particular legislator against Hynes himself. At other times, the opposition came from the representatives of cities and towns in other parts of the commonwealth such as Worcester, Springfield, Westfield, or Pittsfield who almost automatically took opposing stands on any legislation that would benefit Boston. In most of those cases, the Boston legislators themselves were not much help, since their own private ambitions and conflicting loyalties kept them so disunified that seldom were they willing to stand united behind the efforts of their own city.[5]

There was, perhaps, some small consolation in the fact that while old-time political rivalries continued to run high during the early 1950s, traditional religious controversies were showing some definite signs of cooling down in a city noted for bitter denominational feuds that had raged for generations. In the wake of the postwar baby boom, which saw the country's population leap from 130 million in 1940 to 165 million by the mid-1950s—the biggest increase in the nation's history— there was an attendant emphasis on feelings of togetherness among people who shared similar attitudes regarding family and society. It was a time when conformity was the ideal, and when terms like *moderation* and *consensus* were in vogue. In place of the more traditional values of hard work, frugality, and individual self-reliance, there emerged a new "social ethic" based on cooperation, security, and group well-being. Even morality became a social phenomenon as the upsurge of religion could be seen almost everywhere—in the rise in denominational membership, increase in church attendance, prayers at cabinet meetings and breakfast sessions, pious professions of faith by political candidates. Newspapers and magazines gave increased attention to religious topics, motion pictures dealt with a wide variety of biblical themes, and television regularly featured such popular clerical celebrities as Dr. Norman Vincent Peale, Rev. Billy Graham, and Bishop Fulton J. Sheen. Undoubtedly inspired by the interdenominational activities in the armed forces and among the civilian population during the Second World War, by the early 1950s both Protestant and Catholic churches began to explore new ways of reducing old rivalries and encouraging cooperation in religious matters along what came to be called "ecumenical" lines.[6]

At a moment in Boston's history when a new generation of community leaders was making a conscientious effort to break down old social barriers and create a new sense of unity, an attendant change in the traditional religious climate could not help making a subtle but significant contribution. Still a potent force in the affairs of the city in the late 1930s and early 1940s, William Cardinal O'Connell, archbishop of Boston, spent the last years of his life in comfortable splendor. Moving into successively more substantial residences, the prelate ended in an impressive estate in the Brighton section of Boston. He continued to travel extensively all over the world and was greeted by kings, presidents, and popes. Foreign governments honored him; heads of state listened to his words; members of the hierarchy sought his advice. He also maintained his practice of taking long vacations—winters in Nassau, summers at Marblehead—earning him the popular but irreverent nickname "Gangplank Bill" among working-class readers who saw his photographs at regular intervals in the *Boston Post*, shown coming ashore from his latest sea voyage.[7] Residents of Brighton and students from Boston College walking down to the streetcar stop at Lake Street would often pass the prelate seated in solemn meditation in the back seat of his long black limousine while his chauffeur walked his black French poodle along Commonwealth Avenue.

As O'Connell moved into his eighties, old age, failing eyesight, and the complications of chronic diabetes began to take their toll. He traveled less frequently, his winter vacations to the Bahamas became much less elaborate, and by the 1940s he seldom ventured outside his residence except for those formal occasions where his official presence was absolutely required. He reduced his involvement in diocesan management considerably and cut back on such civic responsibilities as serving on the board of trustees of the Boston Public Library. His general condition deteriorated rapidly by the start of 1944, and by April he was confined to bed, where he suffered a stroke and passed away on April 22, 1944.[8] His magnificent funeral at the South End's Cathedral of the Holy Cross was a solemn ceremonial event that marked not only the passing of a prelate but also the end of an era.

The young bishop who succeeded Cardinal O'Connell was forty-nine-year-old Richard J. Cushing, a native of South Boston, who almost immediately proved to be as different from his predecessor in personal style as he was in his ecclesiatical views. He had made a name for himself as an affable go-getter and energetic fund-raiser by directing the local office of the Society for the Propagation of the Faith, an agency that raised money for the support of foreign missions. At the time of his accession to the rank of archbishop, Cushing was a tall, husky, broad-shouldered man, with a gruff voice that had not yet become the high-pitched nasal whine that became his famous trademark in later years. Little concerned with elaborate ceremonies or abstract theology, Cushing was more interested in updating the church and making it more relevant to the everyday lives of ordinary people. He generally avoided the ornate dress and fancy vestments of his exalted office, except when required by the formal rituals of church services and sacramental functions, and usually appeared in public in plain black clerical garb. Breezy, outgoing, and approachable, he welcomed publicity, courted photographers, and posed for television cameras as he mingled easily with people of all sorts, from the rich and the powerful to the poor and the disadvantaged. He said Midnight Mass on Christmas Eve for the inmates of the Walpole State Prison; he accompanied groups of nuns to the amusement park at Nantasket Beach or to ballgames at Fenway Park; he administered First Holy Communion and Confirmation to retarded children at Saint Coletta's School in Hanover; and he sliced turkey at his annual Thanksgiving Day dinner for elderly people at

Blinstrub's Village in South Boston, where he frequently joined in the singing and dancing with his aged parishioners.[9]

More than simply a new man in town with a different way of doing things, however, the new archbishop helped define a new level of human relations in an archdiocese heretofore noted for bitter and sometimes violent conflicts among persons of different religious, ethnic, and racial backgrounds. Distancing himself from the rigid and often confrontational attitudes of his predecessor, early in his career Cushing adopted a more tolerant approach and pledged to refrain from "all arguments with our non-Catholic neighbors and from all purely defensive talk about Catholicism."

That attitude was more than a personal idiosyncrasy or a momentary aberration; it was a reflection of a much broader spirit of unity and cooperation that had developed among a great many American faiths and denominations during the course of World War II. The experience of working together during a major wartime crisis—exchanging altars and pulpits on military and naval bases, sharing Bibles and prayerbooks on the battlefields, conducting interdenominational services, ministering to servicemen of all faiths, minimizing doctrinal differences, accentuating the similarities of their creeds, and announcing their commitments to the principles of the "Four Freedoms"—had prompted many church leaders during the postwar years to develop what became known as an ecumenical movement that would explore new ways of reducing religious rivalries and encouraging a fundamental brotherhood among people of all religious persuasions.

Working in the spirit of ecumenism and preaching the doctrine of universal brotherhood—in great part by his own forthright example— Cushing succeeded in knocking aside many of the invisible barriers that had for so long separated his parishioners from their non-Catholic neighbors. By the time he was appointed cardinal by Pope John XXIII in 1958, Cushing had anticipated many of the far-reaching changes that eventually would be introduced by the reforms of Vatican II. He was already preaching in Protestant churches, speaking in Jewish synagogues, and generally promoting a feeling of fellowship and goodwill among the various ethnic and religious groups throughout the greater Boston area.[10]

Expressions of goodwill and well-meaning gestures of ecumenism might have been enough to create an atmosphere of greater harmony in Boston, but they were not enough to rouse the city out of its lethargy or

*Richard J. Cushing succeeded William Henry O'Connell as archbishop of Boston in 1945, and was elevated to the rank of cardinal in 1958. Gruff, affable, and down-to-earth, Cushing worked in the spirit of ecumenism and sought to heal the city's long-standing social and religious animosities. Especially dedicated to the ideal of service, he brought the solace of religion to the aged and the infirm. Here he is shown serving a Thanksgiving dinner to some elderly people at a local restaurant. Courtesy of the Boston Public Library, Print Department.*

to encourage its leading citizens to take practical measures toward its reconstruction and renewal. During the fall of 1953 Mayor Hynes paid a visit to Israel and the Holy Land, stopping off long enough in Ireland for a brief visit to the home of his forebears in Loughrea, and sending back colorful descriptions of his travels to the *Boston Globe*. It was while he was abroad that the Boston Board of Censorship decided to suspend performances at two of Scollay Square's most notorious burlesque houses—the Old Howard and the Casino Theater. The decision of the board was prompted by actions taken by members of the vice squad after complaints from local civic groups. Plainclothes officers paid their way into the Old Howard, used a sixteen-millimeter camera to take pictures of the stage show, and subsequently produced the evidence before an amused Judge Elijah Adlow in municipal court. The court fined three of the strippers two hundred dollars each for performing a "lewd and immoral" show, and the city eventually ordered the theater closed. "I positively will not tolerate any filthy or indecent shows in our city," declared the acting mayor, city council president Francis X. Ahearn. "Any further complaints of this nature will be met with the most drastic and summary actions while I am acting mayor." Although the fines were appealed, the reopening of the Old Howard—whose box office receipts were already falling off badly—was never seriously pursued. "America's oldest theater was closed," wrote the district's latest historian, "and would stay that way."[11]

This event was not merely a matter of temporary local interest; the city's actions helped to set the stage for the later transformation of the old Scollay Square district into the future site of the Hynes administration's proposal for a new Government Center. But that development was still some years into the future. For the time being, there seemed to be no concerted effort to do anything more substantial about renewing the face of the city than shutting down a popular and generally inoffensive burlesque house.

The unexpected catalyst for bringing together many of the disparate elements in Boston's financial community appeared in the unlikely guise of a young Jesuit priest named W. Seavey Joyce, who had just been named dean of the School of Business Administration at Boston College. Brought up on Dakota Street in Saint Peter's parish, Dorchester, the son of a Boston policeman, Joyce graduated from Boston College High School when it was still in the South End, and in 1931 he entered the Jesuit order. Destined for collegiate pursuits, he received a Ph.D. in economics from Harvard University in 1949 and looked forward to a quiet career teaching in the Boston area, where he could enjoy his passion for the city. "Seavey was not the kind of Bostonian who would have carried back tea and porcelain vases from China," wrote one of his colleagues. "He was the kind of Bostonian who needed to be convinced to go any further than Dedham."[12] A reserved and private person who was more at home in academic pursuits than public relations, his professional competence as an economist and urban planner brought him into the public spotlight as a popular guest speaker, lecturer, and industry spokesman. In a short time his personal charm, sophisticated manner, and public speaking skills made him a favorite among downtown business and financial leaders.[13]

When he assumed his position as dean in 1953, Father Joyce used the occasion of the fifteenth anniversary of the business school's founding to hold an alumni banquet that was successful not only in building stronger alumni relations but also in reactivating the school's advisory council. Looking for something that would give the business school a more attractive public image, as well as carry out the mandate of Boston College's president to "put the school on the map," Father Joyce picked up on a suggestion made by a council member, Arthur J. Kelly—a vice president and treasurer of the R. H. White Company, a well-known downtown clothing and department store—that the school run an all-day conference of business leaders, public officials, and labor executives for a serious consideration of community problems. Kelly's suggestion was heartily endorsed by another council member, Dan Bloomfield, head of the Boston Retail Board, who offered his own expertise as a conference organizer in helping to plan such a conference. When the question of an appropriate theme came up in the course of one late-night planning session, Bloomfield recalls jotting down some words on a scrap of paper outlining the central concepts on which such a conference would focus:

- A delineation of the major survival challenges to an old city
- An appraisal of the city's relationship to a rapidly expanding metropolitan community and to the commonwealth
- A discussion of the elements necessary to a stable and prosperous future[14]

The conference, "Greater Boston's Business Future," was held in May 1954 and proved to be a huge success. More than two hundred persons from the business and public sectors came to the handsome Chestnut Hill campus, on the borderline between Boston and the suburban town of Newton. The participants included such prominent figures as John I. Ahern, vice president of the New England Electric System; O. Kelly Anderson, president of New England Mutual Life Insurance Company; Ephron Catlin, Jr., chairman of the First National Bank of Boston; Thomas H. Carens, vice president of the Boston Edison Company; Carl Gilbert, vice president and treasurer of the Gillette Company; Sidney Rabb, chairman of Stop & Shop, Inc.; and William H. (Billy) Sullivan, Jr., president of the Metropolitan Coal and Oil

Company. A highlight of the program, which received considerable coverage in the Boston newspapers for several days, was a lecture by Joseph A. Healey, director of the Massachusetts Special Commission on Taxation, denouncing plans that were reported to be in the works to provide special tax concessions for investors who would develop an area of the city into what was being called the "Back Bay Center." Such special tax arrangements, Healey charged, would be "unconstitutional, unfair, and unwise." They would give some people a "free ride" at the expense of others, would create dissatisfaction among taxpayers, and would inevitably lead to retaliation by other communities.[15]

The subject of Healey's heated remarks on tax abatement policies went to the heart of a problem that continued to plague the city's early attempts to attract outside investors and developers. Back in 1949, when the John Hancock Mutual Life Insurance Company opened its twenty-six-story office building near Copley Square, many people saw the impressive tower as a harbinger of a bright new city. Indeed, as Russell B. Adams has pointed out, the building's first tenants—the Massachusetts Investors Trust and the American Research and Development Corporation—seemed to symbolize precisely that combination of capital and brainpower that was needed to spark a true urban revival. But the glow of future promise quickly died out. Instead of providing incentive for further growth, the Hancock tower stood for many years as a beacon of caution to those foolish enough to invest their future in Boston. When the Hancock officials received their first tax bill from the city, they were absolutely stunned by the enormity of the costs they had unwittingly incurred. Once word got around—and it got around fast—there was no insurance company, or any other major corporation, that would undertake any major construction in the city of Boston.[16]

This history of unwise and inflexible tax policies helps to explain why the prolonged struggle to transform the tangle of abandoned Boston and Albany freight yards in the Back Bay stands as an illustration of Boston's delay in joining in the nation's postwar building boom. The "whole shebang," as one local writer put it, started in May 1951, when Hynes first learned that the Boston and Albany Railroad Company, a subsidiary of the New York Central, had finally decided to dispose of its twenty-eight and a half acres of land in Boston's Back Bay section, bounded by Boylston, Dalton, and Exeter streets, and Huntington Avenue. The following spring, at a conference of mayors in Washington, D.C., Hynes was told by Mayor Haydon Burns of Jacksonville, Florida, that the Prudential Insurance Company had decided to build a regional office in Jacksonville, but was also quietly looking around for a regional office somewhere in the northeast. "There popped into my mind," wrote Hynes, "a vision of a Prudential Building on the Boston and Albany land in Boston."[17]

A short time later, Hynes remembered, George F. Oakes, vice president of the R. M. Bradley Company, one of Boston's leading real estate firms, and one of the candidates who had run against him in the 1949 mayoral election, came "bounding" into his office in City Hall. He had just heard that the Boston and Albany officials had put a $4.5 million price tag on their railroad property and were willing to give

Back Bay Train Yards, *a 1939 oil by C. Roy Morse, captures the atmosphere of an urban wasteland with his brooding study of smoke-filled freight yards in the Back Bay area looking east toward downtown Boston with Boylston Street on the left. This sprawling expanse of Boston and Albany property was the area that was eventually selected by the Prudential Insurance Company as the site for its Boston office. Courtesy of The Bostonian Society.*

Oakes an option at that figure. He wanted to get going right away, but first he wanted Hynes to give him assurances that the assessed valuation of the property would be brought down to the sales-price figure. "This was a fly in the ointment," sighed the mayor, only too conscious of the political implications of such a move, especially since Oakes's dream of a $75 million complex of buildings along the lines of New York City's Rockefeller Center was still vague and general, founded mainly on an "inexhaustible supply of optimism."[18] Realizing that his chances of getting a special tax arrangement would be much better if he could give an indication of who would be using the property and exactly how it was going to be used, Hynes told Oakes of his confidential information regarding Prudential's interest in a northeast site, and asked him if he had any "pipe-lines" to that company. Oakes recalled some friends in New York who were acquainted with a man named Roger Stevens, who had just created a considerable stir in the real estate market by putting together a syndicate that worked with Prudential in purchasing the Empire State Building. Oakes met with Stevens personally, persuaded him to pick up the time option offered by the Boston and Albany, and began discussions with Prudential. "This is an opportunity which could not be found anywhere else in the country," Stevens declared, promising to develop a business and civic center that would be "one of the world's finest."[19]

Early in 1953 Stevens and Oakes began to design ways to develop the railroad property as a single commercial unit, but in the existing financial climate of the city Hynes had to admit that general interest in the plan "was at a low ebb." Hoping to stimulate interest, Stevens arranged a meeting with Prudential officials at their Newark headquarters, and when Hynes returned home from the meeting he was satisfied that Boston "was not out of the running." He was especially pleased that Prudential's president, Carroll Shanks, had turned future discussions over to the executive vice president, Valentine Howells, whom the mayor found to be "gentle, patient, and discerning" in his contacts with the city. "This certainly explodes any myth that Boston is all done for, and isn't a good financial risk," commented the mayor as he looked forward to the start of a new era in the city's economy.[20] In the fall, George Oakes arranged a special luncheon at the Sheraton Plaza Hotel, complete with an exhibit of project models, as a means of showing Prudential officials the "solid support" of local businessmen in favor of a Prudential building in Boston. The luncheon, he hoped, would also serve as a convenient forum if Shanks decided to make a formal announcement of Prudential's intentions. The city would "officially do all in its power to make what you see here an actuality," Hynes promised the visitors. "This can be a turning point of a bigger, better, busier Boston," he said, taking over a slogan originally used by John F. Fitzgerald when he campaigned for mayor against James Jackson Storrow in 1910. "We can and should be part of it." Carroll Shanks spoke encouragingly about Boston and its prospects, but he really gave no hint of his company's long-range plans. Hynes was disappointed. Not only did he fail to get the commitment from Prudential he had hoped for, but he also failed to stimulate much local enthusiasm for the whole idea. Although he described the attendance at the luncheon as "respectable" and "fairly representative," he had to concede that Boston businessmen "did not exactly storm" the meeting. All in all, he wrote, the atmosphere was "lukewarm."[21]

The mayor found that he was running into stiff opposition from downtown merchants, hotel operators, and property owners who were unhappy at the prospect of outside competition, and who condemned any special tax arrangements to outsiders and newcomers as unfair and discriminatory. In order to encourage the development of the old railroad yards, Mayor Hynes had taken the position that the city would have to fix the tax assessment on the property at the amount of the sales price, $4.5 million. Roger Stevens made it clear that this type of tax concession was absolutely necessary if his venture were to be profitable. No investor looking to make money, he said, would come to Boston as long as the city continued "its present high tax rate and unsound real estate base."[22] Hynes indicated that he was personally willing to negotiate a special tax arrangement with Stevens, but old established firms in the city continued to dig in their heels. While the proposed Back Bay Center along Huntington Avenue was not much more than a mile and a half walking distance from the traditional sales and retail sections of Washington and Tremont streets, downtown businessmen and financiers feared that this new-fangled development was simply one more move that would only add to the frightening stampede already drawing too many paying customers out of the central city and into the suburbs.

The heart of Boston's commercial and financial economy had always been located at the extreme end of the peninsula, close to the waterfront, where for generations tight-lipped Yankees exchanged silent greetings as they passed each other along State Street, Congress Street,

Court Street, and Devonshire Street, intent on the serious business of making more money. No doubt about it; here was the core of the city, the center of things, and by God it was going to stay that way! There was no way such businessmen could be persuaded to support any new efforts to change the way things had always been. Corporate investors were insistent on staying in close touch with their financial advisers, bankers, lawyers, and advertising agencies for the usual man-to-man negotiations on important issues. Legal restrictions usually kept bankers and utility executives from moving out of the city, and heavy investments in downtown real estate properties kept other large corporations comfortably close to their valuable holdings. Newspaper publishers had a commitment to their downtown identities, as well as a concern for keeping economic activity alive and well in the heart of their circulation area.[23]

This emphasis on remaining close to the heart of "old" Boston was not only a matter of dollars and cents—although that, of course, was something that could never be overlooked—but was also a question of a style of living that downtowners saw as an integral part of the Boston mystique that should be preserved at all costs. They valued their associations with the private clubs, the libraries, and the bookstores. They wanted to stay close to the theaters, the art galleries, the concert halls, and the fine restaurants that added zest to what could easily have been a dull and prosaic existence. They viewed the downtown area as an indispensable focal point of communication and culture that inevitably attracted the kinds of intellectuals and artists, writers and architects, physicians and scientists, who were so essential to maintaining a vital and attractive urban—and urbane—center. All these advantages would inevitably disappear, they believed, if that vital center should become so diffused that it would lose its unique appeal and its singular magnetic qualities. After two years of negotiation and debate, Mayor Hynes's proposed tax arrangement came before the Massachusetts Supreme Judicial Court, which, in a 1955 advisory opinion, came to the decision that such an arrangement would be unconstitutional.[24] Here was precisely the kind of complicated issue Father Joyce and his associates hoped to analyze and resolve in order to move things forward for the development of a modernized city.

The success of the May conference at Boston College, and the intense conversations it stimulated among participants who were concerned about the ways in which the prevailing climate of fear and suspicion still prevented a resolution of the city's problems, suggested an important direction in which Father Joyce's business school might be able to move on a permanent basis. Robert Ryan, executive director of the Massachusetts Development Corporation, arranged for a series of meetings between Father Joyce and representatives of the college with local business executives, starting out in July with a luncheon at the Algonquin Club attended by Ryan himself; Norman MacDonald, executive director of the Massachusetts Federation of Taxpayers; John Galvin, executive director of the Boston Citizens' Council; and Ephron Catlin of the First National Bank. At a subsequent meeting at the First National Bank—at which Father Joyce and members of his staff, together with Ryan, Catlin, and Galvin, were joined by Billy Sullivan, the future owner of the New

*Civic leaders meet at a Citizen Seminar conducted at the Chestnut Hill campus of Boston College, March 8, 1955, to discuss Boston's relations with the metropolitan district and with the commonwealth of Massachusetts. From left to right: Christian A. Herter, governor of Massachusetts; Rev. W. Seavey Joyce, SJ, dean of the Boston College School of Business Administration; and John B. Hynes, mayor of Boston. Courtesy of the University Archives, Boston College.*

England Patriots; Joseph A. Lund from the R. M. Bradley real estate development company; and a Boston lobbyist, Tom Joyce—it was obvious that the ice had been broken when all parties frankly admitted that a major obstacle to any future plans for rebuilding a new Boston was the historical division that existed between the "Boston Irish" and the "Boston Blue Bloods." The immediate challenge, they agreed, was to move away from those ancient fears and traditional conflicts that for so long had paralyzed progress in the city, and to bring together men of goodwill from both sides to engage in open discussion of the pressing questions facing the city.[25]

After considering various locations, the members felt that the campus of Boston College would represent an acceptable, neutral site— a rallying point—for a series of meetings or seminars that would bring together leaders from the public and private sectors to discuss common problems. They also agreed to establish a twenty-member planning committee, with John Galvin as chairman, in order to create some kind of permanent mechanism to ensure that these seminars would continue on a long-range basis. A graduate of Boston College, a public relations consultant, and an avid historian of Boston politics, Galvin had served as a navy captain in the Pacific during World War II. After the war he became the executive director of the Boston Citizens' Council, a group of influential citizens organized to spark action on the problems of Boston. Under Galvin's direction, the planning committee worked out a series of meetings to be held on the Chestnut Hill campus, which would be known officially as the Citizen Seminars on the Fiscal, Economic, and Political Problems of Boston and the Metropolitan Community. Under the sponsorship of Boston College, these Citizen Seminars would provide continuing opportunities for participants to discuss "the major challenges confronting the city, and to chart the course for a stable and prosperous future." Here, for the first time, was a catalyst for the kind of concerted action that was desperately needed to save a declining Boston from imminent economic collapse.[26]

Father Joyce's intense concern for the future of Boston was heightened not only by his own attraction to the city's special ambience but also by a particular episode he liked to tell his friends about in later years. Despite his interest in twentieth-century urban economics, he had an almost eighteenth-century aversion to things mechanical and combustible. He was well into his forties, for example, before he agreed to take driving lessons (much to the terror of the entire Jesuit community), and he absolutely refused to travel by airplane.[27] When he was required to go to San Francisco in April 1956 to attend a meeting of the American Association of Collegiate Schools of Business, he insisted on making the transcontinental journey by train. He had just arrived on the West Coast and was congratulating himself on having cheated the paragons of progress one more time, when he received an urgent telephone call from the governor of Massachusetts, Christian Herter, asking the business school dean to represent him at an important economic conference in Michigan, and making available his personal plane to get him there from California on time. Father Joyce could hardly turn down the governor's request, so he put aside his fear of flying long enough to make the Michigan conference and then start the return trip to the Bay State.[28] As the plane neared Boston and banked lazily to begin its approach to Logan Airport, the priest overcame his aversion to heights long enough to look out the window at the scene below, which he now saw from a distance and a perspective he had never before experienced. As he gazed down on the low-lying protuberence of land beneath him, which was completely undistinguished, had no distinctive skyline, and not a single identifiable structure except the old Custom House tower, he exclaimed in a startled voice: "Where's Boston?"[29]

Many other people at the time must have been asking the same question, because when Father Joyce sent out invitations to the first of his new series of conferences on the future of the city, he got an enthusiastic response. The time had clearly come for bringing together public and private interests to change the city for the good of all its citizens. The first Citizen Seminar took place on October 26, 1954, with Rev. Joseph R. N. Maxwell, SJ, president of Boston College, giving an official welcome to the three hundred guests. Mayor John B. Hynes delivered the opening address, "Boston, Whither Goest Thou?," in which he hailed what he perceived as a "new spirit" that had been awakened in Boston. "You feel it. It is in the air," he said. "This meeting here today is a manifestation of that new spirit." The city, he admitted, had been "treading water" and had followed the line of "least resistance," but the time had finally come to "begin moving forward."[30]

Nine months earlier, on January 4, 1954, in his annual address as mayor of Boston, Hynes had taken the unusual step of asking the members of the city council to give their "invaluable" assistance in supporting before the state legislature the passage of a set of city-sponsored modernization bills that could prove to be "extremely beneficial to our city." His was a remarkable gesture, because no previous mayor had ever proposed to any city council, either collectively or individually, that they contact the General Court to help Boston's legislative package. Hynes wanted their backing, he told them, for legislation that would strengthen the city's financial position, eliminate inequities in the deficit assessments of the Metropolitan Transit Authority (MTA), which placed an undue burden on Boston, provide more effective regulation of traffic and parking, and construct a municipal auditorium as part of the projected Back Bay Center—all of which, he felt "reasonably confident," would come to pass and be recognized as "the outstanding improvement in our city for many long years."[31]

By the time Hynes came to speak at Boston College in October, 1954, after a brief summer trip to various religious sites in Europe with Archbishop Cushing and three hundred pilgrims from Boston, many of his ideas had had time to mature, and now he was taking the opportunity to present his views in greater detail and a more orderly fashion.[32] In laying out his plans for a rejuvenated city, Hynes immediately came to grips with what he saw as the single most troublesome issue that stood in the way of large-scale rebuilding and redevelopment—the city's tax policy. Pointing out that the valuation and assessment of properties in Boston in 1954 was some $400 million *less* than it had been back in 1930, he emphasized the necessity for developing a policy that would lower the tax rate, broaden the tax base, locate new sources of revenue other than property, and attract such outside sources of investment as those who were currently proposing to spend up to $75 million developing the unused railroad yards in the Back Bay.[33]

Having proposed a modernized and broadened tax base, Hynes then launched into a description of a renewed and revitalized city along the same general lines as what was going on in several American cities at that time. For the so-called New York Streets section of the South End, he described his plan for urban development that would wipe out most existing structures in a twenty-four-acre zone and change it over to "light industrial and commercial use," with a new street pattern and facilities for off-street parking and loading. The federal government would assume two-thirds of the cost (about $2.9 million) while the city of Boston would assume the remaining one-third (about $1.4 million). After discussing his plans for a new and modernized zoning code for Boston, the building of a second harbor tunnel, and the construction of a new municipal office building, Hynes then went on to expand on his plans to create a World Trade Center that would restore Boston to its historic role as a center for international trade and commerce. After that, he elaborated on plans to construct a Back Bay Center on the site of the old Boston and Albany railroad yards along Huntington Avenue that would include commercial properties, office buildings, luxury shops, a major hotel, parking for thousands of vehicles, and a "convention hall–auditorium" that would be designed to attract "large, free-spending convention groups" to the city of Boston. To see such a complex come into being, however, the mayor took issue with Joseph Healey's critical remarks at the May conference about the dangers of tax concessions, emphasizing instead his own conviction that some kind of "tax protection plan" was absolutely necessary to ensure profitability. He admitted that opposition to this idea came from "old established business interests in Boston," and indicated that he was "sympathetic" with such objections. Nevertheless, he insisted that such special tax arrangements were the only way in which investors and developers could be encouraged to come in and help change the face of the city. "If we are determined to get the things done in Boston which must be done," he concluded, "our city, ten years hence . . . will once again be in the forefront of the great cities of the land."[34]

As groups of businessmen, politicians, educators, and labor leaders began to discuss the problems of Boston and speculate more seriously about ways in which the city could be revitalized, they undertook to examine more closely the ways in which other major cities had gone about tackling the job. During the summer and fall of 1955 Boston leaders visited the massive program of rehabilitation then under way in the city of Pittsburgh. They met with Richard King Mellon (of Mellon National Bank, Gulf Oil, and Alcoa) and with members of the Mellon-backed Allegheny Conference on Community Development, the group headed by Leland Hazard, vice president of Pittsburgh Plate Glass, who had come to Boston College earlier that year to speak at the May 19 meeting of the Citizen Seminar on the subject of what "dynamic business leadership" had done for the city of Pittsburgh.

Referring to the work of the leading businessmen who made up the Allegheny Conference in acting as a catalyst for urban renewal, Hazard had urged his listeners at the seminar not to sit around waiting for some kind of an official appointment from the governor or the mayor. No one appointed us, he stated bluntly, "we appointed ourselves." Once a city had a dynamic steering body headed by a small group of "men of influence and power," he said, the efforts of those men must not be "fragmented" but rather "integrated into a single purpose" if the city is to be saved. He then went into a detailed description of how such a group had gone about remaking Pittsburgh—getting the cooperation of the municipalities; obtaining the necessary enabling legislation; appointing a full-time director ("an engineer with imagination"); naming a public relations director; clearing the slums; moving and rehousing the people; upgrading streets, utilities, and transportation facilities; preserving historical monuments; and maintaining the distinctive culture of the area. Pointing out that sound politics was the glue that held everything together, Hazard urged his listeners to put aside old animosities for the good of Boston as a whole. The salvation of a city is "good politics," he said, and explained that Republican businessmen in Pittsburgh came to the realization that when a city's future is at stake "petty politics must be cleared away with the slums." A city does not endure by the work of "hirelings," Hazard said in his concluding remarks. "A city endures when its least and greatest citizens love it alike, and will live and work and die that it may be glorious."[35] The spirit and tone of Hazard's remarks obviously stimulated the imagination of the conference participants that day and prompted many of them to go to Pittsburgh to see for themselves what had taken place. "If any speaker can be singled out as the inspiration for the changes to come," John Galvin later recalled, "it was Leland Hazard . . . who declared that cities will not last 'if we do not care.' "[36]

As they toured Pittsburgh, the visitors from Boston studied the ways in which Mayor David L. Lawrence had played a key role in rescuing Pittsburgh from pollution and decay. An Irish-American who had come up through the ranks of Pittsburgh's tough Third Ward to serve as mayor for an unprecedented sixteen years, Lawrence joined forces with Richard Mellon and his committee of business executives in their determined plans to remake the city. While the members of the Allegheny Conference provided the money and the plans for reconstructing grimy downtown Pittsburgh, Lawrence himself was busy on the political front enforcing antipollution laws and smoke-control measures, while lobbying at the state capital as well as in Washington, D.C., for the funds necessary to build roads, bridges, and dams. Expressing surprise at an unlikely coalition between old-time ethnic politicians and modern business executives that would have been unthinkable in their own hometown, Bostonians asked the mayor what he and Richard Mellon had in common. Lawrence replied, "We have the same hobby: Pittsburgh." The visitors from Boston got the message, and when they got back home they began putting some of the things they had learned into practice.[37]

Once established on a firm footing, the Citizen Seminars continued on a regular basis and became an established forum where businessmen and bankers, lawyers and educators, labor leaders and political figures, historians and journalists could come together and begin to know and trust each other. During one of his appearances, Governor Christian Herter spoke approvingly of the way in which leaders of the city were given the opportunity to come together to express "freely and fully" whatever was on their minds, to "fraternize" at the social hours and dinners, and to explore the "large and complicated political problems" that had brought then together.[38] According to the *Boston Herald*, here were opportunities where "old foes" met in an atmosphere of goodwill to discuss some of the most pressing issues of the day. Economics, finance, and tax policies; public transportation, foreign trade, aviation, and shipping; fine arts, architecture, sports facilities, and cultural resources; police protection, public housing, and urban renewal; religion, education, and social welfare; labor, management, and political organization—these and literally hundreds of other stimulating topics formed the agenda of the seminars over the course of some thirty years, an agenda that got participants talking about what could be done to save the city. "This is part of a revolution that is quietly taking place in Boston," remarked one newspaper reporter after sitting in on one of the early seminars. "The citizens of Boston are indeed on the march. For the first time there can be intelligent optimism about the city's future."[39]

But one voice cautioned against putting too much emphasis on the future and not giving enough attention to the past. Speaking at a December 1957 Citizen Seminar at Boston College, Lewis Mumford, Bemis Professor at MIT's School of Architecture and one of America's leading business planners, startled his audience with the suggestion that Boston's "backwardness" could well be its "principal asset." In contrast to a number of previous speakers who had projected ambitious designs of modernistic skyscrapers, streamlined office buildings, and intersecting highways as a means of rebuilding the city and reversing the distressing flight to the suburbs, Mumford urged members of the seminar to turn away from such futuristic visions and hold on to the promises of the past. During the 1890s, Mumford recalled, Boston's economy had faltered, and as a result, the city was left with "fewer skyscrapers, with fewer newer buildings, with fewer new economic enterprises" than had developed in such cities as New York, Chicago, and Minneapolis. "If Boston avoided some of the economic prosperity of the years that followed the [18]90s, it also avoided some of the mistakes," he added. "If Boston had been prosperous, Boston would have been uninhabitable by this time." As Mumford spoke, there were only two "tall buildings" in downtown Boston—the Custom House tower along the waterfront, finished in 1915, and the John Hancock tower in the Copley Square area, completed in 1947. Compared to the exuberant skylines of other cities, Boston's was positively flat; but at the same time the very absence of numerous skyscrapers and extensive corporate structures offered an opportunity for physical expansion and development that might not otherwise have been possible.[40]

The planners of the seminars sought ways of expanding discussion of Boston's future to an even larger and more varied audience. Taking advantage of several grants from the Ford Foundation, which were augmented by funding from a group of local citizens under the leadership of Carl Gilbert, president of Gillette, Boston College created both a research bureau and a public television series. Under the initial direction of Joseph H. Turley, the new Bureau of Business Research took on several projects for the Governor's Committee on Transportation, the United States Fish and Wildlife Service, and several private organizations, while at the same time publishing a bulletin of current business conditions. When Turley left to join the Gillette company in 1960, the bureau changed its name to the Bureau of Public Affairs and during the next eleven years, under the direction of Robert T. M. O'Hare, expanded its operations to involve itself in broader problems of the state and the greater Boston community. Working closely with the Citizen Seminars, the bureau pressed for the establishment of a Metropolitan Planning Council, which was finally established by law in 1963, with Father Joyce appointed by Governor Endicott Peabody as its first president and Bob O'Hare as one of its first members.[41]

In hopes of gaining even wider acceptance of the need for municipal change, members of the Citizen Seminar group worked through the vehicle of public television. During 1955–56 a series of twelve television programs was presented over station WGBH-TV (Channel 2) titled "The Challenge to Greater Boston," dealing with the problems facing the metropolitan area. Donald White, associate dean of the Boston College business school, served as moderator of most of these programs, in which Mayor Hynes and many other prominent business and civic leaders participated as panel members. Two years later Father Joyce himself acted as host for another television series on WGBH, called "City in Crisis," which comprised twenty half-hour programs organized along the lines of a town meeting. For the next three years the popular series continued under the title of "Metropolis," with speakers at the Citizen Seminars going directly from the Chestnut Hill campus to station WGBH for informal presentations of what they had already said earlier in the day.[42]

The Citizen Seminars program did much to bring together disparate elements of Boston's corporate and financial community, outlined the major issues that needed to be addressed in projecting the renewal of the city, and established a rational basis for a future urban agenda. Many years later, after he had retired from public life and was reflecting on the beginnings of the New Boston, John B. Hynes paid tribute to the Boston College Citizen Seminars as a unique vehicle for enabling many citizens to rise "from doubt to comprehension." By providing a public forum where political and financial problems could be aired in an objective atmosphere, said Hynes, the seminars "pried open windows long and tightly closed. They have permitted the uninhibited circulation of thought, opinion, and judgment on matters affecting the present and future course of our urban society."[43] "The Boston College seminars were crucial in combining the political and business communities," agreed Mayor John Collins's future Boston Redevelopment Authority administrator, Edward J. Logue, more than a decade later, "and helped mightily in knitting together a city which sometimes seemed to find division the natural order."[44]

Nevertheless, it still remained for the mayor of the city to provide the political leadership needed to translate these wonderful but theoretical ideas into positive action. It would appear that, first, in his annual address in January 1954, and then nine months later, in his keynote address to the Citizen Seminar at Boston College, Hynes had been in the process of pulling together, at least in his own mind, the basic elements of a long-range agenda for a completely new Boston. If the city could form an effective working coalition of government and business leaders, readjust its tax system, and put its economy on a solid footing, then it could clear its slums, revitalize its blighted areas, rebuild its downtown business district, create a modern highway system to allow automobile and truck traffic to bypass the congested downtown area, build a second harbor tunnel to East Boston and Logan Airport, design a World Trade Center to attract vendors and distributors from all parts of the world, and furnish the city with a huge convention center to accommodate major professional and industrial conferences. In that event, Boston would then be able to put an end to the flight from the central city, attract homeowners and customers back from the suburban shopping malls, promote a vigorous commercial activity, and attract substantial investments by outside corporations that would have real confidence in the city's future.

Hynes had the vision; he had the encouragement of many downtown business and financial leaders; he had the backing of major colleges and universities; he had the moral support of big-city mayors and government leaders in other parts of the country who urged him to accomplish in Boston what they had achieved in their own cities. The question was, however, could Hynes get the solid political support he needed from the city bureaucracy, as well as from the state legislature, to put these plans into operation? Was this just talk, just pie-in-the-sky dreaming, or could he actually pull it off? Perhaps the upcoming mayoral election of 1955 would give the general public some clearer idea of just how strong Hynes was at the polls after a full four-year term as mayor—and, by contrast, just how strong those elements were who thought Hynes was going too far and too fast in his elaborate and even quixotic plans for a New Boston.

# 5.

# Trial and Error

As John B. Hynes prepared to run for reelection as mayor of Boston in 1955, his major challenge came from forty-four-year-old John E. Powers, the leader of the Democratic minority in the Massachusetts Senate, who had set his sights on the School Street office. Born in South Boston in 1910, Powers was only eight years old when his father, a streetcar motorman, was killed in an accident. The young man grew up in an atmosphere of poverty, sacrifice, and hard work that was only intensified by the impact of the Great Depression. In 1938 he ran successfully for state representative, and from that date until 1955 he was never defeated for public office. During his long political career, Powers became a familiar figure in every part of the city, although one writer classified him as "South Boston personified" because of his particular association with his hometown district. In the neighborhoods, he was frequently called upon by people who needed personal assistance and political favors; in the state legislature, he built a reputation as a friend of organized labor and an expert in parliamentary procedures. After moving up steadily in the ranks of the house leadership, in 1946 he was elected to the state senate, and now he was prepared to make his move for the city's highest office.[1]

Once the 1955 mayoral campaign got under way, Hynes and Powers marshaled their resources and carefully paced themselves for a long contest, paying little attention to the preliminary election in September, in which eighty-one-year-old James Michael Curley and another contender, Chester Dolan, were eliminated with little difficulty. Instead, they concentrated on the main event in November. The low turnout in the primary, however, with less than 40 percent of the registered voters showing up at the polls, combined with Hynes's lackluster performance—only 39 percent of the vote, compared to 28 percent for Powers—indicated that the incumbent was by no means assured automatic reelection and that the final outcome was far from certain. This would be Boston's first experience without Curley as a finalist in a seriously contested run-off election under the new Plan A system, and no one was exactly sure how it would turn out.[2]

Powers opened his attack against Hynes on a broad front. Often sounding like Curley, whose endorsement he received when the old warrior bowed out of the race after the September primary, Powers portrayed the election as a contrast between "two philosophies of government." One philosophy, he said, was dedicated to "State Street and the banking interests to which the present Mayor has been consistently subservient." The other (obviously his own), he stated, was a philosophy of government "dedicated to the people of Boston." Powers promised to end the rule of the city "by people who neither live nor pay taxes in Boston." Powers went on to raise a highly emotional issue by claiming that Hynes and his budget-cutting policies had led directly to the deterioration of services at the Boston City Hospital and, more specifically, to the deaths of fourteen premature infants. As Curley had done before, Powers called voters' attention to the support Hynes was getting from prominent downtown Republicans and criticized the incumbent for planning to arrange "giveaways" for large commercial property interests in the city. The crusty challenger from South Boston called upon the Democratic majority to turn out the mayor and his Yankee bedfellows.

Hynes at first avoided getting into a mud-slinging contest with his belligerent opponent; he seemed content to emphasize his record as an honest mayor who had ridded the city of its earlier reputation for "venal government," who had laid the groundwork for a "prouder Boston," who had improved delivery of municipal services, and who had acquired for the city a much higher credit rating. All too conscious that even if he won he would have to continue to work with Powers, who would remain as Democratic leader of the state senate, Hynes obviously tried to parry Powers's charges without getting too deeply involved in personal confrontations. As election time neared, however, and as the campaign heated up in its final weeks, Hynes began to lash out at his opponent more vigorously. Characterizing Powers as a would-be political boss who "wants to sit in the Mayor's chair as a Czar or Caesar," Hynes suggested that Powers had ties to the underworld and cited his role in the demise of the Massachusetts State Crime Commission. He even went so far in one television speech as to refer to Powers as the "darling of the mob."

It was the Republican-sponsored *Boston Herald*, however, that placed the contest in starkest terms by charging that Powers was cut from the same stripe as James Michael Curley. His election would mean a "reversion to Curleyism: the same old political manipulation of the Mayor's office for selfish ends that brought the city to its low estate before Mr. Hynes took over. It is no accident," declared the *Herald*, "that Curley turned his support to Powers."[3] John Hynes had shown himself to be a leader of "imagination and integrity," agreed the *Boston Traveler*, also endorsing the incumbent. "Surely Boston would not want to turn aside from the Hynes program of progress," it told its readers. "Surely Boston would not want a return to Curleyism."[4]

In the November election, Hynes defeated Powers by a vote of 124,500 to 111,400—virtually a replay of the 1949 contest. Not only was the number of votes separating Hynes from Powers about the same as the win over Curley six years earlier, but Powers also captured ten of the eleven wards Curley had taken. It was clear that although the cast of characters had changed, the same old battle lines still held firm.[5]

At Symphony Hall on Monday morning, January 2, 1956, before Governor Christian Herter and some three thousand civic and business leaders who had come to attend the start of his unprecedented third consecutive administration, and watched by countless thousands of citizens throughout the commonwealth on their television screens, Mayor John B. Hynes received the oath of office from Supreme Court Justice Stanley E. Qua in simple but impressive ceremonies. In pronouncing the invocation at the start of the program, Archbishop Richard J. Cushing somewhat playfully leavened the otherwise somber atmosphere of the morning not only in asking the Lord's blessings upon the mayor and the members of his administration, but also in pleading with the Almighty for better railroad service—a none-too-subtle reference to the furor over reports by the New Haven railroad that it was going to abandon passenger service on its Old Colony Line, which served commuters south of Boston. "Make our railroads run regularly, on time, and comfortably," he intoned in his familiar nasal whine, "so that visitors may come here with ease, pleasure, and profit to themselves and us, and our own citizens may go abroad from a proud city to bring afar reports of the good things we cherish in this region."[6]

When time came for his own inaugural address, Hynes resumed a more serious tone and expanded on his vision of a revitalized Boston. Enumerating the many accomplishments of his first six years in office, he pointed to the success of his reduction of city departments from thirty-seven to twenty-two, which he said was proving "most efficient." After praising the Boston College Citizen Seminar series as an awakening of "civic pride and civic conscience," he promised further studies of urban issues by such local institutions as Harvard University, Boston College, and the Massachusetts Institute of Technology. He complimented Governor Herter for his proposal to create a Port Authority that would incorporate the assets of the Mystic River Bridge, the Sumner Tunnel, and the Logan International Airport, a move that Hynes said would be beneficial to Boston's progress. Furthermore, he continued, the eventual completion of the Central Artery would be a development that was sure to bring down the cost of doing business in Boston by improving the flow of traffic in and out of the city. For a long time Boston had failed to act as a "magnet" for business, he reminded his listeners, and that had meant a great loss to the city. "Happily," he announced, "that situation has taken a turn for the better." Business corporations from other parts of the country were once again beginning to look for opportunities in Boston, and there was a new feeling of confidence in the city's destiny. "Present prospects for new business in our city are better than they have been for a generation," he told his audience. "I am confident that Boston is on its way to an economic rebirth."[7]

But the future would be bright, he warned, only if the city held expenditures in tight check, and only if the state legislature refrained from passing any bills that would "pry open the floodgates of municipal expenditures." He expanded at considerable length about the financial problems of municipal government, the rising costs of the school system, and the growing budgets for such things as salaries, retirement benefits, and pensions—all at the same time that property valuations were continuing to go down and city income was drying up. Boston badly needed "another source of income" if the city was to meet its obligations as well as the "reasonable requests" for employee salaries and expanded services. Until such time as the state legislature came up with "a new source of municipal income," therefore, he announced he would be "extremely hesitant" about any further spending. He promised that he would resist any major budget increases and would turn aside a "never-ending stream" of pay demands by city employees until the "income picture of the city is brighter."

Almost as soon as the inaugural ceremonies at Symphony Hall were concluded, Hynes drove over to Jamaica Plain, where he personally swore in John F. Collins as a newly elected member of the Boston City Council. Stricken with polio during the last great epidemic of that dread disease, which swept the city during the summer of 1955, young Collins sat in his wheelchair, surrounded by his wife and four little children, to take the oath of office. The following day he was present at the initial meeting of the city council at City Hall, where Edward J. McCormack, nephew of the popular Massachusetts congressman John W. McCormack, was unanimously elected as president of the council on the first ballot. The only thing to spoil an otherwise upbeat week came when Mayor Hynes, nattily and conservatively attired as usual, arrived at his office in City Hall punctually at nine o'clock the morning after his inauguration, only to be informed by his secretary that a man with a foreign accent had just called and said, "Tell the mayor his office is going to be bombed at three o'clock." Hynes burst into laughter, said "What for?," and proceeded with his daily routine of business while members of the Boston police department searched the building without success for the rest of the day.[8]

The time bomb that was eventually to unsettle Hynes's final four years in office was not to be found in City Hall, however, but ticking away in the senate chambers of the Great and General Court, where an angry and unforgiving Senator John E. Powers sat as senate minority leader. Powers often made his political strength and personal hostility evident whenever the mayor attempted to put some of his fiscal ideas into legislative form. According to Michael Hourihan, Hynes's part-time lobbyist on Beacon Hill, Powers used his influence as minority leader to get himself appointed to the Joint Legislative Committee on Municipal Finance so that he could harass whomever city hall sent there to press for Boston bills—even the mayor himself. "Powers would heckle me and ask all kinds of questions," complained Hourihan, who claimed that on occasion Powers would become so abusive or ask such irrelevant questions that senate committee chairman Fred Lamson of Malden and

Connie Kiernan from Lowell would step in and put a stop to the questioning.[9]

In these sessions Hynes and his lobbyists got little help from the legislators from their own city. Indeed, on a number of occasions the few Republicans from the Boston area actually supported Boston bills more loyally than the more numerous Democratic legislators, who either were badly divided by conflicting loyalties or tried to barter with the mayor for their support. This bartering, observed Joseph Slavet of the Boston Municipal Research Bureau, took the form of demands "for jobs, favors, and sometimes business deals with the city." In addition, according to Slavet, whose close relationship with Boston mayors made him privy to much of the inside maneuvering among politicians, such bartering was even greater among legislators from other parts of the commonwealth. Each legislator had a limited amount of patronage from the state and probably little or nothing from his own local community. Those suburban legislators thus viewed Boston as a grab bag of jobs, appointments, abatements, and city contracts, and they expected the mayor of the city to respond to their needs in return for their votes.[10]

Then, too, the recurring rumors that Hynes would take advantage of his close friendship with the Republican governor, Herter, and of his numerous associations with downtown business interests to make a run for the office of governor produced further political complications on Beacon Hill. Despite constant attempts on the part of Hynes to refute such rumors and insist that he wanted nothing else than to be mayor of Boston, he was often regarded with suspicion by those who either had ambitions of their own or wanted to throw their support to some other candidate. Consequently, the legislature routinely voted down Boston bills that tried to save the city money. When Hynes attempted to transfer some of Boston's burdens—such as requiring cities and towns in the Metropolitan Transit District to reimburse Boston for the expenses of the Boston Public Library, or to allocate the MTA deficit among the cities and towns according to population rather than passenger count (which worked against Boston), or to charge some part of Suffolk County expenses to Chelsea, Revere, and Winthrop, instead of having Boston bear the total cost—such attempts were summarily voted down.

Hynes recognized the various forces working against his legislative proposals and was the first to complain that Boston legislators did not perform well on Boston bills. "They had their own little factions. They weren't reliable," he reflected. "In many cases they would not even understand the bill, or they had their own reasons for not going along, or they were unfriendly." But generally he did not become more aggressive or more inventive in trying to secure passage of his legislation, nor did he make any serious attempt to fashion his proposed legislation with much greater care or precision. He still rarely appeared before legislative committees to argue for his own measures, fearing that such appearances would appear undignified and potentially embarrassing. He merely shrugged matter-of-factly, seldom spoke out in public to blame those who opposed him or to criticize those who did not support him, and usually expressed the hope that "private discussion" and friendly persuasion would later change some minds.[11]

In 1956 the Boston Citizens' Council, the Boston Retail Trade Board, the Greater Boston Chamber of Commerce, the Boston Real Estate Board, and the Boston Municipal Research Bureau joined in putting together a comprehensive package of legislation designed to assist Boston, and they worked hard on Beacon Hill to get some of their important measures through. Boston had its greatest legislative success at this time in getting ameliorating legislation passed, but the sponsors were careful to see that all such bills were filed either by one of their own respective organizations or by some individual legislator friendly to their cause. They did not carry Boston's name or the name of Mayor John B. Hynes, for it was generally acknowledged that any such bills would have been killed in the bloody aftermath of Powers's defeat at the hands of Hynes.[12]

In addition to tending to his fiscal responsibilities, Hynes also took stock of various physical developments in the city, some still in the preparatory stages, others not yet begun at all. The construction of the Central Artery was going along at what many critics complained was a snail's pace, but gradually one segment was linked to another, and when only a final layer of blacktop remained to be applied, the public was assured that once the expressway was completed the drive between Freeport Street in Dorchester and downtown Boston would be reduced from its present half hour in rush-hour traffic to only five minutes. In May 1959, four months before the Central Artery was officially opened to traffic, Harold D. Hodgkinson, chairman of the board of Filene's, Edward R. Mitton, president of Jordan Marsh Company, and other local business leaders paid a visit to the construction sites and announced that the Southeast Expressway represented a "turning point in the history of Boston." But influential business leaders wanted to be absolutely certain that a great many of the automobiles traveling along the new Central Artery would be able to use exit ramps and turn off into the downtown area to do their shopping at the well-known department stores along Washington and Tremont streets, which were trying desperately to maintain themselves against the influence of suburban shopping malls. What was "acutely needed" now, Hodgkinson emphasized, was much more parking space in the city itself.[13]

It would be some time, however, before any new parking spaces would be available. Plans to construct a major parking garage underneath the Boston Common were still dragging along at a slow and painful pace, as various interests, including the financier Bernard Goldfine and the *Boston Post* publisher John Fox, vainly sought to obtain the necessary private sources of funding for the project. In 1958, however, the dispute over whether the garage should be built by private promoters such as the Motor Park group or by some public agency created by the City Council ended when the General Court finally accepted Mayor Hynes's recommendation and established a three-member Massachusetts Parking Authority, headed by George L. Brady, to undertake the construction as soon as possible.[14]

The disposition of the unused railroad yards along Huntington Avenue—the so-called Back Bay Center—was another project that remained to be resolved. Particularly frustrating were the continuing conflicts with state legislators and downtown business interests over the question of providing special tax concessions to attract outside business interests to invest their money in such a project. For a while Hynes had been optimistic about working out a favorable tax arrangement with Roger Stevens and his group of New York developers despite the opposition of older downtown business interests. But the negative opinion handed down by the state supreme court in 1955 discouraged the investors, and after another year of fruitless negotiations, Stevens and his New York backers eventually decided they were getting nowhere and prepared to pull out of the deal completely. "It had become all too clear that no development worth its salt would or could happen," said Stevens, "unless capital investors could be certain that they would not be victims of a tax monster with a voracious appetite."[15]

Here was an issue that frustrated not only the mayor but also many of Boston's financial leaders, who despaired of any significant progress as long as it remained unresolved. Robert Ryan, vice president of Cabot,

Cabot, and Forbes, reemphasized the point already made by Roger Stevens that no one would invest private funds in the city until there was assurance of a chance of "return on investment." Boston's abnormally high tax rate, its reliance on the property tax, and its overassessment of business properties, he said, prevented this kind of return.[16] Charles Francis Adams, Jr., president of the Raytheon Corporation, agreed that the tax burden on business had to be eased if there were to be substantial growth in the public sector. Each year, he complained, the city's economic structure "groans more audibly" under the additional burdens imposed on it.[17]

Prospects for development in the Back Bay seemed to disappear completely when a new executive took over the New York Central and closed out the Stevens option. But the Prudential Company quickly stepped in, underwrote the option, and made it possible for Stevens to hold on to his option rights, which he subsequently assigned to Prudential. When Prudential went ahead and consummated a purchase agreement, it took title to the twenty-eight and a half acres of railroad land and thereby made its first overt move toward selecting Boston as a future home for its northeast office. Needless to say, Hynes was delighted with the news, and on January 31, 1957, the Boston Chamber of Commerce arranged a civic luncheon at the Sheraton Plaza Hotel to celebrate the occasion and to hear Prudential's president, Carroll Shanks, deliver the good news in person. Through the grapevine, rumors had reached the ears of many local businessmen that the Prudential had decided to build in Boston, recalled Hynes, and as a result the luncheon meeting was jammed with enthusiastic guests and visitors. When Shanks finished speaking, said Hynes, everybody in the hall was a "believer," and everyone was convinced of Boston's "imminent emergence from the encircling gloom into a new cycle of progress."[18] But the bothersome tax issue, raised by what the mayor called "tax-minded pragmatists," continued to be a stumbling block in subsequent discussions, as Prudential negotiators also demanded tax concessions as a way of ensuring a profitable enterprise. Now that the state supreme court had ruled tax concessions to be illegal, Hynes and his people had the task of trying to come up with a special tax formula to cover new construction projects tied to the development's revenues rather than its actual property value.

The Prudential was not the first organization to run into the discouraging problem of tax assessment in Boston, nor would it be the last, although in the past ways were found to get around the various technicalities of the law. As far back as the Curley administration, for example, a number of companies had worked out "letters of agreement" with the mayor's office, providing special tax arrangements as a means of encouraging investment in the city. Similar kinds of arrangements were arrived at during the Hynes administration as well, especially with Hynes's deputy, John Breen. Breen once told Jerome Rappaport, who was then one of a number of potential investors seeking relief from Boston's "astronomical" real estate tax, that when you deal with changes in a big city "you have to have a geological sense of time." In Rappaport's case involving the West End development, Breen wrote a letter to the federal Housing and Home Finance Agency explaining that the city could not assess a corporation on the basis of such things as operating costs, financing costs, and mortgage costs, and indicating that the city was prepared to do business on the basis of the gross income. The agency was willing to endorse this formula, and the resulting letter of agreement became popularly known as the "golden handshake."[19]

Prudential, however, viewing such arrangements as much too informal and unreliable, continued to press for a more formalized contract through the legal process. Fearing that the ill-fated Prudential project was fast approaching the point where it would be referred to in the future as the "Great Boston Pipe Dream," Mayor Hynes called a meeting in his office in March 1958 in an attempt to finalize some kind of tax agreement that would be satisfactory to Prudential and to the city of Boston. Representatives present agreed to a tax formula, the substance of which was that the ultimate assessment imposed on the entire project when constructed and rented would result in a tax not in excess of 20 percent of gross revenues actually received by Prudential or charged to it by itself for space occupied by the company. They also agreed to a provision for a graduated scale of assessments for the estimated seven-year period of construction prior to receipt of rental income. Although it was recognized by all present that this agreement was still not legally binding, Prudential accepted the pact in the hope that it would be honored by any future city administration.[20] This arrangement, filed with the legislature by Governor Foster Furcolo, would authorize the Massachusetts Turnpike Authority to take over the railroad property on Huntington Avenue, use a portion of it to construct a highway extension into downtown Boston, and set aside another portion of it for the kind of development proposed by the Prudential Company. The MTA would then give the necessary tax breaks to the Prudential investors to ensure the profitability of their multimillion-dollar investment.

On the basis of this agreement, Prudential went ahead with its planning. On January 9, 1959, a freezing cold day, the president of Prudential, Carroll Shanks, was personally present to watch a two-ton wrecking ball, swinging from a ninety-foot boom, proceed to pulverize the walls of Boston's seventy-eight-year-old Mechanics Building, a large, barnlike structure that had housed a succession of dog shows, boat shows, auto shows, and flower shows, to make way for a $12 million convention-exhibit hall that would be part of the Prudential project.[21] Work on construction of the $150 million Prudential Center itself started three months later, at 9:30 A.M. on April 12, when Mayor Hynes turned the first spadeful of earth, then stepped aside while a huge power shovel went to work in earnest.[22]

While construction of the Prudential complex was getting under way, however, conscious of the potential legal problems with older downtown business interests, and mindful of the 1955 advisory opinion that had nullified the original project with Stevens and the New Yorkers, Governor Furcolo sent the tax arrangement plan to the Massachusetts Supreme Judicial Court for another advisory opinion. Once again, the court rejected the latest version of the proposed tax formula involving the turnpike authority as unconstitutional, with the result that in August 1960 a disgusted Prudential Insurance Company halted work on its Back Bay project. All Hynes had to show for his efforts was a massive hole in the ground in the middle of the Back Bay.

While Hynes was trying to cope with such unfinished business as the Central Artery, the underground Boston Common garage, and the Prudential Center, his administration was also moving forward on new projects designed to renew the face of the city. In view of the expanded need for low-income housing in the postwar decade, the Boston Housing Authority created a number of public housing projects in several outlying neighborhoods. The Fidelis Way project in Brighton (1950), the Cathedral project in the South End (1951), an extension of the Mission Hill project (1952), the Bromley Heath project in Jamaica Plain (1954), the Franklin Field project in Dorchester (1954), and the enormous Columbia Point project on the site of a dump just outside South Boston (1954) were only a few of the dozen new housing projects that were calculated to reduce both demographic pressures as well as social tensions by bringing together groups of poor and low-income families into separate, isolated areas. According to the critic Jane Jacobs, these structures were typical of the approach of the 1950s—antiseptic and institutional, designed without imagination and with little concern for the lives of the people who lived in them. In later years most of these socially and racially segregated projects would be judged as unmitigated disasters; at the time, however, they were looked upon as progressive achievements for both the residents and the community at large.[23]

In its plans to modernize the central business district in the downtown area, the City Planning Board had assumed early on that the renewal of blighted areas immediately abutting downtown Boston was an essential part of the overall process. In that respect, both the South End and West End were obvious and natural targets for slum clearance and urban renewal, in keeping with the terms of federal legislation that only recently had been updated. Changes in federal housing policy in 1954 not only substituted the term "urban renewal" for "urban development" but also allowed up to 30 percent federal funding for nonresidential and industrial projects, provided that they were in line with a "workable program" that laid out land-use plans, zoning specifications, relocation of displaced residents, building codes, and citizen participation. These legislative changes made it possible for the planning board to move ahead with a large-scale slum clearance project in the so-called New York Streets area—a narrow strip of land along Broadway in the northeast corner of the South End, with streets named after the Indian tribes of colonial New York—located just south of the present Massachusetts Turnpike Extension at East Berkeley Street, Harrison Avenue, and Shawmut Avenue. In keeping with the terms of the housing policy, the objective was to clear about thirteen acres of land in which "slum dwellings" predominated and convert the area into industrial use, while relocating some 858 families, of which 594 (70 percent) were deemed eligible for public housing.

The parents of the black social activist Mel King were among those notified that the "slum" they had called their home for many years was going to be "renewed." After demolishing the buildings in the community, King recalled, the city let the area stand empty for several years before actually redeveloping it as a commercial property.[24] The offices of the *Boston Herald* would later occupy the ground where the King family home once stood.

This initial South End project, which Hynes described in his opening speech at the Boston College Citizen Seminar in October 1954, had moved into the purchase and demolition phase in 1955, with the planning board confidently asserting that the undertaking would mean the addition of industrial and commercial enterprises that would create new jobs, make more productive use of the land, and provide the city with additional tax revenues. The historian Lawrence Kennedy compares the forced evictions of people in the New York Streets area and the West End to the eviction of Irish immigrants from the Fort Hill area back in the late 1860s. In both cases, he writes, "the residents of a poor neighborhood adjacent to downtown were swept aside in the pursuit of higher property values and the economic vitality of the commercial core."[25]

At the same time that they were moving ahead with their plans to renovate the South End, members of the Hynes administration were also working on plans to redevelop the West End. That area, located directly behind Beacon Hill near the Massachusetts General Hospital, extending down to the Charles River and up to the North Station, was one of the city's oldest sections. Here, successive waves of immigrants—first colonial settlers; then the Irish in the middle of the nineteenth century; later the Italians, Jews, Greeks, Poles, and Russians at the turn of the century; and still later Albanians and Ukrainians—had turned the area into a seething and colorful melting pot. At one point it was home to as many as twenty-three thousand residents, although by the mid-1950s that number had dwindled to an estimated seven thousand people located in about twenty-eight hundred apartments or houses. Geographically connected with downtown Boston, the West End was an obvious choice for renewal because it was within easy walking distance of both the center of city and state governments as well as the business and financial districts. As Herbert Gans pointed out in his classic sociological study of the area's Italian-American community, *The Urban Villagers* (1962), the idea of redeveloping the West End actually dated back to the turn of the century, when the area had already acquired a reputation as a densely populated, low-income neighborhood. In 1907 Edwin Ginn, a Boston publisher and civic leader, built a model tenement in the West End, known as Charlesbank, in the hopes of encouraging commercial builders to become more creative in their structural designs. In the late 1930s Nathan Straus, a well-known advocate of public housing, suggested that the entire West End be cleared and replaced with public housing units. Although no action was taken, the creation of the federal slum clearance program after World War II led the Boston Planning Board to suggest that the fifty-two-acre West End, along with the North End and the South End, was an appropriate location for clearance.[26]

In 1950 the Boston Housing Authority applied to the federal government for money to support the formulation of a preliminary plan to redevelop the West End. The BHA began a formal study the following year, but not until April 1953 was it able to report that it had completed its plan. On April 11, 1953, Mayor Hynes formally announced a West End Project that would include low-rent housing for 1,175 families, 200 middle-income apartments, and 640 high-rent apartments. A front-page newspaper account of Hynes's plan reported that during the three years the project was under construction, a total of 2,248 families would be "displaced." Many of those persons, readers were assured, would find new quarters "in the new low-rent housing units."[27]

In the case of the South End, relocation had not been seen as a particularly serious problem since the area was relatively small (thirteen acres) and the number of families (858) clearly manageable. From the time the redevelopment of the much larger West End was first suggested, however, relocation was definitely an issue, and residents were constantly assured that they would have little difficulty finding housing they could afford. "You do *not* have to worry about finding a new place to live," the Urban Redevelopment Division of the BHA informed tenants in an eight-page, mimeographed brochure widely circulated some time in late 1953 or early 1954. "The Housing Authority has made plans to rehouse every family that would have to move. . . . Apartments in public, low-rent housing projects . . . will be made available," residents were told. "Families displaced by the West End project will be given top priority to get into public housing."[28] As time went on, however, and as financial investment took precedence over community resettlement, references to the availability of public housing became fewer in number and less explicit in description. By the time tenants finally received their official eviction notices in the spring of 1958, there was no mention at all of low-rent public housing.[29]

By 1956 the BHA had secured federal and state approval for its undertaking, and by July of the following year it had received the authorization of the Boston City Council and of Mayor Hynes. A number of local business leaders, however, felt that a stronger and more vigorous hand was needed to pull together the various elements of the city's redevelopment program and to establish Boston's role as a "headquarters city." One executive from Arthur D. Little, Inc., a management consulting firm, seconded the chamber of commerce's suggestion that a "full-time professional coordinator" be put in charge of an "independent Urban Development Authority" that would be separate from the housing authority.[30] Thomas Hennessy, a vice president of New England Telephone, urged the appointment of a strong director, and Robert Ryan of Cabot, Cabot, and Forbes urged the mayor to form a committee of "the best brains and the most effective leaders in the community" in order to move the program ahead. He wanted to see the kind of people in charge who would represent "the highest level of economic power in the community."[31]

State and federal authorities, too, indicated that they were not entirely satisfied with the city's handling of the project, and finally they insisted that management be transferred from the housing authority to a newly constituted development authority. In September 1957, therefore, the state legislature created such an organization—the Boston Redevelopment Authority—to deal exclusively with matters pertaining to redevelopment.[32] From then on, the BRA would replace the BHA as the designated local public authority in handling federal redevelopment funds and in taking over responsibility for executing established policy in the New York Streets area, as well as in the projected West End project.

The new BRA was a semiautonomous board, with four of its members appointed by the mayor, one by the governor, and Kane Simonian serving as executive director and secretary of the board. The son of immigrant parents from Armenia, Simonian had grown up in East Boston, attended East Boston High School, and obtained a degree in economics from Harvard University. After serving in the army during World War II, he was working in the Boston office of the Veterans Administration in 1951 when Hynes asked him to be director of urban renewal for the Boston Housing Authority. Six years later, Simonian moved up to become executive director of the newly created BRA.

The mayor's choice for the first chairman of the new agency was Joseph A. Lund, a vice president of the real estate firm of R. M. Bradley, the trustee and chairman of the Urban Land Institute's research committee, and an executive committee member on Boston's Committee for Economic Development, which had prepared a study of the city's economic future. Quoting New York's innovative planner, Robert Moses, Lund agreed when he took over the position that the city's urban renewal program must not be subject to unnecessary delays by "carping armchair critics and constipated comma-chasers."[33]

Hynes's other nominees to the board included Msgr. Francis Lally, a popular Catholic priest who was the editor of the archdiocesean weekly newspaper, *The Pilot*; James G. Colbert, former political editor of the *Boston Post*; and Stephen E. McCloskey, a well-known labor union executive. Melvin J. Massucco, the photographic editor of the *Record-American*, was Governor Furcolo's first nominee to the board. That three of the five members were associated with influential Boston newspapers was not at all coincidental. Appreciating the novelty of the undertaking, Hynes wanted to see that the board got as much public support as possible.[34]

Once the reorganization was accomplished, the state gave final approval to the plans. In October 1957 the new BRA commissioners held an informal hearing in the West End regarding the project they were taking over from the Boston Housing Authority. Some two hundred residents from the West End attended the hearing, most of them strongly and vocally opposed to the whole idea of redevelopment. Despite the dirt and congestion, inhabitants of the West End still regarded their neighborhood as a warm, friendly, and familiar community in which to live and raise their families. Long after the area had been cleared, a number of old-time residents still came back and reminisced nostalgically about what a wonderful neighborhood the West End had been to grow up in, and swore they would never have moved away from it of their own accord.

"The narrow streets and crowded tenements have taken on an aura of romance," observed one newspaper reporter as he listened to the heart-warming stories of boys and girls, blacks and whites, Jews and gentiles, playing together and going to school together, early Sunday masses at Saint Joseph's Church, the crowded synagogues on the high holidays, everyone looking out for everyone else, the strong and tangy odors of cooking that permeated the atmosphere of that working-class ethnic community.[35] Herbert Gans, who lived in the neighborhood from October 1957 to May 1958 while working on *The Urban Villagers*, readily conceded that the West End was by no means a "charming neighborhood" inhabited by "noble peasants," but by and large, he insisted, it was "a good place to live," an enclave of working-class people struggling with the problems of low income and poor education.[36] "The West End was something else," recalled another former resident. "It was

*A scene of the old West End in 1952 looking south along Auburn Street at the corner of Chambers Street. The obvious difficulty of the fire engines trying to make their way through the narrow streets of the neighborhood dramatizes the reports of critics who complained that the congested area was susceptible to a major conflagration and insisted that the only solution was "total clearance." Courtesy of The Bostonian Society.*

beautiful and unique; and one of the city's crimes against itself is that the West End's narrow mysterious European streets and alleys are not there for the old men to walk, for me to walk, for everyone else to walk."[37]

But it was precisely those narrow "European streets" and those dark alleys that caused city officials such great alarm. Younger, more conservative, and more professional observers viewed the district as an impoverished, overcrowded, and dangerous slum area, an explosive tinderbox that should be wiped out as soon as possible. Kane Simonian maintained that the streets of the West End were so narrow, and the dangers of fire so great, that people actually burned to death because fire engines could not get through to them; and fire fighters had to carry old women and children over rooftops in order to get them safely to the ground.[38] That assessment of the safety hazards and the "fire traps" of the old West End was repeated almost verbatim by Monsignor Lally, who reminded modern historians that many sons and daughters of immigrant residents had already begun moving out of the area "long before urban renewal was even on the planning board."[39]

Indeed, the neighborhood was so congested that families had to rent "garages" for fifty cents a month in an empty store just to get a bit of space to store their baby carriages. Using measurement standards developed by the American Public Health Association, city inspectors reported that 80 percent of the structures in the West End were substandard or marginal; over 60 percent of the structures were reported to be infested with rats; 75 percent contained other types of vermin; 80 percent had no rear stairways; and 80 percent lacked any type of outside fire escape. The inspectors also displayed statistics showing that welfare rates were higher in the West End than in other localities, and that both disease rates and crime rates were higher as well.[40] On paper, at least, the West End certainly seemed to fit the official definition of a slum, and on the basis of those kinds of reports the BRA concluded that the area was "so clearly substandard" that the only way it could be restored was by "sweeping clearance of buildings."

Members of the newly formed BRA listened closely to the arguments at the public hearing and were especially impressed by the objections they heard from old-time residents, although Monsignor Lally later said he was surprised to find opposition at that time "not as intense" as he had expected.[41] After much soul-searching, however, the BRA board concluded that the process had gone too far to be reversed, and its members decided to go along with the plans initiated by the BHA. In January 1958 the city and federal governments signed a contract that would require the federal government to pay two-thirds and the city to pay one-third of the costs of purchasing the land, of relocating the residents, and of clearing the site for the developer.

In retrospect, it seems as though the entire city was solidly behind the clearance of the West End. The project was not the work of a small group of wild-eyed liberals or idealistic do-gooders, nor of greedy developers or crooked politicians. "It was not an overnight local pipe dream," insisted Monsignor Lally. "You must remember that the project had the backing of city planners, the mayor of the city, city officials, most newspaper dailies, and the cardinal."[42] Most of those people were mature citizens who had emerged from the New Deal and World War II with the conviction that government was a benevolent force in modern society and could be trusted to do the right thing. Public programs involving such enterprises as schools, hospitals, parks, playgrounds, sanitation, slum clearance, and urban redevelopment were generally regarded as appropriate areas for the kind of swift and effective government action that had resuscitated the national economy and produced victory over the Axis powers.

"The people were getting poorer, the tenements were falling down, the fire hazard was increasing," one Boston banker summed it up. "There's only one way you can cure a place like the West End, and that is to wipe it out. It's a cancer in the long run to the community."[43] Seen in the light of this familiar medical analogy, a process the political analyst John Mollenkopf aptly referred to as "social surgery,"[44] the "clearance" approach seemed the most obvious and efficient way of dealing with the complex problems of a district like the West End, and there was a general assumption that the process would be conducted in a humane and compassionate manner.[45]

But some observers suggested that the West End became an easy prey because it was made up in large part of "unorganized, uneducated immigrants" who did not know the system and who were incapable of stopping the wheels of progress. It was simple for bankers and real estate developers, in league with city hall politicians, to take the immigrants' land, demolish their homes, and uproot the poor people who had lived in peace with each other for so many years.[46] This type of complaint gained considerable credibility when it became evident that the "new" West End would be designed for wealthy and upper-middle-class residents from the suburbs and not the poorer immigrant groups who were being displaced. Although some twenty-five years later Monsignor Lally still insisted that vocal opposition to the project had developed "after the fact," he had to admit that West Enders came to feel that they had been "sold a bill of goods" and had been betrayed. "They complained that the new housing went to middle-class professionals, that it was a conspiracy against them," Lally conceded.[47]

When federal and local authorities had signed a contract for the area, the BHA put the project out for bids. One of the bidders was a three-person group, consisting of Theodore Shoolman, a local investor who owned and managed a number of downtown office and commercial buildings; S. Pierre ("Pete") Bonan, a New York financier and builder;

and Jerome Rappaport, the former assistant to Mayor Hynes and at that time a practicing attorney. Although Kempner Realty Corporation of New York originally offered the highest bid of $1.75 per square foot, almost $1 million higher in total than what Shoolman and Bonan's second-highest bid of $1.15 per square foot would bring in, on June 16 the newspapers announced that the lesser offer would be considered by the Boston Housing Authority. When it was subsequently reported that the Kempner offer had been withdrawn, the charge was immediately raised by angry critics that "the fix was in" and that Mayor Hynes had engineered the switch behind the scenes as a political reward for his friend and former secretary. Rappaport's close friendship with Hynes and his frequent involvement in tax abatement cases gave the project what one writer called a "bad political smell."[48]

Rappaport and his associates vehemently denied these rumors and insisted they won the contract solely on the merits of their proposal—especially in the absence of any other serious competitors. "I thought everyone would be excited about this new opportunity to build, and that they would all be rushing in with competitive bids," recalled Rappaport, who was at pains to emphasize that no one at all was seriously interested in investing in any kind of Boston project at that time. "There was so little interest in getting involved that the housing authority actually had to go out and advertise in such places as the *New York Times* and the *Wall Street Journal* for investors to come in, present plans, and put up bids for the land." According to Rappaport, the original low bidder, Max Kargman's First Realty of Boston, was not really a "developer" at all in the usual sense. Kargman went so far as to offer a low bid of only a penny—"one cent!"—in the expectation that there would be no other bidders, then pulled out when he had second thoughts about the profitability of the venture. Rappaport insisted that he himself had taken the venture seriously and worked out his bid carefully. "It was all done out in the open; there was no politics involved," he insisted. "Although I was a good friend of John Hynes, he had nothing to do with my getting the bid. It simply was not his style."[49]

Employing the services of Victor Gruen, a successful New York architect, Rappaport's plans for the West End eliminated most of the interior streets within the forty-six-acre site in order to accommodate five residential complexes consisting of some 477 apartments. Each complex would contain a twenty-three-story tower building, a sixteen-story concrete slab apartment building, and a row of three-story town houses consisting of twenty-seven apartments with private terraces.[50] Each of the town houses would rent for about forty-five dollars a room, a figure that placed the project firmly in the luxury-housing category at a time when forty-five dollars was the price most working people paid for an entire five- or six-room apartment in the Boston area.[51]

With the building of the fashionable Charles River Park complex, the die was cast, the future of the old West End was gone forever, and a critical step had been taken in establishing the character of urban renewal in Boston. The nature of the renewal process became almost irreversible when it was decided to create luxury apartments aimed at attracting well-to-do tenants from the suburbs, designed to generate handsome profits for the developers, and organized to furnish additional income for the city. A more balanced mixture of high-rent and low-rent apartments might not have restored the old West End to what it had been, but at least it would have provided an opportunity for some families to remain in a neighborhood they loved and where they had spent all of their lives.

Getting the bid was one thing; getting the necessary funding, however, was something else. When the investors went to the local Housing and Home Finance Agency office to get a commitment for Federal Housing Administration (FHA) insurance on the loan, the people at the agency were shocked at the idea that someone would want to invest in a Boston project. "Why don't you go to Indiana, or some place like that?" they asked. It took some two and a half years, according to Rappaport, of sweating it out with the Boston office of the FHA, which also couldn't understand why anyone would want to build in Boston. When they were finally informed that the FHA would insure the loan on the West End project, the investors then found they couldn't persuade any of the Boston banks to provide them with such a loan. Ironically, however, it was the news that the Prudential Insurance Company was serious about its plans to build a new branch office in the Back Bay that unexpectedly provided the investors with their money. The Pru's projected fifty-two-story building would be higher than any other building in the city, higher even than the John Hancock building in Copley Square, and constituted a major bid for the Boston market. Even though the complicated tax-abatement controversy with the city was still unresolved, John Hancock decided it had to do something to counteract the Prudential move and demonstrate its own interest and concern with the New Boston. Consequently, "in a manner that had never been intended and never anticipated," Hancock agreed to furnish Rappaport's group with the financial support they so badly needed.[52]

To those who lamented the passing of the West End and the dislocation of its people, Jerome Rappaport would forever be the evil genius who designed the devastation and carried it into effect. Thirty years later, critics were still insisting that the fix was in, and that Rappaport had connived with his former boss at city hall to obtain the contract, convert the West End into high-priced luxury apartments, and establish the basis for a multimillion-dollar investment enterprise at the expense of the poor and the underprivileged. Clearly the emphasis had shifted from concern for the health and safety of the residents of the West End to the progress and prosperity of the city as a whole. It had become clear that redevelopment in the downtown area would not be designed to provide housing for low-income people or displaced residents of the West End. At a time when housing was plentiful and rents comparatively low, the planners and developers assumed that those people could easily find other places to live, move in with relatives and friends, or find places in one of the housing projects recently constructed at Mission Hill, Brighton, the South End, or Columbia Point. The purpose now was, rather, to provide a bright new shiny environment for the type of people who would patronize downtown department stores, dine at expensive restaurants, and make purchases at fashionable boutiques. With so many new suburban shopping malls siphoning off profits from the old downtown department stores, the heads of such established concerns as Jordan Marsh and Filene's, along with members of the chamber of commerce, saw the redevelopment of the West End and the creation of a whole new residential area in the downtown area as a strategic way of bringing middle-income families—"quality shoppers"—back to the heart of the city.

"Everybody thought it was right," said Kane Simonian. "All the Boston newspapers backed the idea—the *Post*, the *Globe*, the *Herald*, the *Record*—they all supported it."[53] A popular *Herald* columnist, Bill Cunningham, wrote a front-page article calling the West End "definitely a slum area," a "cesspool," and praising plans that would replace it with modern housing, parking areas, and gardens "of which the entire community will be proud."[54] The *Globe* also gave its unqualified support to the project with a lengthy and detailed article by Robert Hanron assuring its readers that if the West End could be switched from "dilapidation to delight," as had happened on New York's East Side, then it could be the "trail-blazing spark" that would revitalize the entire city.[55] Jerome Rappaport, too, agreed that if Boston were to be saved it was essential for middle-income families to be persuaded to move back into the city. "That's why we built the townhouses, two-bedroom and three-bedroom units," he explained.[56] "This marks the start of a tremendous revitalization of the West End of Boston," Mayor Hynes announced. "The development will attract and bring back to Boston hundreds of families who have left the city because of a lack of suitable and attractive urban living conditions."[57]

Surveyors started coming into the West End in January 1958, and by the next month a site office had been set up to handle relocation surveys and other procedures for relocation and clearance. After the site office had been established, the BRA proceeded to carry out proposals to determine the prices to be paid the owners of structures, and to conduct a relocation survey to aid in the resettlement of the tenants. After the BRA had taken over the land under eminent domain, it also became responsible for the supervision and maintenance of the buildings, as well as for the collection of rents. In accordance with federal law, it made plans to assure that every West Ender would be relocated into a "decent, safe, and sanitary" dwelling unit elsewhere—in public housing if the family's income made it eligible, or in whatever apartments West Enders could find either on their own or with the assistance of the BRA if they were not eligible for public housing.

In spite of these bureaucratic activities, however, a number of residents still did not think that anything would really happen. For many years there had been a good deal of talk about all kinds of projects and programs destined for the West End, and when articles again began to appear in the local papers many residents did not pay much attention. A small group of young West Enders, it is true, did organize a Save the West End Committee, and for several years carried on opposition to the project with the support of Joseph Lee, a prominent Beacon Hill resident whose father had been the founder of the public playground movement and who had opposed other city modernization plans in the past. "Blasted be the poor, for theirs is the kingdom of nothing," Lee intoned in his bitter version of the Beatitudes. "Blasted be the meek, for they shall be kicked off the earth."[58] But the angry protests fell on deaf ears, and the committee was never able to galvanize enough support among the residents to make it an effective agency.

People in the West End simply did not take the project seriously. Rumors, always rumors, they scoffed. Some people did get nervous and began moving to other places, especially young couples who wanted to bring up their families in the suburbs anyway. But most people concluded that it was just a lot of talk—nothing ever happened. And besides, even if the authorities did come in and do some urban renewal, nobody could *make* them move if they didn't want to, could they? And so, with a definite feeling that city officials always talked a great deal but never got around to doing anything, most of the old-timers in the district sat back, relaxed, and believed it would all go away.

But it didn't. On April 25, 1958, all residents of the West End received registered letters from the city of Boston notifying them that the BRA had taken over the property by eminent domain for the purpose of eliminating a "substandard" and "decadent" area, and that demoli-

*A view taken by Boston photographer Robert Severy in 1963 showing the extensive demolition taking place in the vicinity of Pitts Street in the West End, with the Hotel Madison and the Boston Garden in the background. Except for the Old West Church, the first Harrison Gray Otis House, Saint Joseph's Church, the Massachusetts General Hospital, and the Charles Street Jail, nothing else in the entire 52-acre neighborhood was left standing. Courtesy of The Bostonian Society.*

tion would begin immediately.[59] Once it had been decided that the area would be demolished, the city stopped cleaning the streets and collecting the garbage; landlords stopped making repairs on their property; and the district truly began to look like the kind of slum described in the reports of the city inspectors. Then the earthmovers rolled in. By the time schools closed in June, the movement of people out of the neighborhood had begun; by November twelve hundred of the twenty-seven hundred households were gone. By the summer of 1959 the exodus was in full flood; by the summer of 1960 only rubble remained on the site. The relocation process, which had originally been expected to take at least three or four years, was completed after little more than eighteen months.

Despite belated protests and appeals by West Enders and their political representatives, the hastily organized reappearance of the Save the West End Committee, and the sporadic violence of some local youngsters who made a few half-hearted attempts at sabotage—damaging machinery, stealing equipment, breaking windows, harassing workers—it was too little, and much too late. Opponents found there was no effective way of fighting city hall. In no time, the wrecking crews were at work demolishing houses, bulldozing entire city blocks, and displacing residents for whom no adequate provisions had been made. Only a few important historic sites, such as the Old West Church, the first Harrison Gray Otis House, and Saint Joseph's Roman Catholic Church, were rescued from destruction and stood in what Herbert Gans called "lonely isolation" in the center of an area that was totally and entirely demolished.[60]

On December 10, 1959, Mayor Hynes announced that the BRA had unanimously voted to approve the lease agreement with Charles River Park, Inc., for the redevelopment of the West End. In less than two years, he reported proudly, more than 40 percent of the approximately nine hundred structures had been demolished and more than 80 percent of the families in the area had been relocated. He took the occasion to compliment the BRA for "expeditiously" and "efficiently" relocating more than twenty-three hundred of the twenty-seven hundred families residing in the area, "all of which had been accomplished with a minimum of complaints and handicaps."[61]

The apparent ruthlessness with which the demolition program was carried out in the West End produced such a wave of horrified revulsion that the future of any further "urban renewal" projects in Boston was much in doubt. Even more than the physical destruction that had wiped out one of city's oldest neighborhoods, people everywhere were appalled at the heartless way in which former residents—most of them elderly, many of them refugees and displaced persons from World War II, a number of them unable to speak English—had been uprooted from their modest homes and apartments with the payment of a "fair market value" for their property and with no adequate guarantees for the future. Convinced that their own objectives were humane and progressive, and that the city's policy of compensation was fair and equitable, officials and developers appeared to assume that alternative housing was readily available at reasonable rates in various parts of the city and that a few individual inconveniences could be put down as the inevitable price for a bright new future. While there is apparently no written record that families were actually promised that they could return to subsidized housing in their old neighborhood once the renewal project was completed, most of them certainly believed they had been assured that would happen. Indeed, given the earlier experience of the Old Colony housing project in South Boston, where preference was given to families whose homes had been demolished to make way for the new project, such an option was viewed as both a natural and a moral obligation on the part of the housing authority. But no such accommodation was made, and former residents were forced to make whatever arrangements they could elsewhere. Most families packed up and left without calling upon the BRA for help or advice, instead moving in with relatives or finding places of their own in similar ethnic neighborhoods in Somerville, Everett, East Cambridge, and Medford.[62]

"What really happened to relocated families is hard to know because the official information is so unreliable," states a 1989 MIT study of redevelopment in several large American cities. Of all the families, individuals, and businesses evicted from 1949 through 1963, according to the study, only about half received any relocation payments at all. Those who did receive pay got an average of $69 per family, $45 per individual, and $1,405 per business firm. By and large, people forced out of their homes by redevelopment had to move into places that occasionally were better in many respects, but were charged rents that were at least 20 percent higher—although researchers found that from one-fourth to one-half the relocated families moved into homes that were substandard despite the higher rents. Psychologists who studied the consequences of such relocation reported that some 40 percent of the victims suffered severe, long-term grief reactions, including symptoms

*With former mayor John B. Hynes standing by, on March 9, 1960, newly elected mayor John F. Collins blew the whistle to signal the start of the West End development project. An estimated 7,000 residents—most of them poor and elderly, many of them refugees from World War II who were unable to speak English—had been uprooted from their homes and apartments without alternative housing and without adequate guarantees for their future. Courtesy of the Boston Public Library, Print Department.*

of depression, distress, and a sense of helplessness. They told interviewers: "I felt like taking the gaspipe"; "I lost all the friends I had"; "I didn't feel like living any more"; and one elderly Jewish woman from Russia described the process as though the Cossacks themselves had come riding into her neighborhood.[63]

"The West End symbolized all that was wrong with city planning in the 1950s," wrote Lawrence Kennedy, "because it bulldozed the homes of poor people and replaced them with an enclave for the wealthy."[64] Residents of other sections of the city and of the outlying neighborhoods, taking note of what had happened to the residents of the West End, became determined not to allow the bureaucrats, the technocrats, the bankers, the financiers, and the real estate developers to come in to destroy their communities and displace their people. "The experience of the West End," observed the eminent historian Walter Muir Whitehill, "created a widespread conviction that if urban renewal were necessary in Boston, some less drastic form must be devised."[65]

With the demolition of the old West End under way, and with visions of new apartment complexes and soaring modern towers rising from the ashes, the future disposition of those properties that adjoined the West

End was of considerable importance. That was especially true of those close-packed areas sprawled between the outer fringes of the downtown business district and the approaches to the North Station—Bowdoin Square, bordering on the West End itself; Scollay Square, lying in the middle, at the end of Washington Street; and Haymarket Square, bordering on the North End, just off Faneuil Hall. Here was a series of contiguous areas, centrally located, that professional planners and real estate developers could see as an ideal location for Mayor Hynes's often-repeated pledge to create a new Government Center for the city. If successful, such a development would not only provide an attractive addition to an ongoing program of urban development, but it would also enhance the real estate values of the nearby West End. The possibility of replacing views of dingy buildings, run-down hotels, crowded streets, and open-air markets with an inspiring vista of attractive govern-

*The cupola of the Old West Church faces Cambridge Street in the foreground, and behind is a cluster of hotels, medical centers, high-rise towers, and the fashionable apartments of the Charles River Park complex that replaced the working-class tenements of the old West End. Most of the familiar streets were eliminated in order to accommodate five residential complexes designed to attract middle- and upper-income families back to the heart of the city. Photograph © 1992 by Peter Vanderwarker.*

ment office buildings was certainly something that would induce upper-middle-class families to leave their comfortable homes in the suburbs and move back into fashionable and well-furnished apartments developers were preparing for them in the West End.

Many of the same ideological conflicts and philosophical disputes that broke out over the redevelopment of the West End also erupted when the general public learned about plans to build a new Government Center in the heart of Scollay Square. To many old-time Bostonians, "good old Scollay Square" was such a distinctive and identifiable part of Boston that it had become one of those historic areas—like Beacon Hill, the Back Bay, the Boston Common—that should never be changed. So much affection and so many memories had grown up around Scollay Square, with its Old Howard theater, its Crawford House, its tattoo parlors, its movie theaters, its saloons, its transient sailors, its slapstick vaudevillians, and its well-known stripteasers, that there was strong opposition to any plan to tear it down in the name of progress.

But for many other Bostonians, however, especially younger ones, Scollay Square had become an outworn anachronism, an embarrassment—something out of the Gay Nineties or the days of Prohibition speakeasies—that should be done away with as soon as possible. "Much of it seems nostalgic and colorful to people looking back at it," observed Jerome Rappaport, "but in actuality it was horrendous. It was a terrible eyesore that needed to be changed."[66] Its crooked streets were regarded as traffic hazards, its dilapidated buildings were viewed as firetraps, and its atmosphere of tasteless vulgarity was looked upon as an embarrassment to a city that was trying to reestablish itself as a center of culture and refinement. The idea of a brand-new Government Center in this run-down location, a place with shining, new, modernistic buildings proclaiming the rebirth of the city and symbolizing the start of a new political era in Boston's history, appealed to many opinionmakers. Still, there were those who could not resist a condescending smile at Hynes's persistent efforts to convert this sow's ear into a proverbial silk purse, and H. Daland Chandler, a well-known architect, provoked chuckles among his Back Bay friends at the Tavern Club by evoking Coleridge's poetic vision of Xanadu in a whimsical piece of verse:

> In Scollay Square did Johnny Hynes
> A stately civic group decree
> Where sailors and their Valentines
> Now skip it, trip it, fancy free.[67]

The proposed Government Center was no laughing matter to Hynes, however, and on January 15, 1958, he led a delegation to Washington, D.C., where conferences with Franklin G. Floete, the United States administrator of general services, produced approval of a new federal building to be erected in Boston on a lease-purchase arrangement. Approval of the Scollay Square area for a federal building, however, was contingent on the development of the center to include a state office building and a new city hall, as proposed by the Boston City Planning Board. Also required was full city participation in the project, as well as agreement on the price of the land for the federal office building. Overall, the cost of the development was put at $175 million. The state and city office buildings were estimated to cost between $18 million and $25 million each, while the federal building was expected to cost nearly $29 million.

The day after Hynes returned from Washington with the good news, Governor Furcolo sent a special message to the state legislature asking for speedy action on a bill to permit the state to construct a new state office building in Boston as part of Hynes's proposed Government Center. This was a particularly important move, because ever since it had first been rumored that the federal government was thinking of putting up a thirty-story federal office building, a number of state legislators had wanted it located in the Back Bay, on a site near Copley Square, where John Hancock would later build its present-day high-rise structure. Three days after the gubernatorial election in November 1956, Harold D. Hodgkinson, chairman of Filene's, had paid a visit to governor-elect Furcolo and asked him about his plans for such a building. Without the slightest hesitation, Furcolo had responded, "I favor the old Scollay Square area near the present State House." And in January 1957, a year before Hynes's Washington trip, Furcolo had included the request for a state office building in his annual message to the legislature. Hodgkinson, himself a strong advocate of the downtown Scollay Square location, was delighted, and thereafter considered Foster Furcolo as one of three men (the other two being John B. Hynes and John F. Collins) who could claim responsibility for the eventual success of Boston's Government Center.[68]

As the Government Center project moved into the planning stages, however, the general services administrator in Washington began expressing growing dissatisfaction with the location being assigned by the Boston planners for his federal office building. He was not happy with the original site along Sudbury Street, apparently feeling that it did not give his federal building a prominent enough position among the other structures. Mr. Floete was seriously reconsidering the original Back Bay location, and for a time he even suggested the possibility of a site at the corner of School and Washington streets, where the *Boston Post* had been located before it went out of business in 1956. His suggested changes produced a wave of local reaction. Downtown real estate and business interests protested the construction of such an office building in the midst of the traditional commercial center of the city, while planners and investors complained about locating the federal building completely outside the parameters of the original design.[69]

After nearly six months of further negotiations, the only plan that would apparently satisfy Floete was one that switched the proposed new city hall to where the federal office building was supposed to be on Sudbury Street, and that gave the central spot along Congress Street to the federal government. At this, the Boston planning consultants got their backs up, and their angry frustration at the "wandering" federal office building spilled over at a noisy meeting of the Civics Progress Committee at Mayor Hynes's office. Moving the federal building to the site originally designed for the new city hall would be "detrimental to the entire scheme," protested Professor Frederick J. Adams, the chief planning consultant, whose adamant position was supported by letters from the city's Architectural Advisory Committee, as well as from members of the consulting firm involved in the project. Expressing their annoyance with the "hop-skip-and-jump" game being played by the federal authorities, the Boston people spoke about "calling Mr. Floete's bluff." At the same time, however, they did not want to risk breaking their ties with Washington completely, because they viewed the federal building as something that would help preserve the unique character of the project as a government center. Besides, the federal government was clearly a "known client" whose support and participation would help make the project both a civic and a commercial success.[70]

By this time, however, Hynes's second four-year term was coming to an end, and a crisis of confidence was brewing in Boston that had many similarities to the one in Washington, D.C. Nineteen fifty-nine was a year filled with tension, suspicion, and uncertainty. It was the last year of Dwight D. Eisenhower's eight years in the White House, and fears of nuclear confrontation were sweeping through Western Europe and America in the wake of the Berlin crisis. At home there were disturbing signs that the Eisenhower prosperity, the much-heralded "age of affluence," was finally curving downward. There had already been one serious recession in 1957–58, and a number of observers predicted that another financial setback was probable before the year was out.[71]

At the state level, political affairs were also showing similar signs of instability and agitation. Although the Democrats had taken over control of both the executive and legislative branches of state government in 1958 for the first time in Massachusetts history, relations between Governor Furcolo and Democratic legislators degenerated into a constant round of what the local press referred to as "bickering and backbiting."[72] Furcolo's persistent efforts to push through a 3 percent sales tax as a way of providing some relief from oppressive property taxes and income taxes soured relations between himself and his fellow Democrats almost from the time he took office. Powers, who became president of the state senate at the opening of the 1959 session and was more belligerent than ever, made any long-range effort to reform the state's fiscal structure a practical impossibility. Many political observers pointed to a Republican victory in a special election for a state senate seat in the New Bedford area in the fall of 1959 as an example of how the Furcolo administration was hurting Democratic chances to capitalize on their political success.[73]

None of this did anything to help the political climate in Boston as Hynes entered his final year as mayor. According to his son Richard, Hynes had made it clear that he had absolutely no intention of either running for another term as mayor or entering his name in any other state or local contest, but there were moments when the thought of running for governor obviously crossed his mind. After all, given the confused picture of state politics in 1959–60, and with secretary of the commonwealth Joe Ward lining up as the Democratic state candidate, Hynes confided to Kane Simonian that it would be "impossible for me to lose." Then, leaning back in his chair, he chuckled: "But what do I know about running the state? I've been mayor of Boston for nearly ten years now, and I'm just beginning to learn something about running the city. No, it's not for me." Being governor of the state, concluded Hynes, was a job for someone who was more at home in the board room, or on the national scene—not for someone "who can just run a city."[74] Although a few people thought he still might change his mind and make a run for the governorship, most took him at his word and saw him as the proverbial lame duck.

For all his bright visions, earnest promises, and hard work, nothing seemed to be coming out right for Johnny Hynes—indeed, everything seemed to be going wrong. Still lacking substantial federal funding, the BRA undertook a redevelopment project in a blighted seven-acre residential area in the Whitney Street district of Roxbury, off Huntington Avenue. Financed entirely by the city of Boston, the BRA cleared the site and demolished the old buildings, replacing them with a series of high-rise apartment buildings that would not be completed for five or six years.[75] No work at all was taking place at the Prudential site on Huntington Avenue, however, and nobody was working at the excavation for the proposed convention center, as state legislators argued over the propriety of a tax arrangement scheme and planners looked for ways of getting around the state supreme court's latest negative ruling. Nothing had happened to begin construction on the long-awaited parking garage underneath Boston Common, as investors, insurance companies, and state legislators weighed their relative advantages. Not a single piece of scaffolding had yet gone up on the Government Center project, as last-minute details with state and federal governments had yet to be finalized and federal administrators were still vacillating about the actual location of their building. Hynes's slum-clearance program in the New York Streets area of the South End was being criticized as too small to have any appreciable effects on the city's future; his West End project was being roundly condemned for its wholesale destruction of an entire neighborhood and its heartbreaking treatment of the displaced residents.

With the growing realization that there had been no real changes in either the financial basis or the physical structure of the city during the ten years of Hynes's term as mayor of Boston, civic leaders began to show signs of a distinct crisis of confidence in his mayoralty. Few people ever questioned Hynes's personal honesty or integrity, but an increasing number were reluctantly questioning his ability to bring about substantive changes in a city that simply refused to be changed—especially after it was clear that he was not going to run for another term. Strange things can happen in the last year of a political figure who has suddenly lost all titular claims to power, patronage, and privilege, and this was certainly true of John B. Hynes. A definite air of pessimism began to replace the rising spirit of optimism that had greeted Hynes's early efforts at renewal. Critics complained that Boston in 1959 was not a great deal better off than it had been in 1949 when Hynes first took over after his defeat of Curley.

When Hynes had gone to the state legislature in 1957 for a $45 million refunding loan to bail out Boston, he had been forced to agree to reduce the number of city employees by 15 percent, reduce temporary personnel by 15 percent, and conduct an overall property tax equalization survey.[76] But many critics felt that the mayor's efforts at retrenchment were too little and too late. At an early 1959 meeting of the Citizen Seminar, Richard Chapman, the president of Merchants National Bank, attacked Boston for "unchecked extravagance" and dismissed the promises Hynes had made to get the refunding bill passed as "so tardy and trivial that it now becomes necessary to step up the tempo to far more urgent action."[77]

Despite persistent efforts by Hynes and his supporters to persuade the state legislature to expand the tax base, the property tax still remained the mainstay of the economy. In the decades after World War II, the cost of government had increased at a phenomenal rate. Substantial borrowing was needed in order to replace old buildings, enlarge state hospitals, provide new state colleges, pay for park and recreation programs, and match federal funds for the burgeoning highway program. In 1950 state expenditures already totaled about $290 million, and the expansion of state services as well as the multiplication of state employees forced taxes steadily upward. The commonwealth's financial plight was seriously aggravated by the startling jump in the state debt, which topped $1 billion for the first time in 1956.

No concerted effort had been made to bring the state's fiscal problems under control, although almost every governor during this period—Bradford, Dever, Herter, Furcolo—expressed shock and concern over the extravagant spending in state government and the financial crisis of the commonwealth. While the introduction of a sales tax would have broadened the tax base and diversified the sources of revenue, the state legislature was consistent in its refusal to accept a sales tax as a viable alternative. Governor Bradford's proposal of a 2 percent sales tax had been quickly beaten down; Governor Dever had been forced to resort to large-scale borrowing to finance his projects; Governor Herter expressed himself as sympathetic to a sales tax bill, but never campaigned for one; and during Governor Furcolo's administration a sales tax bill once again went down to defeat at the hands of Democrats and Republicans alike.[78]

Boston clearly felt the brunt of the growing tax rate brought on by increased expenditures, ambitious bond issues, and substantial borrowing. Census returns indicated that the city's population had dropped to just below seven hundred thousand, a loss of more than one hundred thousand people (13 percent) in only ten years. Most of those who moved out of the city belonged to the middle class, and their jobs as well as the stores they usually patronized were now found increasingly in the suburbs. With retail sales still falling off in the downtown business district, with employment rates at an all-time low, and with new commercial construction all but nonexistent, the city's tax base in 1959 was 25 percent smaller than it had been back on the eve of the Great Depression, even as municipal spending continued to rise. When Boston tried to raise desperately needed capital by floating a new bond issue late in 1959, Moody's Investor Service lowered the city's bond rating from A to Baa, making Boston, among cities in the United States with over half a million people, the only one assigned this poor rating.[79]

Moody's revaluation immediately sent alarm signals flashing through the downtown financial community, which now became more and more convinced that the city was headed for the shameful specter of municipal bankruptcy. If the city did go into receivership, then the banks and the corporations were determined to have some kind of mechanism in place to scoop up the pieces and manage the disaster in order to preserve some semblance of fiscal solvency. That effort was orchestrated by business leaders such as Charles A. Coolidge, a senior partner in Ropes and Gray; Gerald Blakeley of Cabot, Cabot, and Forbes; Lloyd Brace, the president of the First National Bank of Boston; Paul Clark, the chairman of John Hancock; Erskine White, the president of New England Telephone; Stanley Teele, the dean of the Harvard Business School; and Ralph Lowell, the board chairman of the Boston Safe Deposit and Trust Company, who characterized the group as "men interested in the welfare of Boston."[80] Popularly known as "Mister Boston" because of the wide range of his civic and philanthropic involvements, Lowell became the chairman of this new group, with the First National's Ephron Catlin serving as treasurer. The financial group convened in utmost secrecy, regularly holding its meetings in a boardroom near the vault of Lowell's Safe Deposit and Trust Company, but a few scraps of information leaked out to the press, which quickly dubbed the group "the Vault," although the members preferred to call themselves by the more conservative label of the Boston Coordinating Committee.[81]

The decade-long tenure of John B. Hynes as mayor of Boston, the longest consecutive service of any mayor in the city's history, presents some fascinating paradoxes. For a man who had never run for public office before 1949, the former city clerk proved to be a champion vote-getter and giant-killer. He demonstrated that his initial success in defeating the charismatic James Michael Curley in 1949 was no fluke by virtually burying the old boss in a 1951 rematch, and then in 1955 defeating John E. Powers, who seemed well on his way to becoming the most powerful Democratic politician in Massachusetts. As the years went by, the former political unknown gradually acquired a status and reputation outside the commonwealth that was often denied him at home, where his talents were usually underestimated. Twice elected as president of the United States Conference of Mayors, and an early protégé of Pittsburgh mayor David Lawrence, he was regarded as the "dean" of big-city mayors, traveling widely at home and abroad, and becoming a friend of such prominent international figures as Mayor Willy Brandt of West Berlin. But for all his achievements, Hynes was unable to overcome the outmoded fiscal structures and the old-time political feuds that made it impossible for him to fulfill the hopes and dreams he had of creating a rejuvenated New Boston. "Like other mayors of the past, I regret my inability to accomplish more," he said on leaving office. "Under the circumstances facing me, I did what seemed to be the best for Boston. I did not shirk the job. I tried to be fair in all my dealings and in all my actions." Lawrence Kennedy suggests that because he had spent so much of his life inside City Hall, Hynes was perhaps "incapable of providing the fresh perspective and energy required in a time when government was increasingly responsible for the city's prosperity."[82]

Despite his inability to bring his ambitious projects to completion, however, Hynes remained convinced that his ideas were right and that eventually they would be put into effect. It was inevitable, he was sure. The rebuilding of Boston would actually come about, and the face of the city would undergo real and substantial change. "Give a look . . . a long look," he urged his fellow Bostonians with almost prophetic clarity, at a moment in the old city's history when the downtown area still looked as it had for generations. "Take a walk . . . a slow observant walk through the streets from Bowdoin to Pemberton to Scollay to Adams to Dock squares," he insisted. "Make a mental picture. . . . For soon this

historical part of the old town of Boston will undergo a transformation
. . . a rehabilitation, a rejuvenation. Soon it will be tenderly laid away in
our chest of cherished memories."[83]

There was not the slightest question in John Hynes's mind that the
old Boston was about to pass away, and that a New Boston would
become a reality. He might not be the one to make that change, but
somebody else certainly would.

# 6.

# A New Beginning

When John B. Hynes made it clear that he would not run for another term as mayor of Boston, it was virtually a foregone conclusion that his successor would be John E. Powers, who had gone on to become president of the Massachusetts senate in 1959 after having been defeated by Hynes four years earlier in the mayoral campaign of 1955. With Hynes out of the way, and with a war chest of no less than one hundred thousand dollars, the backing of thirty-three of forty-one state senators, the support of prominent Democrats, the endorsement of leading newspapers (even the Republican *Herald* came over), the personal friendship of Cardinal Cushing, and the efforts of large numbers of city workers and neighborhood volunteers, there was general agreement that Powers would undoubtedly sweep the preliminary election in September and then go on to defeat his remaining rival easily in November.[1]

Indeed, while the Prudential Insurance Company continued to negotiate with the outgoing Hynes administration concerning an arrangement to reduce taxes on its proposed Back Bay project, it also made it a point to keep Powers abreast of the talks and obtained a promise that when he became mayor he would abide by whatever terms were agreed upon. Prospects of victory appeared so inevitable that Powers became positively obsessed with the exhilarating possibility of being president of the state senate at the same time he was mayor of the city. He saw himself holding on to both jobs for the better part of a year.

"Can you picture a Boston Mayor who was also a Senate President appearing before a legislative committee!" he later exclaimed to one interviewer. "I think we could have solved a lot of problems."[2]

Originally three other contestants faced Powers in the September primaries, but none of them seemed to pose a serious challenge to the veteran South Boston politician. Besides a former state representative and current member of the state legislature, James W. Hennigan, Jr., and former state representative and two-term member of the Boston School Committee, John P. McMorrow, only a longtime local favorite, Gabriel F. Piemonte, a former state representative and four-term member of the Boston City Council, seemed to offer any serious competition. Because of his citywide name recognition, as well as his popularity in the Italian-American strongholds in East Boston and the North End, many pollsters figured that Piemonte, with his billboards pledging to "$TOP WA$TE, RI$ING TAXE$, HANDOUT$ AND POLITICAL JOB$," would come in second in the preliminaries and be Powers's opponent in the November finals.[3] Then there occurred one of those unexpected developments that make the study of Boston politics so fascinating. According to a *Boston Globe* reporter, Joseph Keblinsky, a group of city hall newspapermen were gathered around the familiar oval table in the mayor's office one afternoon, "just gabbing," discussing the various advantages of Powers in the upcoming mayoral elections, while Hynes was busily scratching match after match trying to get his pipe lighted. Pausing for a moment, Hynes raised his head and "as though thinking aloud," said quietly: "I wonder how John Collins would do against Johnny Powers for Mayor?" "Two reporters leapt to their feet as though they had been sitting on hot coals," wrote Keblinsky, "and chorused: 'John Collins is the only guy who *can* beat John Powers!' . . . Hynes was smiling smugly," Keblinsky continued. "He had sent up his trial balloon, and it was soaring." Up to that time, the name of Collins, who was register of probate, had not even been mentioned. But the *Globe* ran a story stating that John Collins might be a candidate for mayor, and not long after that Collins announced his candidacy.[4]

Although few people gave the latest candidate any serious consideration, the best-laid projections of the pollsters suffered an embarrassing upset on September 22, 1959. By the narrow margin of only twenty-five hundred votes—a difference of only two percentage points—Collins edged out "Gabe" Piemonte for second place, thereby becoming Powers's challenger in the November election and presenting the electorate of the city with a candidate about whom they knew very little. Born July 20, 1919, in Boston's Roxbury section, John Frederick Collins was the first-born of three sons of Frederick B. ("Skeets") Collins, a mechanic who worked for the Boston Elevated Railway, and Margaret (Mellyn) Collins, both Irish Catholics. Collins attended local Roxbury schools, graduated first in his class at Suffolk University Law School in 1941, and passed the bar the same year. When the United States entered World War II he enlisted in the army and rose from private to the rank of captain in the counterintelligence corps. After his discharge in 1946 he ran successfully for a seat in the Massachusetts house of representatives, and the following year married Mary Patricia Cunniff from Jamaica Plain and began a family that eventually numbered four children. After being reelected to the house in 1948 Collins became something of a maverick in neighborhood politics when he came out in support of John B. Hynes in his first mayoral contest against Roxbury's favorite son, James Michael Curley. Campaigning for Hynes in the heart of Curley territory was not without its hazards, however, and on one occasion, while delivering a campaign speech in Jackson Square, Collins was struck with an "unidentified vegetable that I suspect was a tomato." Turning in the direction from which the missile had been fired, Collins called out: "Let me tell you this. When Johnny Hynes wins, none of you guys will ever be welcome at City Hall as long as I am a member of the legislature. Why don't you recognize that Curley's day is over, wise up, and join up with Hynes?" Hynes went on to win his election, and a year later Collins was elected to the state senate, where he served two terms, making a name for himself for sponsoring tough anti-Communist bills and strict narcotics legislation.[5] In 1954 Collins captured the Democratic nomination for state attorney general, running on a campaign against gambling, bookies, and organized crime. Although he lost the election to the Republican incumbent, George Fingold, many people felt that this bright, young man had a future in Massachusetts politics.

In the summer of 1955, however, it looked as though the promising political career of John Collins had come to a sudden and tragic end when, during the course of a campaign for a seat on the Boston City Council, he and three of his four children were stricken with bulbar poliomyelitis. Although the children fortunately recovered with no permanent effects, their father was almost totally paralyzed. He was near death, and prospects for his recovery were so slim that the best hope his doctors could give him was that, if he did survive, he would face a lifetime of complete inactivity. With the primary election for the city council race only a few weeks away, Collins was advised to withdraw from the campaign, but his answer was: "Under no circumstances . . . we'll just have to work harder." His wife, Mary, took over the management of the campaign with the help of his brothers Leo and Paul, his cousin Arthur Coffey, and such loyal friends as Charlie "Chick" Artesani, Paul Burns, Phil Chapman, Billy Devine, Tom Griffin, and Henry Scagnoli, while John himself directed things from his hospital bed. About the only saving feature of this period of "enforced recuperation," according to Collins, was that it gave him an exceptional opportunity to read all kinds of books about the history of Boston, as well as a number of scholarly studies about urban planning—most of which he found to be without any real value or practical interest. But it was during this time of thoughtful reflection that he maintains he gradually developed a "mental model" of what he thought could be done with the city of Boston if he ever got to be mayor.[6]

Mary Collins already had some experience in campaigning, having begun working on behalf of her husband during the first year of their marriage. Starting in 1947, when he ran for the Massachusetts house, she did door-to-door visiting, leaving his card at each house, and she did the same sort of work when he ran for the state senate. "As a young lawyer, you're unknown in most parts," she explained, "so you have to leave your card and just hope."[7] Now, with her husband recuperating, she took to the campaign trail again, visiting homes, giving talks, attending luncheons, hosting dinners, and playing tape recordings prepared by the candidate. Although he became one of eighteen finalists chosen in the September primary, there were few who gave him much of a chance to win one of the nine council seats in November. But Collins refused to accept defeat. The campaign went on into the final months, with his wife continuing to handle the numerous facets of the drive. She helped prepare a television speech for her husband in which he predicted that he would win and promised that he would personally be at the first meeting of the city council in January. "I really had to hustle around and get everything going," recalled Mrs. Collins, "it happened at such a busy time of the year," no doubt referring to the fact that she was not only actively campaigning but also shopping for a new house—one without stairs—while her family was recovering. "I think if you can say firsthand what you know will be done, and that you've actually seen it," she said, "it helps."[8]

John and Mary Collins's unflagging faith and determination produced results. In the November elections, John Collins finished third
among the nine council finalists. Two days before Christmas, he left his
hospital bed; in January he took the oath of office at his Jamaica Plain
home; the following day he showed up at the first meeting of the Boston
City Council, as he had promised. After serving on the council for a
year, Collins resigned to accept from Democratic governor Furcolo a
vacancy appointment as register of probate and insolvency for Suffolk
County, and the following year he won a full term as register of probate
in his own right. On the surface, it appeared that the thirty-nine-year-
old politician, cut off in his prime by a crippling bout with polio, would
now settle down as a career bureaucrat in a safe and comfortable job he
could probably hold on to for the rest of his natural life.[9]

In 1959, however, Collins surprised almost everyone by announcing
his candidacy in what appeared to be an impossible race for the Boston
mayoralty against such well-known and experienced campaigners as
Powers and Piemonte. But after his surprising victory in the September
primary, voters began taking a second look at this dark-horse candidate
who had come out of the pack and ended up in second place. Was there
really a chance that Collins could give an old warhorse like Powers a run
for his money? Was there any chance at all that this newcomer might
actually win? In reality, several factors operated in favor of the unknown
challenger.

First, his courageous comeback from polio, much in the tradition
of Franklin D. Roosevelt, created a measure of both sympathy and
respect that worked to his political advantage, although there was always
the possibility that people would be repelled by seeing the candidate for
mayor in a wheelchair. "It was obvious," said Collins, "you couldn't
miss it; you couldn't conceal it. It was simply a fact of life. If ever the
subject came up, I would say, 'You run a city with your head, not your
feet.' The way we handled it in our first televised speech was to have an
opening scene where they could take a full shot of the back of the
wheelchair, so people couldn't say we were trying to conceal it from
view. After that we had them take 'tight' shots from the waist up so that
we could not be accused of using it to influence the voters. I never felt
my disability would be a handicap in running the city. I still don't think
it was."[10]

Second, at a time when the medium of television was just becoming
an influential factor in American politics—the famous Kennedy-Nixon

debates were less than a year away—Collins was able to convey an honest, clean-cut, wholesome image to Boston voters, exuding what one writer described as the "carefree, sunny charm of a curly-haired parochial choir boy grown older," while Powers, on the other hand, came across as the kind of tough, arrogant, old-time politician—a "little Napoleon"—that the voters of Boston had rejected when they defeated Curley in favor of someone like Hynes.[11] Collins and his campaign managers quickly fastened on this contrast between a relative newcomer to Boston politics and his veteran political adversary. The preliminary election of September had not only cut out Piemonte from the pack, however; it also sent out a surprising political signal. Powers had drawn only 34 percent of the vote—far short of the 50 to 60 percent his managers had confidently predicted. Those who watched the returns carefully were quick to note that the candidate who was regarded as a shoo-in was by no means as popular as everyone had assumed. Collins suddenly assumed a level of credibility as a viable candidate he did not have earlier.[12]

As they went into the crucial stage of the campaign, the two finalists emphasized their experience, their professional qualifications, and their positions on matters of public policy. On the basis of his long record of public service, Powers presented himself as a farsighted candidate who could reconcile the concerns of both organized labor and downtown business interests. He advocated a program of long-range planning for Boston's economic development and put together an impressive group of "expert advisers"—civic leaders, businessmen, and economists from local universities—who drew up position papers on various topics and formulated a program designed to save the city money and secure state and federal funding. He came out in opposition to a limited sales tax, an idea then being proposed by Governor Furcolo, and insisted that strict management of city government, collection of delinquent taxes, and the elimination of abuses in the tax-abatement system would make it possible to balance the budget without any new taxes.[13] Collins, on the other hand, supported the proposal of a limited sales tax as one of the few practical ways of bringing in a new source of much-needed revenue to lower the city's burdensome tax rate. This plan was something that Hynes had been hinting at for years, but had never mustered the courage to fight for openly. By making it central to his campaign, Collins was sending out early signals that he was cut from a different mold than the previous mayor.[14]

Collins's advocacy of the sales tax also led a great many business leaders to reexamine their position on the outcome of the election. A sales tax had long been supported by the financial community as a sound and reasonable alternative to the high property tax, but none of the city's politicians had been willing to stick their necks out and go along—until Collins. The business leaders perceived that here, finally, was an Irish Catholic politician who understood the business point of view, and who might work with them for both their and the city's benefit. In contrast, Powers made it clear, in public and in private, that he had little sympathy for the businessman's concerns; indeed, in all likelihood he would seek even higher assessments on downtown real estate as a way—the only way, under the circumstances—of balancing the books. Although it was obviously too late, and possibly quite dangerous, to cut their ties with Powers at this stage of the game, many businessmen, by letting it be known that they preferred Collins to Powers, added their weight to several others who had already come into the Collins camp.

One early supporter was Henry Shattuck, described by the writer Alan Lupo as "the bachelor Brahmin from the Back Bay."[15] A lawyer, accountant, and reformer, Shattuck was a member of the city's most prestigious clubs, financial institutions, and law firms, and Collins regarded him as a "rare individual" who was always interested in the welfare of the city "regardless of politics." Robert Cutler, a well-known downtown banker and a close associate of President Eisenhower's, was another prominent GOP figure who came out early for Collins.

Collins remembers calling up Henry Shattuck to tell him that he was running for mayor and that he would like to talk with Shattuck about supporting him. "Well, I don't think it's necessary for you to do a lot of convincing," replied Shattuck. "I think you're eminently qualified to be mayor, and I'll support you. Now, what would you like me to do?"

"I would like you to sign an ad for me," said Collins.

"Of course I will," Shattuck responded. "May I have the privilege of reading the ad before I sign it?"

"Of course," said Collins, with a happy smile, and counted one more valuable supporter on his side.[16]

As Collins stepped up his campaigning and tried to emphasize his intention of saving money and reducing the cost of municipal government, he called for a "no hire, no fire," policy of not filling vacancies

when they occurred in city administration; he also promised to imple-
ment the tax-equalization survey of industrial, commercial, and apartment properties that was currently being conducted by the city assessor's
office. Criticizing Powers for his close association with the downtown
political and financial establishment, Collins promised to "bring government to the people" by establishing a fifteen-member community council in each of the twenty-two wards as a means of creating closer
relations between the office of the mayor and the people in the neighborhoods.[17]

As the campaign went into its final stages, the contest centered
much more on personalities than on issues. Some commentators were
sympathetic to Collins's "lonely and gallant uphill fight," but were
forced to concede that Powers clearly "had the edge."[18] Continuing to
cast himself in the sympathetic role of the underdog, the outsider, and
the champion of those ordinary citizens who had little or no access to
city hall, Collins appealed to the "little people" to help him in his
struggle against what he called "power politics." Playing cleverly and
effectively upon his opponent's last name, he called upon voters to "Stop
Power Politics: Elect a Hands-Free Mayor." Slowly and almost impercep-
tibly, the Collins people shifted from denouncing Powers simply as a
power-hungry political boss making deals with wealthy contributors and
influential businessmen, to insinuating that he was a person of questionable character consorting with unsavory and even criminal elements in
the community.

That shift was a device that the Hynes people had used effectively
against Powers four years earlier, and the suggestion that the politician
from South Boston might have ties to the underworld once again put
him on the defensive. Not one cent of "bookmakers' money" had been
contributed to his campaign, Collins boasted, adding that "there are
only two men in the race."[19] Furious at the puns on his name and the
charges against his integrity, Powers insisted that never before had the
people of Boston witnessed a "comparable smear of lies and character
assassination—all by one man."[20] He struck back at Collins, accusing
him of having an "anti-labor" record, maintaining that he had consistently favored the interests of the big insurance companies, and claiming
that he had received $65,000 in legal fees from the BHA in 1955 when
he was a candidate for the city council. "I know of no man in the past
quarter of a century who has profited more from politics than he has."[21]
Collins branded this latest charge as an "absolute lie" and challenged

Powers to swap public copies of their income tax statements, claiming that Powers had pocketed $140,000 from a recent testimonial dinner and diverted the money into his campaign funds.[22]

Despite heavy odds and confident predictions by the Powers people that their candidate was sure to get at least 50 to 60 percent of the vote, dedicated Collins supporters refused to concede defeat, insisting that the tide was beginning to run in favor of their candidate. "Ourselves we knew, or sensed, that we had rounded third base the second Friday before the election," recalled Hirsh Freed. That was when Senator Wayne L. Morse of Oregon, who had been visiting Boston at the time, told the Collins people that while every professional politician he met told him that Powers was an "easy winner," he was assured by every cab driver, bellhop, and chambermaid at the hotel in which he was staying that they were casting their vote for Collins.[23] Buoyed by this kind of report, the Collins backers kept up their incessant attacks on Powers, especially bringing into question his integrity by pointing out that he had sponsored a bill to legalize pinball machines, and continuing to insist that no "bookmakers' money" had been contributed to the Collins campaign fund.

It was within the context of these implications of illegal gambling and bookmaking that a seemingly unrelated incident occurred that had a decisive influence on the outcome of the mayoral race. At two o'clock in the afternoon of Friday, October 30, only four days before the election, agents of the Internal Revenue Service raided several bookie joints in East Boston, one of which was a barroom that belonged to a former featherweight boxer named Salvatore Bartolo. Nine hours later, on the eleven o'clock news, John Collins appeared on television, claiming that Powers was a personal friend of the alleged gambler and displaying photographs of Bartolo's Ringside Café in East Boston with a large "POWERS FOR MAYOR" sign over it. According to Collins, the photograph had been brought to him by Connie Fitzpatrick, a member of district attorney Garrett Byrne's office, who had seen the flashing police lights while he was returning from Logan Airport, drove over to Maverick Square, and snapped a series of pictures outside the barroom. Although Collins insisted he was so sure of victory at this late date that he did not feel the need to use the photograph, his political advisors, reminding him of how he had lost the attorney general's race in 1954 as the result of a last-minute political editorial in the *Boston Post*, urged him to use every bit of ammunition he had available.[24] Collins's damaging photograph, along with others that appeared in the newspapers the next day, recalled Hynes's charges of four years earlier that Powers was "the darling of the mob."

The photos also formed the basis for large front-page cartoon-advertisements in the newspapers on election day, Tuesday, November 3, showing Powers getting punched in the face by a huge boxing glove marked "T-MEN," cheered on by crowds labeled "People and Collins." Underneath the cartoon were the words "Stop Power Politics. Vote Collins."[23] It was a skillful, devastating, eleventh-hour maneuver, and it produced results. Despite a feverish round of speeches, rallies, radio addresses, and television appearances, John E. Powers went down to defeat in perhaps the biggest upset in Boston's political history. Although Powers swept wards 6 and 7 in his home district of South Boston by margins of 60 and 70 percent, all the other wards of the city tipped in favor of Collins, allowing the challenger to become the next mayor of Boston by some twenty-four thousand votes and leaving the Powers supporters stunned and bitter at this "dirty trick." "COLLINS VICTORY ROCKS BOSTON POLITICS," proclaimed the *Boston Traveler* in banner

*Following a bookie raid by federal authorities on an East Boston tavern that displayed a "Powers for Mayor" sign, John Collins's supporters ran a cartoon on the front page of the newspapers on election day showing John E. Powers getting punched by "T-Men" and suggesting that he was tied in with gamblers. There are many Bostonians who still believe that the bookie raid was a decisive factor in Collins's surprising defeat of Powers in the 1959 mayoral election. From the* Boston Globe.

headlines, while its companion paper, the *Herald*, called the outcome of the election the "most staggering upset" in recent history.[26]

Newspaper reporters and editorial writers provided a variety of reasons to explain Collins's upset victory—sympathy for his handicap, the influence of the women's vote, enthusiasm for a new face, the impact of the bookie raid. "Power politics . . . is definitely out of vogue in Boston today," concluded the *Christian Science Monitor*.[27] But a later political analyst, Murray Levin, noting an eleven-point falloff in voter turnout since the 1955 elections, insisted that the election of 1959 was not so much a vote in favor of Collins as a vote against Powers, by an electorate that had become "alienated" from the existing political system. Levin reminded his readers that the election took place in a community where feelings of political alienation, frustration, and disillusionment with the political process were widespread. Voters who felt powerless and disenfranchised turned against Powers, who became stereotyped as a leader of a powerful and corrupt group of politicians, businessmen, and "unsavory elements" who were out to govern the city for their own personal enrichment. The upset, concluded Levin, was to a large extent "a response to feelings of political alienation."[28]

Other political scientists, however, see the term *alienation* as little more than a new way of expressing an old and familiar form of voter apathy, earlier described as particularly common among "socially and economically disadvantaged groups"—usually in big cities.[29] Collins, especially, rejected the "alienation" theory and insisted that his election was the result not of cynical and negative responses, but of positive and thoughtful decisions on the part of the voters for a candidate who promised a continuation of the kind of honest, dignified, and responsible government ushered in by Hynes.

And so, as the old order prepared to give way to the new, preparations were begun for an orderly transition of power. On Friday, January 1, 1960, a group of newspapermen accompanied Mayor Hynes as he went to his office in City Hall for the last time to clean out his desk and remove his personal belongings. The reporters had composed a fancy-worded resolution, elaborately engraved on parchment, conferring upon him the title of honorary member and dean of the city hall press room, and they presented it to him at a special ceremony attended by all the members of the press corps.[30] Looking around at the various objects that had accumulated in the course of ten years, including some fine Oriental rugs, one reporter asked: "Are you leaving all these things behind, Mr. Mayor?" "Yes sir," Hynes replied, "I'm taking only things that have my name on them." One of those things was a red-leather swivel chair the employees of the city clerk's department had given him when he became mayor "in his own right" in 1950. The only thing he said he'd really like to have—"if the city would sell it to me for $3.62 or something"—was an old, dust-covered 1922 Underwood typewriter he had used when he was city clerk. "I used to pour my soul into that thing," he recalled. But the nostalgia of the moment was rudely interrupted by the clang of fire alarms and the sound of fire engines. At 9:37 a fire broke out at the front door of City Hall, on School Street. A short-circuit had ignited Christmas decorations when a workman inserted new bulbs into sockets soaked from recent rains. The decorations burst into flame, and heavy clouds of smoke billowed through the ancient building as firemen rushed up the steps with their hoses and poured a stream of water through the adjoining office of the Inaugural Committee set up to prepare for the mayor-elect to take over. The short-lived excitement provided an unusual climax for the day as Hynes finished shaking hands and saying good-bye to his friends and co-workers, put on his hat and coat, and walked down the steps as mayor of Boston for the last time.[31] What no one could know at the time was that Boston was about to enter a whole new era, and that the 1959 election marked the true end of the Curley era. The old politician had died on November 12, 1958, most of his loyal supporters had retired, and there was a new generation of voters for whom James Michael Curley was only a fascinating part of history. His ghost might continue to haunt the city for many years to come, but Boston would henceforth plan its future in different ways and with different people.

At ten A.M., Monday, January 4, 1960, John Frederick Collins, forty years old, was formally sworn in as Boston's fifty-second mayor before some three thousand family members, friends, and well-wishers at a ceremony held at Symphony Hall. This was the first time in ten years that Boston had had occasion to inaugurate a new mayor, and the event was conducted with appropriate decorum. Mayor Collins appeared in ceremonial morning suit, with 150 ushers similarly attired. Because Cardinal Cushing had a bad case of laryngitis, Bishop Jeremiah Minihan delivered the invocation, after which Chief Justice Raymond S. Wilkins administered the oath of office as former mayor John B. Hynes looked on in obvious approval.[32]

*"Welcome, Mr. Mayor," says retiring Boston mayor John B. Hynes to his
successor on November 25, 1959. This was John F. Collins's first visit to
the old City Hall on School Street since his upset victory over state senate
president John E. Powers three weeks earlier. Collins spent ninety minutes
talking with Hynes, discussing physical changes and other matters relating
to the office he would occupy after the first of the year. Courtesy of the
Boston Public Library, Print Department.*

Delivering his inaugural address, Collins struck a decidedly optimistic note, tempered by a stern cautionary warning. Despite the serious
financial crisis that had lowered the city's national credit rating, he said,
he was ready to meet the challenge by launching what he called "Operation Revival." "Survival is not enough," said the new mayor. Our goal
is not simply to keep the city alive, but to revitalize it; "we must restore,
rebuild, and redevelop." The problems of Boston, he argued, could be
divided into two categories: those of Boston's own creation, which are
within its own control, and those originating elsewhere, which are
beyond Boston's power to control. Focusing, therefore, on the city's own
problems, Collins pointed to two issues that were causing most of the
trouble: the rising expenditures of municipal government, and the rising
property tax rates, which were oppressing the working-class voters.

Collins spent most of the remainder of his address explaining how he would deal with each of those two critical problems. As far as the municipal bureaucracy was concerned, he promised a series of cost-cutting studies of city government, department by department, that would reduce overlapping functions and increase efficiency. He would approve no general pay increases for city workers; he would demand "immediate economies" in the school committee budget; and he would call upon the state to give the mayor and the city council more fiscal control over the police department. As far as the rising tax rate was concerned, Collins insisted that cities should have new sources of revenue, repeating his campaign demand for a state sales tax. To bring the government closer to the voters, he proposed a new Bureau of Public Information and Citizens' Relations and promised to establish a series of citizens' community councils in local areas to improve communications between city hall and the neighborhoods. In addition, he assured the electorate in the communities that he would reorganize the parks and recreation department to improve the parks, playgrounds, and recreation facilities throughout the city.[33]

While the new mayor stated that the subject of urban renewal had his "earnest, constant, and deep concern" and constituted a "major portion" of his program for Boston, he indicated that time did not allow him to elaborate on that subject in the full manner it deserved. Nevertheless, he then made a specific point of informing his audience that he planned to appoint a development administrator "of proven experience and ability" who would be directly responsible to the mayor. The "full-time job" of this administrator would be to coordinate all renewal activities—slum clearance, rehabilitation, conservation, code enforcement, housing, and promotion of all kinds of "taxable development." The administrator would also "expedite and accelerate" the plans and programs of the Boston Redevelopment Authority, the City Planning Board, and all other agencies operating in that field. The new administrator would make sure, said Collins, that Boston, "which now ranks far too low among the major cities in federal renewal grants," would obtain its "just share" of financial assistance from the federal government. It was an impressive and unusually detailed job description to be included in an inaugural address, and it was obviously putting the city on notice that very shortly there would be a new executive officer, with extraordinary powers, serving as the mayor's right-hand man in all matters pertaining to urban renewal.[34]

After the inaugural ceremonies were over, Collins was driven to City Hall, where he swore in his department heads at 11:30. Later, he was host at the nearby Parker House at the traditional 1:30 luncheon reception for city councillors and school committee members. As he said good-bye to newspaper reporters at the end of the long day, the new mayor told them he would be at his desk bright and early, at nine o'clock the next morning. "And we'll see who else shows up for work on time," he said pointedly, "and who does not!"[35]

Despite his dire predictions of reduced appropriations and tightened budgets—or perhaps because of them—the business community generally hailed Collins's program for the city. Presidents of the Greater Boston Chamber of Commerce and the Greater Boston Real Estate Board termed the mayor's Operation Revival as "courageous . . . encouraging . . . hopeful . . . heartening" and assured the new mayor that he would have the "wholehearted support" of the business and financial leaders. Although state representatives and senators from the Boston district were less enthusiastic—Senate President John E. Powers regarded some of the legislative proposals as "old hat" and described others as "political improbabilities"—most agreed to support whatever would help Boston. Representative Robert H. Quinn of Dorchester had high praise for Collins's program; Charles W. Capraro of the North End said it was "farsighted"; Senator James W. Hennigan, Jr., of Jamaica Plain, one of Collins's rivals in the fall, said he would support the legislative proposals; and Representative John T. Driscoll of Dorchester, who had been neutral in the campaign, pledged his full cooperation.[36]

Before long it became clear that things would be different at City Hall with John Collins in charge. "The very first day, when I came into the first floor of City Hall in my wheelchair, not from the School Street entrance but from the annex side, I got this awful stench of urine. 'Good Lord,' I thought, 'every hobo from Scollay Square's coming in here and using the place as a public toilet!' Well, I gave order to assign keys to the employees on this floor of the building. Public toilets would be located somewhere else, not here. . . . Then I looked around and saw that the floor was pitch black. 'Who's in charge of this place?' I asked. 'Let's wash this filthy floor. Let's find out whether this floor is really black, or whether there's some other color underneath!' By the way, that floor turned out to be light green and white when it was eventually cleaned up." Collins noticed that the handsome front doors of City Hall had also become black and filthy owing to age, neglect, and years of unattended pigeon droppings. When he was informed that nobody at City Hall had the facilities to clean them up, he called a local monument maker at Forest Hills cemetery and asked if he had the kind of equipment that would clean up bronze doors. When the man said yes, and offered to loan it to the city, Collins told him that if he ever wanted to get his equipment back in one piece he'd better send some of his people to do the job themselves. And so they did, recalled Collins. In fact, not only did they restore the beautiful bronze doors, but they also cleaned up the statues of Benjamin Franklin and Josiah Quincy on the outside lawn while they were at it.

A short time later, John Hynes paid a visit to the new mayor at City Hall and complimented him on the condition of the building. "John," said Hynes, "I think you're going to be a very effective mayor—maybe even a great mayor."

"That's awfully kind of you to say," replied Collins, "but why do you say that?"

"I walked in and out of this old building every day for forty years," responded Hynes, "and every day it looked exactly the way it did the day before. I never realized how *dirty* the building was getting. You walked in here, and you've only been in here a few days," he said, "and already it's changed."[37]

While this episode can be dismissed as simply an amusing anecdote or an interesting personal idiosyncrasy, it can also be seen as a typical expression of a generation that saw cleanliness and orderliness as goals of a truly progressive society. The urban planners and architects of the 1950s would tear down whole districts, entire neighborhoods, and replace them with neatly designed and meticulously planned buildings and parks that were symbolic of their creators' love of orderliness and their aversion to the chaos and clutter so typical of the traditional urban environment of the time.

But if getting City Hall cleaned up surprised many people, they were in for an even greater surprise when on January 11, little more than a week after Collins's inauguration, the newspapers carried the startling announcement that the city of Boston was $4 million in the black as a result of "good financial management and a running audit of the departmental expenditures." Despite all the lamentations that had been going on for the past year about the lack of funds, the terrible condition of the city's finances, and the near-panic belief that the city was on the verge of municipal bankruptcy, city auditor Joseph P. Lally disclosed that Boston had finished the year 1959 with a surplus of $4 million and had also reduced its gross debt by $12 million. "For the first time in many years," said Lally, "we find ourselves in the delightful situation where we have taken in more than we have spent." Although the tax rate and the evaluation of real property were still serious problems to contend with, "contrary to the general and erroneous impression, we are not in a financial mess. . . . Boston is in good financial shape." In commenting on Lally's unexpected disclosure, Collins expressed his pleasure at the good news, but announced that the surplus would go into a special account and would not be used in computing the current year's tax rate.[38]

In much the same way that he set out to clean up City Hall, Collins also took immediate steps to modernize and improve the inner workings of city government. Just as he reached out for professional help in cleaning the floors and polishing the doors, this time he contacted local businessmen and bankers for assistance in bringing in modern management procedures. Specifically, he turned to that group of financial leaders who had recently formed the Boston Coordinating Committee—"the Vault"—in anticipation of the city going into receivership in the declining months of the Hynes administration. At an early meeting with the group at its headquarters on Franklin Street, just a short distance from City Hall, Collins informed them that he wanted to reform the city's assessing department and put it on a professional basis as soon as possible. At the time, the department had part-time assessors—employees who would work as city assessors in the morning, and then go off to work as lawyers and real estate people in the afternoon. Collins felt that that was not only an inefficient way to run a department but also a method open to serious conflicts of interest. His objective, therefore, as he explained it to the members of the Vault, was to force those employees to give up either their outside interests or their city jobs. In order to complete such a transformation, Collins indicated, he needed the services of a few outside people, especially people with computer backgrounds, to put the department on its feet while the personnel changes were taking place. He told them that if he could get a few well-trained people working in the assessing department, not full-time, but one or two days a week, he could begin to wrap it up in only a few weeks.

"Charles Coolidge was there at the meeting, taking notes," recalled Collins, "and he knew exactly what I was talking about; and Carl Gilbert of Gillette's, he knew too." So they turned to one another and began asking questions: "Don't you have some data-processing people at your place?" "Don't you have a couple of people at your shop you could spare?" "Couldn't we come up with four or five people?" It was finally agreed that the various banks would loan some of their people to the city on a temporary basis. The banks would continue to pay their salaries, but they would be on part-time loan, working with the people at city hall until the job was done straightening out the department.[39]

Even thirty years later, Collins was sensitive about misunderstandings that had soon cropped up about his relationship with the Vault. For one thing, the idea circulated that the Vault had moved into the financial vacuum of the last days of the Hynes administration and had become the shadow government of the city. Not so, insisted Collins. About a week before the mayoral election, a large number of business leaders, including members of the Boston Coordinating Committee, had interviewed him in a private meeting room at the Copley Plaza hotel, even though it still seemed likely that Johnny Powers would be an easy winner. Once the election was over and he had won his upset victory, Collins asked Don Hurley, chairman of the Committee for Civic Progress, to reconvene the same people in the same hotel room on a Saturday afternoon. Since no one could run the city alone, the new mayor told the business leaders, he would obviously need their help and cooperation, and he promised he would consult with them the same way he would consult with the community leaders of Charlestown, Roxbury, and South Boston. As a practical means of maintaining contact with the business community, he suggested he meet with members of their coordinating committee once every couple of weeks in order to learn about any point of disagreement or any positive suggestions to help the city. "I want you to understand, however," said Collins, "that you are not going to direct the mayor or the city. I do not accept dictation." Regarding rumors making their rounds in some quarters that there might be a withholding of corporate tax revenues from the city, Collins stated that he would regard any such attempt to interfere with the normal operations of the municipal government as a criminal conspiracy and would give any such person the opportunity to testify before a grand jury that he would have summoned. "Now I don't want to talk about this matter again," he said pointedly, "because I know that any such rumors are specious."[40]

Concerning stories that the members of the Vault called the shots and dictated city policy during the remainder of his administration, Collins later was equally adamant about this "figment of the imagination." "Let me set the record straight on that," he said. "Every two weeks, at four o'clock, we would meet to set the agenda. It was I who set the agenda at these meetings, identified the problems to be discussed, and determined how they were to be dealt with."[41] Regardless of where the initiative came from, the close association that developed between the mayor of Boston and influential leaders of the city's business and financial establishment would go far in providing the kind of stability needed for any further progress in the physical development of the city.

But if the new mayor was getting support and encouragement from the downtown business and financial community, he was getting little of either from his rivals on Beacon Hill. "As an Irishman gets older, he is subject to a peculiar form of amnesia," goes an old Boston saying. "He forgets everything except his grudges." With his archenemy, Senate President John E. Powers, still burning with a righteous anger that would never really subside for the rest of his public career, Collins could not have been unaware that his efforts to get his legislation through the Great and General Court would probably be at least as stormy as his predecessor's. It was obvious to anyone who had been observing the erratic course of Boston politics that the continuing feud between the president of the state senate and the chief executive of the city spelled trouble. Any chance for Boston to get the legislation it needed for its future development depended in large part upon relations between two "fellow Bostonians and fellow Democrats," commented the staff writer Michael Liuzzi in a series of articles for the *Christian Science Monitor*. Unless those two political leaders were able to get together and present a "solid front," he observed, there seemed no hope for overcoming the traditional resistance of legislators from outside the city to any bill labeled "Boston." After a series of interviews with both men, however, Liuzzi came to the conclusion that such a solid front was virtually impossible. The scars from the recent mayoral contest were still too fresh and too painful, and it was clear that neither man was ready for a reconciliation. Powers insisted that he was not using his influence against Collins's bills, blaming outside legislators who had been voting against Boston bills "for years" and who would continue to do so "regardless of what I do or say." There was no doubt in Collins's mind, however, that Powers was deliberately engaging in retaliatory tactics, and "if he keeps on killing our legislation," Collins declared, "something will have to be done."[42]

The first year of his term as mayor of Boston was a frustrating one in terms of his relationship with the legislators on Beacon Hill, as he tried to save money for the city, reduce the municipal budget, and broaden the tax base as he had promised in his inaugural address. When he tried to get the fire commissioner appointed to the traffic commission in place of the head of parks and recreation, for example, his proposal went down to defeat in the senate by a nine-to-three vote, even though the fairly innocuous bill had been passed by the house. The following week he asked the state legislature to give the mayor of Boston full control of the city's police budget, a request that would enable him to force the police commissioner, Leo J. Sullivan, to make substantial cuts in the department's 1960 budget. Not only did the legislature refuse his request, but it would not even allow Collins the opportunity to testify on behalf of his own bill. It was pointed out by veteran political observers that Sullivan's wife had been an active campaign supporter of state senator Powers—a fact that undoubtedly did nothing to help the bill's chances of a sympathetic hearing. When Collins attempted to have a portion of Suffolk County's costs assessed on the three other cities besides Boston that made up the county—Chelsea, Revere, and Winthrop—once again his bill was shot down in flames. The house voted against it 150 to 59, with only twenty-two representatives from outside the city voting with the Boston delegation; the next day the senate rejected the bill, with only six senators from outside Boston voting in its favor.[43]

By far the most devastating defeat was one the legislature inflicted jointly on both Governor Foster Furcolo and Mayor John Collins. Early in January Furcolo proposed a 3 percent limited sales tax, the proceeds of which would be used solely for the reduction of local real estate taxes. Collins had campaigned for mayor on such a sales tax, and so he came out in favor of the governor's proposal in the expectation that its passage would help reduce the city's $101 real estate tax by anywhere from $15 to $21 per thousand. Since the bill was energetically supported by the Boston newspapers, by the entire business community, and by a variety of good-government associations, the governor had every expectation that it would pass into law. He expressed his belief that even Powers would give it his support: "I'm satisfied Senator Powers is not going to vote against what Mayor Collins wants, and what is good for Boston," he said confidently. In this he was sadly mistaken. Powers made an announcement that he was "unalterably opposed" to any such sales tax and was prepared to campaign against it the length and breadth of the commonwealth. Once again, one of Collins's "Boston bills" was badly defeated—there was no sales tax.[44]

Unlike Hynes, who had not been particularly inclined to take on the powerful members of the state legislature and engage in the distasteful rough-and-tumble battles and dirty in-fighting of Boston politics, Collins had no such qualms. He organized his plans, devised his strategy, and prepared to go up against his critics on Beacon Hill. One of the first things he did was to make sure there would be no surprise attacks as he moved toward his main objective. Soon after his election as mayor, he went up to the state house for a private meeting with Governor Volpe and made it "perfectly clear" that he had no intention of running against him for governor. "He believed me," said Collins, "and from that time on we got along extremely well." In fact, the two men often spoke on the telephone together—"we each had each other's private number," according to Collins. Eventually Collins's friendship with the governor worked in Boston's favor by enabling the city to obtain $5 million in state funds to fill in the Fort Point Channel (thereby giving Boston new taxable land), and by giving the mayor control over the appointment of the Boston police commissioner (and the police budget)—a power previously exercised by the governor.[45]

Although there was not much Collins could do about smoothing over relations with the president of the senate, he went out of his way to cultivate the powerful speaker of the house, John F. Thompson. Using Representative Robert H. Quinn as his liaison with the speaker, the mayor developed a cordial relationship that became particularly strategic early in 1963 when Thompson became involved in a bitter power struggle with Governor Endicott Peabody, who made a serious effort to oust the "Iron Duke" from his post as house speaker. During the ensuing speakership campaign, an extremely close race, Collins contacted a number of state representatives from Boston who were reportedly going to vote against Thompson and persuaded them to change their votes. Speaker Thompson retained his post, Governor Peabody suffered an embarrassing setback, and Mayor Collins made a future enemy. For the time being, however, his relationship was further solidified with Speaker Thompson, who subsequently appointed Bob Quinn as majority whip. Not only did the appointment put Quinn on the road to the speakership, and later to the attorney general's office, but Collins's role in the campaign also provided the mayor with additional support among influential committee chairmen on Beacon Hill.[46]

Now that he had both flanks covered, Collins was ready to move toward his main objective—the legislature itself. Collins had served four years in the house and four years in the senate before being named register of probate in 1957. He was a member of the club, he knew the game, he understood well the workings of the legislature, and he was determined to win over its assistance. He had every confidence that the two men he selected to serve as his legislative lobbyists on the hill would be effective—the attorney Paul J. Burns, a Boston College Law School graduate, and a former state representative, Louis N. Nathanson, a Harvard Law School graduate. Both men worked hard at their jobs, became well liked at the state house, and on one occasion even Senator Powers agreed that Burns had done "an outstanding job," although he could not resist adding that since Burns was working for Collins he had "a heavy burden to carry." Collins kept in touch with his lobbyists "several times a day" whenever there were important bills up for voting. He himself would get on the phone to some legislator whose vote was in doubt or who opposed a particular bill the mayor wanted passed. At the same time, he established a policy of cooperation between all segments of his administration and state legislators who contacted city hall on behalf of their constituents. His "intelligent use of courtesy and attention" to the needs and requests of legislators produced a number of victories on Beacon Hill as a result of the respect Collins achieved among legislators.[47]

To back up the efforts of his lobbyists even further, Collins made the trip from City Hall to the State House to make a number of appearances before legislative committees, and he encouraged members of his various departments to lend their support whenever it would help. The new mayor made a concerted effort to talk to as many knowledgeable people as possible. He held lengthy conferences with both Joseph Slavet, the executive director of the Boston Municipal Research Bureau, and his successor, Joseph Barresi. He discussed bills with William Kerr, an assistant corporation counsel, as well as with other experienced members of the law department that had handled the city's legislative efforts since Curley's time. This sort of consultation paid off in the preparation of his bills and the accumulation of the kind of statistical data and technical information needed to guide them through the legislative process.

In addition to talking with businessmen and civic leaders, Collins also developed considerable skill in using the news media. Twice a day, four days a week—at 10:00 A.M. for the evening papers and at 3:30 P.M. for the morning editions—he met with the members of the press. Except for an occasional visit from Channel 4's veteran newscaster Arch Macdonald, television reporters had not yet become a regular part of these sessions. Recognizing the increasing influence of television, however, Collins conducted monthly TV shows and organized a variety of public meetings not only in Boston but in other sections of the commonwealth. Bob Quinn helped him set up corned-beef lunches with groups of fifteen or twenty legislators from all over the state every day—"except Friday," quickly cautioned Collins, a devout Catholic, who would never think of eating meat on Friday. The luncheons were one more technique of cultivating widespread friendship and support. "I can recall Senator Moakley saying it was the first time he had ever been in the mayor's office. It made them feel important—sought after." Collins admitted that the routine of daily luncheon meetings became "a pain in the neck," but they proved to be quite effective in developing a new working relationship.

Collins understood the traditional reticence of representatives from other parts of the state, convinced as they were of the waste, inefficiency, and corruption they perceived to be endemic to the big city, to support any measures that would help Boston, and he took steps to counteract it. As soon as possible, he established a Massachusetts League of Cities and Towns, with Kenny O'Rourke, who had been in Washington heading up the National League of Cities, as its executive director. He had hopes that this apparatus would give him the benefit of a more unified and sympathetic support for his efforts on Beacon Hill. In addition, he was able to impress outside legislators with his tight-fisted fiscal policies and by his cost-cutting approach to city government. In addition to collecting delinquent taxes and unpaid hospital bills, his "no hire, no fire" policy cut $13 million from budget requests and reduced the number of city employees by more than three hundred. These efforts to change Boston's image as a big-spending community did a great deal to convince rural and suburban legislators that the city was finally being run by "an honest mayor in an efficient manner."[48]

As he turned from his efforts to establish some dependable measure of legislative support to the broader subject of urban development, it was with amazing swiftness that John Collins was able to come up with precisely the man who fit so closely the description he had outlined in his inaugural address. Looking for someone who could direct Boston's renewal efforts along more professional and imaginative lines, Collins followed up on a suggestion made by Joseph Slavet that he recruit a young man named Edward J. Logue, who was then running the urban renewal program in New Haven, Connecticut. A native of Philadelphia, a graduate of Yale, and a lawyer by training, Logue had begun working for Richard Lee, the newly elected mayor of New Haven in 1954, and the following year had taken over the direction of the urban renewal effort in that city. Supported by a strong mayor with broad-ranging powers, and operating in a city of such manageable size that "what was proposed could be delivered," Logue had achieved impressive results, which attracted a steady flow of federal dollars. Those were achievements that made the thirty-nine-year-old urban planner attractive to Collins right away. "Logue had done an excellent job down in New Haven," Collins said. "He was a generalist, he knew the rules of the game, and he'd dealt with the federal people. And the chemistry was there between us."[49] With his shrewd political instincts, Collins also selected Logue because he was an outsider. Given the Byzantine intricacies of Boston politics, the mayor confided to Logue, only an outsider could start with a clean slate. "They start keeping score on everybody local too early," he explained, and his origins from outside Boston would give him a head start.[50]

Attracted by Collins's offer to come to Boston and try his hand at renewal in a city of larger dimensions, Logue made it clear that he would settle for nothing less than a salary of thirty-thousand dollars—ten thousand more than the mayor himself was paid. Collins agreed without any hesitation. Although there was apparently some discussion about going to the members of the Vault to make up the difference in Logue's salary, Collins was violently opposed to that idea. He was adamant that only city money be used. Logue eventually received a salary of twenty-five thousand dollars out of federal funds as head of the BRA, but insisted that the remaining five thousand dollars come from the budget of the mayor's office so that Collins "could fire me any time he wanted."[51]

In March 1960 Logue arrived in Boston as a consultant to conduct a survey and to prepare a development program for the city. Assessing the current status of redevelopment, he found that except for the ongoing project in the New York Streets area of the South End, the controversial

*Determined to make the New Boston the centerpiece of his administration, Mayor John Collins brought young Edward J. Logue up from New Haven, Connecticut, to take over all facets of planning and executing the city's urban renewal program. Here, at the BRA exhibit at the Home Show, Collins watches Logue describe to representatives from the Builders Information Bureau and the Home Builders Association the plans for a hundred-acre waterfront development project. Courtesy of the Boston Public Library, Print Department.*

project that had just been concluded in the West End, the Prudential Center project, and the Government Center project—all individual projects initiated by Mayor Hynes—there was, for all practical purposes, "no overall plan or program to change the city, and certainly no public or civic organization equipped to do it." Logue felt that several things were necessary for a successful redevelopment program in any city: a comprehensive planning design; substantial federal funding; a highly professional staff; extensive consultation with the residents involved; and effective leadership at the top. "Somebody's got to be in charge," he insisted. Logue found none of those essentials in what he called the "bifurcated" operations of the Hynes administration, where planning was kept separate from execution, and where a series of committees and departments functioned with little overall direction or responsibility.[52]

But before launching any new programs of his own, Logue was convinced that, if only for the sake of credibility, it was necessary to finish the projects already on the drawing board. He believed the effective completion of those pending projects would not only put the new Collins administration on a sound footing right at the start but would also inspire the kind of public confidence needed for developing future plans and more ambitious projects. "Getting Prudential Center built was essential if any of our other plans were to go forward," wrote Logue, emphasizing a point with which the new mayor concurred. "I never thought the Pru was a great building," Collins said some years later. "It was not as nice as it should have been. But it was a loss leader. We had to prove that somebody had enough confidence to put something in there."[53]

Back in the fall of 1959, by the time his last term of office was coming to a close, Mayor Hynes had been convinced that he had worked out with the representatives of the Prudential Insurance Company a satisfactory and mutually advantageous tax arrangement whereby Prudential would get special tax breaks through the agency of the Massachusetts Turnpike Authority. In the closing days of 1959, however, a twenty-seven-page ruling by the state's Supreme Judicial Court struck that arrangement down on constitutional grounds and threatened the whole future of the project. Counsel for Prudential again pointed out that his company had to have an "iron clad tax structure" before it would be fully satisfied, and threatened that unless some new solution was worked out by August, all work on the project would be suspended.[54] On Beacon Hill there was a flurry of frenzied excitement. On January 1, 1960, even though it was New Year's Day, Attorney General Edward J. McCormack held a news conference with a number of other state officials to discuss the legal ramifications of the discouraging court ruling. Assuming an optimistic tone—"I feel a lot better about it than I did yesterday"—McCormack professed to see a promising loophole in the court's ruling and suggested that, since the railroad was discontinuing its passenger service, the unused yards might well be classified as a "blighted area" and thus provide an urban-renewal basis for a new agreement. Key business and political figures called for thoughtful consideration and promised all kinds of assistance. Governor Furcolo announced he was ready to submit a new plan to the state legislature; Charles A. Coolidge, president of the chamber of commerce, indicated that his colleagues were ready to map a "new course of action"; House Speaker Thompson promised full cooperation; Senate President Powers assured voters that new legislation to save the Prudential Center would be drafted "within 48 to 72 hours"; and the newly elected mayor, John Collins, promised to get the advice of "experts" to solve a problem that needs "sober deliberation. . . . Don't push the panic button," he urged the general public.[55]

Despite all the assurances of prompt and speedy action, however, weeks and then months went by as legislators debated the exact wording of possible tax concessions, and a battery of nineteen lawyers wrestled with the constitutional provisions of the bill that was finally filed with the General Court on May 3, 1960, by Governor Furcolo in a last-minute effort to save the multimillion-dollar Prudential project for Boston. The newest piece of legislation proposed a $300 million package plan that tied together the $100 million extension of the Massachusetts Turnpike from Weston to Boston, the construction of a twenty-five-hundred-car garage on the Back Bay Prudential site by the Turnpike Authority, and the leasing of the space above the foundation ("air rights") by Prudential for eighty years. In leasing these air rights, the Prudential project would participate in the tax-exempt status accorded the Turnpike Authority. In return, to compensate the city, the Prudential Company would eventually pay to the city, through the authority, service charges amounting to $3 million a year, more, if 20 percent of the gross annual income from the project exceeded $3 million. The $3 million figure was about the same amount agreed on two years earlier by Hynes and the Prudential representatives. As a matter of policy, Collins let it be known that he would abide by his predecessor's decision in this regard.[56]

Speaking on behalf of his corporation, Fred Smith, vice president and special assistant to the president of Prudential, urged swift passage of this new arrangement in terms that to John Fenton of the *New York Times* "amounted to an ultimatum." After having already spent some $6 million on foundation work, the people at Prudential had become disturbed over reports that some Boston sources were "restive" over the original tax agreement, said Smith, and unless the newest tax arrangement was "tied up in a guarantee," he warned, they were prepared to "pack up and get out." Prudential authorities also made it clear that they would insist on a formal "court test" of whatever legislative proposal was produced before they would regard any further agreements as binding.[57]

It was at this point that Cardinal Cushing, in a comment released by the Archdiocesan News Bureau, added his considerable influence on behalf of the new arrangement, stating that the completion of the Prudential Center, together with the extension of the turnpike, would play an important part in the "rejuvenation of Boston."[58]

Here was a situation where Logue could demonstrate his ability to work out imaginative solutions to complicated problems, and where Collins could show his own determination to move an unfinished project off the drawing board and into completion. Consulting with a number of Boston's business leaders, Logue discussed the possibility of taking the Prudential project out of local hands and using the powers of federal legislation as a tactic to achieve positive results where previous attempts had failed. In seeking an opinion from the state's Supreme Judicial Court, he asked about the possibility of using the urban-renewal powers of the Boston Redevelopment Authority to declare the abandoned railroad site in the Back Bay a "blighted area" and then proceed with appropriate clearance and development plans as part of a necessary public undertaking instead of an exclusively private and commercial venture. This time the court's reaction was a positive one, and early in August 1960 it handed down a ruling stating that the latest piece of legislation concerning the construction of the Prudential Center was constitutional. Within twenty-four hours, the Legislative Committee on Municipal Finance reported the measure favorably.[59]

Logue was delighted, not only that the court ruling put the Collins administration in a much better position to finalize special arrangements with the Prudential group, but also that his vision of a larger and more powerful BRA would almost inevitably result from the decision. Right away he began to exert pressure on the members of the state legislature for the passage of a bill that would abolish the old City Planning Board and transfer its functions to what would become a much more greatly expanded BRA. In a short time, the Massachusetts General Court passed a law entitled "An Act Concerning the Development and Redevelopment of Blighted Open Areas, Decadent Areas, and Substandard Areas by Urban Redevelopment Corporations, with Special Provisions for Projects in the City of Boston"—better known as Chapter 121A. The new legislation, which gave the BRA the function of planning urban renewal and development as well as the power to carry out such plans, proved to be the key to the resumption of the Prudential Center and to the subsequent success of the whole revitalization of Boston. Under the provisions of the bill (as Logue had earlier explained it to the justices), the expanded BRA would declare the site to be a blighted area and turn it over to the Prudential Company, which would develop it in such a way that it would be useful to the public and beneficial to the entire community.[60]

Once the court ruling had been issued, construction on the new Prudential complex began in earnest. The master plan, designed by the California architect Charles Luckman, appeared heavily influenced by the work of the Swiss architect Le Corbusier. "It was Modern with a capital M," wrote Yvonne Chabrier in an article concerning future changes to be made in the Pru.[61] In the spirit of one of Le Corbusier's utopian urban designs, the Prudential Center sat on a concrete platform raised some sixteen feet above the surrounding street level. The signature building, the Prudential Tower, constructed of glass and steel, rose to a height of 743 feet (fifty-two stories), dominated the cityscape, and was surrounded by a cluster of plain, flat-roofed buildings sitting on the same central platform. Ring roads encircled the entire complex, creating a virtual island where people could work, live, park, and shop without ever crossing a street. Typical of the modernistic architectural designs that would eventually characterize the New Boston throughout the downtown area, the Prudential complex was literally a "city within a city," as Chabrier observed, that reversed the traditional fabric of the old city, where buildings normally "line the streets and surround the open spaces."[62] Even though the Prudential complex kept the city divided almost as effectively as the former railroad yards it had replaced, everyone hailed the new enterprise for the momentum it seemed to have given to the idea of a "New Boston." As one BRA official later reflected: "The Prudential Center was conceived in the fifties to give a new, slick, shiny image that would attract new development."[63]

It was during these same early months of 1960 that another long-standing project began coming to life—the underground garage. Although it had been agreed back in 1950 that a garage would be built underneath the Boston Common, the work was just getting under way

*The 52-story Prudential Tower, rising out of the abandoned railroad yards in the Back Bay, was the first major work of construction to take place in Boston in many years. Heavily influenced by the modernistic designs of the Swiss architect Le Corbusier, with its severe lines and its use of glass and steel, it was regarded by many people as the turning point in the movement to transform the old, run-down city into a truly new Boston. Photograph © 1991 by Peter Vanderwarker.*

about the time that John Collins was taking over as mayor. The official groundbreaking ceremonies did not take place until March 3, 1960, a day when the city was hit with one of the fiercest blizzards in history, leading one cynical reporter to suggest that a "jinx" had hung over the Boston Common underground garage "since the very idea was broached."[64] Once construction was under way, the inhabitants of Beacon Hill and Charles Street complained continuously about the noise, the dust, and the incessant banging of pile drivers from morning till night. It was the "earthquake tremors" of those evacuations that provided the background for the bitter ruminations of the poet Robert Lowell one morning in March as he contemplated Augustus Saint-Gauden's inspiring tribute to Colonel Robert Gould Shaw and the gallant members of the Fifty-fourth Negro Regiment on the edge of the common directly across from the golden dome of the State House. As he reflected on Boston's glorious past, he heard behind him "yellow dinosaur steam shovels" grunting away as they cropped up "tons of mush and grass to gouge their underground garage."[65]

Back Bay residents became even more irate when they heard that the contractor was seeking permission to continue his thunderous operations throughout the nights as well as the days, and their loud protestations raised even more serious objections about the way in which the Massachusetts Parking Authority was exceeding its authority and refusing to obtain the kind of permit from the city of Boston normally required for any similar type of operation on the Boston Common— "even for the construction of a chicken coop." Although the parking authority's chairman, George L. Brady, was repeatedly warned by the corporation counsel Arthur Coffey that he must obtain such city permits at the risk of court action, Brady argued that he was not obliged to comply with local standards. The Massachusetts Parking Authority was an agency created by the state legislature, he maintained, and operated under national building codes that were as "inclusive, safety-wise" as the local building regulations of the city of Boston.[66]

Work on the underground garage continued, and the three-level structure beneath the ancient common was finally completed just before Thanksgiving Day 1961. Hardly had the garage opened for business, however, when there were rumbles of discontent among members of the Massachusetts Parking Authority, who were disturbed about allegations of questionable practices raised by Brady, who subsequently resigned in a fit of anger. In December state attorney general Edward McCormack (who, his critics pointed out, was eyeing the U.S. Senate nomination coming up in a few months) arranged for a Suffolk County grand jury probe into the alleged disappearance of some $346,000 in fees, commissions, and contracts.[67]

It was a colorful and juicy scandal that entertained newspaper readers for months to come, and it contributed to the city's unfortunate reputation for municipal graft and corruption. The story was especially embarrassing at a time when the members of the new Collins administration were trying to convince the federal authorities to participate in an important project they hoped would truly energize the movement toward a New Boston—the proposed Government Center.

7.

# "The Stars Were Right"

With the Prudential Center under way, the Central Artery completed, and the underground garage in the process of construction, the way looked clear for the completion of the much talked-about Government Center in the area formerly occupied by Scollay Square. Although Hynes's effective role as mayor of Boston had come to an end once Collins won election in November 1959, Hynes had been determined to use his final weeks in office trying to persuade the federal government to forget about the possibilities of a Back Bay site and to construct its office building as an integral part of the Government Center project. Once again he had led a delegation of prominent business and political figures to Washington in an effort to impress the general services administrator, Franklin Floete, with the importance of the Scollay Square location and the significance of the Government Center design to the future development of Boston.[1]

A tweedy, pipe-smoking man who reminded one of a college professor, Floete told his visitors that he recalled Scollay Square from his Harvard days, mentioning that the Old Howard had been one of his "favorite haunts." All in all, however, he expressed doubts about the ability of city leaders to get their act together, and he boasted that in all probability he could get his federal office building constructed in the Back Bay long before they could get around to completing their plans for their Government Center. Anxious to counteract his pessimistic view and demonstrate as much unanimity as possible on the Scollay Square site, the New England congressional delegation in Washington voted unanimously for the Government Center site, with representatives Edith Nourse Rogers and Joseph Martin, Jr., making the motion. After Hynes left office in January, Collins, continuing to press the issue, also headed a delegation of business representatives to Washington. U.S. Congressman John W. McCormack threw his considerable weight in favor of the Government Center location and arranged a personal meeting between Floete and Collins. "Franklin," said McCormack, addressing Floete by his first name, "the mayor of Boston and the people he represents desire this project. Like most other political figures and businessmen, I did not support Collins in the last election," said McCormack in his typical forthright manner, "but I will do so in every way from this day forward."[2]

Among the local business leaders who were following the erratic course of the Government Center proceedings with much interest was Jerome Rappaport, who had invested heavily in the West End project, and who was now eager for a successful commercial development in the Scollay Square district and the adjoining properties that would obviously enhance the value of his own holdings. He recalled coming home one day, "cussing and complaining" about how long the Government Center project was taking, about the delays, the changes in plans, the lack of progress, and the stupidity of the general services administrator in Washington. His mother-in-law, Edith Vahey, was in the room, heard him complaining about the head of the GSA, and asked, "Do you mean Franklin Floete?" Rappaport stopped in surprise, and said yes; whereupon she informed him that Floete had been her first husband. Immediately, Rappaport used Mrs. Vahey's influence to get in touch with Floete, spoke to him personally on the telephone, and found that he was still uneasy about having "his" brand new federal building located in the run-down, unsavory area he remembered from his college days as Scollay Square. Rappaport explained to Floete how the city was planning to completely rebuild and refurbish the entire area and construct a whole new government center in which his federal building would be the "centerpiece," a veritable "beacon" in a "marvelous" location.[3]

So, while Hynes was traveling regularly to Washington with Collins and paying visits to Congressman McCormack and other influential political figures, Rappaport was working through the good services of his mother-in-law. Whether the decisive player was Hynes, Collins, McCormack, Rappaport, Mrs. Vahey, any of them, or a combination of all of them is almost impossible to determine with any degree of certainty. But eventually Franklin Floete contacted Mayor Collins and informed him that not only was the federal government prepared to have its building erected as part of the Government Center project, but it would also undertake to clear the small triangular area of land lying between the West End and the proposed Government Center in Scollay Square. Once the federal government had agreed to support the Government Center project, the state legislature followed suit. On August 10, 1960, the house passed and sent to the state senate a bill authorizing construction of a $50 million complex of state buildings, including a $26 million state office building in the proposed Government Center. The lopsided vote of 155 to 42 was far more than the two-thirds that would be necessary whenever the legislature would be called upon to authorize the bond issue.

With the federal government and the state government committed to the completion of the Government Center, the stage was now set for the city of Boston to finalize the process—something Logue declared to be the Collins administration's "highest priority," not only because of the space needs this particular project would fulfill, and the hundreds of local jobs it would undoubtedly produce, but also because of the "catalytic effect" it would have upon the whole attitude of Boston about itself.[4] Logue was convinced that the city had to move quickly to maintain momentum in the completion process, as well as to give clear evidence that the new administration was solidly behind the Government Center project. The longer he delayed coming up with a specific plan, he realized, the more skeptical developers would remain about investing their time and their money, and the more worried merchants, property owners, and families in the Scollay Square district would become about their future.

And there was no doubt at all in Logue's mind—the entire district had to go if anything was to be accomplished. "Whatever charms old Scollay Square may have had," he later wrote, "the area had clearly fallen on 'hard times.' " He determined to move forward, therefore, on three different fronts at the same time: (1) to acquire the property right away and relocate its inhabitants as soon as possible; (2) to prepare an overall project plan; and (3) to negotiate with those public agencies whose support was essential. In January 1961 the process began in earnest; by June, Logue was ready for the acquisition hearings. At the same time, he was in the process of engaging a consulting firm of architects and planners to work with the Boston Redevelopment Authority in preparing the overall plan for the Government Center, to "delineate each disposition parcel and establish controls which would limit height, bulk, and setback, and establish a pattern of relationships between each building." Several firms were considered and discussed with Mayor Collins, who suggested that I. M. Pei and Associates be retained—"a very good firm," wrote Logue, "but one which had not yet established the national and international reputation it has today." Logue recommended the mayor's suggestion "enthusiastically" to the BRA board, which promptly gave its approval. The Government Center project was the first time in an American urban renewal program that "early acquisition" of all the property was approved before the official plan was accepted, according to the historian Lawrence Kennedy.[5]

It had been agreed that the centerpiece of the Government Center plan would be a new $30 million City Hall, set prominently in a broad open space. The idea of holding a national competition for the design of this structure was suggested by James Lawrence and Philip Bourne of the Boston Architectural Group and put forward by Robert Morgan, president of the Boston Five Cent Savings Bank, a man originally brought in by Hynes to become chairman of the Government Center Commission and invited by Collins to continue in that capacity. "Morgan had the rare quality of getting people to do what was wanted," according to H. D. Hodgkinson of Filene's, "making them enthusiastic over his leadership while keeping a firm hand in the direction of the master plan in all its details." Although Logue himself was not particularly in favor of a competition, Morgan felt that it was one practical way of keeping the job out of the hands of some political architect who would inevitably be called upon to make a substantial campaign contribution. Collins agreed, and Morgan formed a five-person committee to conduct the competition, consisting of four architects who had received their early training in the Boston area, and one lay person, Hodgkinson. This would be the first open United States architectural competition for a major public structure since 1909.[6] The competition was announced in November 1960, and out of 256 submissions, eight finalists were chosen by the committee. The eight finalists were then reviewed by the members of the original committee, with two more persons added:

Sidney Rabb, head of Stop & Shop, and O. Kelley Anderson, president of the New England Mutual Life Insurance Company.

The result was a unanimous decision in favor of three young members of the Columbia University architectural school, Gerhard M. Kallman, Noel M. McKinnell, and Edward F. Knowles, whose names would be officially announced and whose prizewinning design would be unveiled before Mayor Collins and an invited audience of some four hundred people—architects, city councillors, artists, public officials, business and financial leaders—late in the afternoon of Thursday, May 3, 1962, at the Museum of Fine Arts.[7] When Mayor Collins dramatically lifted the curtain to reveal a mockup of the design for Boston's new City Hall, "surprise was evident in every line" of his face. Like so many of the other guests present that evening, the mayor had undoubtedly been expecting to see a model of a traditional structure consonant with such nearby historical buildings as Faneuil Hall, the Old State House, and the Bulfinch State House on Beacon Hill. Instead, he saw before him a strikingly modern design, low and huge, with what Walter Muir Whitehill has described as "Mycenaean or Aztec overtones" in its soaring massiveness, and borrowing heavily from the work of the Swiss architect Le Corbusier.[8] The sight of the winning design was greeted in the halls of the museum with a scattering of applause, a few audible sighs of approval, and some "less than complimentary remarks."[9] Logue, who was watching, saw the look of shock and astonishment on the mayor's face: "I could almost hear him thinking to himself 'My God, what's that?' But he didn't blink, because he believed in the process." Quickly recovering what another observer called his "executive composure," Collins immediately announced the new design to be "exciting and monumental." "I believe in this century it is a really historic event," he said, "a design that will live for many years."[10]

Neither then, nor now, were there any neutral feelings about the design of the new City Hall. People either loved it fervently or hated it passionately. There was no middle ground. On the one hand, Albert Bush-Brown, a professor of architecture at MIT, hailed its innovative character and said that it spoke to the demands of the twentieth century for better urban government. "No bows to the Georgian. No weak-kneed copying of the State Housedom. Or the Faneuil Hall roof," he wrote in response to those who had hoped for a traditional colonial design along the lines of the shrinelike Independence Mall in Philadelphia. "Nothing but a whole-hearted affirmation of a new time, new

*Developed by architects from the Columbia University Graduate School of Architecture in response to a nationwide competition, the design for Boston's new City Hall was unveiled on May 3, 1962, at the Museum of Fine Arts. The structure immediately provoked a wave of controversy. Critics complained that the modernistic design was inappropriate for the city's heritage. Supporters argued that it symbolized the transformation of Boston from a colonial past to a challenging future. Photograph © 1991 by Peter Vanderwarker.*

social needs, and the new technology and new aesthetics to declare faith in the civic instrument of government."[11] The Boston Society of Architects recorded themselves as enthusiastically in favor of the design; William Wurster of the University of California Architectual School, who served as chairman of the selection committee, predicted that "the world will beat a pathway to see this building"; and one Bostonian would go "all the way back to the Doge's Palace in Venice" to find a public building of equal importance.

On the other hand, howls of protest went up in many parts of the city demanding that the design be rejected as entirely inappropriate for such a recognized center of American history. Stanley Parker and a group of eighteen noted architects signed a petition asking that the design not be accepted; Edward Durell Stone, speaking on May 12 before the annual meeting of the Society of Military Engineers, claimed that the structure looked "like the crate that Faneuil Hall came in"; and an appeal from a number of prominent citizens, organized as the

Citizens' Committee for a Bostonian City Hall, complained that the design was "thoroughly lacking in composition, scale, and architectural feeling," and had absolutely no regard for "the background and environment" in which it would exist.[12] Other critics labeled it "terribly confused," "a hodgepodge," a "Cheops Tomb," a "pigeon cage," and a "Chinese pagoda," while *Horizon* magazine, a publication devoted to architecture, remarked that its style ranged from "WPA post-office colonial" all the way to "Neo-Fascist Federal."[13] But there was no turning back. Despite the storm of controversy created by the modernistic design, Collins and Logue pushed on with their plans for a new City Hall and a new Government Center as a small but essential part of a truly New Boston that would eventually encompass the entire city.

The Prudential Center, the Central Artery, the Boston Common underground garage, and now the Government Center—all finally under way after years of painful and frustrating delay. But these were all Hynes's projects; everybody knew that. Collins and Logue brought them to completion, it is true, but weren't they just carrying out someone else's ideas, finishing off someone else's plans? What about Collins himself? What did he have to offer the city? What was Logue's contribution to be? Why had he been brought up from New Haven? Why was he needed? These, in fact, had been some of the questions Ed Logue himself asked when he first arrived in Boston early in 1960 and looked around the old city. After a few days, he had gone back to Collins in obvious discouragement and said: "Mr. Mayor, there's nothing here for me. There's no job. There's no program. There's no nothing."[14]

In a way, he was right. It is true that urban renewal had begun to take place under John Hynes—some new buildings, a major real estate development, some public housing. But the young city planner saw immediately that those enterprises had been undertaken in piecemeal fashion, largely as responses to specific problems, with inadequate federal funding, few professional designers, and little relationship to any comprehensive plan or model. John Collins had come in with a much more sweeping vision of what a contemporary urban renewal program entailed, however, and one of the reasons he brought Logue up from New Haven was to take what was already on the drawing board and fit it into a more elaborate and far-ranging urban landscape. The surrounding neighborhoods were to be an essential part of that landscape, and he wanted Logue to consider ways in which the entire Boston area, not just the downtown locations, could be developed as complementary parts of a new and modern metropolis. Logue finally agreed that he would stay a while longer as a consultant and conduct a "survey," but it was clear that at this point he did not expect dramatic results.[15]

Because he really did not know Boston very well, Logue spent the next few weeks walking—wandering through the Public Garden and Boston Common; trudging up Beacon Hill; finding the route to Sullivan Square in Charlestown; making his way across to City Square. "I didn't just walk," he said. "I talked. I listened. I learned." In the course of his meanderings, he saw the obvious problems of the city—the lack of new buildings, the shortage of housing, the absence of enthusiasm in a place that had "very little confidence in itself." At the same time, however, he also began to notice that behind those problems Boston was unique, a "walking city in a very special way, like no other in this country." For all its problems, he had to admit that Boston had a certain distinctive character and a number of definite advantages. It had a walkable downtown area, it had established residential communities, it had a series of traditional ethnic neighborhoods, its housing stock was basically sound, and it had an established mass transit system. "It was a place without much spark," he observed, "but the stars were right for a great leap forward."[16]

For the next few months, Logue continued his walks around the city, became more familiar with the outlying neighborhoods as well as the downtown area, spent long nights analyzing documents and reports at City Hall, consulted with Mayor Collins, and conferred at length with the planning director Donald Graham and his city planning staff. On April 12 he participated in a session of the Citizen Seminar at Boston College devoted to the subject of urban renewal, where he aired some of his preliminary ideas and perceptions, and by June he was ready to start putting together a development program of his own that was both ambitious and comprehensive. A former World War II bomber pilot, Logue confronted his responsibilities to the future with sentiments similar to those recalled in similar circumstances by Clark Clifford in his memoirs: "Liberals like me thought the postwar world required us to address many long-deferred problems, from race to education to housing and better working conditions."[17] Insisting a quarter of a century later that he was still an "old-fashioned, dyed-in-the-wool, Franklin D. Roosevelt, New-Deal liberal," Logue assumed his responsibilities firmly committed to the ideal of an enlightened government activism that would improve the quality of life for all citizens. Calling to mind the advice that the celebrated architect Daniel H. Burnham had once given him years earlier—"Make no little plans, they have no power to stir men's blood"—he was determined to come up with a plan that would be on a scale large enough to "make some difference."[18]

In conceptualizing his own ideas, and perhaps either consciously or unconsciously influenced by Burnham's famous Plan of Chicago, which was composed of six main items, Logue formulated a plan that would be based on six major principles: (1) the plan would have to be both comprehensive and action-oriented; (2) it would require a great deal of money; (3) it would require a highly qualified professional staff; (4) it would require the support of both political and civic leadership; (5) it would require a new and more imaginative administrative organization; and (6) it would require the creation of a new and powerful post of development administrator. Logue outlined his plans to the mayor at the mayor's Myrtle Street home, at an informal meeting attended by Collins, Don Graham, and Carl Gilbert of Gillette's. When Logue finished with the presentation of his plan, Collins exclaimed: "Hell, I could have come up with that myself!" Rather than being upset at this, Logue took the remark to mean that with his swift mind and quick perception Collins instantly comprehended the nature of the plan and understood its practical applications.[19]

On September 22, 1960, Mayor Collins publicly announced a dramatic "Ninety Million Dollar Development Program for Boston." The plan, prepared by Logue but approved and presented by the mayor, was based on the conviction that the government would take an active leadership role in developing the city. It projected an ambitious program of urban renewal that proposed to rehabilitate a quarter of the entire acreage of Boston, an area housing half the city's entire population. The mayor proposed to rebuild the city under ten separate plans encompassing not only all of downtown Boston but also such surrounding neighborhoods as Charlestown and the South End, as well as South Boston, East Boston, Roxbury, Jamaica Plain, and the Parker Hill–Fenway area. Anticipating an estimated $60 million in federal funds, along with the city's share of $30 million over six years, the program was designed to eliminate slums, reduce blight, improve public housing, build schools, establish more efficient traffic patterns, and assist neighborhood social, civic, and educational organizations. Painfully conscious of the frightening West End experience, which was still fresh in the minds of many communities, Collins and Logue went out of their way to emphasize that their program would be planned in consultation "with the people who live in those communities," and pointed out that they would be taking a "rehabilitation" approach instead of resorting to "the bulldozer." In discussing future improvements in the North End, for example, an area uncomfortably close to the West End, Collins acknowledged that that historic neighborhood had "a flavor and a way of life which should be preserved, not destroyed." Any kind of "clearance" project would be "an outrage," he wrote. "The City would never be the same."[20]

No American city had ever committed so much cash to urban renewal at one time. Yet the question, Collins insisted, was not whether Boston could afford to spend the money, but whether it could afford not to. "Too much of Boston's greatness lies in the past," he said. Now the city had more of its share of "slums and blights," and that decay was "sapping the great strength and beauty, vitality and charm, which it still possesses in abundance." In outlining the various individual projects envisioned in his $90 million program, Collins was confident that he now had not only the blueprint for progressive change, but also the mechanism for putting such a program into effect. After the advisory opinion of the state supreme court earlier that year gave the go-ahead for special tax arrangements with Prudential, the state legislature had passed Chapter 121A, which gave the BRA expanded powers. Not only could the BRA plan and execute specific projects, but it could also act as a central agency to direct and coordinate the activities of the numerous other agencies that inevitably would be involved in the broadranging reconstruction of the city outlined in his program. Functioning as an overseer, the BRA now had exactly the authority Collins wanted for it. After all, who else was qualified to supervise? "Who, if not the City of Boston," the mayor asked, "is to coordinate the activities of the State Department of Public Works, the Turnpike Authority, the Port Authority, the MDC, and the railroads as they make their presently uncoordinated plans about what to do for Boston?"[21]

From the very outset of his campaign to transform the character of the city, Collins was careful to take influential community leaders into his confidence and make them an integral part of the process. Before Collins, one of the subtle yet significant changes John Hynes had introduced in the course of his ten years as mayor was the breaking down of the almost pathological hostility that had grown up between Irish politicians and members of the downtown business community—a bitter and adversarial relationship that had grown even worse during the years of Curley and his political supporters. Slowly and deliberately, Hynes had cultivated the friendship and support of leading members of the downtown elite, named them to prestigious positions, consulted with them frequently, and appointed them as members of special advisory commissions whenever complicated issues arose involving private interests and public policy. BRA director Kane Simonian regarded this as an important change in Boston's changing fortunes, and he praised the manner in which the mayor sought the advice of recognized leaders. "Hynes didn't go out and bring in stumblebums," he said. "He went out and brought in first-class people."[22]

Not only did Collins maintain those same types of personal relationships, but he also went on to work them into an even more formidable, though unofficial, part of municipal operations. Every other Thursday afternoon at four o'clock he met with Ralph Lowell, Charles Coolidge, Lloyd Brace, Carl Gilbert, and other influential members of the Boston Coordinating Committee (the Vault) in the boardroom of the Boston Safe Deposit and Trust Company on Franklin Street. He gave the merchants of Boston, through the Retail Trade Board, the responsibility of planning the central business district, and then worked closely with the members of the newly formed Central Business District Committee, having Edward Logue attend their meetings and assigning the deputy mayor, Richard Beattie, as full-time liaison. This committee was an association of downtown business and civic leaders that Edward R. Mitton of Jordan Marsh and Harold D. Hodgkinson of Filene's helped organize with a subsidy of more than half a million dollars. Headed by Charles Coolidge and working with a city planner, Victor Gruen, as consultant, the committee assumed the role of monitoring the overall design of business expansion in the downtown area, as well as making sure the traditional downtown shopping area remained where it was, in the light of new construction and potential competition developing in the Back Bay. The committee came to a unique agreement with the administration—a "memo of understanding" signed by Collins, Logue, and Coolidge—that no downtown project would be undertaken by the city unless it had the approval of the Central Business District Committee.[23]

Collins also responded to the anxieties of such prominent Bostoni-

ans as Walter Muir Whitehill of the Boston Athenaeum and Harriet
Ropes Cabot of the Bostonian Society, who feared that indiscriminate
demolition would destroy historic buildings in the Beacon Hill area.
Collins and Logue met with these people and helped form the Boston
Historic Conservation Committee, which would conduct surveys, make
reports, and provide valuable inventories of historic buildings, monuments, and sites. The information provided by the conservation committee was forwarded to a group of young "preservation planners" in the
office of the BRA, who used it to influence the movement toward
preserving entire streetscapes and districts rather than individual buildings and monuments.[24]

In this same mode of incorporating members of the community
into the decision-making process, Collins assigned to the Greater Boston
Chamber of Commerce, under the direction of Frank Christian of the
Merchants National Bank, the task of rehabilitating the dilapidated
waterfront area along Atlantic Avenue, as well as developing the old
Faneuil Hall district along with the adjoining open-air market. The
chamber of commerce went to work almost immediately, and on June
26, 1962, it held a large reception at the Sheraton Plaza hotel to unveil
models for an elaborate renewal project along the waterfront. The plans
proposed the realignment of Atlantic Avenue with pedestrian malls,
walkways, and a new state-of-the-art aquarium; the building of residential apartments and condominiums, with recreational and boating facilities; the removal of the wholesale food industry from the area and the
creation of sites for new office buildings along lower State Street; and
the rehabilitation of many old granite and brick warehouses and their
adaptation to new commercial purposes. The waterfront project would
demonstrate to the world, said Christian, that Boston was a city of
"great vitality and beauty." Collins agreed that the proposal demonstrated what a "united community can accomplish when the leadership
forces are working energetically and unselfishly toward common goals."
The following day, Logue made a public announcement expressing his
pleasure with the proposed waterfront project and assuring the chamber
of commerce that the BRA would proceed to file an application for
federal funding.[25]

In addition to cooperating with businessmen and financiers, Collins
also drew upon the expertise of those various professional and academic
groups that had shown an interest in urban development during the
Hynes years and that continued to demonstrate their concern with

current activities. He created an advisory committee of architects, drawn from the ranks of the Boston Society of Architects, with which Logue and the BRA consulted on "every one of our proposed buildings," and whose professional advice he sought on designs under consideration. "Their advice and, in my judgment, their mere existence," Logue wrote some years later, "raised the quality of the design."[26] Collins also benefited from the work of urban planners at Harvard and MIT; he participated actively in Citizen Seminar programs still going on at Boston College; and in an interesting development, he even asked the Harvard economist Arnold Soloway for a copy of the report that Soloway and a number of other prominent academicians had drawn up for Collins's rival, state senator John E. Powers, during the 1959 mayoral campaign. Not only did Collins receive a copy of the report, but according to one observer he actually incorporated many of the economic proposals in the plans of his subsequent administration.[27]

In looking for the right person to direct the overall operations of his sweeping program of urban renewal, Collins made no secret of his choice of Edward Logue to be his development administrator. Almost immediately, however, his decision struck a sour note among members of the board of the BRA, who seemed willing enough to work with this bright young man from New Haven, but who saw no reason why things could not continue as they had under their first director, Kane Simonian. The board was particularly alarmed by the extraordinary powers Logue demanded in addition to the title. He insisted that the board be allowed to approve or reject any of his plans, but not to change them, and that he himself be authorized to hire and fire the professional staff he needed without the tenure restrictions of the civil service system.[28] Such powers would so obviously undermine the powers board members had been exercising since 1957 that they dug in their heels and refused to go along.

Seeing that there was a "Boston political battle royal" in the making, Logue temporarily sidestepped a confrontation by proposing to serve as development administrator for a ninety-day trial period, during which time Simonian would continue as director. Logue insisted that at the end of that period either he be given full authority or he would leave the agency. "I made it clear," he wrote, "there would be no extension."[29] During the next ninety days, Logue and his staff worked day and night at "top speed" to get the outside funding they needed.

"My personal reputation for long hours and hard work really became established," Logue recalled, when early one morning he signed out of City Hall at 2:14 A.M. The night watchman took a look at the figures Logue put down and decided to play them in the numbers. Although they did not show up the next day, the following day they did, and at once "my name was talked about in every office in City Hall."[30]

Logue and his people pored over documents, collated statistics, prepared rough drafts, and prepared the cumbersome applications for federal funds, although he freely admitted that "any informed skeptic" would have been justified in believing that the federal government would never give Boston enough money "at one crack" to get such a large-scale operation off the ground. And Logue found a number of such skeptics sitting in the Boston City Council, including "one gentleman from South Boston" (chairman Bill Foley) who made it clear that he was "irreconcilable" in his opposition to all aspects of the program. Nevertheless, Logue made out his applications, applied to the "Feds," made telephone calls, had lunch with regional officers, and then accompanied Mayor Collins to New York for a meeting with the "head Fed himself," David Walker, head of the Urban Renewal Administration for Housing and Home Finance.[31]

Logue's strategy worked: "The mayor came home with the bacon." Logue's painstaking preparations, his professional contacts, and his successful track record in New Haven helped persuade the Urban Renewal Administration to allocate nearly $30 million for Boston. "The money was in the bank," he exclaimed with obvious delight. "Almost no one believed it could happen."[32] The federal government's willingness to set aside such an amount of money at a time when capital grant funds were becoming scarce was "a rare and striking tribute to the Mayor, the Redevelopment Authority, the City Council, and to a united community's support for a major building effort," Logue reported. He felt that the accomplishment gave special recognition to "the seriousness of Boston's situation and of its historic importance in the life of our nation."[33]

The remaining question now was: "Could we get a mandate to begin?" To help generate the kind of popular mandate he felt was essential to the success of the program, Logue called a public meeting in the historic Old South Meeting House on Washington Street, to which he invited not only the prominent business, professional, and financial leaders of the downtown area but also representative community leaders

from Charlestown, the South End, Roxbury, and other residential neighborhoods. "It was a most unusual gathering, and filled the ancient hall,"
wrote Logue, who took much satisfaction from the subsequent support
the mayor's new program received from the press and from television.
"The program was launched and on its way," he declared.[34]

As far as his own official position was concerned, Logue was more
convinced than ever, especially after the ninety days of frantic activity
getting federal funding, that it was absolutely crucial for him to get the
necessary authority to run the program or else "the venture would not
be worthwhile." He insisted that either he get the appointment and the
extraordinary powers he wanted, or he would leave Boston. "I'll turn
this city upside down if they try to screw around with me," he told the
Globe's Tom Winship. Because he had recently been contacted by a
member of the new Kennedy administration and asked to consider a
position as an urban renewal administrator, Logue felt more confident
than ever about his nonnegotiable demands. A majority of the five-man
BRA board, however, still did not see the necessity of changing the
structure of the organization and refused to accept Mayor Collins's
decision to put Logue in overall command as development administrator. When some BRA members raised questions about the legality of
lowering Kane Simonian in rank in order to make way for Logue,
Collins insisted that he wasn't lowering Simonian, he was simply putting
Logue above him. "When we decided to make five-star generals in World
War II," he argued, "it didn't lower the rank of the four-star generals."[35]

Only a short time before the date of the BRA board meeting at
which the vote would be taken on his appointment, Logue received a
telephone call asking him to come to a meeting of the Boston Coordinating Committee. He chartered a plane, flew from New Haven to
Boston, and arrived at the offices of the Boston Safe Deposit and Trust
Company on Franklin Street, where the members of the Vault were
waiting. They had obviously been informed about the upcoming vote
and were interested in learning more about Logue and the powers he
demanded as administrator. Logue told them how he had developed his
plans, had acquired the $28 million in federal money to put those plans
into effect, and had his staff ready and eager to go. Still, he insisted,
either he got everything he had specified, or he would go to Washington
and take a job in the Kennedy administration. The job in Boston was his
first choice, and if given the appointment he would turn down the
Washington job and stay in Boston. Asked about divisions within the

board, Logue said that Monsignor Lally was a good friend and loyal supporter who would give him his vote, and that real estate man Joseph Lund would undoubtedly vote in his favor. Jim Colbert, former political editor of the *Boston Post* who had pretty much had his way in directing the affairs of the board, would definitely vote against the new appointment. Colbert, said Logue, was "a piece of work"—"he didn't like me and I didn't like him." And Steve McCloskey, the labor union man, would follow Colbert's lead, as he always did. The swing vote, Logue told the Vault members, was Mel Massucco, Governor Furcolo's appointee, who often voted with Colbert and McCloskey. As photo editor with the *Record-American* newspaper, Massucco was regarded as having neither the prestige nor the power that Colbert had at the *Post*. At that point, according to Logue, having laid before the members of the Vault the situation as he saw it, he stood up, said his goodbyes, and left the meeting.

On January 25, 1961, the BRA board held its scheduled meeting. As expected, Lund and Lally voted in favor of making Logue the administrator; Colbert and McCloskey voted against him. The tie was broken when Massucco voted in favor of Logue. "Who got to him, when they got to him, how they got to him, I don't know to this day," professed Logue. "All I know is that the vote came out three to two in my favor."[36] Considering the close personal relationship that he had developed with the mayor, it is almost impossible to believe that Logue never learned what happened. The answer was not that difficult. After the meeting with Logue, Mayor Collins had simply put in a telephone call to Hap Kern, publisher of the *Record American* and Massucco's boss, and that was that.[37]

As development administrator, Logue was now responsible only to the mayor and the BRA board, which could accept or reject his proposals, but could not change them. He had the authority to propose and execute renewal plans, develop comprehensive plans for the city, propose capital improvements for all municipal departments, hire and fire staff, and set salaries for new personnel without regard to civil service tenure. Collins and Logue now had the administrative mechanism they wanted to launch their Ninety Million Dollar Development Program for the city.[38]

Pushing ahead with speed and determination, Logue took immediate steps to move the Government Center project from the theory of the

*A view of Dock Square in the mid-1920s showing Odin's Block (center) and Bendall's Lane Block (behind), with Devonshire and Exchange streets entering at right, and Washington Street on the left. At the rear right is Faneuil Hall, with the central market building barely visible at the outer edge of the photograph. This was a portion of Scollay Square that was eventually cleared for the construction of Boston's new Government Center. Courtesy of The Bostonian Society.*

drawing board to the reality of concrete and steel. Logue had promised the citizens of Boston that the new approach to urban renewal during the Collins administration would be more competent and more sensitive and would involve more discussion with the residents. Few of those characteristics were apparent in his approach to the wholesale clearing out of the old Scollay Square district to make way for the new Government Center. Even though the project had not yet received formal approval from the Boston City Council, in February 1962 the bulldozers came rumbling in, the streets were torn up, and small businesses dutifully packed up and moved out in advance of the wrecking ball that smashed down one block after another in scenes painfully reminiscent of what had happened in the West End only a few years earlier.

"Perhaps most ironic was the plight of several hundred families who had moved into the Scollay Square project after being kicked out of the West End," wrote David Kruh. Receiving only two hundred dollars for moving expenses, almost half the families evicted from Scollay Square moved to such cities as Medford and Somerville, north of Boston. In an effort to rescue at least one historical site from demolition, Francis W. Hatch, of the Harvard class of 1919, and a group of fans had formed an organization known as the Howard National Theater and Museum Committee, asking the city to save the Old Howard and convert it into a performing-arts center where operas and plays could be presented. Although Logue was dubious about its prospects for survival, he recognized that the boarded-up burlesque house did have "a sentimental hold on an earlier generation of Bostonians," encouraged the committee to submit a formal proposal, and even had I. M. Pei's firm sketch a design for a restored theater "in the best Boston tradition."[39]

The question of the theater's survival became moot, however, when a three-alarm fire "of undetermined origin" burst out in the Old Howard about noontime on June 25, 1961. Engine Company Number 4 responded promptly; a second alarm was sounded to combat the blaze; and by the time the fire chief arrived on the scene, a third and final alarm had been sounded. Despite the efforts of men and equipment from fifteen engine and seven ladder companies, the fire swept through the interior and left only the charred remains of the granite facade, which was torn down that same day. Many fans suspected foul play, the head of the restoration committee thought it "incredible" that the fire should happen at that particular moment, and Frank Hatch wrote a bit of verse that closed with: "Some Coward / Closed the Old Howard. / We don't have Burley any more." Even Logue could see the possibilities: "It's the only time in my life I've ever been accused of arson," he wrote. "I plead innocent."[40]

If some Bostonians failed to save the Old Howard from what appeared to them to be the indiscriminate and insensitive onslaught of the BRA's heavy equipment, some other Bostonians had better luck with another part of the district that was threatened by the direction in which the new Government Center project was moving. On the south side of what would become City Hall Plaza was a curved, red-brick building that had been constructed in 1841 and named for the Yankee merchant and developer David Sears. The Sears Crescent Building was not only a historic monument in its own right but also a landmark that defined the path that Cornhill Street took when that famous street was first laid out in 1816 by the developer Uriah Cotting. Cornhill enjoyed a glorious history as the location of William Lloyd Garrison's publication *The Liberator*, the focal point of thirty years of abolitionist agitation before the Civil War, and in more recent times the renowned center of antique books and secondhand bookstores in Boston.[41]

Rumors that the Sears Crescent was to be torn down and old Cornhill Street removed from sight sent many prominent Bostonians into paroxysms of rage. Kane Simonian recalls one morning when the door to his Tremont Street office burst open and in stalked the eminent Boston historian Walter Muir Whitehill, his face florid, his great white beard bristling. "How *dare* you destroy that old and venerable building!" he roared. "How dare you tear down the Sears Crescent!" With that, he went on to denounce Simonian, the BRA, the mayor of Boston, and anyone else who would dare to think of demolishing one of the great historical landmarks of Boston. Simonian at length explained to Whitehill that he had nothing to do with that kind of decision—that it was entirely in Ed Logue's hands—and at that point, he recalled, "Whitehill put on his hat, stormed through the door, and was off to the City Hall Annex to see Logue himself."[42] According to Thomas Boylston Adams, Whitehill subsequently closeted himself for hours with several cigar-chewing "pols" in the old City Hall, fighting to convince them that saving the Sears block would preserve "that essential link between the past and the future" that had made Boston such a distinctive city.[43]

Delegations visited the mayor, committees descended on the BRA, and floods of letters poured into city hall, such as that from one gentleman who expressed alarm that the famous Brattle Bookshop, "caught squarely in the path of the razing crews now restive in Scollay Square," would eventually be demolished by the "seemingly irresistible juggernaut of progress." While he agreed that the idea of the Government Center in general was "good for Boston," he pleaded with city authorities to show some discrimination: "We ask you, Mayor Collins, to take a strong stand at Cornhill," he wrote, closing with the cry: "*Vive la Brattle Bookshop!*"[44]

This was one time when the popular voice was heard, and the city backed down. "At my request, the Redevelopment Authority staff has completed a feasibility study for the rehabilitation of the Sears Crescent on Cornhill," wrote Mayor John Collins, expressing the hope that "it will be possible to retain this building."[45] Despite alterations that had to be made in the original design ("I wish I had known this was historically significant," complained the architect I. M. Pei. "It will cost thousands to change the plans now"), the plans were changed and the Sears Crescent was saved, refurbished, and made an integral part of the project. Logue eventually conceded that in many ways the Sears Crescent would be a "ready made link between the past and the present." Its height and mass would complement many of the other large buildings in the Government Center project, while its red brick facade would enhance the red brick paving planned for the plaza of the City Hall.[46]

As he worked out the general configurations of the Government Center location, Logue determined that it was essential to create an open area around the Old State House at the head of State Street. Not only would such a space prevent one of the city's most beautiful and historic buildings from being completely overshadowed by the high-rise

*This aerial view of Boston's new Government Center, taken from the Custom House tower, dramatizes the contrast between the traditional architecture of Faneuil Hall in the foreground and the modernistic designs of the new City Hall directly in the rear, and the more recent John F. Kennedy federal office building to the right. Some Bostonians criticize the new architecture as being incompatible with neighboring buildings. Others argue that the differences add refreshing contrasts to the Boston landscape. Photograph © 1991 by Peter Vanderwarker.*

office buildings going up in the surrounding financial district, but it would also provide for a safer and more efficient flow of traffic in that congested area where Congress, Court, Devonshire, and State streets converged. For this reason, in a highly controversial decision denounced by his city council critics as a "sweetheart deal," Logue proposed demolishing two buildings on three-quarters of an acre at the corner of State and New Congress streets, a site known as Parcel 8, in order to create some breathing space around the Old State House. On the remaining site, set back fifty feet from State Street in a landscaped area, he proposed a thirty- to forty-story privately financed office tower that would reportedly yield twice the current rate of tax money to the city as the two previous structures.[47]

The idea of bringing more tax money into the city's coffers from private investment was an indispensable part of Collins's urban development program, as it had been with Hynes's earlier efforts to bring in outside developers and promote commercial investment. Like the new Prudential tower and the War Memorial Auditorium in the Back Bay, the projected federal, state, and city structures in the Government Center complex would provide a series of brand-new buildings to enhance the nondescript Boston landscape. It was also hoped that, like dropping the pebble into the proverbial pool, the new buildings would create a prosperous ripple effect. The prospect of such impressive new structures would be bound to attract other enterprises—hotels, banks, law offices, insurance companies, corporate offices, apartment houses, condominiums—that would not only bring in substantial new tax revenues on their own but also spin off various supplementary enterprises—restaurants, clothing stores, pharmacies, boutiques, specialty shops, bookstores, computer centers—that in turn would be bound to upgrade many run-down parts of the city, provide new sources of employment, and raise personal incomes.

Already there were encouraging signs that private investors were becoming excited about what was happening in the city and tentatively exploring ways of taking part in the transformation. As the Prudential tower and the massive War Memorial Auditorium began to go up on the site of the old abandoned railroad yards along lower Boylston Street, for example, the Sheraton Corporation, seeing the opportunities that increased tourism and enlarged convention groups would bring, proceeded with plans for an adjoining twenty-nine-story Sheraton Boston hotel. Located directly behind the Prudential project, the First Church of Christ Scientist caught the "contagion of improvement" and in 1963 approached Logue and the BRA requesting assistance in improving the area surrounding its Mother Church, whose impressive architectural features had been obscured for many years by unflattering boarding-houses, neighborhood stores, and third-rate movie theaters. After discussions, the church retained the services of I. M. Pei's firm to conduct a planning study of some thirty acres in the Huntington Avenue and Massachusetts Avenue areas, promising to integrate the church's development efforts with the BRA's long-range plans.[48]

Across the city, in the Scollay Square area, the pace of commercial development was starting out much more slowly. It became fashionable in later years to suggest cynically that urban renewal was largely motivated by the prospects of profitable real estate investments. The future building boom that would develop in Boston during the 1970s and 1980s should not be allowed to color the events of the 1950s and 1960s, however. From all accounts, nobody wanted to invest in Boston during these years. Companies had to be persuaded to invest—lured, seduced, and cajoled by any means possible. The people at Prudential, for example, had to be continually reassured lest they lose interest in the Back Bay site and take their business elsewhere. Jerome Rappaport had a difficult time finding a local institution that would even underwrite his financing for the West End project. Twenty years later, it is true, developers would compete for opportunities to invest in the burgeoning city—but that was only after the New Boston had established itself as a viable enterprise in the late 1960s and early 1970s.

The BRA had projected a major office building directly across from the new City Hall, but local developers were still extremely hesitant about investing their money in a Boston enterprise. Finally, Dorchester-born Norman B. Leventhal entered the picture and agreed to take on the assignment. A product of the Boston Latin School and a graduate of MIT, where he earned an engineering degree, Norman and his brother, Robert, had gone into the contracting business and eventually built the Beacon Construction Company into a going concern.[49] "The Leventhal firm took it when no one else would," according to Logue, and started work on a long, low, crescent-shaped structure that would eventually separate Government Center on the west from the Suffolk County Courthouse on Pemberton Square.[50] Developed by the Leventhals, designed by Welton Becket and Associates, and constructed by the Beacon Construction Company, the project was divided into three separate

204 BUILDING A NEW BOSTON

phases, showing that even at this point the developer was uncertain about the success of the Government Center itself. As each of the three units was completed, the construction firm put up a "TO BE CONTINUED" sign on the building's blank wall for passersby to read as they watched the project slowly swing along from Bowdoin Square to Tremont Street. Constructed of red brick and gray granite, One, Two, and Three Center Plaza complemented the graceful arc of the Sears Crescent to the south and blended in with the coloration of the new City Hall and its expansive brick plaza, making it, in Logue's words, "a handsome background building, nicely linking Beacon Hill and its new neighbors."[51]

As time went on, private investors gradually became more confident about the commercial possibilities of a New Boston, and began making plans to participate in the city's renovation. A group of British investors, Boston British Properties, Inc., undertook construction of a thirty-four-story office building on nearby Franklin Street, and when the State Street Bank and Trust Company moved into the lower floors it gave its name to the new structure. The firm of Cabot, Cabot, and Forbes took over construction of the forty-story New England Merchants National Bank building at 28 State Street, on the controversial Parcel 8 site, and a short time later began work on another forty-story tower on Washington Street at the head of State Street for the Boston Safe Deposit and Trust Company, to be known as the Boston Company building. The First National Bank would build itself a thirty-seven-story tower on the corner of Franklin and Federal streets, and the National Shawmut Bank began planning a building at the corner of Franklin, Federal, and Devonshire streets, thus making historian Walter Muir Whitehill confident that this particular area of Boston would continue to maintain its traditional reputation as "the financial center of Boston."[52] As the waterfront project began to take shape at the foot of State Street, two luxury apartment towers, an office building, and a parking garage were being designed by I. M. Pei in the area of India Wharf. Close by, the New England Telephone Company anticipated building a large office structure, while the Employers Group Life Insurance Company had similar plans.[53]

Even local civic groups began catching the contagion of renewal when word got around that the famous Old Corner Book Store on the corner of School and Washington streets was in danger of being torn down because of its scandalously neglected condition. John Codman, chairman of the Beacon Hill Architectural Commission, organized an

Old Corner Committee to develop plans to purchase and restore this singular example of early eighteenth-century architecture. Collins, declaring that "a City's future is but a logical extension of its past," gave his personal encouragement to the group's efforts, as did Logue and the BRA. Considerable funds were raised, and the old building was eventually restored as a functioning bookstore, with the *Boston Globe* renting offices on the second floor. Here was a small but exciting example of how a famous structure could be preserved as a historic site and still function as a self-sufficient commercial venture that paid taxes to the city.[54]

The new construction in downtown Boston, tangible signs of progress and success, obviously gave Mayor Collins great personal satisfaction as well as professional pride, and so on June 24, 1963, he announced his candidacy for reelection to a second term as mayor of Boston, asking the voters to retain him in office for another four years "so that together we may complete the job we have started." Using an efficient staff, a carefully designed set of strategies, and some fairly sophisticated political surveys,[55] Collins built his campaign around the major achievements of his first four years. He pointed out that he had produced four successive tax cuts, which had brought the tax rate down from $101.20, when he first took office, to the present rate of $96.00. In the process, he had also reduced the city budget 3 percent, at a time when state and federal budgets were on the rise. Furthermore, he emphasized, as a result of his ambitious urban renewal program he had promoted a vast building boom that brought in an anticipated $2 billion in new construction, created thousands of new jobs, and greatly increased family income. He made a special appeal to Boston's elderly voters, reminding them that he had initiated a program of housing for the elderly, and that he had come out in support of President Kennedy's Medicare bill.

Collins also courted business support, and in a special letter seeking financial contributions he cautioned members of the business community that if they did not actively support him, no future mayor would consider it "politically feasible" to cut expenditures and run a "clean government." Strong financial backing at the very outset from people interested in "good government," he argued, would allow him to avoid political commitments, reduce campaign costs, and continue programs for the betterment of the city. Pointing to his recovery of Boston's "lost reputation" and creation of a "new face for Boston" that had been recognized by *Look* magazine in April 1963 when it had named Boston as one of eleven "All-American" cities, he listed the new public and private structures already under construction, and some of the new projects scheduled for the future. "LET'S FINISH THE JOB" read the headline on a slick campaign flier that showed Collins being sworn in, in August 1963 in Houston, Texas, as president of the American Municipal Association.[56]

Running against Collins in the September primary were four other candidates, including two city councillors—Gabriel Piemonte and Patrick ("Sonny") McDonough—a local representative, Julius Ansel, and a man named William P. Foley, who obviously hoped to capitalize on the name of the popular incumbent city councillor William J. Foley, Jr. It was assumed that McDonough could count on a strong following in the South Boston wards that had supported Collins's old rival, senate president John E. Powers; Piemonte, by contrast, was expected to draw heavy support from the predominantly Italian-American districts in the North End and East Boston. Both men attacked Collins for going too far in his renewal program, cutting essential services to the citizens, neglecting to provide housing for people who had lost their homes, and making "sweetheart deals" with wealthy private investors. Despite those charges, Collins maintained considerable strength across the city, and in the September primary took seventeen of the city's twenty-two wards, with Piemonte emerging as his November opponent. Piemonte took his second-place win as a sign of success, and in a hoarse voice promised his supporters at an election-night rally at the Parker House that they would all "march on to victory" in November. Meeting with his own people at his Province Street headquarters across from City Hall, Collins expressed his gratitude to the people of Boston for his impressive showing, calling it a "people's campaign and a people's victory."[57]

During October the tempo of the campaign stepped up considerably, focusing not so much on the mayoral race (which many virtually conceded to Collins after his strong performance in the primary) as on the races for the city council and the school committee. Support for Collins and his urban renewal programs in the nine-member city council was razor-thin, and the election of even a single candidate, one way or the other, could make the difference between success or failure for the Government Center project. Up to this point the mayor had been able to count on only four "sure" votes—from council president Peter Hines, Christopher Ianella, James Coffey, and Frederick Langone. Five others had stood steadfastly against him—Bill Foley, Johnny Kerrigan, Gabriel Piemonte, Sonny McDonough, and John Tierney—and even now were holding up final approval of the Government Center. With Piemonte and McDonough running for mayor and therefore out of the council race, the November election was crucial. Writing a front-page editorial in the *Boston Globe* on Monday, November 4, the day before the election, Robert Healy came out with a virtual endorsement of Collins, spelling out the importance of the council race and its implications for Collins's programs. "Boston progress" is the issue in the campaign, he wrote, and "the city's economic life depends on it."[58]

The school committee race also generated a great deal of excitement, over the appointment of a new superintendent of schools as well as over accusations by the National Association for the Advancement of Colored People that the Boston school system was guilty of de facto segregation. The chairwoman of the school committee, Louise Day Hicks of South Boston, campaigned vigorously in favor of the traditional neighborhood school system and refused to acknowledge the NAACP's charges. Mrs. Hicks had already shown herself an impressive vote-getter in the September primary, getting the support of sixty-three of every one hundred voters, and was obviously planning to demonstrate the same level of support in November.

Collins's well-oiled machine moved ahead with its organized system of telephone calls, letters, bumper stickers, buttons, fliers, and posters, with Collins himself making effective use of radio and television slots. At no time during the campaign did he appear on the same platform with his opponent, Piemonte, and he judiciously ignored the charges, coming out of mimeographed neighborhood newsletters, that Collins and his "liberal" supporters had not only produced a "communist and socialist" interference with the rights of the city but had also shown themselves sympathetic to the "agitation of Negroes" who were being used for "Communist aims and purposes." Urban renewal, they claimed, was "the Curse of Boston" because it violated the Constitution and the Bill of Rights and benefited only "private developers" at the expense of ordinary taxpayers.[59] This rhetoric was typical of a growing feeling of anger and resentment that was coming out of several blue-collar neighborhoods against investors, developers, speculators, liberals, social reformers, do-gooders, and "outsiders" coming into their working-class communities, tearing down their family houses, putting up high-rise luxury apartments, and threatening to change the traditional character of their life and society.

Against this rising tide of local dissatisfaction, the campaign finally came to a close on Monday night, November 4, with the usual windup festivities. Collins forces staged a huge rally at the Mary E. Curley School in Jamaica Plain, where crowds of workers and well-wishers cheered their candidate lustily; Piemonte's friends and supporters held an equally impressive rally in front of Burden's Drug Store on Hanover Street in the North End. After that, as many as possible traveled over to Mattapan for the traditional midnight rally in front of the G & G Delicatessen, where both candidates made final appearances.[60]

The next day, Tuesday, November 5, John Collins swept the boards, taking nineteen of the twenty-two wards in the city and defeating Piemonte by a vote of 107,617 to 72,842—a plurality of 34,775 votes.[61] But it was Louise Day Hicks who was the top vote-getter in the city, getting nearly 20,000 more votes than Collins and making certain that the incoming school committee reflected the view of most the city's white voters that their school system should remain unchanged. While the outcome of the city council contest was close, with the election of Catherine Craven of Hyde Park providing another antirenewal vote for Foley and Kerrigan, observers felt that the election of Barry T. Hynes (the son of former mayor John B. Hynes) and the attorney George F. Foley would provide the decisive measure of support Collins needed. The Globe's Robert Healy told readers that the election had given Collins a "go signal" for his program for a New Boston, although he recognized that the margin in the council was still "thin." Collins himself felt comfortable with his victory, and believed that his solid 60 percent majority over Piemonte was proof that the people of Boston wanted to keep their city "going in a forward direction as a first class city, a first rate city."[62]

Now that the campaign was over and he was safely reelected to another four years in office, Collins could relax for a while, enjoy the company of his family, attend a few parties and dinners, catch up on the flood of letters and congratulatory telegrams that had poured in, including a thoughtful note from Lady Bird Johnson thanking Mary and John Collins for their hospitality when she and Vice President Lyndon B. Johnson had recently visited Boston. Like everyone else, the Collins family began to make preparations for the upcoming holiday season. Thanksgiving was only a few weeks away, and the downtown stores were already decorating their windows for their annual Christmas displays. Suddenly, on the afternoon of November 22, 1963, the sounds of Yuletide carols were violently choked off by the tragic news of the assassination of President John F. Kennedy. Bostonians everywhere seemed too shocked to believe and accept the horrifying details out of Dallas, Texas, that came over their television screens and their radios. "Boston was a stunned city," wrote the mayor's press secretary, "a city of deep deep sorrow." As mayor, Collins immediately ordered the cancellation of all municipal functions. "Does that include the Christmas Festival?" he was asked. "Until the thirty-day period of mourning has ended, it most certainly does," he responded.

In front of City Hall, Christmas decorations that had been put up only that morning were taken down. Where a few hours earlier every window in the building had been ablaze with lights, now those same windows were plunged into darkness as electricians went from office to office removing the installations. Through the medium of television, which made the details of the tragedy all the more poignant, Bostonians joined millions of other American families as they watched the president's casket borne by caisson to Saint Matthew's Cathedral, where the funeral Mass was said by Cardinal Cushing, after which the somber cortege made its way to Arlington National Cemetery, where an eternal flame was lit. Waiting an appropriate and respectful period of time after the funeral, Mayor Collins finally gave permission to start the 1963 Christmas Festival, with the provision that activities be kept within the limitations imposed by the knowledge of the city's "tremendous spiritual loss."[63] It was ironic that a year that had started out with so much hope and accomplishment should have ended with so much grief and pain.

# 8

# Progress and Populism

On January 6, 1964, John F. Collins was sworn in for a second four-year term as mayor of Boston. Seated in his wheelchair on the stage of Symphony Hall, he took the oath of office according to the traditional ceremonies, but then caught the packed audience of three-thousand listeners by surprise with an inaugural address that was nothing less than a blistering attack on Governor Endicott Peabody and the leaders of state government for being "grossly inadequate" in their responsibilities "not only to Boston, but to all cities and towns in the Commonwealth." Frequently interrupted by applause, Collins blasted state house officials for handing out some $20 million in pay raises while ignoring the pressing needs of the city of Boston. Boston schools received only 8 percent of their total costs from the state, he pointed out, and he blamed the state for doing nothing to help ease the critical transportation crisis or to come up with alternative tax proposals. While Boston was busy cutting taxes and holding down budgets, the state was going "merrily along the road to its own fiscal disaster," not only spending all its own money but also dipping into funds earmarked for the cities and towns.

"For an inaugural speech, it was a scorcher," wrote Joseph Keblinsky in the *Boston Globe*, while Robert Healy offered the interesting speculation that Collins's attack against Chub Peabody was actually a tip-off that Collins already had his eye on 1966. In two years, Healy suggested, Collins would be looking at two options—either challenging Peabody for a four-year term as governor, or considering a six-year term as United States senator if Leverett Saltonstall decided to retire.[1] Senate president John E. Powers saw Collins's outburst in more simple and pragmatic terms, however, and declared the mayor's angry speech as nothing more than "the beginning of a sales tax drive." Defending Peabody for having done an "outstanding job" as governor, Powers said that Collins should not complain about the "financial fix" of Boston if he had no solution of his own. Insisting that he was not speaking as a "political antagonist," Powers criticized the mayor for "overextending himself" by attacking the governor and the state legislature.[2]

Seeming to enjoy thoroughly the furor he had created with his inaugural address, Collins prepared to take up where he had left off and get the Government Center project off the ground. Fresh from his easy victory at the polls, he had every right to expect that a new and more friendly city council would finally give him the formal approval of the $200 million Government Center that the council had denied him by a five-to-four vote on two previous occasions. Suddenly, however, an unexpected turn of events brought him up sharply and reminded him of the peculiar vagaries of Boston politics. In the course of a public hearing in the council early in May 1964, Councillor Frederick Langone jumped to his feet when he learned of a proposed new ramp from the Central Artery that would exit in front of the mouths of the two East Boston tunnels, run along Cross Street, empty into the already congested Haymarket Square, and in the process work an inconvenience on his family's undertaking parlor on Hanover Street in the city's North End. "I am certainly not going to go along with that ramp," Langone protested loudly, and thereupon withdrew his support from the whole Government Center project.[3] Langone's announcement threw the city council meeting into a turmoil that went on until Councillor Catherine Craven, an ardent foe of the project, scooped up her papers, got to her feet, and announced: "This is the end. I can tell you how I'm going to vote"—and walked out of the hall.[4]

After weeks of discussion, debate, and private manipulations, on May 26 the Boston City Council finally gave its formal approval of the Government Center in a five-to-four vote in which Langone agreed to go along with Peter Hines, Christopher Ianella, Barry Hynes, and Bill Foley in support of the mayor—possibly mollified by Edward Logue's offer to Langone's brother, Joseph, of a "very desirable location" for his funeral parlor, then located on Merrimac Street. The new parcel of seventy-five hundred square feet would be on Hawkins Street, directly across from the welfare building and the Boston Edison substation, and according to Logue could accommodate a two- or three-story building with adjoining parking space.[5]

After Collins signed the measure, the matter went to the appropriate federal agencies for their approval, despite a pending lawsuit by owners of the office building taken over by eminent domain on Parcel 8.[6] Critics of Parcel 8 had brought suit against Logue and the Boston Redevelopment Authority, asking the court to cancel the votes of Hynes and Foley and to disqualify Langone because of a conflict of interest involving the family funeral business. On July 24, however, Superior Court Judge Felix Forte denied a request for an injunction, and the following day BRA officials, with a federal loan-and-grant in hand of more than $65 million for the Government Center project, took possession of the office building at 10 State Street and brought the bitter Parcel 8 controversy to a virtual close.[7]

Certainly a great source of personal satisfaction as well as a formal tribute to the civic accomplishments of John Collins came in June 1964 when Harvard University made him the recipient of an honorary doctor of laws degree, the first twentieth-century Boston mayor to be so honored. Hailing John Frederick Collins as a "courageous rebuilder of an old Boston," the citation declared that his leadership as mayor "had given Boston a new spin."[8] Just a century earlier, Harvard had conferred an honorary degree of doctor of divinity upon John Bernard Fitzpatrick, the Roman Catholic bishop of Boston, not only to honor the prelate personally as a "scholar, gentleman, and divine," but also to give public recognition to the patriotism of the Irish soldiers who were performing so gallantly in the Civil War.[9] In a similar vein, while the overseers of Harvard were undoubtedly recognizing the talents and achievements of Collins himself, it would seem that they were also using the occasion to symbolize the passing of an older and more adversarial relationship between the Yankee and the Celt, the Protestant and the Catholic, and the beginning of a new and more cooperative relationship between both groups as they worked together to create a New Boston. The mayor received congratulatory letters and telegrams from all parts of the city— from old friends, former teachers, and parish priests in Dorchester, Roxbury, and Jamaica Plain, as well as from more recent colleagues and associates in the banks, law offices, and investments houses of downtown Boston, including one letter from the attorney Oscar Haussermann, who warmly congratulated his friend on his "canonization" by Harvard.[10]

Prospects that Collins's second four years in office as mayor of Boston would be less rancorous than his first four brightened in November 1964 when Republican John Volpe came back to win a second term as governor of Massachusetts, defeating his rival, Francis X. Bellotti, who had successfully challenged Peabody for the Democratic nomination. Many observers saw great possibilities in the election of a governor who had established such good personal relations with the mayor two years earlier, and who shared so many political interests in common—especially their enthusiasm for a sales tax. This new "undeclared alliance" between Volpe and Collins, asserted an editorial in the *Boston Herald*, offered the "brightest hope for Boston." Never before in recent memory, said the Republican newspaper, had a chief executive of the commonwealth and the chief executive of the city seemed so close together in their thinking about Boston's problems and needs. "The Mayor did not endorse Mr. Volpe," the paper pointed out, "but his failure to endorse Mr. Bellotti amounted to the same thing. A pact was sealed."[11] While there is certainly no evidence of anything as formal as a "pact," it is clear that after his previous two years of abrasive contacts with Chub Peabody, Collins could look forward to a period of more amicable relations with his friend John Volpe, the first person elected to a four-year term as governor under Article 82 of the amendments to the Massachusetts Constitution.

And indeed, the start of the new year seemed to augur well for the future. Beginning on Sunday, February 21, 1965, a committee headed by Eli Goldston, president of Eastern Gas and Fuel, launched a week-long series of activities heralding the formal dedication of the War Memorial Auditorium adjoining the Prudential Center in the Back Bay, calculated to make Boston a major center for national and international conferences. One of the largest facilities of its kind in the country, the auditorium boasted 150,000 square feet of exhibition space, seating facilities for as many as six thousand people, a large meeting room with a capacity of nine hundred, and a series of smaller rooms and exhibit areas. On Sunday, numerous veterans' and military organizations, complete with bands and marching units, were on hand with Mayor Collins for the formal dedication of the structure. Special "Boston Medals" were struck and conferred upon such notable Bostonians as the manager

214 BUILDING A NEW BOSTON

of the Boston Celtics, Red Auerbach; the conductor of the Boston Pops, Arthur Fiedler; and the businessman-attorney Charles Coolidge for their "distinguished achievements" on behalf of the city. On Monday a series of floats dramatized the city's scientific and technical achievements; on Tuesday the focus of celebration was international trade, commerce, and shipping; Wednesday was education day, with exhibitions by college students that closed with a performance by the Harvard Glee Club and the Radcliffe Choral Society; and Thursday was given over to the arts, with a day-long display of painting and sculpture, followed by a presentation by the New England Opera Company.[12]

It was a gala week that was calculated to impress Bostonians with what had already been accomplished in the creation of a New Boston, and to raise their hopes and expectations for even more substantial successes to come. "For its size, Boston is the most renewal-minded city in the country," reported the influential London *Economist*, which quoted the words of the federal urban renewal commissioner calling the eleven integrated projects in the mayor's Ninety Million Dollar Development Program "a laboratory demonstration of renewal techniques." "The bull-dozer is peculiarly inappropriate to an historic shrine like Boston except in sparing doses," the journal wrote in praise of the selective approach Collins and Logue had taken to the renewal process; "preservation and rehabilitation take first place."[13]

The initial focus of Collins's Ninety Million Dollar Development Program was on the downtown area—the Back Bay, the Prudential Center, the War Memorial Auditorium, the Boston Common underground garage, the Scollay Square district, the Government Center, the financial district, the waterfront area—attracting federal funds, encouraging local investment, and bringing in outside developers. The long-range ambition of the program, however, was to extend many of those same techniques of renewal and rejuvenation into the various neighborhoods surrounding the central city. It would be difficult for the administration to boast of a proud New Boston when the refurbished downtown business district and Government Center were still hemmed in by a series of run-down old neighborhoods populated by blue-collar workers, low-income people of color, and a depressing collection of the homeless and the disadvantaged. The city's new program was designed to transform those valuable locations into clusters of attractive communities with the kind of shiny new town houses and modern apartments that would bring middle-class families and well-to-do professionals back to the city, where they would make Boston once again an appealing place to live and a convenient place to work.

The question, of course, was where to begin. In 1951, when the Plan A system had been introduced, the city had abolished district representation, reducing the city council from twenty-two members representing the various wards of the city to nine councillors elected at large. Heavily populated wards could usually depend on the support of popular Irish and Italian candidates to safeguard their interests, while smaller wards had to depend on the goodwill of at-large members of the city council for whatever they needed. With Frederick Langone and Christopher Ianella sitting in the council, for example, no urban renewal projects were scheduled for either the North End or East Boston.

The BRA had in mind a $30 million program to reverse the structural decline of the aging South Boston neighborhood, just across the channel on the south side of the city, under the heading of a "General Neighborhood Renewal Plan." Estimating that some 47 percent of the district's housing stock was badly in need of repair or demolition, especially in the lower end, the plan called for 22 percent of that housing to be torn down, some new housing constructed, and the remaining dwelling units rehabilitated. The BRA was especially critical of the fourteen public school buildings in South Boston, most of which had been built before 1900. It scheduled six of the schools for immediate demolition, and most of the others for substantial repairs and improvements. In addition to assistance for commercial enterprises and private homeowners, the BRA also called for a "Special Development District" for industry, with better zoning, safer streets, and more effective access roads.[14]

Suspicious South Boston residents, however, fearing that these ambitious plans would disrupt their old neighborhood, destroy the traditional family character of their community, and displace old-time residents as they had seen happen in the West End, stopped the BRA plans cold. They had been willing to go along with the Boston Housing Authority's earlier public housing projects because they had known that their displacement would be temporary, that they would have first preference in moving back into the new apartments, and that they would enjoy the company of their friends and relatives with whom they had previously shared the original two- and three-decker houses that had been taken down. They had none of these assurances from the current

BRA, and based on what they had seen happen in the West End, they saw no reason to trust the authority.

Even the most ardent advocate of urban renewal hesitated to push the matter any further. The influential city councillors Bill Foley and Johnny Kerrigan, both from South Boston, had long ago gone on record as opposing large-scale urban renewal in any form. In his critique of the idea of progress, *The True and Only Heaven*, the social critic Christopher Lasch maintained that with their drive for individual advancement, material success, and social mobility, upper-middle-class liberals have generally failed to appreciate the values of lower-middle-class culture, with its emphasis on family, church, and neighborhood. Certainly that was the belief of opposition leaders such as Foley, who sensed the distinct air of superiority with which technocrats and bureaucrats regarded their own values as compared with those of residents in a working-class neighborhood such as South Boston, whom they regarded as uneducated and reactionary.[15] "Logue interferes in the lives of people and tells them to fix up their homes," complained Foley. "He says people shouldn't be allowed to live in lower-class neighborhoods. He wants to make poor people middle class, just like him."[16] Mayor Collins often regarded Kerrigan as the most serious roadblock to renewal projects in the peninsula district, but Monsignor Lally was of the opinion that it was Foley who kept the BRA from "even thinking of going there."[17]

The nearby neighborhood of Charlestown, jutting out on the north side of the city, was a similar Irish Catholic working-class district, but here Logue hoped to find a less belligerent reception to his plans for upgrading and improvement. During the 1950s the population of Charlestown, once as high as forty thousand, had declined to barely eighteen thousand, while the assessed value of property that back in 1930 had equalled $48.4 million had by 1960 dropped to only $34 million. The deterioration of its real estate property was so great that under the original BRA plan over 60 percent of the homes in Charlestown had been slated for demolition, a figure Logue reduced to a more manageable 11 percent. "What has happened to this historic neighborhood was a shock to me," he admitted to one Charlestown audience. "Not the Monument, not the Square, but just a few blocks away on the slopes of this hill are slums as bad as any I have ever seen." Certainly, he felt, hard-pressed residents would jump at the chance to have the city repair old houses, construct new homes, furnish new schools and playgrounds, stem the drain of young families to the suburbs, and restore Charlestown "to its former glory."[18]

Furthermore, Logue believed that he had put together the necessary clout to bring his BRA projects into the neighborhood without undue protest or opposition. Pointing to the success of his projects in the downtown area, he was able to get the support not only of local business interests in Charlestown, who anticipated higher real estate values and substantial profits from the upgrading of the neighborhood, but also of such powerful labor groups as the Teamsters and the Longshoremen, who saw the obvious employment opportunities in transportation and construction.

In addition to this solid economic support, he could also rely on the moral support of Cardinal Cushing, as well as that of the BRA's chairman of the board, Monsignor Lally, who had actually taken up residence at Saint Catherine's Church in Charlestown. At the start of the Collins administration there had been a "certain coolness" between the new mayor and the cardinal. A close friend of former mayor Hynes and an enthusiastic supporter of Powers, Cushing had been greatly disappointed at the way in which Collins had defeated the senate president in 1959. Before long, however, a warm and cordial friendship developed between the cardinal and Collins, certainly helped along by the consideration shown by the mayor to Monsignor Lally.[19]

A bright lad from Swampscott who had attended Boston College and then went on to study for the priesthood at Saint John's Seminary, Frank Lally had quickly caught the attention of local church leaders, who saw his potential appeal to younger and more sophisticated members of the archdiocese. Cushing came to have a warm spot in his heart for this young priest, who was often able to articulate the crusty old prelate's gut instincts in matters of civil rights and interfaith relations. After serving as assistant editor of *The Pilot* for four years, in 1952 he was appointed editor of the weekly newspaper, which he turned into a highly respectable Catholic publication that won him many admirers in the downtown business community. Elevated to the rank of monsignor at the relatively young age of forty-one, Lally shared the cardinal's desire to see a new and modernized Boston, and when asked by Hynes to serve as a member of the BRA board he accepted the post with Cushing's approval. Collins later appointed him chairman of the board.

With the blessings of the cardinal, the support of Lally, and the backing of the pastors of the district's three Catholic churches—Saint

Catherine's, Saint Mary's, and Saint Francis de Sales—Logue felt he would have little difficulty persuading the residents that progress could be brought to their old neighborhood in a thoughtful, efficient, and completely humane fashion.

But the longtime residents of Charlestown—those "Townies" whose families had lived together for generations in good times and bad under the shadow of the historic Bunker Hill monument—had no intention of letting a bunch of outside liberals, Ivy League social engineers, and money-hungry real estate developers simply walk into their community and start tearing down the comfortable and familiar structures of their life and society. Like their friends and relatives across the way in South Boston, they too had seen the terrible things those people had already done, and they were determined to prevent them from doing the same things in Charlestown. They had seen the city bring in bulldozers and wrecking crews to demolish the old West End and then heartlessly throw poor old people out of their homes without a care as to where they would go or what they would do. Logue protested in vain that he had had no part in the West End fiasco, that he had not yet arrived in Boston when it happened. But it was people just like him who did it, Townies countered, and they were not going to do it to Charlestown!

Then, too, there was the Bunker Hill housing project, built back in 1940. When it first started out, the city planners had said it was going to be a real neighborhood project, a place for hardworking, low-income residents of Charlestown to live in comfort with their friends and neighbors—just like the Old Harbor and Old Colony projects across the way in South Boston. But then in the 1960s the outsiders went to work and changed the ground rules. Local residents saw their project become a dumping ground for people—mostly "outsiders" and increasingly of different skin colors—who were poor, unemployed, dispossessed, and disadvantaged. From a place originally designed for local white families with low incomes, the project became a place where no-income, one-parent families were assigned to live in a community that did not want them and that despised them as "riffraff" and "project rats." The Townies no longer accepted the project as part of their traditional community, and always blamed outside bureaucrats and real estate speculators for ignoring the history of the neighborhood and the customs of its people in their mad desire for change, progress, and moderniza-tion. Given this background, local residents greeted the elaborate plans of the BRA and the warm-hearted reassurances of Logue with "profound skepticism," and prepared to draw the battle line to preserve their homes, their families, and their way of life.[20]

In laying out his development program for Boston's neighborhoods, Logue insisted that he was committed to what he described as "meaningful community participation." Under the slogan of "planning with people," he proposed to move away from the old bureaucratic "bulldoze and build approach" of the 1950s and show more sensitivity to the needs and desires of the neighborhood itself by holding public hearings, consulting with community leaders, meeting with local advisory groups, and planning with representatives of the neighborhood.[21] His hope was to create the same kind of general consensus that had worked so well in developing the various downtown projects. In Charlestown, however, the announcement of open meetings became the clarion call for organized opposition by irate Townies who saw only hidden dangers in the extensive changes proposed by the outsiders.

In January 1963 a thousand members of the local Self Help Organization–Charlestown (SHOC) packed into a public hearing to protest the BRA's plans in what Logue described as a "tumultuous" manner.[22] Month after month, meetings of Logue and his staff with civic groups and fraternal organizations were countered by the noisy demonstrations of what he called "a highly vocal minority" whose sound trucks drove through the streets of the town warning about the dangers of urban renewal and calling upon residents to "Save Our Homes."[23] The acrimonious climax came in March 1965 when advocates of both sides poured into the armory atop Bunker Hill to attend the final hearing, which raged on for three hours until one of the pastors suddenly called the question: "All those in favor of a renewal plan for Charlestown, please stand!"[24] When the chairman declared that a majority—albeit a narrow one—had responded in the affirmative, Logue had his vote to proceed. But it was hardly the consensus he had hoped for.

The same kind of bitterness and recrimination marked the city's plans for the North Harvard Street project in the Allston-Brighton section of town, where Logue's redevelopment plans ran head-on into violent conflict with local neighborhood groups. The BRA's plan called for the demolition of fifty-two structures in a section of Allston-Brighton called Barry's Corner, a ten-acre neighborhood located at the corner of North Harvard Street and Western Avenue, only a short distance from the Harvard Business School. Maintaining in their official surveys that the houses in the district were "substandard," and that the neighborhood as a whole was in a "particularly run-down condition," the BRA classified the area as "blighted." Three months later, the city council approved plans to demolish all the homes in the area and replace them with a $4.5 million, three-hundred-unit, ten-story luxury apartment complex.[25]

The first indication the residents received that the BRA was planning to demolish their neighborhood had come in the spring of 1961. "It came like a bolt—we learned about it one night on the Channel 4 news," recalled one homeowner. "The city made no effort to inform us before that announcement." Longtime residents deeply resented the ways in which the city had categorized their neighborhood as a rundown slum. "The word blighted means rot and decay," protested Father Timothy Gleason, pastor of Saint Anthony's Church. "There is nothing rotten, nothing decayed in Barry's Corner."[26]

When Logue and other members of the BRA board finally came to the neighborhood on June 27, 1962, for a public meeting at the Thomas Gardner School—a full year after the initial announcement—they ran into a firestorm of protest. Monsignor Lally tried to discuss the realities of urban renewal in calm and reasonable terms, but residents found his words "callous" and his lack of understanding unacceptable. Some measure of the emotional level of the evening came as local Catholics, usually pious and respectful, exploded in rage against the popular priest: "Shove it, Lally!" "You are a disgrace!" they shouted. "Take the collar off!" "You're a pious hypocrite!" As they gathered up their papers and left the hall, Lally, Logue, and the other members of the BRA board were "visibly shaken" by the hostile treatment they had received, reported the local press.[27]

Despite strong neighborhood opposition, plans for the demolition process went forward without any apparent obstruction. Woefully underrepresented in the nine-member at-large Boston City Council after the retirement of Francis X. Ahearn in 1957, the Allston-Brighton community found it had to depend largely on community action and public opinion. Outraged residents organized the Citizens for Private Property, which sent out a flood of angry press releases denouncing the city's actions. Together with civic groups, church leaders, local politicians, and Harvard students, they appealed to the mayor, the city council, the General Court, and the state planning board for help. Despite BRA assurances that "every effort is being made to assure that the residents now living in the area are provided with suitable new homes," local homeowners refused to cooperate willingly. "We are categorically against the acquisition of one man's land for the sake of private profit for another," they declared, accusing the BRA of actually stealing their homes.

Signs exclaiming "To Hell with Urban Renewal" went up all over the neighborhood as residents engaged in picketing, sit-ins, and public demonstrations, determined to hold on to their homes until they were "driven out by force." After the Allston-Brighton cause suffered a major defeat in January 1963, when the city council formally approved the BRA plan by a five-to-four vote, the neighborhood responded by driving over to Dorchester and picketing Mayor Collins's home. In August 1964 residents of Barry's Corner turned out en masse when alerted by automobiles driving through the neighborhoods with their horns blaring. Armed with brooms, shovels, sticks, and spades, these local "Minutemen" cheered as they put to rout several members of an appraisal team sent in by the BRA. But these were only delaying tactics. The appraisers returned later with police protection, and the preparations for Barry's Corner proceeded as planned.[28]

In August 1965, in a last-ditch effort to head off demolition, the residents sent a delegation to Washington to appeal to their congressional representatives and to place their case before the federal Department of Housing. But it was no use, and one by one the houses in Barry's Corner began to collapse under the weight of the wrecking ball. The final act in this human tragedy came in October 1969, when BRA officials and more than fifty Boston policemen arrived on the scene to forcibly evict the last three families who still remained in their homes and refused to leave. In front of their homes along North Harvard Street paraded a hundred sympathetic protesters chanting anti-urban-renewal slogans and shouting their determination to support the three holdout families. After a flurry of shoving and fistfighting, the police finally dispersed the demonstrators, carted off several protesters to the police station, and evicted the last of the residents.[29]

The David-and-Goliath struggle going on between the small Allston-Brighton neighborhood and the powerful BRA attracted extensive media attention and caused such embarrassing publicity for the city that finally, with just nine of the original fifty houses still standing, Mayor Collins ordered the suspension of further demolition and appointed a blue-ribbon panel to look into the controversy. Although the panel urged the BRA to reopen the bidding process and to return the deeds of the

Outraged residents of the Barry's Corner section of Allston-Brighton attempted in many ways to prevent the destruction of their homes by the BRA during the 1960s. They organized citizens' groups, issued impassioned press releases, appealed to city and state authorities, and traveled to Washington. When it became apparent that their efforts were to no avail and that the BRA was going ahead with its plans, residents responded by putting up angry signs of protest on their lawns and on their houses. Three Cats Photos. Courtesy of Bernard Redgate.

*The demolition in Barry's Corner was devastating to families who stood by and watched the destruction of their homes. In some cases, Boston police were called in to forcibly evict families who refused to leave their homes willingly. Three Cats Photos. Courtesy of Bernard Redgate.*

*Despite the vocal opposition by angry homeowners, church leaders, and civic organizations in the Allston-Brighton area, families were evicted and their homes were demolished. Three Cats Photos. Courtesy of Bernard Redgate.*

nine remaining houses to their original owners, the federal Department of Housing and Urban Affairs refused to go along with that approach, and the demolition of the remaining structures moved forward according to plan.

Once again the BRA had achieved its stated goals; but once again residents failed to see where the supposed improvements were in the best interests of themselves or of their neighborhood. Something that helped bring down the level of the tensions was the selection of a local nonprofit corporation as the developer of what was now called the North Harvard Street Development Area. The Committee for North Harvard (CNH), cosponsored by five local churches and with a board that included a number of Allston-Brighton community leaders, gained support with a proposal to construct 212 units of moderate-income housing. But the local newspaper could not let the destruction of Barry's Corner go by without a final word of warning: "The BRA and the city must use this dramatic example of inflexible policies and structured thinking to prevent such a tragedy from recurring," wrote the editor. "The rending of stable communities cannot possibly benefit anyone in the long run," he said. "It can only add to the degradation of human beings at the mercy of their government and take us a step further in the ruination of urban America."[30]

In view of the fierce and unremitting resistance he encountered in Charlestown and again in Allston-Brighton, there is little question that Edward Logue looked to the South End as perhaps a more receptive area for urban development—especially after being informed by his planning administrator, Donald Graham, that the highly regarded black community leader Muriel Snowden had approached him with the suggestion that the South End be placed next on the BRA's agenda. "We decided you couldn't plant flower boxes and make the community better," explained her husband, Otto Snowden. "You had to have some basic changes: new buildings, schools, streets—plow everything. That's why we supported urban renewal." "The condition of the city was in such a shape that something had to be done. Some direction had to be taken," agreed political leader Royal Bolling, Sr. "And it's one of those things that it's easier to see the mistakes after the fact than it is before. I've always thought—and still think—that it was a positive influence for Roxbury."[31]

The area these local black leaders were talking about was an expanse of some six hundred acres lying southwest of Boston's central business district. Tufts University's New England Medical Center was on its northern fringes, while Boston City Hospital and the Boston University Medical Center were located on its southeastern border. Along the southwest ran Massachusetts Avenue, and to the northwest lay the Christian Science church headquarters and the Prudential Center complex, which was in the process of construction.

The South End was one of the country's largest and most diverse communities. Decades before the Civil War, developers had erected a series of fine bow-front houses, shady parks, and elegant apartments to accommodate an anticipated influx of upper-class residents. The construction of the nearby Back Bay area, however, totally eclipsed the South End as the future center of fashionable society in Boston. To protect their investments, developers converted town houses to multiple dwellings and turned private homes into rooming houses for working-class families, enterprising clerks, and transient salesmen. By the late 1890s and early 1900s the South End had become a neighborhood of tenements and boardinghouses, a catch basin for thousands of newcomers crowding into its narrow streets. Yankees and Irish now had to make way for Greeks and Italians, Syrians and Lebanese, and thousands of Jews who arrived in Boston at just about the same time that the city's black community had decided to leave the neighborhood where they had lived since the eighteenth century, on the north side of Beacon Hill, and make the South End their new home.

For old-time residents as well as for new arrivals, the South End was a warm, polyglot, and closely knit community of churches and social clubs, grocery stores and restaurants, tailor's shops and shoemaker's shops, schools and reading centers, drugstores and flower shops.[32] Describing the New York Streets area where he grew up as a boy, the black activist Mel King recalled the different stores in the neighborhood and the variety of families who lived upstairs over them. "On the corner of Seneca and Harrison, there was an Armenian store with olives in barrels out front, and a fish market next door. The next block down on the corner of Oneida was Leo Giuffre's bakery, I think. There was a synagogue on Oswego. Bikofsky's bakery was on the corner of Lovering and Harrison, and Saroka's Drug Store a block down on Davis Street."[33]

By the 1920s and 1930s, however, signs of deterioration had begun to appear, and they only worsened during the terrible Depression years. Upwardly mobile younger families moved to other parts of the state in search of better jobs and better homes, leaving behind older and poorer people who were in serious need of medical treatment, social care, and subsidized housing. The influx of roomers, transients, drifters, and homeless people greatly increased the incidence of gambling, alcoholism, crime, and prostitution. Real estate values dropped, blight accelerated, and along many of the main streets boarded-up stores became the outward signs of bankruptcy and ruin. A steady drop in population from 57,000 in 1950, to 35,000 in 1960, to 22,000 in 1970 forced schools to close and churches to move away. City authorities came in and took over houses. "People would sell houses to them, or abandon houses—and they'd knock them down and just let the grass grow," remarked Amanda Houston. "It was the first time we began to see empty overgrown lots, dirty lots. And we began to see dirty streets and the lack of services."[34]

The celebrated black artist Allan Rohan Crite, a lifelong resident of the South End, recalls standing with his friends and neighbors and watching the bulldozers and cranes "reduce the old wood-frame houses into splinters" and transform the familiar brick houses "into clouds of rubble." The wrecking crews brought massive destruction to streets that were once filled with people, he wrote, "alive with children and the busy chatter of black people, the cries of the vendors of fruits and vegetables and fish, and ice, wood and coal and oil."[35] Barrooms, pawnshops, and poolhalls proliferated, creating depressed skid-row areas where street people, derelicts, and alcoholics slept under the shadow of the Boston Elevated Railway.[36] For many years the South End remained neglected as a mere residential appendage of Boston, divided by arteries, railroads, and the Boston "El," whose overhead structure rained soot down on the houses and the residents as the elevated trains came rumbling through their community.

Unlike other Boston neighborhoods, where one particular ethnic group predominated—the Irish, the Italians—the South End had no single group to exert political clout and thus had to be satisfied with one of the at-large members representing its interests at city council meetings. For that reason residents became particularly apprehensive when, having witnessed the terrible things city leaders had done to the inhabitants of the West End, they heard rumors that those leaders were planning a similar program of demolition in the South End. And indeed, many city planners did see the demolition of the South End as the logical next step in cleaning up blighted areas around the central city. In the early 1950s, during the Hynes administration, they had already taken over two small chunks along the north side of Dover Street (now East Berkeley)—the New York Streets area, between Washington and Albany streets, to be used for light industry, as well as the Compton–Village Streets neighborhood, where they had created the Castle Square housing project.[37] Clearly, it was only a matter of time before the forces of urban renewal moved into the whole area—especially after the completion of the new Prudential Center in 1965 brought the South End closer to the heart of Boston and made it "infinitely more attractive as an in-town residential district."[38] Its strategic location, positioned near major downtown institutions that wanted protection from the growing influx of minority groups, made the South End a logical choice as one of the next areas for large-scale urban renewal.

Only too well aware of the new interest in their old neighborhood, but conscious of what had gone on in the West End, both longtime residents and new middle-class arrivals formed neighborhood associations to force the city to abandon any plans for wholesale demolition. The South End House and several other local settlement houses had already formed the United South End Settlements (USES), which in turn helped organize and coordinate a number of neighborhood associations, including the South End Planning Council, the South End Businessmen's Association, Interagency, and the South End Neighborhood Conservation and Rehabilitation Committee. Working together, in September 1961 the South End Planning Council and USES formed the twelve-member South End Urban Renewal Committee (URC), with Royal Cloud, a resident homeowner, as chairman. By December the URC had been expanded to include five businessmen, five professionals, five people from South End institutions, and twenty-three local residents. South Enders were protesting in advance any unnecessary destruction of basically sound buildings and calling for the preservation of a long-established neighborhood.[39]

By this time John Collins had taken over as mayor of Boston, and his development director, Edward Logue, had become extremely sensitive about the adverse effects the West End project had on the reputation of the BRA and the whole future of urban renewal. Emphasizing his personal commitment to "planning with people," he assured residents at the outset that he would avoid a program of wholesale demolition and would preserve as much of the original South End as was practicably possible. In fact, however, in order to achieve the upgraded property values, the moderate and high-rent housing, and the influx of salaried homeowners and well-to-do tenants who would transform the South End into the kind of respectable middle-class neighborhood they saw as their ultimate goal, members of the BRA realized they would have to engage in precisely the kind of substantial demolition and wholesale clearance they had promised to avoid. To justify their actions, especially in light of the widespread public revulsion against what had happened in the old West End, city planners projected an image of a neighborhood so "pathologically disorganized," as one recent analyst phrased it, that its recuperation would require nothing short of drastic "social surgery."[40]

Social reformers inveighed against the numerous "vice dens" that pockmarked the area and lamented the various skid-row areas where panhandlers roamed the streets by day and the unconscious bodies of drunks lined the sidewalks by night. Largely ignoring the lively elements of multiracial and ethnic community life in many parts of the South End among Syrians, Greeks, African-Americans, and Puerto Ricans, whose activities revolved around their churches, social clubs, restaurants, stores, and taverns, planners chose instead to draw up lists of depressing statistics on the disproportionate amounts of crime, violence, disease, alcoholism, and welfare dependency. In reports remarkably similar to those that had been prepared for the old West End prior to its demolition, committees reported that over 37 percent of South End males between the ages of sixteen and sixty-five were not in the labor force; that 78 percent of the households did not have automobiles; and that the neighborhood had nearly 30 percent of Boston's tuberculosis cases.[41]

While compiling their statistical justification for extensive renewal, city planners were also working to establish the personal relationships necessary to make the scope of their intervention acceptable to the residents. Conscious of the Collins administration's promises of "planning *with* people rather than planning *for* people," Logue and his staff set about building a neighborhood constituency of recognized local leaders to support their planning efforts. In forming those support networks, planners repeated their earlier promises that the BRA's renewal efforts would stress rehabilitation, not demolition, and would also provide low-rent housing for those residents who were displaced as well as adequate relocation assistance for those who might be forced to move into other neighborhoods. "Anybody who wishes to stay in the South End," one BRA staffer assured the members of the Boston City

Council, "we believe we have adequate facilities for them." "Even though the basic aims of urban renewal precluded fulfillment of these promises," observed John Mollenkopf in his study of the renewal process, "planners had to make them anyway to get their projects moving."[42]

In pursuit of his goal of a broad public consensus, Logue orchestrated an elaborate process in which BRA staff members consulted with the South End Urban Renewal Committee (URC) as well as with the impressive network of neighborhood homeowners' councils and associations that had been created in the last years of the Hynes administration. These groups constituted the major neighborhood leadership at the time, although they actually represented only a small fraction of the total number of residents. Logue's view of consensus was that any plan that had the political support of neighborhood residents "was by definition the right plan for that area."[43] In the course of literally hundreds of meetings where staffers undertook to hammer out a comprehensive renewal project for the South End, the BRA was actually using the process to organize the community in support of its own renewal objectives. As one observer noted: "The BRA was able to find within the South End a group of elite homeowners and tenants (who could afford a moderate or high rent) who aspired to make the South End a respectable middle-class neighborhood, a goal also held by the BRA."[44]

Because the URC disapproved, Logue and the BRA scrapped an early "Green Strip" plan that would have divided the South End into "problem" and "nonproblem" areas—skid row on one side, a "family" area on the other side, with a strip of community facilities down the middle. In response to community pressures, he also agreed that demolition would be reserved only for a small number of structures, which were beyond repair and located along heavily traveled streets. Remaining federal funds and private investments would be redirected to constructing new housing, salvaging old buildings, repairing the district's infrastructure, and beautifying its streets.

In January 1964 the BRA came up with a plan called "The Concept" that would divide the South End into residential and industrial/institutional ovals. This time, since the final project had been presented and discussed before a total of 155 groups, and since so many neighborhood groups had been involved in the planning process, there was general agreement that the results were satisfactory, and those who attended the August 1965 public meeting voiced overwhelming approval for the plan. Logue was completely satisfied that there had been extensive community participation and that the residents were solidly behind him. After all, of the 149 testimonials heard at the meeting, only 20 came out in opposition to the plan, and most of those came from people outside the South End.[45]

The final plan called for the rehabilitation of more than three thousand structures and the construction of over three thousand new private rental units, three hundred new public housing units for families (to be built on scattered sites, with no more than fifty units per site), five hundred new public housing units for the elderly, three new schools, and seven new playgrounds, along with improvements in parks, roadways, and street lighting. It was the nation's largest renewal project, endorsed by the Boston City Council and approved by the federal government in the spring of 1966.[46]

Although in developing his renewal plans for the South End Logue did not run into the stone wall of opposition he encountered in the streets of Charlestown, a delayed reaction among blacks, Hispanics, and low-income tenants quickly grew in size and intensity during the late 1960s and became a major force in Boston politics by the 1970s. City Councillor Foley, a consistent foe of urban renewal, had already gone on record in warning that the BRA had no intention of making anything but a "shameful token effort" in the South End for the majority of those "displaced" who were poor. Conceding that Logue's plan would eventually rehabilitate the area, he predicted that it would come about only "at the expense and through the misery and suffering and pain of between 10 and 15 thousand poor people. It is as simple as that!"[47] Critics such as Foley continued to believe that the progrowth coalition of ambitious politicians, wealthy urban developers, and upper-class social reformers would bring about ostensibly "progressive" changes in the working-class neighborhoods at the expense of traditional life-styles, familiar surroundings, and close-knit relationships.

Other members of the city council leveled serious attacks at the BRA for its failure to provide new housing at moderate cost for city residents. "We are tearing down homes without replacing housing for this same economic group," exclaimed Gabriel Piemonte. "We have moved thousands of families with no thought, no interest in providing suitable housing replacements. Progress doesn't give us the right to trample over human beings." Patrick F. McDonough declared urban renewal to be a "failure" because of its insistence on building public projects instead of low-cost housing, and Peter Hines, too, came out strongly against the direction in which he saw the BRA heading. "Our urban redevelopment program, when it comes down to doing something for the people, has been a miserable failure," he said. "We are headed on the wrong track with the urban renewal authority married to projectitis."[48]

A large segment of the South End population also suspected, from the very beginning, that BRA leaders had made up their minds to ignore the interests of the poor and the homeless and were targeting their efforts mainly at the town house crowd—those young architects and professionals who were purchasing apartments and renovating town houses in their efforts to upgrade and "gentrify" the community. There was a sentiment among blacks, Puerto Ricans, the poor, the elderly, and the homeless that they had either been ignored or elbowed off in increasing numbers toward Roxbury. Furthermore, since HUD money was slow coming through from Washington for the construction of new housing, old buildings were being torn down faster than new ones could be put up. A number of families, therefore, usually tenants rather than homeowners, were displaced and not relocated. Many actually had to leave the South End and find new places to live elsewhere. "As one area was demolished, families were forced to move on," recalled Mel King, who was working with youngsters at the South End's Lincoln House at the time. "From the New York Streets, families generally moved to Castle Square; from there, when it was renewed, most white families went to South Boston, Dorchester, and Jamaica Plain. Black and Portuguese families moved to Washington Park, Lower Roxbury, and North Dorchester. Some families had to move four and more times in the face of renewal pressure."[49]

Already a significant number of black people had moved across into northern Mattapan, a neighborhood that was considered the largest Jewish community in New England. Even as late as the mid-1950s some fifty thousand Jews were still living in this section, served by some eight congregations, almost all of them Orthodox.[50] During the 1950s and 1960s, however, younger Jewish families began moving out of Mattapan into such nearby residential suburbs as Milton, Randolph, and Canton in search of better homes and more adequate school systems. The drop in Jewish population to some ten thousand was reflected in a 1967 newspaper article that reported that in the course of the eight years after 1950 at least six synagogues had been disbanded and nine Hebrew schools had shut down. In 1968 a consortium of twenty-two Boston savings banks, organized as the Boston Banks Urban Renewal Group (B-BURG) and working with Mayor Kevin White's administration, allocated some $50 million in mortgage money to encourage low-income black families to buy homes in Mattapan. Partly as a result of this gesture, which many critics feel may have been well intentioned but badly flawed, some four thousand more black people entered Mattapan between 1968 and 1970, moving down along Blue Hill Avenue from Grove Hall toward Mattapan Square. By 1972 the number of Jewish residents in the area had dropped to fewer than twenty-five hundred, and the subsequent flare-ups of racial fears, panic selling, speculation, blockbusting, and redlining greatly accelerated the movement of remaining Jewish families out of their familiar neighborhood, completing the changeover of a once predominantly white district into an almost all-black neighborhood.[51]

Back in the South End itself, black resentment grew as many of the expected improvements failed to materialize. There was no sign of any of the three new schools that had been promised for the area, road repairs and street lighting were behind schedule, construction had begun on only a fraction of the proposed subsidized housing, and rehab money was going mostly toward the renovation of upper-middle-class town houses. Between 1960 and 1969, the total number of occupied low-rent dwelling units in the South End project dropped from 14,012 to a low of 7,277 in the early 1970s.[52] The disenchantment of lower-income residents was exacerbated by rising real estate values, skyrocketing mortgage rates, and mounting rental fees that drove even more low-income families out of the South End toward lower Roxbury, creating a widening gap between old-time residents, usually blacks and Spanish-speaking people, and the predominantly white, middle-class professionals who were moving in. In view of the location, the basic quality of the housing stock, the market potential, and the availability of funding sources, the South End offered more potential for return on a modest investment than any other area in Boston. Real estate investors rapidly acquired the Victorian housing stock, evicted the old tenants (usually elderly and poor), and reconverted the structures to single-family or rental apartment use. To encourage further private investment, Mayor Collins persuaded the city's mortgage lenders to put an end to their redlining of the South End and promised not to raise property tax assessments on rehabilitated properties.[53]

Like so many others, John Collins saw the economic development of the South End not only in terms of immediate financial profit but also as a practical way in which long-term social progress and upward mobility could be measured. Successful urban renewal had certain visible attributes—streets that were clean, traffic that moved freely, restaurants and shops that did a thriving business, houses that were well kept, apartments that were carefully maintained, real estate values that were clearly on the rise. These were the tangible signs of urban progress that would be upset by signs of the poor and the homeless, by derelicts, drunks, and transients. And so these disturbing elements were moved out of sight, pushed along out of the South End into congested parts of nearby Roxbury. "Large families were squeezed into small apartments which had never been the best Roxbury had to offer," recalled one observer; "absentee landlords milked the buildings for profit, maintaining them only minimally."[54]

The displacement created hard feelings and conjured up bitter memories of what had happened in the West End, as noted by later specialists in urban affairs. A 1965 article in *Boston Magazine* pointed out that only a small segment of the South End community ever actually belonged to any of the advisory groups with which the BRA had consulted, and estimated that over 80 percent of the residents of the South End had neither seen nor heard of Edward Logue's final renewal plan.[55] In his study of neighborhood planning, Langley Keyes claimed that Logue made it a practice to deal with carefully selected members of the powerful and influential elements in the community, and he insisted that the BRA director was more concerned with having his plan approved than "maximizing citizen participation."[56]

Both Logue and Collins were determined to get their projects through "come hell or high water," insisted Robert Coard, who worked in the BRA office, but whose reports critical of what was going on in the South End he maintained were shunted aside by the director. "They would ride over any local objections in order to achieve what they considered a better community, which was nice spanking new housing," he complained bitterly. "And they did not have the kind of regard for the human disaster that occurred in terms of the removal of lower-income people who were in the communities."[57] "The advocates for low-income groups lost out to the more stable neighborhood organization interests," agreed Morton Rubin, an urban sociologist, in 1971. "The new Urbanites became more influential, and pushed hard for the South End as a 'Bright New Place' rather than as a 'Social Agency.' "[58]

234 BUILDING A NEW BOSTON

The efforts of coalition politics to bring into black and ethnic neighborhoods the sweeping renewal process that had worked so well in the central business district produced a powerful countermovement that Daniel Bell has called a "community revolution."[59] Angry black residents used street parades, sound trucks, protest marches, and public demonstrations of all kinds to call attention to their needs and demands. The movement of the BRA and its urban renewal projects into both black and white neighborhoods had accelerated the growth and development of angry community forces that by the mid-1960s were complaining that the programs of Collins, Logue, and the rest of the city apparatus were paying too much attention to beautifying the well-to-do downtown business and financial districts while ignoring the more mundane needs of impoverished neighborhoods. Millions and millions of dollars were being spent for the construction of fancy banking institutions, high-rise insurance towers, and elaborate government buildings, while only a fraction of those funds were being allocated for police and fire protection, road repairs, street lighting, low-income apartments, and decent housing projects in the neighborhoods. By January 1968, as John Mollenkopf has shown in his *Contested City*, the BRA had relocated only five hundred families, most to housing outside the South End. Contrary to BRA promises, only twenty-five families had been rehoused in rehabilitated units within the South End. That the first wave of relocation had already exhausted the neighborhood's low-rent relocation resources meant that all future persons displaced would be forced out of the area.[60]

Convinced that they could no longer obtain effective relief or protection from city hall, citizens at the local level began taking matters into their own hands. During the 1960s Boston saw the emergence of a grass-roots political movement designed to force both the officials of government and the representatives of business to take into account the interests of neighborhood residents whenever they prepared any future plans involving their communities. Working-class groups now formed community organizations to prevent what they regarded as the destruction of their neighborhoods, using many of the organizational techniques being employed so successfully during the 1960s by civil rights groups, antiwar protesters, and social activists. Many neighborhoods formed development corporations of their own to help them rehabilitate run-down houses, resuscitate dying businesses, and even bring light industry into their districts. Longtime residents of Beacon Hill sought to preserve the distinctiveness of their old neighborhood with the Beacon Hill Civic Association; businessmen in Mattapan worked to revitalize their community with the Mattapan Square Board of Trade; advisory groups pressured local banks to invest their capital in those neighborhoods in which they were located; and parents fought for meaningful educational reforms through such coalitions as the Boston Home and School Association. Through these and similar associations, community action groups fought against plans to construct the Southeast Corridor through Roxbury, to redevelop the Mission Hill district, to industrialize the Chinatown area, and to further expand Logan Airport. Sometimes they succeeded. More often they failed. But in any case, these local groups gradually became a force that could not be ignored.

"No longer could planning be done exclusively in corporate board rooms and government offices," wrote Lawrence Kennedy. "It now had to take into account the wishes of ordinary citizens."[61] Coalition politics, a new and alternative source of power in Boston, soon came to have a decided influence on how people in the neighborhoods would respond to decisions made by political and financial groups outside their communities. Fights over urban renewal in neighborhoods such as Charlestown, Brighton, and the South End, together with the bitter legacy of the West End, had intensified distrust of experts, bureaucrats, developers, and social engineers. The overall effect of such "renewal" battles, according to Ronald Formisano, was to "erode even further the legitimacy of the powers that be," to create suspicion of "programs sold as beneficial to the common good," and to "fragment the city's constituent elements into combatants in a struggle that has been called 'street-fighting pluralism.' "[62]

The angry complaints of working-class people in such traditionally white neighborhoods as South Boston, East Boston, Charlestown, and Dorchester were many of the same complaints that were coming out of the black and Hispanic communities in the South End, Roxbury, and North Dorchester. Following a trend that social scientists observed in many other American cities during the 1960s, younger and more militant residents representing the interests of "the people" were challenging the leadership of older and more conservative activists for community leadership.[63] Protesting that reasoned demands for economic progress and social improvement by the earlier, silk-stocking leaders of the South End had been well meant but largely ineffective, the younger groups

ıry began to employ more militant techniques to dramatize
and demand from the "white power structure" satisfaction
ds. During the early 1960s Otto and Muriel Snowden might
_____ _____ ıble to speak for the black community, observed Langley
Keyes in his study of urban rehabilitation. By 1967, however, they had
no such "mandate," and in some quarters Freedom House, the symbol
of black Roxbury in the late 1950s, was being called "Uncle Tom's
Cabin."[64] New young leaders such as Thomas Atkins, Ruth Batson, Rev.
James Breeden, Ellen Jackson, Melvin King, Paul Parks, and Bryant
Rollins created organizations that challenged the BRA and the school
committee, sponsored rehabilitated housing, and agitated successfully
for jobs through the United Community Construction Workers, the New
Urban League, and the Boston Job Coalition. This new sense of aggressive determination certainly reflected the changes that were taking place
in the black communities all over the country.

The successes of the national civil rights movement of the late 1950s
and early 1960s promoted among black people a greater pride in their
identity and a growing consciousness of their heritage. Black citizens no
longer accepted the social and economic injustices that had retarded
their progress for so many generations. Inspired by the ideals of Rev.
Martin Luther King, Jr., and the well-publicized victories in various
southern states, black citizens were further buoyed by the enactment of
the Civil Rights Act of 1964, which ensured equal access to public
accommodations and prohibited discrimination in employment. In 1965
the Voting Rights Act encouraged black voter registration, and in 1968
the Open Housing Act banned discrimination in housing. In Boston, as
in other American cities at the time, the black community set out to see
that its members were accorded equal rights in housing, equal opportunities in jobs, and equal access to a good education.

As living conditions deteriorated in the South End and Roxbury,
black residents began to direct a great deal of their animosity toward
Mayor Collins himself for apparently ignoring the deplorable situation
in their community. During his years as mayor so far, Collins had
worked out a generally good relationship with a number of older, well-
established, relatively conservative black leaders in the South End who
had been working not only to obtain social, educational, and economic
improvements for their own people but also to maintain the South End
itself as an integrated community where blacks and whites could live
together in decent conditions. People like Muriel and Otto Snowden,

the founders of Freedom House, were on friendly terms with the mayor, as was Ruth Batson, a longtime activist for integrated education and head of the NAACP's education committee, who appealed to Collins for a more effective police presence in the black community, and whom one city hall aide described as a "close ally" of Collins in dealing with affairs in the black community. Melnea Cass; Ed Cooper, the executive director of the Urban League; the attorneys Harry and Clarence Elam; Wilfred Scott; and Julian Steele were among those to whom Collins and Logue turned for advice and assistance in their plans for urban renewal.

But as the black population increased from about forty thousand in 1950 to well over sixty thousand in 1960, and as more of their members were forced out of the old South End into parts of lower Roxbury and North Dorchester by land clearance, building demolition, project construction, and renewal projects, newer and younger leaders emerged. Most of them from the South and many of them recent arrivals, they were frustrated with the lack of progress and insistent upon more aggressive measures for immediate relief. Collins was frequently shocked and repelled by the character of these new demands, the stridency of the language with which they were expressed, and the unusual manner in which they were often presented. One morning, for example, a group of six mothers from Roxbury, along with their children, staged a sit-in at the mayor's office at City Hall to protest the infestation of roaches and rodents in their apartments and to demand that the city furnish them with temporary housing. After a three-hour wait, they left without seeing the mayor. A few days later, late at night, another group of Roxbury residents drove a truck into Boston and dumped a huge pile of trash and garbage on the front steps of City Hall, much to the disgust of the fastidious mayor, who had worked so hard to clean up the building when he first moved in six years earlier. He sharply criticized this action as "a rude and vulgar exhibition," and ordered a police investigation of the incident.[65]

Black community activists increased their efforts nonetheless, circulating mimeographed leaflets in the streets of Boston calling upon the "Mayor of the 'New' Boston" to speak to the citizens of Roxbury, to put an end to the "slums" in their district, and to provide improved municipal services, including two garbage collections a week. Unless conditions of unemployment, slum housing, dirty streets, and "raggedy" schools were alleviated, they warned, there would be "trouble in Roxbury this summer."[66] In view of the terrible violence that had already

238 BUILDING A NEW BOSTON

erupted in the Los Angeles ghetto of Watts in the summer of 1965, and the bloody race riots that were then plaguing the cities of Newark and Detroit, many people did not regard this message as an idle threat.

In response to a warning sent to him by the board of directors of the Roxbury Multi-Service Center predicting impending riots if "ghetto conditions" were not improved, on Saturday, February 5, 1966, the mayor took a two-hour trip through Roxbury to see what the local *Bay State Banner* called "the worst slum conditions in Massachusetts." The president of the Multi-Service Center's board, Harry Elam, accompanied Collins on a tour that had been planned by assistant director Hubert Jones, pointing out that slum conditions had led to "complete frustration" among the residents of the district and had produced "no faith in the lawful channels." Along with others, he urged the mayor to demonstrate in some public way that he "*does know*" that the Negro in Boston has special problems, and that he "*does care.*"[67]

Clearly, however, the black residents of the South End and Roxbury were not satisfied that Collins and his city administration were doing enough to provide them with adequate health care and sufficient low-income housing to satisfy their basic needs. Ministers of various races and denominations, poverty program employees, African-American social workers, Puerto Rican community organizers, and idealistic white professionals came together to control the actions of the BRA, halt demolition and relocation, and push for more subsidized housing. In pursuit of those aims, community leaders organized three more important neighborhood groups: the South End Tenants' Council, in which Ted Parrish, a black social worker, played a key role; the Emergency Tenants' Council (later Inquilinos Boricuas en Accion), organized by Fr. William Dwyer, a Spanish-speaking Episcopal minister, along with Carmelo Iglesias and others; and in 1967 the Community Assembly for a United South End (CAUSE), which made itself heard at the outset principally through public demonstrations. One of the first of these was the "Tent City" demonstration in 1968, when their supporters occupied a piece of land at the corner of Columbus Avenue and Dartmouth Street, adjacent to Copley Square, where the BRA was planning a seven-story garage with a tower and a plaza. The demonstrators demanded, and finally got, a commitment from the BRA that it would build low- and moderate-income housing on that location instead.[68]

Another dramatic example of the rising tide of discontent within the black community occurred in December 1967, when HUD secretary

Robert Weaver arrived from Washington to speak at Roxbury's Freedom House and personally dedicate the 731 units of public housing that constituted the nation's largest rent-supplemented rehabilitation project. The local black activist Bryant Rollins spoke out, however, interrupted Weaver's prepared remarks, and publicly characterized the federal program as "a robbery of the Roxbury community." It was becoming obvious that residents of the black community were demanding a much greater role in their own redevelopment.[69]

Education, too, was a pressing issue that further convinced black citizens that city leaders were failing to take seriously their demands for equal rights. Even though in 1954 the United States Supreme Court had ruled in *Brown* v. *Board of Education of Topeka* that segregation in the public schools was unconstitutional, more than ten years later Boston's public schools were still predominantly either all white or all black. The Boston chapter of the NAACP, insisting that "segregation in fact" existed in the Boston public school system, demanded that the city immediately take steps to correct that condition. The members of the all-white school committee, in response, flatly denied that any child had been deprived of the right to attend any Boston school because of his or her race, religion, or national background. If some schools in Boston were "imbalanced," they explained, it was simply because black people happened to live in certain parts of the city while white people lived in other parts. Since parents naturally sent their children to the closest neighborhood school, the result was a housing problem, not an educational one.

When the state legislature passed the Racial Imbalance Act in August 1965, however, stating that any school that was more than 50 percent black would be considered racially imbalanced, the onus of segregation was placed squarely on Boston, where over 60 percent of its black students attended schools that were at least 70 percent black. On the basis of this legislation, the State Board of Education insisted that the Boston School Committee come up with some type of plan or formula that would reduce the number of imbalanced schools in the city system. Year after year, however, the school committee held the line, refusing to admit that de facto segregation existed in its school system.

The lack of discernible action by Collins in the school segregation issue, as well as his increasingly public posture as a no-nonsense executive who would not be pushed around by demonstrators and civil rights extremists, only further served to alienate the black community from the city administration and even brought critical remarks from usually friendly sources. "Mayor Collins has remained scrupulously aloof from the dispute between the School Committee and the Negro community," commented an editorial over Boston radio station WEEI on June 24, 1966, which also pointed out that none of the city council members had shown any interest either. "Ignoring the problem won't make it go away," the editorial concluded. "In fact, ignoring it will only make it worse, not better."[70]

Whether the complexities of Boston politics had become too great, the tactics of the neighborhood activists too distasteful, or the prospects of another four years in City Hall too dismal, John Collins seemed to be losing his zest for municipal government. Reflecting a downturn in the economy, as well as an increase in the fiscal responsibilities brought on by new social demands, his annual message in January 1966 was unusually depressing for a chief executive whose messages in the past had been tough and demanding, but generally vigorous and upbeat. Six years earlier, he reminded his listeners, the city of Boston had been beset with many problems, and the people of Boston had been at a crossroads. But the people made the "hard decision," closed ranks, embarked successfully on "Operation Revival," and proceeded to make Boston "*THE* first-rate city." Now it was 1966, he continued, and the citizens of Boston, like those of other large cities, were facing "staggering problems . . . none of which are their own creation." Such new and complicated issues as education, juvenile delinquency, chronic poverty, care of the aged, and "intergroup relations" were draining the resources of the city. In addition, routine municipal costs were also climbing out of sight. Increased Massachusetts Bay Transit Authority (MBTA) assessments, additional pension and retirement costs, added welfare benefits and veterans' services, wage increases for employees, and school and hospital expenses were putting the city in an impossible situation at a time when the costs of the Vietnam War were escalating at an alarming rate. With the total military budget rising from $51.6 billion in 1964 to $82.5 billion in 1969, Congress was cutting back severely on appropriations for urban renewal projects and other publicly financed domestic programs. Not only had the federal government stopped providing adequate local assistance, complained the mayor, but even the state government had turned a "deaf ear" to the plight of the cities. The fact is, he concluded on a melancholy note, that unless tax relief was immediately forthcoming from the commonwealth, the 1966 tax rate would go up to at least $130 because of "unavoidable increases in expenditures imposed on the city beyond its control." If the state legislature did not come up with the assistance, he said, the future was "bleak and repelling."[71]

It was, in fact, well known that Collins would be a candidate for the United States Senate seat previously occupied for the preceding twenty-one years by Leverett Saltonstall, whose retirement had been announced the previous September.[72] It is still not entirely clear, even among some of his closest supporters, why Collins decided to run for the Senate position. "He was a born executive—a get-it-done guy; he just didn't have the temperament for a legislative career," remarked a former aide. "Few of us could really understand why he would give up the mayor's job like that." Writing about "Saltonstall's successor" in *The New Republic*, the Boston journalist Martin Nolan compared the relative merits of the Republican candidate, Edward Brooke, and those of Collins, whom he admiringly described as a "tough, courageous mayor who had united the hostile tribes of a feudal city behind the nation's most ambitious urban renewal program."[73]

In terms of the pragmatic realities of the moment, however, Nolan pointed out that Collins faced certain obstacles in the forthcoming Senate race. For one thing, he could expect no help from the Kennedy clan, which was backing its own Kenny O'Donnell for the Washington post. For another thing, the former governor Endicott Peabody had already announced himself a candidate for the same Senate post, and although John Powers had left the presidency of the state senate to become a clerk of the state supreme court, he was a potent influence at the state level and still sensitive to his embarrassing defeat by Collins seven years earlier. With some of Frank Bellotti's supporters opposed to Collins because they thought he had not done enough to help their candidate in the 1964 gubernatorial campaign, the Boston mayor clearly faced serious opposition from powerful forces on Beacon Hill.[74]

Evidence of Peabody's strong feelings against Collins had surfaced unexpectedly back in November before an audience of some two hundred Democrats at the dining room of the Yellow Aster Restaurant, where a "Meet the Candidates" forum was in progress. According to the newspaperman A. A. Michelson, Peabody suddenly "took off the gloves" and started a "bare-knuckled fight" against Collins. He claimed the mayor had always worked against him, that at his mayoral inauguration in January 1964 Collins had attacked him with a "boorish backhand" for failing to get a tax program passed, and that he had played a major role in his loss of the governorship to Republican John Volpe in November 1964. Collins, charged Peabody, had never sacrificed his personal ambitions for the good of the Democratic party, and even then was gathering campaign funds at a hundred-dollar-a-plate dinner organized by a member of the state Republican finance committee.[75]

As if this lack of support among influential politicians were not discouraging enough, Nolan pointed out that the mayor's position on racial matters was none too strong at a time when the subject of the "Negro revolution" would undoubtedly be a key issue in the campaign. "On Negro rights, Collins has done little," he wrote, although acknowledging that Brooke, an African-American then serving as state attorney general, had done "even less." And on the festering school desegregation question, Collins "took no stand"—although Brooke, who had taken no stand either, was generally regarded by local black leaders as an Uncle Tom.[76] All in all, judging from Nolan's assessment, it appeared that Collins was facing an uphill battle in the move from Boston to Washington.

Collins had already made up his mind as early as 1965 that he would not run for a third term as mayor of Boston. In addition to a personal conviction that no one should hold office for more than two terms (he himself had served two terms in the house, and two in the senate), he felt that the long hours and heavy pressures of the mayor's job were taking a severe toll on his home life, his relations with his children, and his own precarious health. It generally takes an extraordinarily high self-regard for any person to go into politics, and John Collins was no exception. Having received considerable praise from urban planners and political colleagues for his numerous accomplishments during his eight years in office, he felt ready, not for a step down to private life, but for a step up to higher office. He considered himself highly qualified for a position in Washington and felt he would make an excellent senator—one whose more conservative views could offset the liberal policies of the state's other senator, Edward M. Kennedy. Money, too, was a mundane but very practical consideration for the future. Like his predecessor, John Hynes, Collins had also come from a modest working-class family, had little money of his own, operated a small law practice, and received a salary of only twenty thousand dollars a year as mayor of the city. Without heritage or inheritance, his options were decidedly limited, and the prospects of a comfortable seat in the United States Senate conjured up visions of a restful six years recovering from the strenuous pressures of his eight years as a big-city mayor.

It may have been a naive and simplistic view of a senator's responsibilities, but that was the way Collins saw it at the time.[77] On Thursday, May 12, 1966, therefore, Collins officially announced his candidacy for the Senate of the United States, proclaiming that it was absolutely "vital" that the Massachusetts Democratic party offer "the strongest possible candidate" for the federal office. To direct his campaign, he put together a team consisting of Hirsh Freed, Dick Sinnott, Jack O'Neill, Dan Fenn, and Jack Tierney.[78]

In view of Collins's increasing difficulties with the black community, his running against the personable Edward Brooke raised some sensitive issues, which were explored in a twenty-page planning document prepared for his campaign. In addition to a detailed ward-by-ward, precinct-by-precinct breakdown of voters across the state, arranged according to ethnic, racial, religious, economic, and educational characteristics, the briefing document offered some general observations and recommendations. Collins was warned, for example, not to let the race issue take over the campaign, but rather to make a "JFK-type plea à la the Houston ministers"—a reference to Kennedy's appearance in November 1960 before the Greater Houston Ministerial Association to emphasize his position on the separation of church and state and to denounce religious intolerance. Tell the voters not merely to vote for Brooke because he is black or to vote for you because you are white, he was instructed. The election might hinge on a "liberal, issue-oriented group," stated the document, although another "critical group" might well turn out to be "low-income, low-educated, urban Italo- and Irish-Americans and Jews (Ward 14 types)—overwhelmingly Democratic." Some data had been collected that indicated that Italian-American voters were "less anti-Negro" than Irish-American voters.[79]

Collins also worked up a position paper on foreign policy, focusing particularly on the increasingly controversial involvement of the federal government in Vietnam and in Latin America. As far as Vietnam was concerned, he called for the national government to develop a policy of "creative patience" in order to encourage a measure of "stability" that would serve as a prerequisite for the election of a representative government. In the case of Latin America, he announced that he was opposed to any direct military intervention. Instead, he would support programs of social and economic reform that would eventually alleviate the terrible poverty endemic to that part of the world.[80]

The corporation counsel Arthur Coffey, the budget director Henry "Buddy" Brennan, and the city greeter Larry Quayley left their regular assignments at City Hall to work full-time on the campaign, and Roy Covell, the mayor's chief liaison with convention delegates, confidently promised a "landslide victory." Although he admitted there would be a "pretty close battle" on the convention floor in the early stages of delegate balloting, when the votes came in from Suffolk and Worcester counties, as well as from Bristol County, Cape Cod, and the islands, said Covell, Collins would have his landslide.[81]

For all his plans and preparations, however, when the eighteen hundred Democrats met in convention on Friday, June 10, at Boston's huge War Memorial Auditorium to endorse their official slate of candidates, Collins felt the full force of that deep reserve of sullen resentment that delegates from other parts of Massachusetts usually hold in store for the mayor of Boston. Peabody had been working the delegates almost without letup, buttonholing as many Democrats as possible before the actual voting began. "He has shaken every hand of every delegate," observed the *Globe* journalist Robert Healy. "He has gone back time and time again to those who have not made a commitment." It also became clear that the former governor had worked up a great deal of sympathy among those Democratic delegates who felt that he had been "shabbily treated" when Bellotti challenged him in 1964 and helped the Democrats lose the governorship to Volpe.[82]

Despite his own optimistic prospects, and despite fairly solid support from his own Boston delegates, in the initial contest, held on Friday night, Collins received only 717 votes for the nomination, while Peabody surged ahead with a total of 1,089 votes on the first ballot.[83] Conceding defeat, a visibly shaken Collins told the audience that a ghost from the past—like Jacob Marley, "dead these seven years"—had risen from the grave to rob him of the nomination. Flushed and perspiring as he stood beneath the glare of television lights in the smoke-filled hall, Collins blamed his loss on the "revenge" of his old political rival, former state senate president John E. Powers. "The voice was the voice of Peabody," he said in a voice choked with emotion as the jeers and catcalls of the Peabody delegates threatened to drown him out, "but the hand was the hand of Powers." Going back to the theme he used to defeat Powers in

1959, Collins continued: "I have learned tonight—and indeed the hard way—that you can't always win when you're fighting power politics."[84]

Although Powers was obviously delighted with the outcome, he maintained a poker face and refused to admit that his personal efforts on behalf of Peabody had influenced any of the convention delegates. "Even my own district split," he said blandly; Collins "does me more credit than I deserve." Accusing the mayor of "poor sportsmanship," Powers recalled for reporters what he had said back in 1959 when he had been defeated by Collins: "If you don't know how to lose, you have no right to win." Powers went on to predict that if Collins continued his campaign into the September primary, not only would Peabody defeat him again, but the former governor would actually take the city of Boston.[85]

Collins had no intention of dropping out of the race just because he had failed to get convention support. "This is merely a temporary setback," he assured his supporters confidently after the convention, and he promised to come back in the "main bouts" and take both the September primary and the November final. Collins certainly had reason to hope for success in September. According to the *Globe*, his campaign war chest was "bulging," and he had every intention of using those funds to finance an elaborate media campaign including billboards, newspaper ads, radio spots, and television time.[86] Furthermore, he could take considerable comfort in Peabody's past difficulties in primary contests. Of four tries, Peabody had succeeded only once. Even as the incumbent governor two years earlier, he had lost out in the primary to his lieutenant governor, Bellotti.

There was no doubt about it: Chub Peabody was beatable, and Collins was gearing up to do just that. During July and August, he campaigned extensively across the state—Pittsfield, Worcester, Springfield, Fall River, New Bedford, Taunton, Cape Cod, Quincy, Weymouth, Framingham, Cambridge, the North End—giving speeches, making personal appearances, giving radio talks, and opening local political headquarters.[87] But Peabody was hard at work, too, crisscrossing the state, conducting his own personal, on-the-spot, hand-shaking campaign. "At the age of 46," wrote Timothy Leland in the *Globe*, "the former governor is a tireless, non-stop campaigner. He gets up at dawn, and he doesn't stop moving until midnight, and all the time he is shaking hands—at factory gates, on street corners, in subway stations." It was an interesting contrast in personal campaign styles—a classic case of a "media" campaign versus a person-to-person approach.[88]

Right up until the first returns began to come in on the evening of election day, Tuesday, September 13, 1966, Collins and his supporters were certain they had turned things around and would take the race. At 8:40 P.M., however, the first Boston returns came in from Precinct 5 of Ward 17, a residential district of Dorchester composed of predominantly Irish voters. To the shock and consternation of the Collins people gathered around the tables at their campaign headquarters, the district gave Peabody 129 votes and Collins a mere 76. It was only one precinct, to be sure, but it sounded an alarming note. Precinct 3 in Ward 10, Collins's old district when he had been a state representative, came in with 367 votes for Peabody and 249 for Collins. And then Precinct 3 of Ward 11, another of the mayor's home districts, gave 101 votes to Peabody and only 60 to Collins. In a scene right out of *The Last Hurrah*, when the fictional Mayor Skeffington's lieutenants first notice that "small erratic fluctuation, isolated and unexplainable," that gives the disturbing signal to the engineer that something has gone wrong along the track, a cloud of depression began to settle over the Collins workers tabulating the results as the city figures continued to roll in. When Mattapan's Ward 14, Dorchester's Ward 15, Roslindale's Ward 20, and Brighton's Ward 22 all came in on Peabody's side, everybody knew it was all over. At 11:25 P.M. Collins gave his concession speech before a large crowd of cheering supporters at his campaign headquarters, where he pledged to lend his full support "to the entire Democratic ticket" in the weeks to come.[89]

Now that the campaigning was over, the election finished, and his senate prospects gone forever, the mayor seemed to experience a sense of relief. "Verging at times almost on the jocular," as one reporter put it, Collins appeared much more relaxed and exhibited none of the bitterness or rancor he had displayed three months earlier at the convention in his outburst against Powers. It was over; regardless of the outcome he announced that he was "of good cheer," had "no regrets" about his run for higher office, and sat back to watch the outcome of the November finals.[90]

Looking back at the senatorial race from the vantage point of twenty-five years, however, Collins was still firmly convinced that had he been able to gain the Democratic nomination, he would have gone on to defeat Brooke. And had he been elected to the United States Senate, he declared, "it would have been a different America."[91] Although in retrospect that seems an unlikely prospect, in view of the changing times and shifting politics of the late 1960s and early 1970s, it was a dream that obviously helped ease the painful loss and helped him reflect on his plans for the future.

At their own party convention in June, the Republicans had confirmed Edward Brooke and John Volpe as their senatorial and gubernatorial candidates respectively. Hoping to be a gubernatorial nominee himself in 1970—perhaps even earlier if rumors about Volpe's availability as a vice presidential candidate proved a reality—Lieutenant Governor Elliot Richardson chose to run for Brooke's vacated post of state attorney general, allowing the Department of Public Works commissioner, Francis W. Sargent, to get the convention's support as its nominee for lieutenant governor. Although preliminary reports during the summer indicated that a woeful lack of qualified candidates would probably cause the Republicans to lose about a third of both houses in the state legislature, their unified support of the top of the ticket allowed them a clean sweep of the offices of U.S. senator, governor, lieutenant governor, and attorney general. Volpe took every county in the state, lost only five cities and towns to his Democratic rival, Eddie McCormack, and even took the city of Somerville, with its six-to-one Democratic registration. In his race for the U.S. Senate, Peabody lost every county except Suffolk, and even there his majority (twenty-six thousand) was appallingly low for a Democrat. Although he won a few industrial centers such as Chicopee, Holyoke, and Lawrence, most other large cities and towns in Massachusetts went to Brooke, including Peabody's own home town of Cambridge.[92] It was a disastrous year for traditional Democratic leadership in the state, and the outcome of the 1966 elections left most political observers wondering about the long-range direction of the commonwealth, the viability of the state Democratic party, the political future of Mayor John Collins, and the immediate prospects of Edward J. Logue and his plans for a New Boston.

As Christmas approached, the members of the city hall press corps—Joe Keblinsky of the *Globe*, Bob Hannan of the *Herald*, Earl Marchand of the *Traveler*, Bob Aldrich of the *Record-American*, George Merry of the *Monitor*—met in a dirty, litter-strewn room in a corner of the third floor of the old City Hall, just one floor above the mayor's office, and put together a humorous piece of doggerel verse, which they sent to Collins in typewritten form as a Christmas card. Expressing their collective concern about rumors that he would soon retire from public life, and urging the mayor not to retreat ("A guy like you is rayor / And real damn hard to beat"), they tried to draw him out in their concluding refrain:

> We wish for you the very most:
> A Christmas blessed with cheer;
> So tell us, sir, as you we toast;
> *WHAT ARE YOUR PLANS NEXT YEAR?*[93]

Indeed, that was precisely the question many Bostonians were asking as the end of one year ushered in the beginning of another—an election year.

# 9.

# Changing Times

The year 1967 had begun, and for most professional football teams the regular season was over. Buffalo prepared to meet the Kansas City Chiefs for the AFL playoff, and the Green Bay Packers were getting ready to go up against the Dallas Cowboys in the NFL division to see who would appear in the Super Bowl at the Los Angeles Coliseum on January 15. A week earlier the Atomic Energy Commission had exploded a thermonuclear device, code name Greeley, some four thousand feet down a shaft in the desert region of southern Nevada, jolting the seismograph at the University of California at Berkeley with the force of a medium-size earthquake. The United States had been watching the Soviet Union deploy an antiballistic missile system of its own in the arctic regions, and Greeley was considered an appropriate response to that escalation. Space experts were speculating that "old-timers" like forty-three-year-old Walter Schirra, forty-year-old Virgil Grissom, and thirty-nine-year-old Gordon Cooper might well be the first Americans to walk on the moon when the three-man Apollo flight lifted off some time in 1968 or 1969.

The economic condition of the nation was on everyone's mind as the new year began. Throughout 1966 money had been scarce, the labor market tight, interest rates high, and home construction stagnant. Dow Jones industrials closed the year out with a slight dip at 799.10, continuing a depressing lack of business activity that represented a disappointing season. The U.S. Chamber of Commerce and other indus-

249

try groups and lobbyists were getting ready to press for tax credits and other investment incentives in the event that President Lyndon Johnson asked Congress for a tax increase to meet the spiraling costs of the war overseas. In Vietnam the fighting had gone on without ceasing down to the moment when, on the morning before Christmas, the guns fell silent. Although another holiday truce went into effect, American troops mounted a lonely and wary vigil, recalling all too well the surprise Viet Cong attacks during the 1965 Christmas break. Some observers back home clutched at a slim straw when they heard that United Nations ambassador Arthur Goldberg had hand-delivered a note to U.N. secretary general U Thant, emphasizing the U.S. commitment to seek "an honorable and lasting settlement of the conflict and asking the secretary general to take "whatever steps you consider necessary" to bring about a cease-fire. Most political insiders, however, considered that nothing would come of this latest effort, since there had been no substantial change in Washington's position and no visible indication that Hanoi was interested in talking.

Johnson's commitment to fighting the war in Vietnam while continuing his Great Society programs—his promise of "guns and butter"—was proving impossible to maintain. The inflation rate, which had remained fairly constant at about 2 percent through most of the early 1960s, had risen to 3 percent by 1967 and was showing no signs of leveling off. In return for agreeing to tax increases to support the war and contain inflation, conservatives in Congress demanded severe cutbacks in Great Society programs at a time when such programs were desperately needed in large cities with burgeoning immigrant and minority populations. Reductions in welfare payments, elimination of job training programs, increases in unemployment, inadequate public housing, overcrowded schools, juvenile delinquency, inadequate medical care, and unfair treatment by public officials had already produced violent reactions in the black neighborhoods. After the Watts section of Los Angeles erupted in 1965, frightening outbursts occurred in other major northern cities such as Newark, Washington, Cleveland, Detroit, and Chicago.

It was becoming painfully obvious that Boston could not escape the repercussions of racial discontent much longer, and already observers were calculating the time and intensity of such an outbreak. "What will happen in Roxbury-Dorchester, with an estimated 70,000 Negroes, some 10 percent of the city's population?" asked the journalist Ian

Menzies in a special New Year's Day edition of the *Boston Globe*. "Boston escaped racial violence last year and still has a reservoir of good will—but for how long?" he asked. Reflecting a growing attitude among some people that the Collins administration, originally vigorous and creative, had grown old and lethargic, Menzies painted a depressing picture of Boston as it looked forward to the coming year, an election year. The city still "stumbles," he wrote, reflecting the growing complaints of both black and white neighborhoods against the policies of the Collins-Logue administration. Boston was still plagued by "the need for more housing, torn by racial imbalance in the schools, beset by transportation problems, suffering from dirt and neglect in too many areas outside the showpiece plazas." The only hope Menzies could see for avoiding the type of catastrophes that were devastating so many other American cities was more efficient management. "This should be the year, the first of four years, to close the elusive gap of tired-out management, to seek younger men who delight in challenges . . . and make government work exciting and vital." The editorial was a clear signal that some people at the *Boston Globe* felt it was time for Collins to move on and make way for new blood.[1]

Mayor John F. Collins, however, had shown no sign that he had the slightest intention of moving on, and on Monday, January 2, in his eighth annual address as mayor of Boston, he spoke about what he intended to accomplish in the coming year only in positive terms. The previous year had been another "year of progress" for the New Boston, he said, and assured the citizens that "great new advances" were in store during the coming year. In light of the growing problems of the needy, the sick, and the aged, the rising level of racial disturbances, and the continuation of blight and misery throughout the city, however, the mayor warned Boston taxpayers to brace themselves for a "substantial" tax hike that would push the rate much higher than the current $101 levy. Boston's great financial problems, like those of all cities in America, could not be solved on a local basis, he concluded. Out of "sheer necessity" citizens must look to the state and the federal governments for help in meeting problems that the people themselves did not have the means of overcoming. As Collins delivered his address, veteran political observers tried to get some idea of the mayor's plans for his own future, but to no avail. Even those "political sharpies" adept at reading between the lines came out of the city council chambers as confused as when they went in, according to one *Globe* writer. They were unable to detect in

Collins's words any sort of hint as to whether he would be a candidate for a third four-year term. In speaking with reporters later, the mayor still kept everyone guessing by stating that he had not "closed the door entirely" to the possibility of a third term.[2]

There were those who were no longer content to remain patient in the face of the mayor's enigmatic silence, and one response to Menzies's call for new faces and fresh blood came from thirty-eight-year-old Kevin White. Long before 1966 came to an end it was being rumored that the young secretary of state, the only Democrat to escape the Republican sweep of state offices, had become dissatisfied with his dead-end job and intended to run for the mayor's office. Early in January White made his ambitions for higher office much clearer in a *Globe* piece in which he told the reporter Timothy Leland that becoming mayor of Boston would enable him "to make headlines," which, in turn, would give him the leverage "to raise money for a gubernatorial bid." Right from the start, White made it clear that he was interested in becoming governor of Massachusetts, and that the office of mayor was only a stepping stone toward that exalted office.[3]

A month later, on February 15, at a press conference at the Sheraton Plaza Hotel, White made his formal announcement in an address deliberately distancing himself from the policies of his predecessors. "The last two administrations have laid plans and . . . constructed great new buildings," he conceded, but then went on to complain that a great city is not only a place to work but also "a place in which to live and raise a family, and it is precisely here that we have failed." Pointing to the drain of population out of the city as evidence of "acute disenchantment," White promised the "alienated voter" of Boston (an interesting choice of words taken from the 1959 Collins-Powers contest) the opportunity to participate in the processes of government, and held out to the black community the hope of racial harmony. "If we fail to foster and sustain our human relations," he concluded, "then any other achievements will mock our efforts in the future."[4]

According to the author George Higgins, the reason White came out so early and so aggressively was to intimidate Collins into not running for a third term. Collins had not yet announced his own plans, noted Higgins, and White hoped the incumbent mayor would have second thoughts if he realized that he would have a serious fight on his hands and would be faced with the prospect of defending himself "against charges that he was the chief reason why his voters were getting out of Boston."[5]

Politics was clearly in the air, and while Collins continued to remain silent about his future plans as he prepared for a trip to Ireland, a number of other candidates decided to test their strength. Early in May, the longtime city councillor Christopher Ianella, convinced that Collins would not seek reelection, threw his own hat into the ring. Warning that Boston was facing a "grave municipal crisis," he announced that "sensitive, alert, and vigorous leadership" was needed to make the city "preeminent" again. City leaders had failed to provide a "clean, healthy environment, with decent housing, superior education, and attractive recreational facilities," he charged. Those same leaders had also failed to provide safe streets "where no citizen need fear for himself or his family at any hour of the day or night." Ianella put himself forward as the most experienced candidate who could provide solutions to all these problems.[6]

Two weeks later, on May 16, city councillor Barry Hynes, the thirty-three-year-old son of former mayor John B. Hynes, announced his candidacy for the mayor's office, motivated not only by his own political ambitions but also by a desire to reclaim his father's name and reputation from what some members of the family felt was John Collins's claim of sole authorship of the New Boston. The *Boston Traveler* hailed Hynes's decision to run as "courageous" and commended him as the only candidate who had "actually committed himself on some issues" and who had said something "meaningful about where this city is or might be going." The newspaper was especially strong in its praise for Hynes's proposal to expand the school committee from five to eleven members, and then take it out of the hands of "politicians."[7] He recommended naming a panel of professional educators and businessmen who would put together a slate of school committee members and then present it to the mayor. From this list, the mayor would select a school committee, which would then be independent of the mayor. These were the kinds of ideas the *Traveler* felt would improve the political atmosphere of the city and move the New Boston along new and more imaginative lines.

In addition to Barry Hynes and Christopher Ianella, Peter F. Hines became the third city councillor to enter the mayoral contest, while Beacon Hill Republican John Sears, a perennial political candidate and indefatigable public servant, also offered himself as a candidate for the

254 BUILDING A NEW BOSTON

city hall post, although most of his Brahmin friends and associates could see little real chance for victory in a city election with so many Irish Democrats going to the polls.

Refreshed by a short vacation in Ireland, Collins returned to Boston at the end of May to find not only a growing number of candidates planning to replace him but also several discouraging problems awaiting his arrival. First of all, he was being called upon to endorse a school committee overdraft of $226,000 in pay raises for such employees as truant officers, janitors, supply room personnel, and secretaries. Louise Day Hicks of South Boston, the prominent school committee chair-woman and herself an announced candidate for the office of mayor, waited to see what action the mayor would take. On the one hand, if he approved the overdraft he would undoubtedly contribute to the financial difficulties of the city by increasing the budget and raising the tax rate. On the other hand, if he did not approve the committee's proposals he would be accused by Mrs. Hicks of heartlessly ignoring the interests of "the little people" who worked for the school department and who would almost certainly cast their votes for the lady from South Boston.

As if this were not bad enough, the mayor was also getting insistent calls from residents of the Codman Square section of Dorchester who were up in arms about reports that the MBTA was planning to move a considerable amount of rolling stock from its Cambridge yards to expanded storage facilities in Dorchester in order to free up property near Harvard University for the proposed John F. Kennedy Library. Neighborhood leaders demanded that the mayor take action to prevent the increased traffic and ugly environmental impact of such a move, which would inevitably lower real estate values in the area.

And last, but by no means least, Collins returned to confront one of the city's most violent racial demonstrations. Boston had been rela-tively calm during a period when many other cities had exploded in destruction and violence. But on Friday, May 26, members of Mothers for Adequate Welfare had staged a sit-in at the Blue Hill Avenue division of the Boston Welfare Office, protesting that their checks had been cut off without notification, that social workers were hostile to them, and that they were often "pushed around" at welfare offices. When they got no appreciable response, they employed the same tactic the following Thursday, June 1. Some fifty women stationed themselves in the Grove Hall welfare office and remained overnight; when workers prepared to close up for the weekend on Friday afternoon, the protesters chained themselves in the building along with a number of frightened employees. When uniformed members of the Boston police department finally broke into the building at the orders of Mayor Collins, released the hostages, and took the demonstrators into custody, hundreds of black youths from the community went on a rampage protesting police brutality.[8] For several days and nights mobs ranged up and down the streets of Roxbury and North Dorchester looting stores, starting fires, smashing street lights, throwing rocks at police and firefighters as sirens from fire engines and police cars echoed through the night. Although the violence in Boston came nowhere near that experienced in other American cities that year, the devastation it caused among kosher meat markets, fish stores, bakeries, delicatessens, and Jewish bookstores along Blue Hill Avenue caught the city by surprise and led Collins to call the actions of the welfare mothers "the worst manifestation of disrespect for the rights of others that his city has ever seen."[9]

Although the Grove Hall riot had no direct influence on Collins's decision not to run for a third term as mayor, it certainly must have convinced him that he had made the right decision. Collins may well have seen the Boston he returned to from his trip abroad as a city that he no longer wished to govern—if, indeed, it could be governed at all. When he had first taken over as mayor in 1960, an air of civility, as well as an unwritten code of gentlemanly conduct that provided acceptable guidelines of behavior, had still pervaded the political process. He had moved into the mayor's office with a fairly clear consensus, certainly among the movers and the shakers, that the city should be rebuilt; and under his vigorous and capable direction the city had become more prosperous and progressive than ever before in its history. In what had once been old, neglected, and broken-down areas of the city there had sprung up beautiful buildings, majestic towers, high-rise banking institutions, elaborate insurance companies, impressive corporate offices, modern hotels, and expensive restaurants, which together made Boston one of the leading examples of enlightened urban renewal.

Seven years later, however, it was all going up in smoke. Civil dialogue had given way to angry shouts and bitter recriminations. Negotiation had been replaced by confrontation. Compromise had been supplanted by unnegotiable demands. The orderly political process that had once moved along at a leisurely pace was being upstaged by theatrical public demonstrations clamoring for immediate solutions. Day after day it was becoming painfully clear that a person who held public office was no longer a figure of honor and respect, but an exposed target of derision and assault. The idealistic spirit of young John Kennedy—"ask not what your country can do for you, ask what you can do for your country"—had died in a hail of gunfire at Dallas, and Lyndon Johnson's dream of a Great Society was foundering in the rice paddies of Vietnam. The mood of the nation had turned ugly and mean, and the politics of Boston was reflecting much of that same depressing atmosphere. Being mayor of Boston was no longer something to be desired—it was no longer fun.

Confronted with problems that had no solutions, challenged by people who had impossible demands, trying to run a city with a failing tax base, increasing expenditures, and political rivals who played games with serious issues, Collins had had enough. When he announced a special press conference for Tuesday, June 6, rumors immediately made their way around town that he was ready to announce his plans for the future. His reappointment of Edmund L. McNamara as police commissioner, his disregard of pressures to build more police stations, his willingness to support a raise in the tax rate, and his failure to display any effort to mount a campaign—all were taken as signs that he would not run for a third term.[10] But then again, Collins was still playing his cards close to his vest, and nobody was absolutely certain what he would do.

On the morning of June 6, therefore, City Hall was crowded with newspaper reporters anxious to learn the mayor's long-awaited decision. He was originally scheduled to meet at 10:30 with a delegation from the Mothers for Adequate Welfare, but when the women did not show up Collins waited another twenty minutes and then called in the press. Wasting little time with preliminaries, he made his announcement: "I will not be a candidate for mayor." He then went on to explain that he had tentatively arrived at that decision before his recent one-week trip abroad, and then finalized it while he was in Ireland. Appearing relaxed, happy, and even "jubilant," the mayor seemed comfortable with his decision, joked with the throng of reporters, and when asked about his future plans said flatly: "I am not going to have a political future." At 9:30 that night Collins appeared on local television to explain to the citizens of Boston why he was not going to be a candidate, to review his many accomplishments in building a New Boston, and to urge the voters to be "very selective" about the man they chose as his successor: "I pray our Boston shall not pass to those who care not for our city, but only for themselves."[11]

Collins's decision not to run caught many voters by surprise, caused a number of supporters to find the news "disheartening and disappointing," and produced consternation among downtown bankers and businessmen who had been unprepared for such an eventuality. When he heard the news, Ernest Henderson, Sr., of the Sheraton Hotel Corporations, issued a call to various business leaders to attempt a last-minute move to persuade Collins to change his mind, but the mayor would not be deterred.[12] According to a poll conducted for the *Boston Globe* by John Becker's research firm right after the Collins announcement, most downtown leaders somewhat grudgingly admitted they preferred Kevin White to all other candidates who were then in the running. Their preference was something that White himself appeared to accept as a political fact of life, assuming that the downtown investors would surely support him rather than Louise Day Hicks. According to George Higgins, the knowledge that he already had the downtown vote in his back pocket gave him the freedom to play to the neighborhoods and strike "a posture as something of a populist"—a point White himself readily conceded. "I went into the neighborhoods because downtown was already functioning without me," he said. "Collins had brought in the money, he had lowered the tax rate, he had brought in the business leaders—those things were *done*. I could draw on that source like an inheritance."[13]

White issued his first position paper of the campaign only two days after Collins's announcement not to run, making his appeal to the neighborhoods a major plank in his platform. He promised to establish a Neighborhood Services Department, which would employ "coordinators of community projects [and] grievance officers for individuals or neighborhood groups," who would serve as "reporters of human needs to all levels of government." Counting on these local "coordinators" for advice, White further responded to recent neighborhood demands by promising to upgrade the police, increase their pay, build new substations, push new school building programs, and select sites based on educational needs.[14] In the days that followed, White continued to put as much distance as possible between the renewal policies of Collins and his own appeals for neighborhood support. "Obviously, the people of the city judge Boston not only by its skyline but also by its services," he said, emphasizing his theme that Boston needed "people programs" to match the "building programs" of previous administrations. A city capable of attracting hundreds of millions of dollars to revitalize the downtown business area, he argued, was equally capable of attracting public and private funds "to influence new life into the neighborhoods where people live."[15]

Although Collins had decided that he himself was through with politics, he still believed in the prospects of a New Boston and the renewal programs by which that goal could be fully achieved. One day in March, before he had made his plans public, he called Ed Logue into his office and asked him to sit down. "Ed," he said, "I'm not going to go again."

"Christ Almighty, Mr. Mayor," exclaimed Logue, "we're not through yet."

"We'll never be through, Ed. Don't you know that?" replied Collins. Then, with a sidelong glance and a sly smile, the mayor asked, "Didn't you ever think of doing it yourself?"

"Of course I had thought about it," Logue recalled later. "After all, I had worked for some great people in the course of my public career— Chester Bowles (Christ, he wanted to be president!), Dick Lee in New Haven, Nelson Rockefeller in New York, and John Collins in Boston— all of them active, dynamic people who liked to get things done. Of course I had thought about it. And what the hell, I certainly had name recognition. By that time everybody in Boston either loved me or hated me, but they all knew my name. My wife wasn't crazy about the idea, but I decided to take the plunge."[16]

Admitting that he was an "amateur politician" and had made some mistakes during his early years with the BRA, Edward J. Logue launched his campaign and pointed out his many accomplishments on behalf of Boston: how the New Boston he had created had attracted businessmen and investors, brought money into the city treasury, raised real estate values, kept down the tax rate, and created an average of four thousand new jobs in the *construction trades alone every year.*" He promised voters of the city that he would improve education in the face of a "stagnant School Committee," provide better police protection, create safer streets, and build a new sports stadium in the South Station area.[17]

Collins encouraged Logue in his political aspirations, was convinced that he would win, and assured him that he would help him in every way possible in his campaign, although he cautioned that any signs of public support from the incumbent mayor would probably work to his political disadvantage. The eminent Bostonian Henry L. Shattuck contacted Logue almost immediately and offered him his support, representing an important downtown constituency that certainly wanted to see a continuation of the renewal process, but many of his Brahmin colleagues were not so forthcoming. The fly in the political ointment, as far as Logue and Collins were concerned, was John Sears. Although as a lifelong Yankee Republican he had little chance of winning, his personal friendships among his Beacon Hill neighbors were enough to take away some critical votes that would otherwise have gone to Ed Logue, whose home and friends were in the same area. Collins put in a telephone call to his friend John Volpe and asked him if there was anything he could do to persuade Sears not to run in a contest he didn't have a chance of winning. "If Logue doesn't get either the number one or two spot, you know what that means," said Collins, "it'll either be Louise Day Hicks or Kevin White. Now which of those two do *you* like, John?"

"Neither," Volpe responded.

"Well, you're going to have one or the other if you don't get John Sears out of that race," said Collins. But Sears remained adamant, and stayed in the race.[18]

Collins, appalled at the thought of either Hicks or White emerging victorious, later admitted that if he had ever imagined that Kevin White would become mayor of Boston he himself would have considered running for a third term. The main strategy in moving Logue ahead into a challenging position, therefore, had to involve coming up with something that would stop the momentum that was building up for White, who was already claiming by default the support of former Collins backers in the business and financial community.

It was at this point, as the campaign was heading into the September primary, that a young technician from Jamaica Plain named Richard Iantosca walked into the city elections department, registered a formal complaint about Kevin White's nomination papers, and walked out again. Nobody seemed to know who Mr. Iantosca was, and after he left City Hall that day nobody was likely to know, because the young man promptly disappeared from his house and his job.[19] On September 6 Logue issued a statement to the press claiming that something was "seriously wrong" with his opponent's signature papers, since affidavits appeared to have been signed by "different hands." Although he pointed out that this was a clear violation of the election laws, he insisted that White's name should still remain on the ballot, obviously hoping that the adverse publicity would cut into White's support.[20] While White's close associates Ted Anzalone and Dick Dray went in frantic search of the elusive Iantosca, White publicly claimed that Ed Logue was behind the scheme, denounced the effort as a "power play" generated by members of the "power establishment of the city" who did not want the people to choose their own mayor, and claimed that it was only the latest example of the kind of "dirty politics that had alienated the Boston voter from his city government."[21]

In the midst of the charges and countercharges Iantosca's attorneys unexpectedly announced that the challenge would be dropped, undoubtedly prompted by recurring rumors and innuendoes that homosexuality was involved in the Iantosca affair. Whether the stories were true or false, whether they were planted by political rivals or stimulated by mischievous troublemakers, was immaterial. This was a time when even the mere hint of homosexuality was regarded as a political disaster.

There are those who believe that in the long run Logue suffered more by the embarrassing signature incident than White, and Logue himself was the first to admit that the operation had been neither wise nor successful. While he continued to insist that reports from a local handwriting expert absolutely proved that a great many signatures on White's nomination had been forged, letting himself be persuaded by a well-meaning friend to use a person he did not know and had never met to register the challenge was a bad idea that boomeranged and caused him a serious "loss of credibility."[22]

Certainly that view would seem to be supported by the outcome of the primary election in September. Hicks proved she was still the top vote-getter in Boston by coming in first with 43,719 votes, just over 28 percent of the votes cast. White placed second with 30,497 votes, about 20 percent of the total vote. Republican John Sears came in third with 23,879 votes, while Logue pulled in a disappointing fourth with only 23,026 votes.[23] When Logue had first come to Boston at Collins's invitation seven years earlier, Collins had told him that as an "outsider" from New Haven he would have a better chance of getting things done than if he were an "insider" and better known. Bostonians "start keeping score on everybody local too early," he had explained to the young man, showing a keen sense of the reality of Boston politics that would ultimately allow Logue to get a good head start in his renewal plans. But seven years is a long time in Boston politics, and by 1967 Boston voters had totaled up the score on Logue, the consummate outsider (Louise Day Hicks persisted in calling him "The Intruder"), and decided they did not want him for their mayor any more than they wanted Collins and his downtown brand of urban renewal.[24] Under the Plan A system, still in operation, only the top two candidates, Hicks and White, would fight it out in the final election in November. All other candidates were simply historical statistics in the political record. It was time to move into a new phase of Boston political history.

For generations, Boston politics had been divided into traditional and familiar lines of religion and ethnicity—Yankees versus Celts, Protestants versus Catholics, natives versus newcomers—the stuff that history, legends, anecdotes, and classic fiction were made of, from *The Late George Apley* to *The Last Hurrah*. In 1967, for the first time, the issue of race became a new and significant dimension in Boston politics, combining with the seething anger of white neighborhood resentment to form an explosive mixture that threatened the new upper-class establishment of old-line Brahmins and newly arrived Irish Catholics in banks and boardrooms all over the city. Poor blacks and poor whites were preparing to square off against one another in a desperate struggle to get jobs, housing, food, medical care, and educational opportunities for themselves and their families. Federal funds were shrinking, taxes were rising, inflation was causing food and fuel costs to rise, and a frightening recession was causing serious unemployment in working-class communities. Blacks and whites were both fighting for the same piece of pie, which seemed to be getting smaller all the time.

These problems of racial tensions, neighborhood discontent, and serious economic setbacks provided the background for the mayoral elections of 1967. Louise Day Hicks presented herself as the outspoken champion of local autonomy and neighborhood schools. The daughter of Judge William J. Day, justice of the South Boston district court, a married woman with two children, a law school graduate, and a practicing attorney, Hicks had run successfully for a seat on the Boston School Committee, and after a fairly routine first term had been elected by her colleagues as chairwoman of the committee. Her second term had promised to be fairly routine as well until, on June 11, 1964, the local chapter of the NAACP leveled charges of de facto segregation against the Boston public school system, charges that Hicks promptly and absolutely denied. From that point on, Louise Day Hicks became the unquestioned spokesperson of those who felt that the time had come for the "little people"—the white, tax-paying, working-class residents of the neighborhoods—to stand up for their rights and defend their neighborhood schools from the social experiments of black "outsiders," their Ivy League supporters from the suburbs, and the downtown developers who had already done so much to destroy the old neighborhoods of Boston.

The other candidate who emerged from the September primary in 1967 was Kevin Hagan White. As a man whose father and grandfather had served in city government, White came from a long line of active politicians and soon established himself as a resourceful campaigner in his own right. A graduate of Williams College and of the Boston College Law School, he was acceptable to upper-middle-class groups in the city, who saw him as a capable and articulate administrator. As four-time Massachusetts secretary of state and the only Democrat who had survived the Republican sweep in 1966, White was viewed by older members of the downtown Yankee community as an appealing "nonpolitical" candidate in the tradition of Hynes and Collins who could be depended on to keep the process of urban renewal rolling now that Logue was definitely out of the running. And as a reputedly liberal-minded progressive in the flamboyant style of New York's mayor, John Lindsay, White was more than acceptable to Boston's black community as the only viable alternative to Mrs. Hicks. "Kevin H. White, candidate for Boston's top office, has realistically met the issues of this campaign and the issues and problems that confront the city of Boston with a candid and believable approach," declared the black community's *Bay State Banner* in its election-eve endorsement of the former secretary of state.[25]

Most observers agreed that the contest between White and Hicks was a tight race, with the final outcome very much in doubt. Despite the opposition of civil rights groups, black associations, the downtown business establishment, the academic world, and most newspaper reporters, who poked fun at her hats, laughed at her beehive hairdo, counted the sequins on her dresses, and dismissed her as an inconsequential "tea party candidate," Hicks more than held her own. She rallied her loyal constituents in support of local autonomy and neighborhood schools ("You know where I stand," she repeated) and won considerable admiration in traditional ethnic communities for the way she stood up to powerful outside forces that threatened to change their lives and disrupt their close-knit communities. Indeed, so strong a candidate was

*The incoming mayor, Kevin H. White, meets with the outgoing mayor, John F. Collins, after White's hard-fought victory over Louise Day Hicks in 1967. Despite taking office during a disruptive period of antiwar protests, urban violence, and civil rights demonstrations, Mayor White continued the process of urban renewal and completed a number of projects begun during the Collins administration. He called attention to the New Boston by hailing it as a "world-class city." Boston Globe photograph.*

Hicks that the *Boston Globe* broke a seventy-one-year tradition by coming out with a public endorsement of Kevin White.[26] Although her supporters in South Boston's Wards 6 and 7 gave their "Louise" a whopping 11,335 votes to a meager 4,489 for her opponent, White was able to pile up enough votes in the other wards to take the election. Of a total of 192,673 votes cast, White defeated Hicks by a margin of 12,000 and prepared to begin his first term of office during one of the most chaotic and disruptive periods in American history.[27]

As he prepared to take over as mayor of Boston, it was generally assumed that White would resign his position as secretary of state and allow several Beacon Hill politicians to move one notch higher on the state political ladder. House Speaker John F. X. Davoren, for example, anticipated becoming the next secretary of state, thereby making room for Robert Quinn, the house Democratic majority leader, to take over

Davoren's post as speaker. Suddenly becoming aware that a new state welfare reorganization bill would add such crippling costs to the city budget that he would be forced to raise property taxes—a political disaster for any big-city mayor—White announced that unless the state government agreed to assume all welfare costs for the cities and towns of the commonwealth, he would continue to serve as secretary of state until statewide elections could be held the following year. "I was tickled pink with myself when I thought of that," he later told a *Globe* reporter, Michael Rezendes. Despite the howls of protest that reverberated through the State House corridors, the state legislature eventually acceded to White's demands and took over responsibility for the city's welfare costs, thus relieving the new mayor and his successors of the burden of a tax hike.[28]

Before the year ended and his own term came to a close, Collins announced that he intended to move out of the old Second Empire–style City Hall on School Street and into the new futuristic City Hall in Government Center. Obviously unable to resist the opportunity to become the first tenant of the building that epitomized his strenuous efforts to revitalize the city, he told reporters that starting on Monday, December 18, he would be spending his remaining days in office "doing business" in the mayor's office on the fifth floor of the southeast corner of the new building, which was still in the final stages of construction. In anticipation of the move, he arranged for a gala "tea party" on Sunday, December 17—the 194th anniversary of the original Boston tea party—to which he invited "everyone who had participated in the creation of the New Boston." On Sunday, some two thousand Bostonians from all walks of life got a firsthand glimpse of their future $26 million City Hall, although none of the public escalators or elevators were working that day, and stacks of bricks and piles of scaffolding blocked many of the accesses. The visitors found that the five rooms that made up the mayor's executive suite on the fifth floor had not yet been completed, and although the wood paneling and light fixtures had been installed, the carpeting had not yet been put down, workers were still laying the teak flooring, and the heating system was not working. Sitting behind a borrowed desk in his new office, Mayor Collins welcomed visitors to "the most exciting public building in America," spent three hours shaking hands, and asked his guests to register their names in a large book he assured them would "go into the archives."[29]

The following day Collins arrived at the New City Hall at 10:00

A.M., took the private elevator to his fifth-floor office, and spent the next five hours chatting with visitors and conducting routine business while the noise of construction went on around him. About noontime mayor-elect Kevin White arrived, met with Collins for almost an hour, and then toured the building with a group of his own aides, explaining to reporters that he himself would remain on at the School Street building until at least May or June of the following year. Although Collins fully enjoyed his day "reigning in solitary splendor" in his new quarters, he was never able to return. The lack of adequate heating, combined with the chill December winds that blew through the unfinished offices, caused him to come down with a serious case of pneumonia, which kept him bedridden for weeks and prevented him from attending the first inauguration of Kevin H. White.[30]

True to his word, John Collins never again offered himself for public office. There were many in Boston who regretted that decision and found it difficult to believe that such an effective political leader would simply walk away from elective politics.[31] In an end-of-the-year farewell to one of the city's "greatest mayors," who had done so much to create the New Boston, Robert Healy, the *Globe*'s political editor, wrote that Collins's concept of public office had been to "do the job; do it well." As mayor he assumed that it was performance that counted in politics, "not being a good fellow." One of Collins's most significant achievements, wrote Healy, was to build a bridge between the investment community and the body politic. It was on this "bridge of confidence" that Collins had built a New Boston and changed its entire shape, Healy concluded. "Few Boston mayors leave that kind of mark on the city."[32]

There were others, however, who might agree that Collins had indeed changed the shape of the city, but would argue that it had not necessarily been for the better. In the downtown area he had gone along with the prevailing designs of the "new architects," whose modernistic designs seemed incompatible with their historic surroundings, whose windswept open spaces seemed out of place in their confined colonial settings, and whose single-purpose zones had replaced many of the cluttered byways that had been so characteristic of the old city. What Healy called Collins's "bridge of confidence" with the investment community solidified a successful and beneficial downtown alliance, it is true, but it also ensured that the main goal of the mayor's urban-renewal campaign was to transform blighted areas into profitable real estate ventures more suited to the inflated salaries of well-to-do clients than to the limited incomes of blue-collar workers.

That tendency toward upward mobility became even more apparent as the administration sought to bring its ideas of progressive improvement into the surrounding neighborhoods, producing widespread antagonism and violent disaffection. Residents of the white ethnic neighborhoods angrily resented the arrogant manner in which outside social organizers and profit-motivated urban developers planned to renovate the living habits and social customs of old and established communities. Black citizens similarly reacted to the ways in which the Boston Redevelopment Authority pushed longtime residents out of the South End into less desirous locations in Roxbury and North Dorchester in order to make room for expensive apartments and high-priced townhouses. There was no question that the transformation of the New Boston during the Collins administration was both dramatic and spectacular, attracting the admiration of visitors, the raves of urban planners, and the investments of corporations. In terms of its impact on the working classes, the minorities, the poor, and the homeless of the city, however, its long-range social effects were incalculable, and its short-term political effects were yet to be measured.

The official transference of power from John Frederick Collins to Kevin Hagan White took place on Monday, January 1, 1968. For the first time in fifty years, an inauguration of a mayor of Boston was held in historic Faneuil Hall on New Year's Day instead of in Symphony Hall—a symbolic tribute to the significance of the New Boston.[33] Mayor-elect White and his wife, Kathryn, entered the hall at 10:05 A.M., and the entire audience of fewer than one thousand guests, crammed into the ancient chamber, rose and applauded for two minutes. Smiling, confident, shaking hands, and accepting congratulations, White made his way to the stage and was sworn in as mayor of Boston in a ceremony that lasted forty-five minutes. In a brief speech the new mayor outlined a program for the city based on four major promises: to furnish the city with people of exceptional talent; to provide the city with modern methods of government; to be mindful of the "shared needs of the entire metropolitan area"; and to organize an administration that would offer a role in community life "to all who are interested." "The shape of tomorrow's Boston will be our measure," he concluded, "the measure of each of us as men and women, and the measure of the civilization we represent." When the inaugural ceremonies were over, White broke with another precedent by driving to the French Room of the Ritz-Carlton Hotel, instead of the Parker House, for the traditional mayor's luncheon for the incoming members of the city council and the school committee. And no one could recall the last time a Boston mayor had celebrated his installation with a formal dance. But that is just what Kevin White did that evening as close to five thousand guests ignored the subfreezing temperature and swarmed through Boston's new Sheraton Boston Hotel to enjoy what a *Globe* reporter, Christopher Lydon, described as an "uninhibited display of black-tie elegance."[34]

Now that he had been duly installed, the new mayor settled down to confront the complex problems of a dividing city with the help of a close-knit group of friends and associates. Edward T. Sullivan, who had been his deputy secretary of state for the previous seven years, now took over as his director of administrative services. Theodore Anzalone, former state director of corporations under Secretary of State White, now became a mayoral assistant, as did Richard M. Dray, who had been an attorney in the secretary of state's office. Herbert Gleason, a Ward 5 friend and neighbor, became corporation counsel for the new administration; Lawrence Cameron, White's former law partner, joined the team; and Katherine D. Kane, another Beacon Hill neighbor, also came aboard, where she would remain an important part of the White administration for many years. With these members of his "cabinet" and with other young idealists such as Daniel J. Finn, Barney Frank, and Hale Champion, White worked long and hard to keep the city under wraps during those critical years of racial disturbances, civil rights activities, women's rights movements, college demonstrations, and grass-roots political agitation by trying to placate as many of the varied and often conflicting constituencies as possible.

Following through on his promises to involve himself more closely in the affairs of the neighborhoods, White set up "Little City Halls" to make city government more responsive to the needs of the people as well as to give local representatives an opportunity to participate in the political process. Of course, these locations also allowed the new administration an opportunity to establish a strategic network of political bases from which to send out foot soldiers and volunteers to canvass all parts of the districts and solidify political support for Kevin White.[35] To help reduce the level of criticism that downtown city government was ignoring the needs of working people and doing little to resolve neighborhood problems, the new administration spent much more money on

*Kevin White was the first mayor of Boston to recognize the city's growing black population as a new political constituency. During times of racial tensions he visited black neighborhoods, cultivated the support of black leaders, and provided recreational opportunities for young people. Here he meets with Melnea Cass (second from left) and other members of the black community to help launch a drive for the construction of the Harriet Tubman House in the South End. Courtesy of the Boston Public Library, Print Department.*

neighborhood capital improvements and engaged in highly publicized efforts to provide better lighting and more adequate police protection to help reduce crime and vandalism.[36] At the same time, appreciating the political realities of the new racial dimension in Boston politics that had appeared for the first time in the election of 1967, the new mayor tried to keep things cool in the city's restless black community. With his jacket slung over his shoulder, his necktie loosened around his button-down oxford-cloth shirt, White became a frequent visitor to the black neighborhoods, sauntering through the playgrounds, talking with groups of mothers, and maintaining personal contacts with local black leaders. He supplied more black policemen to counteract charges of police brutality, made an effort to give black people the feeling that they were full members of the Boston community, and supported a mobile program called "Summerthing" to supply music and entertainment for young people during the long and dangerous summer months.[37]

All the while, however, White was careful to maintain good relations with the downtown bankers and businessmen of the city, assuring them that he would move ahead with plans for the further renovation and modernization of the city. The new mayor was perfectly conscious of how the remarkable course of urban renewal over the past decade had not only improved the financial standing of Boston but also enhanced its reputation as a model of progressive modernization. It was undoubtedly his consciousness of the effect on the public imagination of the city's revitalization that led White to showcase in spectacular fashion the official opening of the new City Hall. Although he had expected to be in the new building by the summer of 1968, continued delays in construction forced him to stay in the old School Street building for the remainder of the year. He had his own office and several outer offices washed and repainted, stating "I want an environment that is good to work in, and is clean and neat."[38] Only when he was satisfied that the new City Hall was fully operational did he schedule a week-long series of inaugural events beginning on Monday, February 10, 1969. The events would be a way of celebrating not only a new and distinctive architectural structure but also the start of what he hoped would be a distinguished mayoral administration. Unfortunately, the opening ceremonies had to be postponed for twenty-four hours when the Northeast was battered by a howling blizzard that produced the heaviest snows in many years. The next day, Tuesday, February 11, huge snowdrifts still covered the City Hall plaza, but some five hundred invited guests carefully made their way to the central court on the first floor, where oriental rugs and pots of greenery had been placed in strategic locations in an effort to soften the stark background of bare walls and gray concrete slabs.[39]

From the first landing atop the main staircase Governor Francis W. Sargent welcomed the guests, praised the "magnificent" new building, and provoked an outburst of laughter among those who were well aware of Kevin White's aspirations to run for governor in 1970 when he wished the new mayor many years of happiness "right here in City Hall." The tone of the day became more serious, however, when Senator Edward M. Kennedy rose to speak. After paying tribute to the two former Boston mayors who were on the platform—John B. Hynes and John F. Collins—for helping to revitalize the city, and pointing to the promising neighborhood programs already begun by Kevin White, Kennedy then went on to temper the congratulatory mood of the morning with some somber words that perceptively touched on the disturbing signs of social discord and racial tensions. "If the city of

Boston becomes a city filled with crime," he warned, "if it becomes a city lived in only by the very rich and the very poor, if over the next fifty years it gradually becomes an all-black city rather than an integrated city, then our problems will overcome us." In his own remarks a little later, White chose to strike a more optimistic note as he tied the inauguration of the new City Hall in with the inauguration of his own administration. "It is not just an architectural event which we celebrate this morning," he said, standing smiling and confident. "For, if you believe, as I do, that architecture both portrays and shapes men's lives, then you will agree that this building's major significance will be its effect on the people who use it." Although acknowledging that American cities were indeed facing "incredible problems," he expressed his conviction that the completion of the new City Hall would inspire all Bostonians to do "better than we thought we could do" in dealing with those problems—to be "hospitable to change, to try new ideas, to bring people closer to government." After the dedication ceremonies, the guests gathered at a luncheon of lobster Newburg in the reception hall, a low-key gathering with no head table, no special seating arrangements, and no speeches. When he was not table hopping and shaking hands, White sat at a table with former mayor Hynes, while John Collins sat at the next table with the Boston banker Robert Morgan, chairman of the City Hall Commission. After the festivities were over, seventy-two-year-old John Hynes stood alone in a corridor waiting for an elevator. He was a happy man; he had finally seen his great vision for the city come true. Turning with a smile, he remarked to a stranger: "This is something, isn't it? Really something."[40]

It was in keeping with the spirit of continued revitalization that White turned his attention to those areas between the Government Center and the waterfront that Logue had targeted for development back in 1963 but that had run into unexpected delays. On February 6, 1969, only a few days before his inauguration of the new City Hall, White had met with business and civic representatives to formally launch an elaborate $30 million apartment-commercial-parking program to begin upgrading Atlantic Avenue's decrepit waterfront district. Following along the lines of plans and projects developed during the Collins administration, White called the program "one of the largest residential developments to get under way at one time." He announced the construction of two $14 million forty-story apartment towers, as well as a $6 million six-level, fifteen-hundred-car garage in the vicinity of Atlantic Avenue's India Wharf area. At a press conference at the nearby New England Aquarium, White emphasized that the so-called Harbor Towers project was just the beginning. He envisioned a four-hundred-unit moderate-income housing development near the North End; a four-and-a-half-acre public "Marina Park" between Long and Commercial wharves; a four-hundred-room motel overlooking the harbor; and the restoration of the Faneuil Hall market area.[41]

Perhaps of most immediate concern to the mayor was the unsightly Faneuil Hall market area, its narrow streets congested with delivery trucks, broken-down pushcarts, and piles of debris, which lay in all its embarrassing ugliness directly beneath the windows of his shiny office in the new City Hall. "It was an eyesore, right in front of me," said White. "If you can visualize the expanse of window in my office as a mural, it was a mural of disrepair."[42] The remnants of the market district White looked out upon had actually started out as a notable example of early urban renewal begun in the mid-1820s by Boston's second mayor, Josiah Quincy, who almost single-handedly renovated the run-down old market area along the waterfront between Faneuil Hall and the old town dock. Working with unflagging energy and determination, Boston's "Great Mayor" filled in the flats, drained the putrid dock, tore down old buildings, laid out new streets, and brought in Alexander Parris to design an original granite market house two stories high and more than five hundred feet long, with a classical portico at each end. With its equally splendid granite warehouses on either side stocked with supplies from all over the world, its market stalls offering textiles, fabrics, spices, and household wares of every description, and its pushcarts loaded with fresh fruits and vegetables, the new market district remained a bustling part of the city for many years. By the turn of the century, however, the once-elegant market structures had begun to deteriorate as the immigrant populations in the downtown areas swelled to enormous portions. Horsecarts and delivery wagons jammed the narrow, congested streets, and merchants deserted the waterfront area for more promising locations elsewhere.

By the end of World War II the market buildings and the surrounding warehouses had become so dingy and dilapidated that in 1956 the city planning board gave up all hope of renovation and designated the area for wholesale clearance to make way for office buildings. Although the Cambridge firm of Adams, Howard, and Greeley subsequently drew up a plan advising the city to retain the three central buildings as a permanent marketplace, it was not until 1963 that saving and restoring the buildings became city policy, after the BRA administrator, Logue, was persuaded by historians and preservationists that they were worth saving because of their historical significance. Logue then persuaded the chamber of commerce to undertake its renewal study of the entire waterfront area, which he in turn used to secure federal funds for a more detailed plan. It was quite clear in both the chamber's preliminary study as well as in Logue's final plan that the city, having decided to preserve the market area as "one of the finest urban spaces in America," would also renovate the original market buildings rather than tear them down.[43]

In 1966 Roger S. Webb, founder of the Architecture Heritage Foundation, assembled a team, including the noted Boston architect Frederick A. Stahl, to undertake a feasibility study for the reuse of the Faneuil Hall markets. He was already in the process of transforming the old City Hall into what Ada Louise Huxtable of the *New York Times* called "a revenue-producing building that would carry its weight in downtown Boston." In 1968 he began the work of restoring the exteriors of the three Greek Revival market buildings.[44]

While the historic structures themselves were being salvaged, however, the city had no clear proposal about what to do with the new space once it was renovated—how the market area behind Faneuil Hall would actually be used. There were some vague plans about redesigning the old buildings for offices or apartments, but nothing came of them. Despite his own irritation with the condition of the market district, Kevin White took no particular action even after he defeated Mrs. Hicks a second time in November 1971 and embarked on a second term as mayor. "Remember, that was 1972," he later pointed out. "I had a lot of things on my mind at that time, but Faneuil Hall was certainly not one of them. I had lost the race for governor, but now I'm redeemed. I've won the city. I beat Mrs. Hicks again. I'm back in as mayor, and in the meantime I've just been mentioned for vice president with McGovern. So now I begin to think 'Why not me, Lord?' I was fantasizing about becoming president, for God's sake! I wasn't thinking about Faneuil Hall at all."[45]

Someone who *was* thinking about the wider uses of the Faneuil Hall market area was Benjamin Thompson, an accomplished architect, a successful Cambridge restaurateur, and an imaginative businessman who had founded a retail chain called Design Research. In studying the old buildings in the Faneuil Hall market area, he became intrigued by the possibilities of the seemingly useless urban space and began drawing up plans for a downtown shopping mall whose central focus would be food. By the time the BRA was ready to take competitive bids in late 1970, Thompson had teamed up with the Philadelphia firm of Van Arkel and Moss to design a retail center with food as the major theme. Two other developers offered designs that proposed fewer retail outlets but more offices and apartment complexes. Although Van Arkel and Moss received the award, the BRA eventually took back the project when the developers were unable to meet the required deadlines. While Thompson went in search of a more dependable developer, the BRA itself moved ahead under a federal grant for historic preservation and began the actual physical restoration of the rundown market buildings. For the next five years, the historic market district directly behind Faneuil Hall was a clearing of dirt and rubble, cluttered with pipes, beams, and culverts, overrun by bulldozers, earthmovers, and cranes. The old granite buildings were completely gutted, and like gloomy skeletons they stood in the dusk, awaiting the decision that would determine their role in the New Boston.

At the suggestion of a mutual friend, Thompson wrote to James Rouse of Maryland, who had pioneered the enclosed suburban shopping mall in the 1950s and used the Rouse Company to create the racially and economically integrated community of Columbia, Maryland, in the 1960s. Rouse felt the time had now come to reverse the trend to suburbia and wanted to try his hand at creating a profitable shopping center in the heart of some big city. Boston seemed exactly suited to his kind of experiment and he responded eagerly to the ideas of Thompson, who saw a shopping mall as a possible means of not only attracting more investments but also drawing people back to the city once again. Rouse and Thompson agreed to work together and in the spring of 1972, through the agency of Kevin White's close aide Ira Jackson, who had once worked for Rouse's firm, met with the mayor and the current BRA director, Robert T. Kenney, informing them that they wanted to develop the market complex.

Earlier projects such as the Prudential Center, the West End development, and the Government Center complex were impressive to look at, and they had certainly done much to improve the image of Boston. But for the most part, except for an occasional tourist, they attracted only those local residents who had some kind of specific business at those locations. They did little to bring back into the city those middle-class people from Boston's neighborhoods and communities who had become accustomed to driving out to suburban shopping malls, where parking spaces were plentiful, arcades air-conditioned, fast-food restaurants numerous, and all types of stores conveniently at hand. Indeed, the advantages of suburban malls were so obvious that Rouse and Thompson found practically no encouragement or support for their project among bankers and investors who rejected the very idea of a successful downtown mall and who scoffed at the notion that a group of independent merchants—"a bunch of nobodies"—could compete successfully with the big national chains that dominated most suburban malls.[46] But the idea of an attractive and lively shopping mall in the heart of the historic Faneuil Hall market district that would delight tourists, attract local residents, and serve as a natural gateway from the traditional government and business districts of the city to the new public park and restored waterfront areas he had in mind—literally a "walkway to the sea"—clearly captivated Mayor White, and he encouraged the two men with their ideas.

Meanwhile, however, one of the previous competitors for the market project, Roger Webb, submitted a second proposal of his own to the BRA. His plan was to renovate only the two granite warehouse buildings on either side of the Quincy Market, leaving it to the city to improve and manage the central building. Webb and his partners were well-known Bostonians prominent in the field of architectural preservation, and Webb himself had recently gained considerable attention by renovating the old City Hall on School Street as a location for private offices and a chic French restaurant. Webb's proposal did not suggest the kind of retail center envisioned by Rouse and Thompson, but called for office space, specialty stores, and apartment units in the north and south buildings.

In December 1972 Robert Kenney took Thompson by surprise when he told him that he planned to recommend giving the project to Roger Webb at the meeting of the BRA board two days later. Rouse and Thompson immediately contacted their friends in Boston, persuaded the BRA members to postpone their decision, and then organized a high-pressure campaign to persuade Mayor White at least to conduct a careful review of the two proposals before making a final decision. While the mayor agreed to take the matter under advisement, the BRA, the Boston City Council, the Municipal Research Bureau, and a group of downtown businessmen friendly to Rouse who had formed a group called Neighbors of Government Center made studies of the competing proposals. On the one hand, if they selected Webb as the developer, they would save the ancient buildings and maintain the historic ambience of the location, but were not likely to get the kind of retail focus that could attract paying customers. With Rouse as the developer, on the other hand, they felt they would get a large retail magnet in the market buildings that could generate more profits than rental income. Quick to emphasize that particular aspect of his project, Rouse offered to guarantee a return of at least $600,000 a year to the city, which would be paid before debt service and operating expenses. Webb, in contrast, while he proposed to take a limited profit and turn the rest of his rental income over to the city, refused to make any specific guarantees.

While he was still weighing the pros and cons of the two projects, White received a memorandum from Ira Jackson urging him to decide in favor of the Rouse proposal. According to an analysis of the memorandum by Tilo Schabert, a visiting German scholar who did a detailed operational study of the White administration, Jackson made an objective and even "brilliant" comparison of the two competing programs in the main body of his formal review, but then added a handwritten postscript informing the mayor of "a late development." Rouse, it appears, had agreed to " 'donate' $500,000 (free and clear) for the Bicentennial."[47] It was clearly left to His Honor to determine the influence this "gift" would have on the city's final decision. A short time later, the city council committee on urban renewal recommended by a unanimous vote that the project be given to Rouse and Thompson.

As far as Kevin White was concerned, the decision to go with Rouse was not determined by any decision of the city council, not by the reports of research bureaus, and not by the promise of a financial contribution, but solely by the creative imagination and personal charisma of James Rouse himself. Like Ed Logue and so many other men of his time, Rouse had been influenced by his experiences in World War II. "This country has the capacity to do mind-boggling things when we're at war," he once said. "If we look upon the quality of life in cities to be of comparable importance to fighting a war, then we would organize for it in the same way." From all accounts, Rouse was a spellbinder, a "visionary" who often took on projects others didn't think could be done. "If he wants something, others do it," said a longtime associate. "He lifts their sights in a way they've never known."[48]

That certainly seems to have been the case with Kevin White. The mayor had taken an immediate liking to Rouse, but didn't have the same feelings for Thompson, who he felt was out to sell a product at all costs. "Rouse won my heart and mind; Thompson wouldn't know how to get it in a million years," said White. "Webb was certainly good enough, but he was offering a routine proposal. Rouse's ideas captivated me. He turned the market project from simply curing an eyesore into something much more than that. He elevated my mind." The offer of a financial contribution for one of his civic projects was something White dismissed entirely—"that kind of thing wouldn't influence me at all; companies doing business with the city made those kinds of offers all the time, that was nothing at all"—and he scoffed at the idea that the reaction of the city council would affect his decision. "I made it a point never to meet with city councillors; I sent *people* to deal with them."[49]

Having made up his mind to go with Rouse, the mayor invited the developer to take a walk with him through the market district in order to satisfy himself that Rouse's ideas were sound and that he had the best interests of the city in mind. "I felt like what a father must feel like when he's about to give his daughter away to a prospective son-in-law," recalled White. "He's told me how much potential my daughter has, and now I'm faced with giving her away, knowing that I'll never be able to get her back. So I turned to Rouse and said to him in the kind of threatening way that somebody does or does not know what you mean by it: 'I'm going to give you the project, but I'll *kill* you if you do it wrong. Better you don't take it than to take it and blow it!' "

Rouse assured the mayor that he would do nothing of which White would disapprove. He offered to work closely with the mayor, would report to him once a week, and would keep him personally informed about everything he was doing. "You can watch it all the way," he promised.

"Well, you flatter me, Jim, but I'll take advantage of your offer and poke my nose in now and then," White responded. "I don't want to be consulted every five minutes. But Jesus Christ, concentrate on it, and don't short-change me."

White later recalled, "We shook hands, and he had it. It was that simple." Several days later, in March 1973, the BRA officially named James Rouse as the developer for the Faneuil Hall market project.[50]

The ceremonies to dedicate the official opening of the new Faneuil Hall Marketplace were scheduled for Thursday, August 26, 1976, with the weather forecast calling for heat, humidity, and a temperature in the eighties. It was the kind of day when most Bostonians would never think of coming into the city, with its heat, its traffic, and what Mayor Josiah Quincy had delicately referred to 150 years earlier as the "noxious effluvia" of the waterfront location. The merchants were there, many having set up shop only the day before, but the central Quincy Market building was still one-fifth vacant, and the two adjoining warehouse buildings would not be ready for occupancy for another two years. A modest crowd showed up for the opening ceremonies, which began at Dock Square at 11:15 A.M. with the dedication of a bronze plaque, just below the statue of Samuel Adams, honoring seventy-six-year-old Walter Muir Whitehill, the eminent Boston historian and consultant on the market project. The formal opening of the market itself began at 11:45 A.M. as the people stood in front of the Greek Revival entrance to Alexander Parris's splendid market building, with its triangular facade and sturdy classical columns, while members of the Ancient and Honorable Artillery Company stood at attention for the national anthem. Speakers unveiled a seven-foot stone honoring Josiah Quincy, Boston's "Great Mayor," who had dedicated the original market himself. Mayor White then addressed the audience, praised the imaginative work of those who had brought the old market district back to life, and called the occasion "truly an historic event, a rebirth." When the speeches were over, a man in colonial costume, complete with tricorn hat, swung a large handbell declaring the market officially open. After the mayor cut the ceremonial ribbon, James Rouse led a company of red-kilted Stuart Highlanders up the steps and into the building to pipe in the crowd for a champagne reception.[51]

Boston is always having public celebrations, ribbon-cutting ceremonies, and formal dedications of all kinds. Usually the small audience remains politely until the last speech has been given and the closing benediction is pronounced, and then almost immediately disappears. This day it was different. The ceremonies concluded at just about lunchtime, and at that moment a huge wave of people came pouring out of the banks in the financial district, the big department stores in the shopping district, and the various legal offices around Government Center and made their way down into the market district. And they did not stop. Throughout the remainder of the afternoon, the crowds of people kept coming, reaching a total of about 100,000, according to police estimates. "You would have to be made of ice to be unimpressed,"

Mayor Kevin White set out to reclaim the handsome buildings in the historic Quincy Market district, which had deteriorated over the years. He decided upon the plans of architect Ben Thompson and developer James W. Rouse, which created Faneuil Hall Marketplace, an attractive downtown shopping complex. This not only attracted visitors and tourists to Boston, but also drew native Bostonians back from the neighborhoods and the suburbs to the central city. Photograph © 1991 by Peter Vanderwarker.

said the *Boston Globe* in its lead editorial, wondering why it had taken so long for "such a splendid idea" to come about. It was "instant acceptance," according to the *New York Times*, as throngs of people wandered among the quaint pushcarts with their handmade arts, crafts, and jewelry; stared longingly at displays of gourmet delicacies alongside savory offerings of baked beans, homemade bread, chicken wings, and spareribs; made selections of kitchenware products, pottery items, ceramic jugs, woven shawls, and stuffed animals; and mingled with wandering jugglers, magicians, puppeteers, acrobats, and actors dressed up as vegetables.

And the crowds never stopped coming. Faneuil Hall Marketplace was an immediate success, attracting some ten million visitors during its first year of operations—a figure equal to the gate count at Disneyland—and then going up to twelve million in 1978 when the entire complex was finally open. When the banks had been debating whether to lend James Rouse the money to develop his project, they estimated that in order to stay in business he would have to come up with a volume of sales of about $150 per square foot—the same as most successful suburban shopping malls. Quincy Market astonished almost everyone by producing sales of $233 per square foot in its first year, and up to the incredible figure of $500 per square foot by the mid-1980s.

In almost no time, according to leading experts in the field of urban redevelopment, Faneuil Hall Marketplace became the first "nationally recognized popular success in the rebuilding of downtown."[52] It marked a turning point that brought middle-class residents back to town, attracted visitors from all over the world, brought bright lights and open spaces to a part of the city that had always been dark and deserted, and turned the downtown area into a major resource for a thriving metropolis. "When I remember how ugly and rundown this place used to be," remarked a North End resident, Frannie Cintolo, "I can hardly recognize it."[53] The reputation of the Faneuil Hall Marketplace spread quickly and soon became the model for other American cities that were looking for ways of reversing the trend to suburbia and bringing their people back to downtown once again.

The success of the Quincy Market and the renovation of the entire waterfront area from Marina Park and the North End to the New England Aquarium and the South Station is an important element not only in the revitalization of the city but also in an assessment of the role of Kevin White in the development of the New Boston. In the immediate aftermath of his withdrawal from political life in 1983, after four consecutive four-year terms as mayor of Boston, the general consensus seemed to give him credit for continuing the projects envisioned by Hynes and later brought into being by Collins, but contributing little of his own that was creative or original. In his 1984 study of the White administration, *Style versus Substance*, the lawyer and novelist George Higgins accurately reflected the general assumption that White's main contribution to the "breathtaking reclamation of an urban downtown area" was in "expediting" the process, in using his finely honed political skills to "midwife" the complicated changes through the well-known "Byzantine bureaucracies" of Boston politics.[54]

Nothing is inevitable in politics, especially in Boston politics, and when he took office in January 1968 the new mayor had had several options where urban renewal was concerned. He could have cut back on it substantially, reducing his own visibility in the process, and allowed the projects of Hynes and Collins finally to run their course. Or he could have called an end to urban renewal entirely, announced it to have fulfilled its original expectations, and turned his attention to other pressing social and municipal concerns. But he did not. He committed himself fully to what had already been accomplished and proposed to "sell" the New Boston to the city, the state, and the world. With crackling wit and boundless energy, Kevin White publicized the city's physical advantages, promoted its commercial and financial strengths, and capitalized on its unique cultural and educational opportunities. With a keen sense of the town's historical heritage, he emphasized its importance not only to the nation but also to the world. He worked vigorously and creatively to establish Boston's reputation as a world-class city.

Within a short time Boston became one of the most popular cities in the United States, definitely an "in" city, a far cry from the depressed and run-down backwater it had been less than twenty years earlier. Tourists from all over the world were now drawn to the city by the combination of such historical attractions as the Freedom Trail and such modern additions as the bustling Quincy Market complex. Students in droves came to attend the numerous colleges and universities in the Boston area; physicians, scientists, and scholars of every discipline found the research facilities of the region most appealing; business people and financiers were delighted with the new prospects for profitable expansion; and people from many parts of the country came to make their home in what White and his public relations people shrewdly advertised as a truly livable city.

Historical circumstances even contributed to the efforts of Mayor White to put on public display the distinctive features of his city. While the nation was celebrating the two-hundredth anniversary of its independence during 1975–76, Boston captured the attention of Americans everywhere with such spectacular events as the breathtaking arrival of the Tall Ships, the historic visit of Queen Elizabeth II of England, and the gigantic Fourth of July concert on the Esplanade with Arthur Fiedler conducting the Boston Pops and the bells of the city ringing out the final chords of Tchaikovsky's "1812 Overture" as fireworks illuminated the summer sky. That hundreds of thousands of persons of all ages and colors could gather together in various places throughout the city to celebrate the nation's birthday, without incident and without massive police protection, indicated a potential for goodwill and cooperation that many people hoped would continue well into the future. There was no doubt about it. White had picked up on the remarkable accomplishments of Hynes and Collins and proceeded to generate a degree of interest and excitement in the New Boston that had never been seen before.

Furthermore, in his approach to the Faneuil Hall Marketplace and in his renewal plans for the waterfront district, White himself added a distinctive contribution to what his predecessors had accomplished with such successful enterprises as the Prudential Center, the Hynes Auditorium (formerly the War Memorial Auditorium), and the Government Center complex. It is true that Edward Logue and the BRA had taken the initiative in recognizing the historical importance of the market district and the waterfront area, obtained federal funding for a detailed study, and arranged for the physical rehabilitation of the buildings themselves. But it was White who made the final decision that the completed project be not only a fitting tribute to the past but also an exciting and vibrant part of a changing city's future. By selecting Benjamin Thompson as the architect and James Rouse as the developer of the Faneuil Hall Marketplace, White deliberately flew in the face of most experts in the field, who were absolutely certain that the concept of a downtown shopping mall was a losing proposition and bound to be a commercial disaster. White was well aware that he was taking a decided risk, but felt it was his way of carrying through on his campaign slogan that the city needed "people programs" as well as "building programs." In supporting the commercial retailing approach to the market district, he was underlining his belief that an important part of the New Boston was not merely putting up a collection of handsome new office buildings and professional services for the benefit of the elite, but also providing a place where the people of the city from all walks of life could come to walk, to work, and to play—to enjoy historic sights, listen to happy sounds, smell delicious cooking, and shop in a friendly atmosphere.

From Kevin White's point of view, it was the summer of 1976 that marked a turning point in the city's vision of itself. Up to that point, according to White, most people may have heard about the New Boston, but few of them had actually had any firsthand experience with what was happening downtown. It was something that was talked about in the chamber of commerce and in the boardrooms, but the neighborhoods were not part of it—and furthermore, they didn't want to be part of it. But events during the summer of 1976, the Bicentennial year—the arrival of the Tall Ships, the visit of Queen Elizabeth, and the opening of the Faneuil Hall Marketplace—broke things loose. "If these events had happened two or three years apart, it would have been remarkable, but it wouldn't have had such an overwhelming impact on the general public," said White. "But coming back to back in such a short space of time—bang, bang, bang—they brought people from everywhere into the city and changed enormously Boston's sense of itself."[55]

Until then, most people still didn't want to come into the city. They were nervous about what they had heard; they were disturbed about reports of crime and violence; they were afraid. Indeed, according to White, Queen Elizabeth herself was afraid. She didn't want to leave Philadelphia; she didn't want to come to Boston. All she kept hearing was that Boston was a terrible, hate-filled city populated by Irish bomb tossers and people who simply hated the English. She was so afraid, in fact, that her representatives were thinking of canceling her trip. But the queen finally agreed to come, and like so many Bostonians who came into the city to enjoy the festivities, she found Boston "a wonderful city filled with friendly people."

White recalls riding beside the queen in the official limousine while crowds of people lined up along the sidewalks were waving and "cheering their brains out." Her Majesty turned to him with a surprised look on her face and said, "They really like me, don't they? They really like me." That was the time, the turning point, insists White, when the people of Boston as a whole really began to take new pride in their city and realize for the first time what amazing things had been accomplished in such a short space of time.[56] The people had finally grasped that things had changed and that they really did have a New Boston.

# Conclusion

Few would deny that a substantial transformation of Boston's central business district took place during the twenty years from 1950 to 1970, that a New Boston had indeed replaced the old Boston of the prewar decades. But whether this New Boston was a better Boston is a subject that is as debatable as the aesthetic qualities of the new City Hall, which has evoked both paeans of praise and cries of derision. Urban renewal in Boston, as in so many other American cities during the 1950s and 1960s, has been contested and controversial, among the people directly affected at the time as well as among the social scientists and historians who analyze the process today.

Critics of urban renewal have strong objections not only to the heavy-handed ways in which much of it was carried out—citing the West End debacle as a classic example of the ruthless destruction of an irreplaceable ethnic neighborhood—but also to the way in which short-sighted municipal planning, corporate greed, and personal profits callously superseded legitimate community concerns and individual needs. In the early stages of urban renewal, it is true, it was almost impossible to persuade private developers, especially those based in Boston, to invest in the future of a city most of them regarded as a broken-down relic of the past. The possibilities of significant returns on substantial investments seemed extremely remote in a city whose infrastructure had become weakened with age and corroded by disuse. Only after the West End had been cleared, the Prudential Center established, and the Government Center an accomplished fact did it become evident that Boston offered unexpected opportunities for large-scale financial investment and commercial promotion. By the late 1970s and early 1980s Boston found itself in a colossal building boom that continued to transform a poor, run-down old town into a successful, modern metropolis whose soaring skyscrapers often diminished the view of Boston Harbor and almost completely obscured the sight of the State House's golden dome.

Behind some criticism of the ways in which the progrowth coalition of political leaders and business interests reshaped "good old Boston," however, seems to lie the assumption that having done nothing would have been better than taking the drastic steps needed to cure the many ills that had brought the city to its knees. That type of nostalgic criticism tends to ignore the sad deterioration of Boston during the 1930s and 1940s as well as the historical setting of the postwar era in which the urban transition actually took place. No documentary evidence suggests that any of the neighborhoods were undertaking initiatives for substantial reform, that either the city council or the state legislature was organizing plans for urban renewal, that any of the banks or businesses were ready to launch programs for public housing, or that local newspapers or academic institutions were designing projects for relief or renovation. "Residential neighborhood clubs, labor groups, and political party organizations did not spearhead the movement for renewal," writes Jon Teaford in surveying the movement as a whole in the United States. It was all very well for out-of-towners from wealthy suburban communities to visit Boston, enjoy the "European charms" of the West End or relish the sleazy delights of "good old Scollay Square" before going off to their private clubs for lunch, but they did not have to confront the everyday realities of the congested streets, the dilapidated housing, the widespread unemployment, and the crumbling infrastructure of a city on the brink of disaster. "It is something less than sensible to believe that the Boston area is facing a failure of healthy business growth, if the core of the area, the inner city, is facing a life and death struggle for existence," said Mayor John B. Hynes to a meeting of the Citizen Seminar in 1954.[1]

It was a new generation of young World War II veterans who had been torn away from their parochial moorings and who returned to Boston during the late 1940s and early 1950s, after many years of traveling throughout the world, who took up the challenge. They could see with perhaps a clearer perspective than most the disastrous condition of their city and the inefficacy of the political system that had allowed it to happen. As they resumed their jobs, completed their educations, and began their families, it was soon evident that members of this postwar generation were anxious to restructure their run-down city, revitalize its depressed economy, and reform the prevailing system of confrontational politics. Out of the successful and often exhilarating wartime experience of witnessing how modern science and technology could overcome insurmountable obstacles, the members of this new generation were absolutely convinced that the physical transformations of the city was within their grasp.

Their sense of practical accomplishment was further augmented by a sincere and even idealistic spirit of public service, obviously stimulated during the war by such inspirational rhetoric as the Atlantic Charter and the Four Freedoms, and further buoyed after victory was achieved by the promise of a brave new world. As the presidential counsel Clark Clifford recalled in his memoirs of the postwar years, the young veterans "all felt that" having a "larger vision of what the government should, and could, be" provided them with "the dream that we could marshal the power and authority of the government for the benefit of all mankind."[2] It was heady stuff, idealistic notions that convinced them that they finally had the human skills and the professional technology to overcome poverty, combat disease, provide adequate housing, and generally improve the quality of life in their community. In other parts of the country, in cities such as New Haven, Pittsburgh, Philadelphia, Baltimore, Albany, and Chicago, political leaders were already forming critical alliances with business and financial interests to develop long-range plans, seek out federal funding, and bring about major redevelopment efforts in their downtown areas. Certainly the time was right for Boston to undertake similar programs to modernize its neglected infrastructure and to rein-vigorate its stagnant economy.

The defeat of the popular old political warhorse James Michael Curley in 1949, in 1951, and again in 1955 by a political unknown named John B. Hynes provided the first real opportunity to put many of those ideas into practice. In a short time a coalition of liberal Democratic forces came to the support of the new mayor in hopes of bringing a new direction to government and changing the future of the city. Old-timers saw a chance to improve local politics; racial and ethnic groups saw the possibilities of upward mobility; progressive reformers and idealistic college students banded together for effective action; and major univer-

sities provided both talent and expertise. John Hynes's primary contribution was not only his vision of a renewed and revitalized city but also
his sense of personal integrity, which helped convinced many influential
people that this vision might actually be realized.

Hynes's ten years in office, from 1949 to 1959, provided an
important transition period when Boston could gradually recover from
generations of pervasive and pernicious social divisions and religious
rivalries, as well as from the prevailing notion stemming from the Curley
era that Boston politics was innately self-seeking and inevitably corrupt.
During the Great Depression, Boston had been regularly denied significant amounts of federal monies because of the assumptions on the part
of Franklin D. Roosevelt, Jim Farley, Louis Howe, and other members
of the New Deal bureaucracy in Washington that all Irish politicians in
Boston were notoriously crooked and would either waste, steal, or
misappropriate any funds sent to them. The serious efforts of John
Hynes during his first term of office to streamline the operations of
municipal government, together with his own sober and responsible
conduct in office, helped persuade a skeptical public that an Irish
politician could be both honest and competent, and that constructive
reforms in Boston might finally be possible.

Despite his personal integrity and his technical competence, John
Hynes was not able to generate either the political skills or the professional support to bring most of his early renewal projects to fruition.
Although it was clear that many people wanted change, it was also clear
that few really believed that substantial change was possible in a city
like Boston, where old habits die hard. For one thing, despite the
refreshing ecumenism of religious leaders like Cardinal Cushing, it was
still difficult for a predominantly Irish Catholic political system to forget
old rivalries and make common cause with a traditionally Protestant
Yankee business establishment. It would take many years before those
who had grown up in the degrading social traditions of "No Irish Need
Apply" could feel entirely comfortable in a close peer relationship with
those who had known the Irish primarily as stablemen and gardeners.
For another thing, the city lacked not only money but also confidence in
its economic future. Nobody seemed to believe in Boston. The city's
general financial condition was so depressed and its system of tax
assessment so backward that banks held back on loans and mortgages,
developers looked the other way, and investors departed the scene
entirely. All these factors—ethnic tensions, social rivalries, urban paro-

chialism, regional insecurity, and fiscal irresponsibility—were part of the long Curley legacy that created a form of municipal paralysis so insidious that even after ten years in office Hynes was unable to overcome its crippling effects.

And finally, there were the personal characteristics that Hynes himself brought to the office of mayor. By all accounts a kind and compassionate man, he was at the same time decidedly limited by his scant political experience and his narrow range of professional associations. Although urban renewal was taking place in several major American cities during the 1950s, it was still a new process, and few people in Boston had the technical knowledge or the managerial experience to handle it properly. His bright dreams for the renovation of the city notwithstanding, Hynes was a novice, a well-meaning amateur with few professional experts to turn to for advice except those who saw exciting new opportunities for real estate investment and financial profit. Remarkable ideas and innovations were being developed by creative scientists and engineers in the electronics industries along Route 128, but those ideas had little immediate effect on downtown Boston. Hynes may have been capable of bringing together progrowth coalitions to support commercial enterprises like the Prudential Center complex, initiated by corporations that had their own staffs of managers and executives, but he was far less successful in his development ventures outside the central business district.

Working with longtime civil service personnel in the various city agencies, still without adequate funding from either the state or federal governments, Hynes set about the renewal process in piecemeal fashion. The city's move into the New York Streets area of the South End was a hesitant first step toward clearing up a blighted area, but ended with a parcel that provided more room for industrial parking garages than low-rent housing for displaced residents. As subsequent events demonstrated, the case of the West End proved even more disastrous. The almost total destruction of the area displaced hundreds of families, demolished their homes, and replaced them with the elegant town houses and high-rise towers of Charles River Park, which only the wealthy could afford. The city's first major redevelopment effort produced such a violent public reaction that it jeopardized the whole future of urban renewal in Boston.

The task of rescuing the concept of redevelopment from oblivion and moving it into more positive and acceptable directions fell to another surprise mayoral contender, John F. Collins, who in November 1959 defeated the popular front-runner, state senator John E. Powers, and took office at a time when the city appeared on the verge of financial collapse. Using his own efficient and aggressive executive style to establish a strong political base, and enjoying the support of an organized group of downtown financial leaders known as "the Vault," he promised a continuation of urban renewal but assured voters that it would be carried out in a careful, professional, and humane manner.

But Collins wanted more than a warmed-over version of what Hynes had attempted to accomplish. He saw the modern urban renewal process as much more than a series of unrelated enterprises—a building here, a slum-clearance project there—but rather as a conceptual model in which all the parts are designed to fit together to form a compatible whole. Transforming the Boston Redevelopment Authority into a virtually autonomous agency for planning and design, he placed it under the direction of Edward J. Logue, whom he brought up from New Haven, Connecticut. Working in tandem with his energetic young administrator in what one writer has aptly described as a "relationship of peers," Collins displayed great political and managerial skills in transforming many of the programs and projects initiated by John Hynes into elements of a thriving and prosperous new city. With the solid backing of the mayor, Logue and his staff made their plans, drew up their agendas, created political alliances, pursued private investments, acquired federal funding at a time when the administrations of John F. Kennedy and Lyndon B. Johnson looked kindly upon such progressive enterprises, and moved ahead confidently with the revitalization of the city.

In order to establish an atmosphere of confidence and achievement, Logue first carried into effect the several uncompleted projects of the Hynes administration. In the Back Bay, the Prudential Center and the War Memorial Auditorium became the first structures to herald the revival of a part of the city that had been occupied mainly by unused railroad yards. After many years of confusion and delay the Boston Common underground parking garage was finally completed, providing much-needed space for parking in the heart of the downtown business district. Once the complicated issues of funding and status were resolved and a spacious Government Center was created on the rubble of old Scollay Square, a strikingly modern City Hall went up to dramatize the transformation of a run-down old town into a bright New Boston. And like the proverbial magnet, these publicly funded projects attracted many of those private investors and developers who had once refused to have anything to do with Boston, but who now became anxious to undertake ambitious building programs and construction projects.

Building his New Boston had become the central focus of John Collins and his administration. He dedicated himself to the task and worked tirelessly toward its completion, studying proposals, reviewing plans, poring over the wording of complicated contracts well into the late hours of the night in his City Hall office. Collins had not simply cleaned up an old city and erected a series of impressive new office buildings. By turning planning and design over to recognized experts, he took urban renewal out of the hands of local political forces and skillfully used the process to demonstrate the vitality of the New Boston as a leading center of financial investment and business opportunity. The successful alliances he created between the public and the private sectors were recognized throughout the country, and Collins himself was hailed as a great executive who had brought Boston back into first place among the nation's cities. The mood had definitely changed; Boston had acquired the reputation of a city on the move.

The physical changes taking place in Boston during the 1960s meant more than tall buildings and expansive architectural designs, however. Those changes also helped transform the very nature and character of the city itself in such a way that the Boston of the 1970s and 1980s was substantially different from the old Boston of the 1940s and 1950s. For one thing, a number of the quaint, old-fashioned, often eccentric architectural designs and structural patterns that many people had always found so charming and so characteristic of the three-hundred-year-old city had been wiped out in favor of a growing array of modernistic glass-and-steel skyscrapers that many critics found both undistinguished and inappropriate. The question of how far this renewal process could go without completely transforming a venerable city into a sanitized version of hundreds of other American urban centers was one that puzzled architects and residents alike. For another thing, with the kinds of investments that were made and the sort of corporations that were attracted to the New Boston, the city quickly developed a much more extensive service-based economy than ever before. A city whose occupations once revolved around the needs of import and export, commerce and trade, shipping and fishing, now became known for its health services and medical research, its tourism and higher education, its asset management and high-tech professional services. The emphasis on professional skills and managerial occupations requiring a high degree of education made Boston a predominantly white-collar city, and produced an extraordinary growth in jobs and wages during the 1970s and 1980s.

A new wave of well-educated and affluent young people, mostly professionals—engineers, computer specialists, architects, designers, advertising executives, medical technicians—single, or married with few or no children, found the obvious benefits of the New Boston much to their liking. They were attracted by the city's service economy, its numerous cultural and educational institutions, its proximity to rural and recreational areas, and its appeal as a walkable and livable city. In large numbers, this young "gentry" moved into convenient and historical locations that were still in the process of renovation, such as the North End, the South End, and parts of the old waterfront area along Atlantic Avenue. With their professional incomes, however, the newcomers forced up the rents of housing units, raised the costs of apartments, and accelerated the conversion to condominiums. That process of gentrification caused serious financial burdens among the older and poorer inhabitants—elderly Italian couples in the North End, established black families in the South End—forcing many of them to move out of familiar neighborhoods in which they had spent their entire lives.

While the attractiveness of jobs and salaries brought new residents into the city at an unusual rate, many of the newcomers were relatively uninterested in city politics, and a number of them spent only a few years in the city before moving out into the suburbs in search of better schools, larger homes, and greener lawns. The relative transience of the city's new population left an effective degree of political power in the hands of older residents in such traditionally white ethnic neighborhoods as East Boston, South Boston, Jamaica Plain, and West Roxbury, whose representatives wielded a disproportionate influence over city politics. This fascinating contradiction of a younger and better-educated population becoming inhabitants of a city whose important political decisions continued to be made by older and more conservative residents was only one of the potentially explosive political changes taking place behind the high-rise buildings and the soaring skyscrapers proclaiming the accomplishments of Boston's progrowth coalition.

It was when Collins and Logue began to move their urban renewal concepts outside the central business district into the surrounding neighborhoods that the energetic driving force of the progressive reform

*Once the idea of a New Boston had been established and the city's financial condition stabilized, confidence was quickly restored. Boston became an attractive investment site for bankers and financiers, a center for major service industries and high-tech firms, and a mecca for medicine and education. In rapid succession a series of corporate towers and high-rise office buildings went up in the downtown area, completely transforming the Boston skyline. Photograph © 1991 by Peter Vanderwarker.*

enterprise in Boston most clearly began to lose its momentum. By the late 1960s and early 1970s a number of factors came into play not only to blunt the drive for continuing large-scale urban redevelopment but also to bring into question the idealistic conviction of liberal Democrats that an activist government could be a positive force in effecting social improvement, promoting racial equality, and ensuring financial parity. If urban renewal was intended to revitalize the central city, it also served unintentionally to revitalize a number of Boston's white neighborhoods, which had lost a good deal of their traditional political clout as well as their ethnic distinctiveness during the 1950s and 1960s as young families moved away and old families struggled to survive.

Watching all the time, attention, and money being lavished on the downtown business district, white neighborhoods charged that city hall was completely ignoring the interests of the "little people." Local residents complained that they had lost vital services, were forced to pay higher taxes, and received fewer benefits. And on those occasions when the municipal authorities did get involved in the neighborhoods, it seemed always to be at the expense of the working people: residents of East Boston and South Boston complained of terrible airport noises; members of the Italian community in the North End found themselves cut off from the rest of the city by the Central Artery; residents of Chinatown lost precious land to the Southeast Expressway; people in the Mission Hill district felt the impact of expanding hospitals and medical schools.

Even worse than what the Democratic leaders did, the neighborhoods complained, were the ways in which they did it. City authorities always wanted to change things, to improve things—and always insisted that everything had to be done their way. There was always the understanding that "We'll help you, but it has to be on our terms." Neighborhood residents resented being ordered how to use their land, how to build their houses, how to improve their living standards, how to reorganize their schools—often being forced to change when they didn't see any reason for change.

The conclusion was that large numbers of middle-class and working-class white ethnics—long the solid core of the Democratic party— now began to see the central government as their enemy, their opponent. It was something that was continually oppressing them, taking their land away, taking their houses away, telling them where to go, how to behave, how to dress, how to improve themselves, how to raise their standard of living. In anger and frustration, the neighborhoods rejected the lure of better housing, cleaner streets, and newer schools because they suspected a liberal agenda that would ultimately threaten their family values and undermine their working-class traditions. Perceiving a common enemy in the wealthy professional classes of real estate developers, downtown bankers, city hall politicians, and suburban do-gooders, a number of the old neighborhoods came back to life, rediscovered their ethnic roots, reorganized their political forces, and formed a common cause against the Hyneses, the Rappaports, the Collinses, and the Logues. "Not in my neighborhood you don't" became the battle cry of the "townies" who settled back to fight the intrusion of liberals and "outsiders," while their elected representatives manned the battlements at the meetings of the Boston City Council.

In Boston's black community, too, with its expanding numbers and its increasing sense of identity and pride, urban renewal produced similar reactions of fear, anger, and resentment. Forever on the outskirts of the city, isolated and ignored, Boston's black residents had to survive on the sufferance of city hall and the largesse of white politicians. A coterie of black ward bosses worked with local community leaders to hold together a culturally diverse urban neighborhood in the South End in the face of municipal neglect, inadequate housing, and meager public funding. They hoped that the city's much-heralded urban renewal program would finally help revitalize and restore their community, only to find that few of the original residents would be the ultimate beneficiaries. The major objective of the project appeared to be establishing a substantially upgraded residential area in which wealthy professionals could purchase expensive housing and contribute to rising real estate values. Already caught up in national events—the civil rights movement, the rising consciousness of black identity, the freedom marches, the influence of Dr. Martin Luther King—black residents were increasingly sensitive to what they saw as a white-dominated establishment moving into the South End, taking away their land, evicting them from their homes, knocking down their houses, putting up high-priced apartments for white "gentry," and pushing poor black people out of the old South End and jamming them into less desirable sections of Roxbury, which became almost exclusively black.

The anger and bitterness over what they perceived to be promises that were never kept, schools that were never built, and low-cost housing that never materialized caused a wave of new young black militants to rise up in Roxbury, brush aside many of the older and well-established black leaders who had always worked well with mayors like Hynes and Collins, and assume a posture of open anger and defiance against a Democratic city administration they viewed as hostile and treacherous, a government that made promises it either could not or would not keep. Black neighborhood leaders selected their own spokespeople, developed their own agenda, and agitated for their own needs irrespective of the goals and objectives of Collins, Logue, and the Boston Redevelopment Authority.

Reaction to urban renewal, first under Hynes and then to a greater extent under Collins, helped to accelerate the growth of conscious, grass-roots political forces in old, established, white neighborhoods as well as in the newer, expanding, dynamic black communities. The story of twentieth-century Boston is, in actuality, a tale of two cities—literally "two Bostons." During the first half of the century, Boston had been divided by the two major social and religious groups that had constituted its hostile warring factions. One Boston, the central area, was the traditional preserve of the Protestant, Anglo-Saxon, Yankee Brahmin population that occupied the Victorian residences of Beacon Hill and the Back Bay. The other Boston was made up of the more recent communities of the Irish and the Germans, the Italians and the Jews, the African-Americans and the Puerto Ricans, and all the other races and nationalities that had come into the city in the nineteenth and twentieth centuries and settled in the waterfront wards and the surrounding neighborhoods.

Many had hoped that an extensive process of urban renewal might well lessen the differences between these two Bostons and draw closer together the central downtown area and the ethnic neighborhoods. But that did not happen. If anything, urban renewal under Hynes and Collins created an even greater chasm than ever before. For one thing, two decades of seeing an upper-class, progrowth coalition of big-city politicians, downtown financiers, out-of-state developers, and university-trained professionals demolish their homes, displace old residents, and put up high-rent apartment complexes and elegant town houses caused the working-class neighborhoods to withdraw even further from the orbit of municipal influence.

Perhaps even more significant, the manner in which the renewal process was handled changed the major force dividing the two Bostons from religion and ethnicity to race and class. By the 1970s the old rivalries between Protestants and Catholics had been largely forgotten in the wake of more sophisticated times and the influence of modern ecumenism. By the 1960s sons and grandsons of immigrant day laborers had become well-to-do professionals, moved out into the suburbs, invested wisely, prospered greatly, joined the country club, and generally become indistinguishable from the downtown Boston Brahmins who had once been their sworn enemies. They now joined together in politics and in business, lunched together at the Tavern Club, and put together a progrowth coalition designed to build on the ashes of the run-down old city a grand new metropolis with new standards of taste and a better quality of life for everybody. This new controlling class no longer seemed to be speaking the same language of even its own people in the old white neighborhoods, much less that of the blacks, the Puerto Ricans, and the other people of color who lived in communities that were increasingly segregated and isolated from the rest of the city. There were still two Bostons, but from now on the inhabitants were separated by the size of their wallets and the color of their skins.

By the time Collins was leaving office and Kevin White was coming in, city government in Boston was faced with two mutually hostile neighborhood forces—one black, the other white. First becoming apparent early in the twentieth century when the city's African Americans moved into the South End, and then taking shape after World War II when the black population more than doubled, the rival communities came of age during the struggle over urban renewal and then grew to maturity in the tug-of-war over dwindling economic resources in the late 1960s. The new Nixon administration was reducing the federal government's role in the economy, replacing many welfare programs with the president's Family Assistance Plan, and cutting back on aid to state and local communities with his revenue-sharing concept. Not only were the two racial forces that emerged hostile to one another, but both of them were also hostile to the political, economic, and cultural ideology of the downtown "establishment," which each community, in its own way and in light of its own goals, saw as antithetical to its culture, its well-being, its aspirations, and its future.

Taking over as mayor in January 1968, Kevin White was determined to continue good relations with the prosperous downtown business community in order to maintain the momentum of construction and renovation. At the same time, he set out to develop a greater degree of friendship and cooperation with the city's working-class neighborhoods, whose residents were clamoring for more municipal services as well as a greater role in their own affairs. Taking a virtually completed urban model that had been passed along to him by Collins, White developed a conscious effort to discover the human dimension in the impressive new structures of steel and concrete, and to develop those "people" themes that allowed his public relations experts to publicize Boston as a truly "livable" city. From the very first, he demonstrated an imaginative flair for dramatizing the New Boston, advertising its commercial and cultural advantages, and drawing the attention of visitors and tourists to Boston's virtues as a world-class city. The classic example of the White technique came with the way in which he transformed the historic Quincy Market area into the lively Faneuil Hall Marketplace. Going up against the collective thinking of historians and preservationists in his desire to attract large numbers of people to the downtown area, White took a definite risk in selecting the Thompson-Rouse team that turned the waterfront shopping mall into a resounding success. With parties and parades, concerts and fireworks, spectacles and ceremonies, he created a new spirit that drew people of all levels from all parts of the city to discover the excitement of the New Boston.

But White's personal involvement in the details of the urban renewal process began to slip away as the complexities of office grew in both number and intensity. For one thing, he faced the depressing economic realities of a Republican administration that was no longer willing to grant federal funds for large-scale projects where completion would take several years. Now funds would be allocated only on an annual basis for individual projects of a decidedly limited nature. This was not to White's liking. For John Collins, urban renewal was the centerpiece of his administration, out of which would emerge a revitalized and prosperous city. For White, on the other hand, urban renewal was only one of a number of enterprises that he hoped would transform the new metropolis from a cluster of impersonal public buildings into an exciting place for people to live. As he constantly liked to remind his friends, he was definitely no "manager" in the style of Collins, constantly absorbed in the minutiae of administrative operations. Things like building programs and clearance projects were only a small part of the many responsibilities that occupied the attention of a big-city mayor. White preferred to hire people to look after things like that so that he could take care of other and more-pressing issues.

And certainly there were more and more pressing issues occupying White's time midway through his second term. Dissatisfaction in both white and black communities against the policies of the city administration in general and the adverse effects of urban renewal in particular finally boiled over into a violent racial conflict over school desegregation and court-ordered busing that tore the city apart. In his scholarly study of the school crisis, *Boston against Busing*, Ronald Formisano agrees that several neighborhoods that fought against desegregation tended to see the struggle against court-ordered busing as a continuation of the battles they recently had been waging against the onslaught of highway construction, urban renewal, and airport expansion promoted by social planners, downtown bureaucrats, and liberal outsiders. "Antibusing," concludes Formisano, "exuded the same anti-elitism and fierce class resentments that had erupted in these earlier struggles of neighborhood defense."[3]

Faced with crippling federal cutbacks, relentless neighborhood hostility, and bitter racial strife, Kevin White devoted far less of his time and energy to dealing with the details of urban renewal than had his predecessors. He became less interested in using the BRA as an instrument for large-scale physical renovation, and he directed the operations of that agency more toward monitoring and managing the city's overall economy while he took the actual decision-making process into his own hands. Building went on, of course. The momentum had been established, the economy revitalized, confidence restored. Over the course of the next decade at least fourteen new office buildings would go up. Banks, insurance companies, corporate headquarters, medical centers, federal buildings, trade centers, hotels, restaurants, theaters, and stores would turn the old city whose death had seemed imminent only twenty years earlier into a bustling, vibrant, and stylish metropolis.

Although the building went on and the construction continued at an amazing rate, the sales and the deals, the arrangements and the manipulations, the profits and the mergers added little more of substance to the city's distinctive appearance or its unique character. Without the consensus from within or the funding from without, the influence of private enterprise became the more dominant force, as the directing role of city government no longer served its earlier function. Municipal authorities would establish parameters and provide restrictions, they would control heights and modify size, they would interact with racial groups and consult with ethnic constituencies, but they would no longer play a decisive leadership role in projecting long-range plans, stimulating creative urban designs, or shaping the future configuration of the city.

"In all human institutions, as in the human body, there is a hidden source of energy, the life principle itself, independent of the organs which perform the various functions needed for survival," wrote Alexis de Tocqueville. "Once this vital flame burns low, the whole organism languishes and wastes away, and though the organs seem to function as before, they serve no useful purpose."[4] In the course of the two decades from 1950 to 1970 there had been a clear sense of purpose in Boston as well as tangible evidence of a collective energy determined to carry out a successful program of urban renewal. Mayors and administrative officials were articulate about their plans and accountable in their leadership roles; businessmen and financiers were definite in their support; religious leaders were positive in their encouragement; local newspapers took strong editorial positions; universities supplied valuable studies and designs. Working together, they were able to put together a coalition that provided the money, the talent, and the energy to succeed in their stated objectives. In those days even the opponents of urban change spoke out boldly and contributed a visible presence to the scene. Members of the city council defended the interests of the white neighborhoods; militant community leaders fought for the preservation of the black neighborhoods.

By the late 1970s and early 1980s, however, the "vital flame" of municipal leadership had begun to burn low in terms of providing the source of energy needed to inspire any greater vision and to effect any more substantive changes in either the physical appearance of the city or in the quality of life of its citizens. The depressing struggle over urban renewal, followed by the physical and emotional exhaustion of the busing crisis, drained the city of its will and deprived the neighborhood of its energies. Political leaders put the city on a sort of automatic pilot and preferred to deal with the important but more prosaic issues of snow removal, off-street parking, juvenile violence, and drug control. There were no serious attempts to chart new directions for the city, to revive its distinctive cultural and literary heritage, or to develop new strategies for closing the unfortunate chasm that continued to separate the various neighborhoods from each other and from the central city. Businessmen returned quietly to their boardrooms; financiers disappeared into their vaults; the clergy discovered the comforts of the wall of separation; the universities became more involved in tenure decisions than urban planning. A veil of anonymity settled over city government in Boston, and by the 1990s veteran observers were at a loss to identify any significant traces of leadership at any level. The organs of the body politic continued to function, of course, but an apathetic citizenry was forced to wonder from time to time whether they still served any useful purpose.

# Notes

## Introduction

1. *U.S. News and World Report*, September 21, 1964, pp. 52–54.
2. Kevin White, television interview, "Boston Common," WNAC-TV, Channel 7, Boston, June 10, 1990.
3. Margot Stage, ed., *Who Rules Boston?: A Citizen's Guide to Reclaiming the City* (Boston, 1984), p. 37.
4. When I began my research, I was told that there was a collection of Hynes's papers at the Boston Public Library. Consultation with library officials and research staff, discussions with members of the Hynes family, and a thorough review of the papers of assistant library director Francis X. Moloney failed to disclose a single document.

## 1. "A Hopeless Backwater"

1. Cleveland Amory, *The Proper Bostonians* (New York, 1947); Brett Howard, *Boston: A Social History* (New York, 1976). Although a work of fiction, J. P. Marquand's *The Late George Apley* (Boston, 1937) offers delightful insights into the personal and social lives of Boston's Brahmin community.
2. Jane Holtz Kay, *Lost Boston* (Boston, 1980), pp. 282–84; Douglass Shand-Tucci, *Built in Boston: City and Suburb, 1800–1950* (Amherst, Mass., 1988), p. 194.

3. Kay, *Lost Boston*, pp. 282–84.

4. Ibid., p. 284; David McCord, *About Boston: Sight, Sound, Flavor, and Inflection* (Boston, 1948), pp. 112–26.

5. McCord, *About Boston*, pp. 35–47, 75–79; Jeremiah Murphy, *Jeremiah Murphy's Boston* (Boston, 1974), pp. 22–24, 42–44. Sam Bass Warner, Jr., *Streetcar Suburbs: The Process of Growth in Boston, 1870–1900* (Cambridge, Mass., 1962), is an excellent study of the movement of immigrants groups out of the central city and into the surrounding neighborhoods.

6. Leo P. Dauwer, *I Remember Southie* (Boston, 1975), pp. 75–78.

7. Herbert A. Kenny, *Newspaper Row: Journalism in the Pre-Television Era* (Chester, Conn., 1987), is a detailed description of Boston's newspaper row, "the busiest street in Christendom," by a veteran Boston newspaperman.

8. For a delightful anecdotal history of Scollay Square, see David Kruh, *Always Something Doing: A History of Boston's Infamous Scollay Square* (Boston, 1989). Also see A. C. Lyons, *Invitation to Boston* (New York, 1947), pp. 3–48; Dauwer, *I Remember Southie*, pp. 81–85; George E. Ryan, "The Olde Dame," *Boston College Magazine* (Summer 1988), pp. 31–33.

9. Eliot Norton, *Broadway Down East* (Boston, 1978), provides a professional account of the plays and playhouses of Boston from the viewpoint of one of the city's outstanding theater critics. Shand-Tucci, *Built in Boston*, pp. 207–8, provides a fascinating analysis of the architectural details of Boston's major theaters and movie houses.

10. Jeremiah Murphy, *Jeremiah Murphy's Boston*, pp. 75–77. Also see Sam Bass Warner, Jr., *The Way We Really Live: Social Change in Metropolitan Boston since 1920* (Boston, 1977), for a creative analysis of the changing demographics of the city during this period.

11. Edward A. Filene, "Unemployment in New England," in *New England's Prospects* (American Geographical Society, 1933), p. 76.

12. Margaret C. Parker, *Lowell: A Study of Industrial Development* (New York, 1940), p. 126; Dennis Manning, "Reminiscences," in *South Boston*, Boston 200 Neighborhood History Series (Boston, 1976), pp. 14, 15.

13. Parker, *Lowell*, p. 105.

14. Thomas H. O'Connor, *South Boston, My Home Town: The History of an Ethnic Community* (Boston, 1988), p. 182.

15. New England Council, *Transactions in the New England Economy* (Boston, 1954), p. 15.

16. Francis M. McLaughlin, "Boston Longshoremen and the Right of the Sling Load," research paper, Boston College Department of Economics, 1988.

17. Joseph F. Dinneen, *The Purple Shamrock: The Hon. James Michael Curley of Boston* (New York, 1949), pp. 93–117, 129–41. The hasty passage by the state legislature of a statute prohibiting the mayor of Boston from succeeding himself was probably the only thing that prevented Curley from being reelected

right away in 1926—a piece of legislation that was promptly rescinded after Maurice Tobin was elected mayor in 1937.

For a complete, up-to-date biography of Curley, see Jack Beatty, *The Rascal King: The Life and Times of James Michael Curley, 1874–1958* (Reading, Mass., 1992). For many years the only study available was Dinneen, *Purple Shamrock.*

18. Charles Trout, *Boston, The Great Depression, and the New Deal* (New York, 1977), pp. 50–52; James Michael Curley, *I'd Do It Again: A Record of All My Uproarious Years* (Englewood Cliffs, N.J., 1957), pp. 246–48; Beatty, *Rascal King*, pp. 269–70. Beatty refers to Curley's 1930 plan as "a rare piece of statesmanship."

19. Steven P. Erie, *Rainbow's End: Irish-Americans and the Dilemmas of Urban Machine Politics, 1840–1985* (Berkeley and Los Angeles, 1988), p. 117; Dinneen, *Purple Shamrock*, pp. 227–30.

20. Trout, *Boston*, pp. 155–56, 161–62, 171–72; Beatty, *Rascal King*, pp. 368–70; Erie, *Rainbow's End*, pp. 110–11.

21. Trout, *Boston*, pp. 191–93; John F. Stack, Jr., *International Conflict in an American City: Boston's Irish, Italians, and Jews, 1934–1944* (Westport, Conn., 1979); W. Lloyd Warner and Leo Srole, *The Social System of American Ethnic Groups* (New Haven, Conn., 1945), pp. 96–98.

22. James Green and Hugh Donaghue, *Boston's Workers* (Boston, 1979), p. 106; Beatty, *Rascal King*, p. 366.

23. Thomas H. O'Connor, *Bibles, Brahmins, and Bosses: A Short History of Boston*, 3d ed. (Boston, 1990), pp. 191–92; Beatty, *Rascal King*, pp. 337–38.

24. Curley, *I'd Do It Again*, pp. 225–26; City of Boston, *17th Annual Report of the City Planning Board* (Boston, 1930).

25. Charles H. Trout, "Curley of Boston: The Search for Irish Legitimacy," in *Boston, 1700–1980*, ed. Ronald Formisano and Constance Burns (Westport, Conn., 1984), p. 181.

26. Frederic Cople Jaher, "The Boston Brahmin in the Age of Industrial Capitalism," in *The Age of Industrialism in America*, ed. F. C. Jaher (New York, 1968), is a literary essay on the attitudes of Brahmin intellectuals toward the rise of industrial capitalism in Boston and the related growth of immigration and bossism.

27. Curley, *I'd Do It Again*, pp. 220–21.

28. T. O'Connor, *Bibles, Brahmins, and Bosses*, p. 192; Beatty, *Rascal King*, p. 171.

29. Robert H. Lord, John E. Sexton, and Edward T. Harrington, *History of the Archdiocese of Boston*, 3 vols. (Boston, 1945); Annabelle Melville, *Jean-Louis Lefebvre de Cheverus, 1769–1836* (Milwaukee, 1958); Thomas H. O'Connor, *Fitzpatrick's Boston: John Bernard Fitzpatrick, Third Bishop of Boston* (Boston, 1984); Lawrence Kennedy, "Power and Prejudice: Boston Political Conflict, 1885–1895" (Ph.D. diss., Boston College, 1987).

30. Dorothy G. Wayman, *Cardinal O'Connell of Boston: A Biography of William Henry O'Connell, 1859–1944* (New York, 1955), has been updated by James M. O'Toole, *Militant and Triumphant: William Henry O'Connell and the Catholic Church in Boston, 1859–1944* (Notre Dame, Ind., 1992).

31. Cited in O'Toole, *Militant and Triumphant*, p. 121. Also see Beatty, *Rascal King*, pp. 103–7.

32. O'Toole, *Militant and Triumphant*, pp. 237–38. Also see James W. Sanders, "Catholics and the School Question in Boston: The Cardinal O'Connell Years," in *Catholic Boston: Studies in Religion and Community, 1870–1970*, ed. Robert Sullivan and James O'Toole (Boston, 1985), pp. 121–69.

33. O'Toole, *Militant and Triumphant*, pp. 242–44. An amusing but perceptive incident involving the horror with which old-time Catholics viewed the prospect of entering a non-Catholic church can be found in Doris Kearns Goodwin, *The Fitzgeralds and the Kennedys* (New York, 1987), relating to the fears of young John F. Fitzgerald taking visitors into Boston's famous Old North Church.

34. Thomas E. Wangler, "Catholic Religious Life in Boston in the Era of Cardinal O'Connell," in *Catholic Boston*, ed. Sullivan and O'Toole, pp. 254–56.

35. O'Toole, *Militant and Triumphant*, pp. 229–31; Wangler, "Catholic Religious Life," pp. 255–56.

36. O'Toole, *Militant and Triumphant*, p. 54.

37. Beatty, *Rascal King*, p. 107.

38. Elisabeth Herlihy, "Planning for Boston, 1630–1930," *City Planning Quarterly* 6 (1930): 163.

39. Elisabeth Herlihy, *Fifty Years of Boston: A Memorial Volume Issued in Commemoration of the Tercentenary of 1930* (Boston, 1932), p. 54.

40. City of Boston, *10th Annual Report of the City Planning Board* (Boston, 1923), appendix. Also see City of Boston, City Planning Board, *Report on a Thoroughfare Plan for Boston* (Boston, 1930), pp. 12–14.

41. Kruh, *Always Something Doing*, pp. 113–25; Stewart H. Holbrook, "Boston's Temple of Burlesque," *The American Mercury* 58 (April 1944): 411–16; Walter Muir Whitehill, *Boston: A Topographical History*, 2d ed. (Cambridge, Mass., 1968), p. 201; A. C. Lyons, *Invitation to Boston* (New York, 1947), pp. 220–21.

42. Kruh, *Always Something Doing*, pp. 113–15; Whitehill, *Boston*, pp. 196–97.

43. Whitehill, *Boston*, p. 195.

44. Louis M. Lyons, "Boston: Study in Inertia," in *Our Fair City*, ed. Robert S. Allen (New York, 1947), p. 20.

45. Curley, *I'd Do It Again*, p. 306; Beatty, *Rascal King*, pp. 409–15.

46. Vincent A. Lapomarda, "Maurice Joseph Tobin, 1901–1953: A Political

Profile and an Edition of Selected Public Papers" (Ph.D. diss., Boston University, 1968), pp. 38–39.

47. *Boston Post*, November 2, 1941. See Jon Teaford, *The Rough Road to Renaissance: Urban Revitalization in America, 1940–1985* (Baltimore, 1990), pp. 33–34; James Bruner and Sheldon Korchin, "The Boss and the Vote," *Public Opinion Quarterly* 10 (Spring 1946): 1–23; Beatty, *Rascal King*, pp. 433–34.

48. Lapomarda, "Tobin," p. 53.

49. Curley, *I'd Do It Again*, pp. 312–15; Beatty, *Rascal King*, pp. 435–37.

50. Beatty, *Rascal King*, pp. 443–47.

51. Robert C. Estall, *New England: A Study in Industrial Adjustment* (Westport, Conn., 1966), p. 16; National Planning Association, *The Economic State of New England* (New Haven, Conn., 1954), p. 341.

52. Alan Lupo, "Beyond V-J Day," *Boston Globe Magazine*, August 11, 1985.

53. John H. Mollenkopf, *The Contested City* (Princeton, N.J., 1983), pp. 142–44, 154.

54. Lapomarda, "Tobin," pp. 80–84.

55. Alec Barbrook, *God Save the Commonwealth: An Electoral History of Massachusetts* (Amherst, Mass., 1973), pp. 84–85; Beatty, *Rascal King*, pp. 471–72.

56. Barbrook, *God Save the Commonwealth*, p. 86. On August 8, 1948, Tobin was nominated by President Harry Truman to fill the cabinet post vacated by the death of Secretary of Labor Lewis B. Schwellenbach. Tobin accepted, and was sworn in as the sixth secretary of labor on August 3, 1948 (Lapomarda, "Tobin," p. 109).

57. Curley, *I'd Do It Again*, pp. 317–19. In *Rascal King*, pp. 456–57, Jack Beatty claims that money supplied by Joseph P. Kennedy enabled a bankrupt Curley to run for mayor, leaving his congressional seat for young Jack Kennedy to occupy.

58. The controversial case rose out of the questionable activities of a wartime consulting firm called the Engineers' Group Incorporated—a company that Curley had carelessly allowed to use his name. Curley, *I'd Do It Again*, pp. 325–32; Beatty, *Rascal King*, pp. 474–75; Dinneen, *Purple Shamrock*, pp. 296–98.

59. Dinneen, *Purple Shamrock*, pp. 305.

60. Ibid., p. 306.

61. Hirsch Freed, "The New Urban Leadership" (paper delivered at the Boston 350 conference "Hizzoner the Mayor of Boston," John F. Kennedy Library, May 10, 1983).

62. Thomas P. O'Neill, *Man of the House: The Life and Political Memoirs of Speaker Tip O'Neill* (New York, 1987), pp. 50–51.

63. Ibid.

64. *Boston Globe*, November 29, 1947; Beatty, *Rascal King*, p. 481.

65. *Boston Globe*, November 29, 1947. Samuel B. Cutler wrote the piece describing Curley's reception and his "coolness" toward Hynes. Cutler also referred to Curley's rejection of the idea of a conference with Hynes as a "snub." Also see Beatty, *Rascal King*, p. 482.

66. *Boston Globe*, November 29, 1947; Curley, *I'd Do It Again*, p. 335.

67. Mary (Sheehan) Nolan, interview, November 17, 1991.

68. *Boston Globe*, November 28, 1947. During the five months that Curley was in the federal prison, the city of Boston paid the salaries of two mayors—Hynes and Curley.

69. Jack Hynes, interview, March 24, 1989.

70. Hirsh Freed, "New Urban Leadership."

71. Edward McLaughlin, interview, May 22, 1990.

72. John F. Collins, interview, December 15, 1989.

73. Lance Carden, *Witness: An Oral History of Black Politics in Boston, 1920–1960* (Chestnut Hill, Mass., 1989), pp. 27, 63–64. This valuable compilation of oral interviews was commissioned by the Black Studies Department of Boston College as a part of the fifth "Blacks in Boston" conference, April 1989, sponsored by Boston College, the Museum of Afro-American History, and Roxbury Community College.

74. Jerome Lyle Rappaport, interview, January 16, 1990.

75. Ibid.

76. Ibid.

77. Curley, *I'd Do It Again*, p. 335.

78. Beatty, *Rascal King*, pp. 487–88; Dinneen, *Purple Shamrock*, p. 315.

79. Beatty, *Rascal King*, pp. 489–90; Dinneen, *Purple Shamrock*, p. 316.

80. Carden, *Witness*, pp. 48–49.

81. Curley, *I'd Do It Again*, pp. 337–38.

82. *Boston Traveler*, November 9, 1949; John P. Mallan, "The End of Jim Curley?" *The Nation*, October 29, 1949.

83. *Christian Science Monitor*, November 3, 1949; *Boston Herald*, November 1, 1949; *Boston Post*, November 4, 1949.

84. *Boston Globe*, November 3, 1949.

85. Ibid., November 4, 1949.

86. Ibid., November 7, 1949.

87. Ibid., November 9, 1949.

88. Ibid. See also Beatty, *Rascal King*, pp. 495–96.

89. *Boston Globe*, November 6, 1949.


## 2.  *Forming a New Coalition*

1. *Boston Globe*, January 2, 1950.
2. Ibid.

3. Ibid., January 3, 1950.

4. Ibid., January 1, 1950.

5. Marie (Hynes) Gallagher, interview, February 11, 1991.

6. Warner, *Streetcar Suburbs*, pp. 55–56, 68–69.

7. Gallagher, interview, February 11, 1991.

8. Joseph A. Keblinsky, "Johnny Hynes . . . As I Knew Him," *Boston Globe*, January 8, 1970.

9. *Boston Globe*, March 19, 1973.

10. Mollenkopf, *The Contested City*, p. 149.

11. Alan Lupo, *Liberty's Chosen Home: The Politics of Violence in Boston* (Boston, 1977), p. 86.

12. Ibid.

13. Examples of Catlin's outspoken views were conveyed to me by Dr. Donald J. White and Rev. John J. Collins, SJ, of Boston College.

14. Barbrook, *God Save the Commonwealth*, pp. 81–83.

15. Gallagher, interview, February 11, 1991.

16. Kane Simonian, interview, July 10, 1990.

17. Mayor Hynes's sons Jack and Richard told me about their father's friendship with writer Bill Schofield and about his many conversations with Paul Hines about promoting the history of the city.

18. *Boston Herald*, March 14, 1951.

19. *Boston Traveler*, March 8, 1951.

20. Ibid., March 31, 1951.

21. Ibid., June 25, 1951. Also see Richard Berenson's prologue to William G. Schofield, *Freedom by the Bay: The Boston Freedom Trail* (Boston, 1988).

22. An international flavor was added when an American Express Foundation grant funded translations of the official Freedom Trail maps into Japanese and German. See George E. Ryan, "Bill's *Freiheitspfad*," *The Pilot*, October 14, 1988.

23. Carden, *Witness*, pp. 63–64.

24. Rappaport, interview, January 16, 1990.

25. Joseph Fahey, *Boston's 45 Mayors: From John Phillips to Kevin H. White* (Boston, 1975), p. 39.

26. Rappaport, interview, January 16, 1990.

27. *Boston Globe*, September 1, 1951.

28. Ibid., September 21, 1951.

29. Ibid., September 22, 1951.

30. Curley, *I'd Do It Again*, p. 346.

31. Ibid., pp. 346–47.

32. *Boston Globe*, September 22, 1951.

33. Ibid., September 21, 1951.

34. Curley, *I'd Do It Again*, p. 348.

35. Ibid.

36. *Boston Globe*, September 25, 1951.

37. Ibid.

38. Ibid.

39. Curley, *I'd Do It Again*, pp. 350–51.

40. *Boston Globe*, November 3, 4, 1951.

41. Ibid., November 5, 6, 1951.

42. New Boston Committee, "A Fact Sheet" (copy in the State House Library, Boston, Massachusetts).

43. Rappaport, interview, January 16, 1990.

44. *Boston Herald*, December 4, 1940; *Boston Traveler*, August 17, 1957. Also see "New NBC Elected," *New Boston Comments* 1 (Summer 1952): 3; John P. Mallan, "Boston's Curley Bows Out," *The Nation* (October 27, 1951), pp. 350–51.

45. Amanda V. Houston, "Beneath the El," *Boston College Magazine* (Summer 1988), pp. 20–25. Written while Houston was director of the Black Studies Department at Boston College, this essay recounts the personal experiences of a young black woman growing up in the South End.

46. Carden, *Witness*, pp. 14–15.

47. Houston, "Beneath the El," p. 23; Trout, *Boston*, pp. 298–99.

48. Reginald Weems, "Reminiscences of the Jazz Scene," research paper, Harvard University Extension Program, May 1988. Also see Nat Hentoff, *Boston Boy* (Boston, 1986), pp. 110–37, for personal recollections of the music of the South End. *The Autobiography of Malcolm X* (New York, 1964), pp. 39–55, provides a more critical view of Boston's "Harlem" district through the eyes of a young black newcomer from Michigan.

49. Carden, *Witness*, p. 47. An interesting and helpful summary of the changing nature of Boston's black population may be found in J. Anthony Lukas, *Common Ground* (New York, 1985), pp. 57–62.

50. Carden, *Witness*, p. 57.

51. Rappaport, interview, January 16, 1990; Hirsh Freed, "New Urban Leadership."

52. *Boston Globe*, November 4, 1951. A preelection issue featured photographs and brief biographical sketches of all the finalists.

53. *Boston Herald*, November 6, 1951.

54. Ibid., November 4, 1951.

55. Ibid., November 6, 1951.

56. *Christian Science Monitor*, September 18, 1951, August 8, 1954; *New York Times*, September 27, November 8, 1951; "Something New in Boston," *Time*, October 8, 1951, p. 28.

57. *Christian Science Monitor*, July 15, 1954; *Boston Herald*, August 19, 1954; *Boston Traveler*, August 18, August 20, 1954.

58. Cited in Mollenkopf, *The Contested City*, p. 150.

59. Rappaport, interview, January 16, 1990.


3. *Visions and Designs*

1. Mark Gelfand, *A Nation of Cities: The Federal Government and Urban America, 1933–1965* (New York, 1975), pp. 106–7.

2. Ibid., p. 107.

3. T. O'Connor, *Bibles, Brahmins, and Bosses*, pp. 196–97; idem, *South Boston*, pp. 197–98.

4. Russell B. Adams, Jr., *The Boston Money Tree* (New York, 1977), p. 305.

5. T. O'Connor, *Bibles, Brahmins, and Bosses*, pp. 71–72; Kay, *Lost Boston*, pp. 70–71.

6. T. O'Connor, *Bibles, Brahmins, and Bosses*, pp. 92–93; Kay, *Lost Boston*, pp. 131–32.

7. T. O'Connor, *Bibles, Brahmins, and Bosses*, pp. 165–66; Kay, *Lost Boston*, pp. 214–20. For a general history of Boston's planning history from the colonial period to the present, see Lawrence W. Kennedy, *Planning the City Upon a Hill: Boston since 1630* (Amherst, Mass., 1992).

8. Boston Society of Architects, *Report Made to the Boston Society of Architects by Its Committee on Municipal Improvement* (Boston, 1907). Also see Whitehill, *Boston*, 200–201; Kay, *Lost Boston*, 274–75.

9. *Public Improvements for the Metropolitan District* (Boston, 1909); Alex Krieger and Lisa J. Green, *Past Futures: Two Centuries of Imagining Boston* (Cambridge, Mass., 1985), pp. 13–14.

10. *What Boston-1915 Is* (Boston, 1909), a pamphlet published by the Boston-1915 board of directors.

11. Krieger and Green, *Past Futures*, pp. 17–18.

12. *The Boston Contest of 1944* (Boston, 1944), p. 8. Also see Lupo, *Liberty's Chosen Home*, p. 87.

13. Mellier G. Scott, *American City Planning since 1890* (Berkeley, Calif., 1969), p. 435; Herlihy, *Fifty Years of Boston*, p. 61.

14. Allen M. Wakstein, "Boston's Search for a Metropolitan Solution," *AIP Journal* (September 1972), pp. 285–96.

15. *Boston Sunday Globe*, September 22, 1985.

16. Lupo, *Liberty's Chosen Home*, p. 85; Kenny, *Newspaper Row*, passim.

17. Erie, *Rainbow's End*, pp. 145–50, has a valuable analysis of the changing character of the new postwar urban electorate in a number of large American cities, demonstrating that these changes were not peculiar to Boston.

18. Teaford, *Rough Road*, p. 2.

19. Erie, *Rainbow's End*, pp. 140–41. "The new social triumvirate of labor,

capital, and the federal government drove the big-city bosses with their Thanksgiving turkeys off the block," writes Erie.

20. Ibid., pp. 151–57.

21. Teaford, *Rough Road*, pp. 45–47, 50.

22. Bernard J. Frieden and Lynne B. Sagalyn, *Downtown, Inc.: How America Rebuilds Cities* (Cambridge, Mass., 1989), p. 18.

23. Erie, *Rainbow's End*, pp. 158–60.

24. Adams, *Boston Money Tree*, p. 307. Jon Teaford discusses postwar renewal plans in Pittsburgh, St. Louis, Baltimore, Cleveland, Minneapolis, Philadelphia, and Chicago; but there is no mention of any comparable activities in Boston (Teaford, *Rough Road*, pp. 44–45).

25. City of Boston, Planning Board, *General Plan for Boston* (Boston, 1950), pp. 7, 8, 23.

26. *Boston Globe*, May 12, 1955.

27. *General Plan*, p. 56.

28. E. C. Banfield and M. Derthick, *A Report on the Politics of Boston* (Cambridge, Mass., 1966), 6:8–11; Walter McQuade, "Boston: What Can a Sick City Do?" *Fortune*, June 1964, pp. 134–35; *Christian Science Monitor*, July 30–August 12, 1954.

29. McQuade, "Boston," p. 134; "Is Boston 'Beginning to Boil'?" *Fortune*, June 1957, p. 286; Daniel S. Pool, "Politics in the New Boston: A Study of Mayoral Policy Making," Ph.D. diss., Brandeis University, 1974.

30. Quoted in John Patrick Diggins, *The Proud Decades: America in War and Peace, 1941–1960* (New York, 1988), p. 128.

31. Ibid., p. 181.

32. Cornelius Dalton et al., *Leading the Way: A History of the Massachusetts General Court, 1629–1980* (Boston, 1984), pp. 209–10, 232.

33. Barbrook, *God Save the Commonwealth*, pp. 95–96.

34. Dalton, *Leading the Way*, p. 329.

35. Sometime in the late 1950s the original logo of the authority—Paul Revere on horseback—was changed to the present one, an arrow through a Pilgrim's hat. Local wags claim this was Callahan's way of showing how the Irish pierced the Yankee lock on Massachusetts political power. See Peter J. Howe, "Why We Don't Fly out of Hegenberger Airport," *Boston Globe Magazine*, April 23, 1989. Also see Kennedy, *Planning the City*, p. 251.

36. John Strahinich, with J. William Semich, "The Shadow Government," *Boston Magazine*, November 1989, pp. 129–33.

37. City of Boston, Planning Board, *Report on a Thoroughfare Plan for Boston* (Boston, 1930), p. 12.

38. *Boston Globe*, October 19, 1953.

39. Ibid., October 27, 1953.

40. *Chinatown*, Boston 200 Neighborhood History Series (Boston, 1976), p. 12.

41. Paula J. Todisco, *Boston's First Neighborhood: The North End* (Boston, 1976), pp. 51–52.

42. WCVB, Channel 5, Boston, "The Way We Were: The Original Big Dig," *Chronicle* series, September 12, 1989.

43. *Boston Globe*, January 3, 1955.

44. Whitehill, *Boston*, p. 35; Kay, *Lost Boston*, pp. 5, 8.

45. McCord, *About Boston*, p. 43.

46. *Business Week*, May 29, 1948, p. 22.

47. Ibid., July 23, 1955.

## 4. *"Where's Boston?"*

1. John B. Hynes, Interview, September 9, 1969, cited in Daniel Rudsten, "City-State Conflict: A Study of the Political Relationship between the Core City of Boston and the Massachusetts State Legislature," Ph.D. diss., Tufts University, 1973, p. 203.

2. Ibid.

3. Joseph Slavet, interview, July 31, 1969, cited in ibid., pp. 192–93.

4. Norman Weinberg, interview, August 11, 1969, cited in ibid., pp. 195–96.

5. Slavet, interview, July 31, 1969, cited in ibid., pp. 196–97.

6. Thomas H. O'Connor, *Religion and American Society* (Menlo Park, Calif., 1975), pp. 158–62.

7. O'Toole, *Militant and Triumphant*, p. 87.

8. Ibid., p. 251.

9. T. O'Connor, *Bibles, Brahmins, and Bosses*, pp. 202–3; idem, *South Boston*, p. 202.

10. O'Toole, "Prelates and Politicos," in *Catholic Boston*, ed. Sullivan and O'Toole, pp. 57–62.

11. *Boston Globe*, October 31, November 9, 1953; Kruh, *Always Something Doing*, p. 80.

12. Rev. Joseph A. Appleyard, SJ, eulogy at the funeral of W. Seavey Joyce, SJ, May 24, 1988.

13. Ben Birnbaum and Raymond F. Keyes, *Excellence in Education for Leadership: A History of the Boston College School of Management, 1938–1988* (Chestnut Hill, Mass., 1988), pp. 23–24.

14. Ibid., p. 25.

15. Joseph A. Healey, lecture, Conference on Greater Boston's Business Future, May 15, 1954, Boston College Archives.

16. Adams, *The Boston Money Tree*, p. 306.

17. John B. Hynes, "How Hynes Steered the Pru to Boston," *Boston Sunday Globe*, January 11, 1970. Toward the end of his life, Hynes was persuaded to put together a firsthand account of the Prudential Center. His account was

published as a full-page article in the *Sunday Globe* just nine days after the former mayor's death.

18. See Victor O. Jones, "The Man with Faith in Boston," *Boston Globe*, July 15, 1966, for an article showing the influence of Oakes on the rebuilding of the city.

19. A diary of Oakes's, located in the R. M. Bradley Company's archives, shows that from 1953 to 1955 Oakes worked at least 193 days on the Back Bay project. During that time, he made 161 telephone calls to Stevens and held 110 meetings with business leaders. See Jones, "The Man with Faith."

20. *Boston Business*, March 1953, p. 7.

21. Hynes, "How Hynes Steered the Pru."

22. Ibid.

23. Frieden and Sagalyn, *Downtown, Inc.*, pp. 18–19.

24. "Court Trims City's Plans," *Business Week*, May 28, 1955, p. 86; *New York Times*, February 13, 1953; *Christian Science Monitor*, October 11, November 4, 1954.

25. Birnbaum and Keyes, *Excellence*, pp. 25–26.

26. Ibid., p. 26.

27. Appleyard, eulogy.

28. Interview with Dr. Donald J. White, dean, Graduate School, Boston College, May 15, 1989. Dr. White was associate dean of the Business School and accompanied Father Joyce on his trip to the West Coast.

29. Andrew Buni and Alan Rogers, *Boston: City on a Hill* (Woodland Hills, Calif., 1984), p. 134.

30. John B. Hynes, "Boston, Whither Goest Thou?" (keynote address, Boston College Citizen Seminar, October 26, 1954, Boston College Archives).

31. Hynes, interview, in Rudsten, "City-State Conflict," p. 204.

32. On this trip, accompanied by his longtime friend and companion Andrew Dazzi, Hynes sent back a series of charming and informative dispatches that were published in the *Boston Globe* and subsequently reprinted as a small booklet called *The European Odyssey of Mayor John B. Hynes*.

33. Hynes, "Boston, Whither Goest Thou?," p. 8.

34. Ibid.

35. Leland Hazard, "What Dynamic Business Leadership Has Been Able to Accomplish in Pittsburgh" (lecture, Boston College Citizen Seminar, May 19, 1955, Boston College Archives).

36. John Galvin, "Pittsburgh: A Model for the 'New Boston,' " *Boston Globe*, March 15, 1985. Also see Mollenkopf, *Contested City*, pp. 158–59.

37. Galvin, "Pittsburgh."

38. Christian Herter, lecture, Boston College Citizen Seminar, March 8, 1955, Boston College Archives; Mollenkopf, *Contested City*, p. 155.

39. *Boston Herald*, January 13, 1955.

40. Lewis Mumford, "The Future of Downtown" (lecture, Boston College Citizens Seminar, December 11, 1957, Boston College Archives).

41. Birnbaum and Keyes, *Excellence*, pp. 26–27. Joseph Turley rose in the ranks of the Gillette Company and eventually became its president.

42. Ibid., p. 27. Father Joyce eventually became president of Boston College and, during his years of service from 1968 to 1972, continued his lively interest in the Citizen Seminars.

43. Hynes, "How Hynes Steered the Pru."

44. Edward J. Logue, "Boston, 1960–1967: Seven Years of Plenty," *Massachusetts Historical Society Proceedings* 84 (1972): 85.


## 5. *Trial and Error*

1. T. O'Connor, *South Boston*, pp. 203–4. According to his son, deputy mayor John Breen had an understanding with John Hynes that he would succeed Hynes as mayor at the end of his second term. When the 52-year-old Breen dropped dead of a heart attack on October 8, 1957, Mayor Hynes was suddenly left with no logical successor. John Sherman Breen to author, October 8, 1992.

2. *New York Times*, December 20, 1953, September 25, 27, 28, October 2, 1955.

3. *Boston Herald*, May 6, 8, October 18, November 7, 1955; *Boston Post*, November 7, 1955.

4. *Boston Traveler*, October 26, 1955.

5. *New York Times*, November 9, 1955.

6. *Boston Post*, January 3, 1956.

7. *Boston Globe*, January 2, 1956.

8. Ibid., January 3, 1956.

9. Michael Hourihan, interview, 1955, cited in Rudsten, "City-State Conflict," pp. 201–2.

10. Joseph Slavet, interview, July 31, 1969, cited in ibid., p. 196.

11. Ibid., p. 207.

12. Ibid., p. 206.

13. *Boston Globe*, May 22, 1959.

14. Dalton, *Leading the Way*, p. 331.

15. Hynes, "How Hynes Steered the Pru."

16. Robert Ryan, lecture, Boston College Citizen Seminar, January 5, 1957, Boston College Archives.

17. Charles Francis Adams, Jr., lecture, Boston College Citizen Seminar, February 19, 1957, Boston College Archives.

18. Hynes, "How Hynes Steered the Pru."

19. Rappaport, interview, January 16, 1990.

20. Hynes, "How Hynes Steered the Pru." This, in fact, proved to be the case when mayor-elect John F. Collins gave his endorsement to the pact on December 9, 1959, a month before he actually took office.

21. *Boston Globe*, January 9, 1959.

22. Ibid., April 2, 1959.

23. Kennedy, *Planning the City*, p. 167.

24. Mel King, *Chain of Change: Struggles for Black Community Development* (Boston, 1981), p. 20.

25. Kennedy, *Planning the City*, p. 166.

26. Herbert Gans, *The Urban Villagers: Group and Class in the Life of Italian Americans* (New York, 1962), p. 282.

27. "$20 Million Home Project for West End Revealed," *Boston Sunday Globe*, April 12, 1953.

28. Boston Housing Authority, Urban Redevelopment Division, "Urban Redevelopment and the West End: A Pamphlet Explaining the Plans for the West End Redevelopment Project" (Boston, 1951, mimeographed).

29. BRA Notice to Residents, April 9, 1958, signed by Joseph W. Lund, chairman (BRA Archives).

30. Mollenkopf, *Contested City*, pp. 157–58.

31. Thomas Hennessy, lecture, Boston College Citizen Seminar, October 29, 1957; Robert Ryan, January 5, 1957, Boston College Archives.

32. Massachusetts, *Acts and Resolves*, chapter 150 (1957).

33. Joseph Lund, lecture, Boston College Citizen Seminar, January 27, 1959, Boston College Archives. Also see Mollenkopf, *Contested City*, p. 158.

34. *Forty-Fourth Annual Report of the City Planning Board*, Boston City Document no. 8 (1957) (Boston, 1958), pp. 9–10. Kane Simonian, executive director of the BRA, saw this as a shrewd and intelligent move on Mayor Hynes's part to get as much public support for his new undertakings as possible (interview, July 10, 1990).

35. Peter Anderson, "West End Story," *Boston Globe Magazine*, May 24, 1987, pp. 37–38.

36. Ibid., pp. 40–41; Gans, *Urban Villagers*, p. 282.

37. Richard Lourie, "A Whole Other Boston," *Boston Magazine*, April 1985, p. 142. Lourie's article is an idealized and romanticized recollection of growing up as a teenager in the West End during the mid-1950s.

38. Simonian, interview, July 10, 1990.

39. Msgr. Francis Lally, interview, July 1985 (courtesy of Professor Andrew Buni, Boston College).

40. Robert Hanron, "West End Project Could Be Spark to Revitalize Boston," *Boston Globe*, December 20, 1959; Anderson, "West End Story," pp. 40–41.

41. Lally, interview, July 1985.

42. Ibid.

43. "The Lost Neighborhood" (ABC News documentary on the West End, WCVB-TV, Channel 5, November 20, 1962).

44. Mollenkopf, *Contested City*, pp. 169–70.

45. According to public opinion polls during the late 1950s, some 80 percent of the American people said they had "great trust" in government. This figure dropped sharply after the mid-1960s. See Frieden and Sagalyn, *Downtown, Inc.*, p. 55.

46. Gans, *Urban Villagers*, pp. 308–10.

47. Lally, interview, July 1985.

48. An official BHA report, dated May 15, 1956, listed Kempner Realty Corporation of New York as the highest bidder, with Shoolman and Bonan as second highest. Zerman Realty of Boston offered a bid of $1.06; De Mov and Morris of Boston offered $1.00; and Max Kargman's First Realty Corporation of Boston was the lowest, with a bid listed as "indefinite" (BRA Archives, box 330). Also see Mollenkopf, *Contested City*, p. 150.

49. Rappaport, interview, January 16, 1990. Although in 1987 Rappaport identified Kargman of First Realty as the highest bidder in Anderson, "West End Story," p. 46, Joseph Lee in a written rebuttal to *West End Project Report* (March 1953) named Kempner Realty as the highest bidder. Both corporations, along with three others, are named in a Boston Housing Authority document dated May 15, 1956; Kempner Realty is at the top of the list, while First Realty comes at the end. Kane Simonian, executive director of the BRA, confirmed that it was a New York company that withdrew its bid, and agreed that at that time "nobody had any faith in the city; nobody wanted to invest" (Simonian, interview, July 10, 1990).

50. BRA press release, December 10, 1959 (BRA Archives).

51. Anderson, "West End Story," p. 40.

52. Rappaport, interview, January 16, 1990. Rappaport confirmed the story of Hancock's competition with Prudential to BRA historian Lawrence W. Kennedy (*Planning the City*, pp. 164–65).

53. Simonian, interview, July 10, 1990.

54. Bill Cunningham, "2 Great Projects to Change Boston," *Boston Herald*, November 17, 1957.

55. Robert Hanron, "West End Project."

56. Rappaport, interview, January 16, 1990.

57. BRA press release, December 10, 1959 (BRA Archives).

58. Joseph Lee obituary, *Boston Globe*, November 8, 1991.

59. In its original "Declaration of Findings," issued in November 1955 and revised in May 1957, the BRA declared the project area to be "substandard" and "decadent" as defined in Section 26J of Chapter 121 of the General Laws (BRA Archives).

60. Gans, *Urban Villagers*, p. 304.

61. BRA press release, December 10, 1959 (BRA Archives).

62. Chester Hartman, "The Housing of Relocated Families," in *Urban Renewal: The Record and the Controversy*, ed. James Q. Wilson (Cambridge, Mass., 1966), p. 360.

63. Marc Fried, "Grieving for a Lost Home: Psychological Costs of Relocation," in Wilson, *Urban Renewal*, p. 306; Frieden and Sagalyn, *Downtown, Inc.*, pp. 33–34.

64. Kennedy, *Planning the City*, pp. 162–63. Jon Teaford, *Rough Road*, p. 155, also agrees that "to many commentators the West End was a symbol of all that was wrong with urban renewal."

65. Whitehill, *Boston*, p. 202. Some forty years later, sons and daughters of parents ousted from the West End still kept alive the image of the neighborhood and attacked the evils of urban renewal. Supported by donations from a loyal readership that extended into thirty-five states, Joseph Lo Piccolo turned out a quarterly newspaper, *The West Ender*, featuring wistful letters from former residents and criticizing city politics. A teenager at the time of the demolition, Lo Piccolo and his close friend James Campano considered themselves a "government in exile."

66. Rappaport, interview, January 16, 1990.

67. Cited in Whitehill, *Boston*, p. 200.

68. Harold D. Hodgkinson, "Miracle in Boston," *Massachusetts Historical Society Proceedings* 84 (1972): 73.

69. Ibid., p. 74; *Boston Globe*, January 16, 1958.

70. Reporter Michael Liuzzi presented a detailed description of the meeting in the *Christian Science Monitor*, November 10, 1959.

71. Diggins, *The Proud Decades*, pp. 319–21, 336–37.

72. *Boston Globe*, September 11, 1960.

73. Barbrook, *God Save the Commonwealth*, pp. 105–6.

74. Simonian, interview, July 10, 1990.

75. The Papers of John F. Collins, box 192, Boston Public Library. Collins's papers are kept in the Rare Book Room of the Boston Public Library in Copley Square, Boston, Massachusetts. Collins was the first Boston mayor to preserve his official papers and leave them intact in a public repository. The papers are categorized by topic in separate file folders and kept in large cardboard boxes. They represent not only Collins's own mayoral papers but also those of his administrative assistants, his press secretary, his secretaries, and other members of his official staff. Hereafter cited as Collins Papers. Edward Logue, *Seven Years of Progress: A Final Report* (Boston, 1967), p. 85.

76. Mollenkopf, *Contested City*, p. 157.

77. Richard Chapman, Boston College Citizen Seminar, 1959 series, pp. 7–8, Boston College Archives.

78. Dalton, *Leading the Way*, pp. 283–84; Barbrook, *God Save the Commonwealth*, pp. 86, 92, 100, 103.

79. "Boston Bonds Rating Slips a Notch," *Business Week*, December 19, 1959, pp. 90–94; Banfield and Derthick, *Politics of Boston* 6:14–18.

80. *Boston Globe*, December 25, 1959.

81. Ibid.; Stage, *Who Rules Boston?*, p. 37.

82. Kennedy, *Planning the City*, p. 168. In his comparative analysis of redevelopment in American cities, Jon Teaford spends little time discussing the "lackluster" Hynes, whom he regards as "largely ineffective" in sparking the city's revival, but at least doing nothing to "further damage its repute" (*Rough Road*, p. 59).

83. *Boston Globe*, January 7, 1970.


## 6. *A New Beginning*

1. Murray B. Levin, *The Alienated Voter: Politics in Boston* (New York, 1960), pp. 12–14. Professors Murray Levin and George Blackwood of Boston University conducted some five hundred interviews within three days of the election of 1959. From those interviews they analyzed the socioeconomic factors that went into voting behavior that formed the basis of their theory of political alienation.

2. John E. Powers, interview, July 17, 1969, cited in Rudsten, "City-State Conflict," pp. 175, 180.

3. Levin, *Alienated Voter*, pp. 8–9.

4. Joseph A. Keblinsky, "Johnny Hynes . . . As I Knew Him," *Boston Globe*, January 8, 1970.

5. John F. Collins, interview, December 15, 1989.

6. Ibid.

7. Collins Papers, box 52.

8. Ibid.

9. Levin, *Alienated Voter*, pp. 11–12.

10. John F. Collins, interview, February 19, 1991.

11. As a result of his postelection interviews, Murray Levin records such responses concerning Powers as "don't like his looks—tough, ugly looking," "smug—looks crooked," "too cocky," "little Napoleon," "ran a dirty campaign." Responses concerning Collins included "nice quiet manner," "he always had a smile and a handshake," "clean fighter," "a real gentleman," "just the way he spoke, I feel he is honest" (Levin, *Alienated Voter*, p. 44).

12. *Boston Herald*, September 23, 1959.

13. Levin, *Alienated Voter*, p. 18. Powers's list of "experts" included such authorities as Arnold Soloway of MIT, Edward Smith of Boston College, Joseph Slavet, Michael Dukakis, and Herbert Gleason.

14. Levin, *Alienated Voter*, p. 18.

15. Lupo, *Liberty's Chosen Home*, p. 80.

16. Collins, interview, December 15, 1989.

17. Levin, *Alienated Voter*, pp. 17–18.

18. Tom Callaghan used these phrases in an article in a newsletter of Government Research, Inc., Collins Papers, box 4.

19. *Boston Herald*, October 27, 1959.

20. *Boston Traveler*, October 20, 1959.

21. Ibid., October 27, 1959. The reference was to a piece written by James Colbert supporting Republican George Fingold and accusing Collins of being an antilabor candidate.

22. Levin, *Alienated Voter*, p. 21.

23. Hirsh Freed, "New Urban Leadership."

24. Collins, interview, February 19, 1991. Collins professed to know nothing about reports that several photographs had been cropped to eliminate other prominent people standing alongside Powers in front of Bartolo's café—including a well-known monsignor. See Joseph Dever, *Cushing of Boston: A Candid Portrait* (Boston, 1965), p. 233.

25. *Boston Globe*, November 3, 1959; Levin, *Alienated Voter*, pp. 21–22.

26. *Boston Traveler*, November 4, 1959; *Boston Herald*, November 4, 1959.

27. *Christian Science Monitor*, November 4, 1959.

28. Levin, *Alienated Voter*, pp. 58–75.

29. Barbrook, *God Save the Commonwealth*, pp. 128–29.

30. *Boston Globe*, January 3, 1970.

31. Charles L. Whipple, "Hynes Calls It a Day after 10-Year Hitch," *Boston Globe*, January 1, 1960. After leaving office, former mayor Hynes set up his law office at 73 Tremont Street, just up the street from City Hall. He was later named state commissioner of banks and banking by Governor Endicott Peabody. Hynes died on January 2, 1970, at his Druid Street home in Dorchester at the age of seventy-two.

32. *Boston Globe*, January 4, 1960.

33. Ibid.

34. Ibid.

35. Ibid., January 5, 1960.

36. Ibid.

37. Collins, interview, December 15, 1989.

38. *Boston Globe*, January 11, 1960.

39. Collins, interview, December 15, 1989.

40. Collins, interview, February 19, 1991.

41. Collins, interview, December 15, 1989.

42. *Christian Science Monitor*, February 11, 12, 1960. Collins Papers, box 188.

43. Rudsten, "City-State Conflict," pp. 160–61.

44. Ibid., pp. 161–62.

45. Ibid., p. 163. According to Kane Simonian, Mayor Hynes made no effort to acquire the power to appoint the police commissioner. He had no interest in getting involved in such a "hot political potato" (Simonian, interview, July 10, 1990).

46. Rudsten, "City-State Conflict," p. 164.

47. Ibid., p. 183.

48. Ibid., p. 184. Daniel Rudsten based his description of Mayor Collins's political routine on interviews with Collins himself and with Attorney General Robert H. Quinn on July 22, 1969.

49. *Boston Sunday Globe*, September 22, 1985.

50. Logue, "Boston, 1960–1967," p. 84.

51. Edward J. Logue, interview, January 30, 1991.

52. Ibid.

53. *Boston Sunday Globe*, September 22, 1985. Also see Logue, "Boston, 1960–1967," p. 89. Logue said he always resented "being accused of having anything to do" with the West End Project (p. 84).

54. *Boston Traveler*, January 1, 1960.

55. Ibid.

56. *New York Times*, May 1, 1960. After eighty years, title to the property, except for the railroad lines and the Mass Pike extension, would revert to the city of Boston. Mayor Collins considered it essential for the good faith and future stability of the city to accept the arrangement worked out by Mayor Hynes (Collins, interview, February 19, 1991).

57. *New York Times*, May 1, 1960.

58. *Boston Herald*, May 4, 1960; *Boston Traveler*, June 2, 1960.

59. Logue, "Boston, 1960–1967," pp. 89–90.

60. Ibid.; Hynes, "How Hynes Steered the Pru."

61. Yvonne V. Chabrier, "Born Again," *Boston Magazine*, November 1991, pp. 143–44. Many Bostonians recalled Charles Luckman as the former president of Lever Brothers in Cambridge.

62. Ibid., p. 144.

63. Comments by Homer Russell, assistant director for urban design and development, Boston Redevelopment Authority, cited in ibid., p. 144.

64. *Boston Globe*, May 2, 1962.

65. Robert Lowell, "For the Union Dead," *Atlantic Monthly*, November 1960, p. 54.

66. *Boston Herald*, May 6, 1960.

67. *Boston Globe*, May 2, 1962. Brady himself was eventually convicted in the case, but dropped out of sight for several years. Finally he was discovered in a New Jersey hideout and subsequently sent to prison. See Dalton, *Leading the Way*, p. 331.

## 7. *"The Stars Were Right"*

1. BRA director Kane Simonian recalls that he made "dozens" of trips to Washington with Mayor Hynes on behalf of the Government Center project (interview, July 10, 1990).

2. Hodgkinson, "Miracle in Boston," p. 74.

3. Rappaport, interview, January 16, 1990.

4. Logue, "Boston, 1960–1967," p. 93.

5. Kennedy, *Planning the City*, p. 178; Logue, "Boston, 1960–1967," pp. 77, 92.

6. Hodgkinson, "Miracle in Boston," p. 77; Logue, "Boston, 1960–1967," p. 95. Chairman William W. Wurster was from California, Ralph Rapson from Minneapolis, Walter Netch from Chicago, and Pietro Belluschi from Boston. All four architects had studied at MIT or Harvard and knew the city well.

7. "Wonder of wonders," wrote Hodgkinson. "Four professional architects . . . in four widely separated parts of the nation, and three lay citizens produced a unanimous decision for the design of the present City Hall" (Hodgkinson, "Miracle in Boston," p. 77).

8. Whitehill, *Boston*, p. 208.

9. *Boston Globe*, May 4, 1962.

10. Logue, "Boston, 1960–1967," p. 96; Hodgkinson, "Miracle in Boston," pp. 77–78.

11. *Boston Globe*, May 4, 1962.

12. Hodgkinson, "Miracle in Boston," pp. 77–78.

13. Cited in Kruh, *Always Something Doing*, p. 134.

14. Logue, "Boston, 1960–1967," pp. 84–85.

15. Ibid.

16. Ibid., p. 83.

17. Clark Clifford, *Counsel to the President* (New York, 1991), p. 80.

18. Logue, "Boston, 1960–1967," p. 86. Daniel Burnham, chief architect of the World's Columbian Exposition, held in Chicago in 1893, developed the Plan of Chicago (1906–9), which was viewed by some scholars as the single most influential city-planning document of modern times. See Zane L. Miller, *The Urbanization of Modern America* (New York, 1973), pp. 140–42.

19. Logue, interview, January 30, 1991.

20. *City Record*, September 24, 1960; Logue, "Boston, 1960–1967," p. 87.

21. *City Record*, September 24, 1960.

22. Simonian, interview, July 10, 1990.

23. Hodgkinson, "Miracle in Boston," p. 75.

24. I am grateful to Judith B. McDonough, executive director of the Massachusetts Historical Commission, for providing me with background material on

the Conservation Committee. She recalls the ruling of the Louisiana judge who defended the preservation of New Orleans's Vieux Carré district—"le tout ensemble"—as the rationale for protecting an entire historic district.

25. Hodgkinson, "Miracle in Boston," p. 75; *Boston Globe*, June 27, 28, 1962; *Boston Herald*, June 27, 1962; Kennedy, *Planning the City*, pp. 180–81.

26. Logue, "Boston, 1960–1967," p. 87.

27. Discussion with Herbert Gleason, corporation counsel, June 12, 1990, Suffolk University.

28. Logue, interview, January 30, 1991.

29. Ibid.; Logue, "Boston, 1960–1967," p. 90.

30. Logue, interview, January 30, 1991.

31. Ibid.

32. Logue, "Boston, 1960–1967," p. 91.

33. Edward J. Logue, memo to the Boston Redevelopment Authority, December 21, 1960, cited in Tilo Schabert, *Boston Politics: The Creativity of Power* (Berlin, 1989), p. 295.

34. Logue, "Boston, 1960–1967," pp. 90–91.

35. *Boston Sunday Globe*, September 22, 1985; Simonian, interview, July 10, 1990. Simonian brought suit on the basis that the hiring of Logue violated the civil service tenure law, but in May 1961 the state supreme court dismissed the suit.

36. Logue, interview, January 30, 1991.

37. Collins, interview, February 19, 1991.

38. Logue, "Boston, 1960–1967," p. 91.

39. David S. Kruh, "The Temple of Burlesque," *Boston Globe*, June 17, 1991.

40. Ibid.; Kruh, *Always Something Doing*, p. 81; Logue, "Boston, 1960–1967," p. 93.

41. Kruh, *Always Something Doing*, p. 33.

42. Simonian, interview, July 10, 1990.

43. Thomas Boylston Adams, "Walter Muir Whitehill" (memorial read at the Tavern Club, May 8, 1978).

44. Letter from Mr. W. M. Rogers, Cambridge, Mass., February 25, 1963 (Collins Papers, box 229).

45. Collins Papers, box 229.

46. *Boston Globe*, January 20, 1968; Logue, "Boston, 1960–1967," p. 94; Kruh, *Always Something Doing*, pp. 141–43; Teaford, *Rough Road*, p. 148.

47. Collins Papers, box 247.

48. Logue, *Seven Years of Progress*, p. 63; Whitehill, *Boston*, p. 226.

49. David Nyhan, "Boston's Civic Light," *Boston Globe*, August 14, 1990.

50. Logue, "Boston, 1960–1967," p. 94.

51. Ibid.; Kruh, *Always Something Doing*, pp. 138–39. Construction on the

first two phases went smoothly, but the third section was stalled for months in mid-1967 by two disputes: the question of access to the courthouse on Pemberton Square, and a suit by the Moskow brothers, developers who contested the BRA's legal title to the land.

52. Whitehill, *Boston*, p. 216.

53. Logue, *Seven Years of Progress*, p. 32.

54. Whitehill, *Boston*, p. 219.

55. The Collins Papers contain a typewritten copy of a political survey conducted during December 1962–January 1963 by John F. Kraft, Inc., based on questionnaires about issues, problems, officials, and candidates, at eighty random points in each of the city's twenty-two wards. The survey showed that Collins was strong among upper-middle-class, educated voters, and appealed especially to Jews and "others," with Catholics third, and Protestant fourth (Collins Papers, box 4).

56. Collins Papers, boxes 4 and 188.

57. *Boston Globe*, September 25, 1963. Piemonte took Wards 1 and 3 in the North End and East Boston; McDonough took Wards 6 and 7 in South Boston; Ansel took Ward 14.

58. Ibid., November 4, 1963.

59. Peter Hines, president of the city council, forwarded to Mayor Collins on August 8, 1963, the first of a series of mimeographed newsletters (Hines called them "baloney sheets") attacking Collins and his programs. They were published by local groups calling themselves the "Delaware Pilots," after colonial patriots who warned people about the coming of British tax ships (Collins Papers, box 4).

60. *Boston Globe*, November 5, 1963.

61. Once again Piemonte took Ward 1 in the North End and Ward 3 in East Boston, but this time he also carried Ward 6 in South Boston—Johnny Powers's home base—demonstrating that the resentment from the 1959 campaign could "still take a toll against John Collins" (ibid., November 6, 1963).

62. Ibid.

63. Collins Papers, box 52. A careful account of the mayor's reactions to the Kennedy assassination was prepared by his press secretary, Richard Sinnott. Four days after the assassination, Pete De Rosa wrote to John Collins suggesting that Collins consider running for vice president in 1964. De Rosa felt that Collins, as a nationally known urban mayor from Kennedy's home state who made a good appearance on television, would make a sympathetic "favorite son" candidate running on the same ticket with Lyndon B. Johnson (Collins Papers, box 210).

## 8. *Progress and Populism*

1. *Boston Globe*, January 6, 1964.

2. Ibid.

3. Ibid., May 8, 1964.

4. *Christian Science Monitor*, May 11, 1964.

5. Undated letter from Edward J. Logue to Joseph A. Langone, Jr., 58 Merrimac Street, Boston (Collins Papers, box 247). Also see *Boston Herald*, May 26, 1964.

6. *Boston Globe*, June 25, 1964.

7. *Boston Herald*, July 24, 30, 1964.

8. Collins Papers, box 4. The last previous instance of such an honorary degree was Nathan Matthews, mayor of Boston from 1891 to 1895, who was awarded a Harvard LL.D. in 1909.

9. T. O'Connor, *Fitzpatrick's Boston*, pp. 197–98.

10. Collins Papers, box 229.

11. *Boston Herald*, November 18, 1964.

12. Collins Papers, box 221.

13. Ibid., box 195.

14. Boston Redevelopment Authority, *South Boston General Neighborhood Renewal Plan* (Boston, 1962).

15. Christopher Lasch, *The True and Only Heaven: Progress and Its Critics* (New York, 1991). Also see Formisano, *Boston against Busing: Race, Class, and Ethnicity in the 1960s and 1970s* (Chapel Hill, N.C., 1991), pp. 17, 118.

16. *New York Times*, May 1, 1966.

17. There were two John Kerrigans active in city politics at this time. John E. Kerrigan came from South Boston, was elected state senator and city councillor, served as mayor of Boston when Maurice Tobin ran for governor, and was elected once again to the city council in 1951, where he opposed Collins and his Government Center plans. John J. ("Bigga") Kerrigan came from Dorchester; worked as an orderly at the New England Medical Center, where he befriended the convalescing John Collins; became an assistant corporation counsel in the Collins administration; and was elected to the Boston School Committee in 1967, where he subsequently became a leading opponent of busing.

18. Lukas, *Common Ground*, p. 153.

19. Dever, *Cushing of Boston*, pp. 233–34. The papers of Msgr. Francis Lally are in the Archives of the Archdiocese of Boston, Brighton, Massachusetts, but they contain few if any materials relating to his service on the BRA board.

20. Lukas, *Common Ground*, pp. 151, 153.

21. Edward J. Logue, "A Look Back at Neighborhood Renewal in Boston," *Political Studies Journal* 16 (Winter 1987): 341–42.

22. Ibid., p. 342. Also see Kennedy, *Planning the City*, pp. 187–88.

23. Logue, *Seven Years of Progress*, pp. 56–57.

24. Lukas, *Common Ground*, p. 154.

25. William P. Marchione, *The Bull in the Garden: A History of Allston-Brighton* (Boston, 1986), pp. 129–30.

26. Cited in William P. Marchione, "The Life and Death of a Neighborhood," *Allston-Brighton Journal*, August 11, 1988.

27. *Brighton Citizen Item*, July 12, 1962; Marjorie T. Redgate, "Part Two: To Hell with Urban Renewal!" *Allston-Brighton Journal*, September 15, 1988. Bernard and Marjorie Redgate were among the last to leave their homes. Marjorie kept a detailed memoir of events and later, with the assistance of William P. Marchione, published a series of four excerpts from these memoirs in the *Allston-Brighton Journal*, September 8, 15, 22, and 29, 1988.

28. *Allston-Brighton Citizen-Item*, August 8, 1964, cited in Marchione, *Bull in the Garden*, p. 130.

29. The Redgates, the Caseys, and the Hollums were the last of the holdouts in Barry's Corner. For a firsthand account of the evictions, see Marjorie T. Redgate, "Part Three: To Hell with Urban Renewal!" *Allston-Brighton Journal*, September 22, 1988.

30. *Allston-Brighton Citizen-Item*, October 23, 1969, cited in Marchione, *Bull in the Garden*, p. 131; Kennedy, *Planning the City*, p. 188.

31. Carden, *Witness*, pp. 70–71; Kennedy, *Planning the City*, pp. 186–87.

32. City of Boston, Landmarks Commission, *The South End: District Study Committee Report* (Boston, 1977), p. 19; Robert A. Woods, *The City Wilderness* (Cambridge, Mass., 1898), pp. 30–31, 33–49; Warner, *Streetcar Suburbs*, p. 144; Houston, "Beneath the El," pp. 20–25.

33. King, *Chain of Change*, p. 20.

34. Carden, *Witness*, p. 69.

35. *Boston Globe*, January 23, 1991.

36. Landmarks Commission, *The South End*, pp. 21–22; Mollenkopf, *Contested City*, pp. 144–45.

37. Landmarks Commission, *The South End*, p. 19.

38. Lukas, *Common Ground*, p. 168; Laura Shapiro, "Commandeering the South End," *The Real Paper*, October 3, 1973.

39. Landmarks Commission, *The South End*, p. 10; City of Boston, Boston Redevelopment Authority, "South End Urban Renewal," April 1, 1963, p. 6.

40. Mollenkopf, *Contested City*, pp. 169–70.

41. Based on a report by the city's Action for Boston Community Development (ABCD), a community action program begun by the Ford Foundation Gray Areas program in 1961 at the insistence of Edward Logue, cited in Mollenkopf, *Contested City*, pp. 173–74.

42. "BRA staff members made many promises which, by their nature, were

bound to be broken," wrote John Mollenkopf. See *Contested City*, pp. 169–70, 176–77.

43. Langley C. Keyes, Jr., *The Rehabilitation Planning Game* (Cambridge, Mass., 1969), p. 217.

44. Mollenkopf, *Contested City*, pp. 174–75.

45. Logue, interview, January 30, 1991; Keyes, *The Planning Game*, p. 84.

46. Landmarks Commission, *The South End*, p. 10; Lukas, *Common Ground*, p. 169.

47. Cited in Mollenkopf, *Contested City*, p. 176.

48. *Boston Globe*, January 30, 1962.

49. King, *Chain of Change*, p. 22.

50. Yona Ginsberg, *Jews in a Changing Neighborhood: The Study of Mattapan* (New York, 1975), pp. 29–30.

51. Hillel Levine and Lawrence Harmon, *The Death of an American Jewish Community: A Tragedy of Good Intentions* (New York, 1992), pp. 168–71, provides an in-depth study of the Jewish community in the Mattapan area and its eventual destruction by the ostensibly good intentions of those who wished to provide housing for disadvantaged minorities.

52. Shapiro, "Commandeering the South End," p. 8.

53. Mollenkopf, *Contested City*, pp. 178–79.

54. Robert Rosenthal et al. *Different Strokes: Pathways to Maturity in the Boston Ghetto* (Boulder, Colo., 1976), p. 20.

55. "The South End Today," *Boston Magazine*, October 1965, p. 34. According to this article, Mel King ran a sample survey and found that something less than 20 percent of the South Enders had ever seen the plan or knew anything about it.

56. Keyes, *The Planning Game*, p. 219.

57. Carden, *Witness*, p. 70.

58. Morton Rubin, *Organized Citizen Participation in Boston* (Boston, 1971), p. 120.

59. Cited in Mollenkopf, *Contested City*, p. 180.

60. Ibid., pp. 183–84.

61. Kennedy, *Planning the City*, pp. 200–201.

62. Formisano, *Boston against Busing*, p. 165.

63. "Many young Turks were no longer willing to accept the accommodationist stance of leaders they viewed at best as too moderate or at worst as Uncle Toms interested only in lining their pockets with white money" (Teaford, *Rough Road*, p. 179).

64. Langley C. Keyes, Jr., *The Boston Rehabilitation Program: An Independent Analysis* (Cambridge, Mass., 1970), p. 25.

65. *Christian Science Monitor*, March 12, 1966.

66. Collins Papers, box 188; *Bay State Banner*, March 12, 1966.

67. Collins Papers, box 188; *Bay State Banner*, February 5, 1966; italics in original.

68. A 269-unit mixed-income apartment complex called Tent City and costing $36 million opened in 1988. The project was a joint effort of the city, the nonprofit Tent City Corp., Community Builders, and JMB/Urban Development Corp. The complex won the Urban Land Institute's 1990 Award for Excellence "as an inspirational model of the good that comes from sincere public/private partnership" (*Boston Sunday Globe*, November 11, 1990). See also Mollenkopf, *Contested City*, pp. 184–86.

69. Keyes, *The Boston Rehabilitation Program*, p. 1.

70. Collins Papers, box 188. According to *Globe* columnist Timothy Leland, Collins had recognized the black backlash in the city and "courted it openly" in order to carve out for himself the Louise Day Hicks vote in Boston (*Boston Globe*, September 14, 1966).

71. Collins Papers, box 192.

72. *Boston Sunday Globe*, September 5, 1965.

73. Martin Nolan, "Saltonstall's Successor," *New Republic*, January 22, 1966.

74. Ibid.

75. Clipping dated November 3, 1965, in Collins Papers, box 5.

76. Nolan, "Saltonstall's Successor."

77. Collins, interview, February 19, 1991.

78. Collins Papers, box 5.

79. Ibid.

80. Ibid.

81. *Boston Globe*, June 8, 1966.

82. Ibid., June 11, 1966.

83. Barbrook, *God Save the Commonwealth*, pp. 147–48.

84. *Boston Globe*, June 11, 1966.

85. Ibid.; "Collins's underdog position seemed inappropriate and inelegant at the convention, for he was well supported by the Boston delegates," remarked the *Boston Sunday Herald*, June 12, 1966.

86. Collins Papers, box 5.

87. *Boston Globe*, September 14, 1966.

88. Ibid.

89. Ibid.; Barbrook, *God Save the Commonwealth*, pp. 148–50.

90. Timothy Leland, "Collins Concedes with a Smile," *Boston Globe*, September 14, 1966.

91. Collins, interview, February 19, 1991.

92. Barbrook, *God Save the Commonwealth*, pp. 150–52.

93. Collins Papers, box 209. Dick Sinnott, "The Unwelcome Guest," *Boston Globe*, December 24, 1990, provides an amusing recollection of the city hall press corps by Mayor Collins's press secretary.

## 9. *Changing Times*

1. *Boston Globe*, January 1, 1967; George V. Higgins, *Style versus Substance: Boston, Kevin White, and the Politics of Illusion* (New York, 1984), p. 7.

2. *Boston Globe*, January 3, 1967.

3. Ibid.; Kevin White, interview, March 12, 1991.

4. *Boston Globe*, February 16, 1967; Lupo, *Liberty's Chosen Home*, p. 107.

5. Higgins, *Style versus Substance*, pp. 24–25.

6. *Boston Globe*, May 5, 1967.

7. *Boston Traveler*, May 16, 1967.

8. Levine and Harmon, *Death of a Jewish Community*, pp. 98–99. After unsuccessful attempts by welfare manager Dan Cronin to talk to the demonstrators, Mayor Collins ordered Police Commissioner McNamara to break into the building when he learned that one employee, a Mrs. McNeil, had suffered a heart attack (Collins, interview, February 19, 1991).

9. *Boston Globe*, June 3, 4, 1967. Also see Levine and Harmon, *Death of a Jewish Community*, pp. 100–103; Higgins, *Style versus Substance*, p. 63; Lupo, *Liberty's Chosen Home*, p. 108.

10. When asked if Collins was going to run for another term, Arthur Coffey, his campaign manager, replied: "I doubt it. He really hasn't been enjoying the job in recent years. There are too many problems in the city." Cited by Alan Lupo, "The Tired Mayor Syndrome," *Boston Globe*, November 17, 1992. At the time, Elliot Friedman wrote a special feature speculating on Collins's political future (*Boston Globe*, June 4, 1967).

11. See Joseph A. Keblinsky's description of Collins's press conference in the *Boston Globe*, June 6, 1967. The same issue also contained a text of Collins's TV remarks. George Higgins believed that Collins could have won a third term if he had wanted to: "He could probably have beaten Kevin White, Louise Day Hicks, and all the other strays who most likely would have stayed home if he had said he meant to stay in office" (*Style versus Substance*, pp. 96–97).

12. *Boston Globe*, June 6, 1967.

13. White, interview, March 12, 1991.

14. *Boston Globe*, June 8, 1967. According to George Higgins, these "tribunes of the people," created by White, "strikingly resembled ward heelers of bygone and disparaged days of machine politics" (*Style versus Substance*, p. 66).

15. *Boston Globe*, June 12, 1967.

16. Logue, interview, January 30, 1991.

17. Collins Papers, box 188; italics in original. Mayor Collins had begun talking about a new stadium in 1960, and Governor John Volpe signed a bill for it in 1962. In 1965 the Greater Boston Stadium Authority unveiled a model for a "flip-top" stadium that it proposed to build behind South Station. See John

Powers, "Unbuilt Boston," *Boston Globe Magazine*, December 30, 1990.

18. Collins, interview, February 19, 1991. Also see Collins Papers, box 5.

19. Lupo, *Liberty's Chosen Home*, pp. 109–10, contains a thorough and at times hilarious description of the Iantosca affair and the efforts of the White people to uncover the culprits behind it. Also see Higgins, *Style versus Substance*, p. 105.

20. Collins Papers, box 188.

21. *Boston Globe*, September 1, 1967.

22. Logue, interview, January 30, 1991. Also see Higgins, *Style versus Substance*, p. 111. "For Kevin White," writes Higgins, "the Logue-Iantosca affair brought a sympathetic press and no loss of voters, perhaps even a gain."

23. *Boston Globe*, September 27, 1967.

24. Ibid., September 9, 1967. Louise Day Hicks had the "anti" vote, according to reporter Bob Healy. It was against a strong mayor, John Collins. It was against the Boston concept of urban renewal. Then he added: "And it was against Negroes."

25. "Kevin White: Boston's Next Mayor?" *Back Bay Banner*, November 2, 1967.

26. *Boston Globe*, November 6, 1967.

27. Jon Teaford, *Rough Road*, p. 197, makes the interesting observation that two other women followed Hicks's example in 1967. Alfreda Slominsk of Buffalo and Mary Beck of Detroit also ran for the office of mayor—and lost.

28. Michael Rezendes, "Balancing Boston's Books," *Boston Sunday Globe*, March 1, 1992, pp. 73–74.

29. *Boston Globe*, December 18, 1967.

30. Ibid. Also see Lukas, *Common Ground*, p. 196.

31. Collins served for twelve years as a visiting professor at MIT and conducted a successful law practice in downtown Boston. He appeared for a number of years as a panelist on a Sunday-morning television program, frequently served as a consultant for urban enterprises, and contributed occasional articles in Boston newspapers on political and moral issues.

32. Robert Healy, "Collins Leaves a New Boston," *Boston Globe*, December 29, 1967.

33. The last inauguration held at Faneuil Hall had been in 1917, when Andrew J. Peters was sworn in as mayor of Boston.

34. *Boston Globe*, January 2, 1968.

35. Eric Nordlinger, *Decentralizing the City: A Study of Boston's Little City Halls* (Cambridge, Mass., 1972); Teaford, *Rough Road*, pp. 258–59.

36. According to John Mollenkopf's study, Boston spent some $500 million on neighborhood capital improvements between 1968 and 1975. This was six times more than in the previous seven years (Mollenkopf, *Contested City*, p. 207).

37. Martha Wagner Weinberg, "Boston's Kevin White: A Mayor Who Survives," in Formisano and Burns, *Boston, 1700–1980*, pp. 213–39.

38. *Boston Globe*, December 28, 1967.

39. Ibid., February 10, 11, 1969.

40. Ibid., February 12, 1969. Also see Lukas, *Common Ground*, p. 196.

41. *Boston Globe*, February 7, 1969.

42. White, interview, March 12, 1991.

43. Frieden and Sagalyn, *Downtown, Inc.*, pp. 107–8.

44. "Roger Webb," *Historic Preservation* 42 (November/December 1990): 46.

45. White, interview, March 12, 1991.

46. Frieden and Sagalyn, *Downtown, Inc.*, p. 6.

47. Schabert, *Boston Politics*, pp. 174–75.

48. Claire Carter, "Whatever Ought to Be, Can Be," *Parade Magazine*, May 12, 1991, pp. 4–5.

49. White, interview, March 12, 1991. Also see Frieden and Sagalyn, *Downtown, Inc.*, p. 5.

50. White, interview, March 12, 1991.

51. *Boston Globe*, August 26, 27, 1976; Benjamin Thompson, "Making a Marketplace," *Boston Magazine*, August 1986, p. 111; Gurney Breckenfeld, "Jim Rouse Shows How to Give Retailing New Life," *Fortune*, April 10, 1978, p. 90; Michael Ryan, "Boston Learns to Love the Great American Marketplace," *Boston Magazine*, April 1979, pp. 120–24.

52. Frieden and Sagalyn, *Downtown, Inc.*, p. 7; Teaford, *Rough Road*, pp. 253–54.

53. *Boston Globe*, August 27, 1976.

54. Higgins, *Style versus Substance*, pp. 144–45.

55. White, interview, March 12, 1991.

56. Ibid.

## Conclusion

1. Teaford, *Rough Road*, p. 26; Hynes, "Boston, Whither Goest Thou?"

2. Clifford, *Counsel to the President*, p. 86.

3. Formisano, *Boston against Busing*, p. 3.

4. Alexis de Toqueville, *The Old Regime and the French Revolution*, trans. Stuart Gilbert (New York, 1955), p. 79.

# Bibliography

Banfield, E. C., and M. Derthick. *A Report on the Politics of Boston.* Cambridge, Mass., 1966.

Banfield, E. C., and M. Myerson. *Boston: The Job Ahead.* Cambridge, Mass., 1966.

Barbrook, Alec. *God Save the Commonwealth: An Electoral History of Massachusetts.* Amherst, Mass., 1973.

Beatty, Jack. *The Rascal King: The Life and Times of James Michael Curley, 1874–1958.* Reading, Mass., 1992.

Birnbaum, Ben, and Raymond Keyes. *Excellence in Education for Leadership: History of the Boston College School of Management.* Chestnut Hill, Mass., 1988.

Carden, Lance. *Witness: An Oral History of Black Politics in Boston, 1920–1960.* Chestnut Hill, Mass., 1988.

Curley, James Michael. *I'd Do It Again: A Record of All My Uproarious Years.* Englewood Cliffs, N.J., 1957.

Dalton, Cornelius, et al. *Leading the Way: A History of the Massachusetts General Court, 1629–1980.* Boston, 1984.

De Marco, William M. *Ethnics and Enclaves: The Italian Settlement of the North End.* Ann Arbor, Mich., 1980.

Dever, Joseph. *Cushing of Boston: A Candid Biography.* Boston, 1965.

Dinneen, Joseph F. *The Purple Shamrock: The Hon. James Michael Curley of Boston.* New York, 1949.

Erie, Steven P. *Rainbow's End: Irish-Americans and the Dilemma of Urban Machine Politics, 1840–1985.* Berkeley and Los Angeles, 1988.

Ferman, B. *Governing the Ungovernable City: Political Skill, Leadership, and the Modern Mayor.* Philadelphia, 1985.

Firey, W. *Land Use in Central Boston.* Cambridge, Mass., 1947.

Formisano, Ronald P. *Boston against Busing: Race, Class, and Ethnicity in the 1960s and 1970s.* Chapel Hill, N.C., 1991.

Formisano, Ronald P., and Constance Burns, eds. *Boston, 1700–1980: The Evolution of Urban Politics.* Westport, Conn., 1984.

Fried, Marc. *The World of the Urban Working Class: Boston's West End.* Cambridge, Mass., 1973.

Frieden, Bernard, and Lynne Sagalyn. *Downtown, Inc.: How America Rebuilds Cities.* Cambridge, Mass., 1989.

Gans, Herbert. *The Urban Villagers: Group and Class in the Life of Italian-Americans.* New York, 1962.

Gelfand, Mark. *A Nation of Cities: The Federal Government and Urban America, 1933–1965.* New York, 1975.

Ginsberg, Yona. *Jews in a Changing Neighborhood: The Study of Mattapan.* New York, 1975.

Goodwin, Doris K. *The Fitzgeralds and the Kennedys.* New York, 1987.

Green, James, and Hugh Donaghue. *Boston Workers: A Labor History.* Boston, 1979.

Hentoff, Nat. *Boston Boy.* Boston, 1986.

Hepburn, A. *Biography of a City, Boston: The Story of a Great American City and Its Contribution to our National Heritage.* New York, 1966.

Higgins, George V. *Style versus Substance: Boston, Kevin White, and the Politics of Illusion.* New York, 1984.

Hollister, Rob, and Tunney Lee. *Development Politics, Private Development, and Public Interest.* Washington, D.C., 1979.

Huthmacher, J. Joseph. *Massachusetts People and Politics, 1919–1933.* Cambridge, Mass., 1959.

Jennings, J., and M. King. *From Access to Power: Black Politics in Boston.* Cambridge, Mass., 1986.

Joher, F. C. *The Urban Establishment: Upper Strata in Boston, New York, Charleston, Chicago, and Los Angeles.* Urbana, Ill., 1982.

Kay, Jane Holtz. *Lost Boston.* Boston, 1980.

Keller, M. *Historical Sources of Urban Personality: Boston, New York, Philadelphia.* Oxford, 1982.

Kennedy, Lawrence W. *Planning the City upon a Hill: Boston since 1630.* Amherst, Mass., 1992.

Kenny, Herbert A. *Newspaper Row: Journalism in the Pre-Television Era.* Chester, Conn., 1987.

Keyes, Langley C., Jr. *The Boston Rehabilitation Program: An Independent Analysis*. Cambridge, Mass., 1970.

———. *The Rehabilitation Planning Game: A Study in the Diversity of Neighborhoods*. Cambridge, Mass., 1969.

King, Mel. *Chain of Change: Struggles for Black Community Development*. Boston, 1981.

Krieger, Alex, and Lisa Green. *Past Futures: Two Centuries of Imagining Boston*. Cambridge, Mass., 1985.

Latham, Earl, and George Goodwin. *Massachusetts Politics*. Medford, Mass., 1960.

Levin, Murray. *The Alienated Voter: Politics in Boston*. New York, 1960.

Levine, Hillel, and Lawrence Harmon. *The Death of an American Jewish Community: A Tragedy of Good Intentions*. New York, 1992.

Litt, Edgar. *The Political Cultures of Massachusetts*. Cambridge, Mass., 1965.

Logue, Edward J. *Seven Years of Progress: A Final Report*. Boston, 1967.

Lord, Robert H., John E. Sexton, and Edward T. Harrington. *History of the Archdiocese of Boston*. 3 vols. Boston, 1945.

Lukas, J. Anthony. *Common Ground: A Turbulent Decade in the Lives of Three American Families*. New York, 1986.

Lupo, Alan. *Liberty's Chosen Home: The Politics of Violence in Boston*. Boston, 1977.

Mollenkopf, John H. *The Contested City*. Princeton, N.J., 1983.

Murphy, Jeremiah. *Jeremiah Murphy's Boston*. Boston, 1974.

O'Connell, J. B. *The Boston Plan*. Cambridge, Mass., 1979.

O'Connell, William Cardinal. *Recollections of Seventy Years*. Boston, 1934.

O'Connor, Thomas H. *Bibles, Brahmins, and Bosses: A Short History of Boston*. 3d ed. Boston, 1991.

———. *South Boston, My Home Town: The History of an Ethnic Community*. Boston, 1988.

O'Toole, James M. *Militant and Trumphant: William Henry O'Connell and the Catholic Church in Boston, 1859–1944*. Notre Dame, Ind., 1992.

Pleck, Elizabeth. *Black Migration and Poverty: Boston, 1865–1900*. New York, 1979.

Rabinowitz, A. *Non-Planning and Redevelopment in Boston: An Analytic Study of the Planning Process*. Seattle, 1972.

Rosenblum, J. W. *The Boston Redevelopment Authority*. Cambridge, Mass., 1969.

Rubin, Morton. *Organized Citizen Participation in Boston*. Boston, 1971.

Ryan, Dennis. *Beyond the Ballot Box: A Social History of the Boston Irish, 1845–1917*. Amherst, Mass., 1989.

Schabert, Tilo. *Boston Politics: The Creativity of Power*. Berlin, 1989.

Schragg, Peter. *Village School Downtown*. Boston, 1967.

Shand-Tucci, Douglass. *Built in Boston: City and Suburb, 1800–1950.* Amherst, Mass., 1988.

Shannon, William V. *The American Irish: A Political and Social Portrait.* New York, 1963.

Solomon, Barbara. *Ancestors and Immigrants.* Cambridge, Mass., 1956.

Stack, John F., Jr. *International Conflict in an American City: Boston's Irish, Italians, and Jews, 1935–1944.* Westport, Conn., 1979.

Stage, Margot, ed. *Who Rules Boston?: A Citizen's Guide to Reclaiming the City.* Boston, 1984.

Stainton, J. *Urban Renewal and Planning in Boston.* Boston, 1972.

Sullivan, Robert E., and James M. O'Toole. *Catholic Boston: Studies in Religion and Community, 1870–1970.* Boston, 1985.

Teaford, Jon. *The Rough Road to Renaissance: Urban Revitalization in America, 1940–1984.* Baltimore, 1990.

Thernstrom, Stephan. *The Other Bostonians: Poverty and Progress in an American Metropolis, 1880–1970.* Cambridge, Mass., 1973.

Todisco, Paula J. *Boston's First Neighborhood: The North End.* Boston, 1976.

Trout, Charles H. *Boston, the Great Depression, and the New Deal.* New York, 1977.

Warner, Sam Bass, Jr. *Province of Reason.* Cambridge, Mass., 1984.

———. *Streetcar Suburbs: The Process of Growth in Boston, 1870–1900.* Cambridge, Mass., 1962.

———. *The Way We Really Lived: Social Change in Metropolitan Boston since 1920.* Boston, 1977.

Wayman, Dorothy G. *Cardinal O'Connell of Boston.* New York, 1955.

Whitehill, Walter Muir. *Boston: A Topographical History.* 2d ed. Cambridge, Mass., 1968.

———. *Boston in the Age of John Fitzgerald Kennedy.* Norman, Okla., 1966.

Whyte, William. *Street Corner Society: The Social Structure of an Italian Slum.* Chicago, 1943.

# Index

*About Boston*, 87
Adams, Charles Francis, 19, 71, 74, 120
Adams, Frederick J., 143
Adams, Russell B., 98
Adams, Samuel, 277
Adams, Thomas Boylston, 200
Adams, Howard, and Greeley, 271
Adlow, Elijah, 96
Advertising Club, 49
African-American community, xii, 26, 29–30, 49, 57, 59–61, 224, 228, 230–31, 235, 237–40, 262, 268, 293–96; militancy, 234, 237, 294
"Age of affluence," 144
Ahearn, Daniel, 50–57
Ahearn, Francis X., 62, 84, 96, 220
Ahern, John I., 97
Albany, New York, 74, 286
Aldrich, Robert, 247
Algonquin Club, 103
Alienated voter, 160, 252
All-Boston Committee (ABC), 62, 63
Allegheny Conference, 74, 107, 108
Allston-Brighton, 219, 220, 221, 224

American Association of Collegiate Schools of Business, 105
American City Planning Institute, 82
American Municipal Association, 206
American Public Health Association, 130
American Research and Development Corporation, 98
Ancient and Honorable Artillery Company, 277
Anderson, O. Kelley, 47, 186
Ansel, Julius, 206, 322*n*57
Anzalone, Theodore, 260, 267
Archdiocesan News Bureau, 177
Architectural Advisory Committee, 143
Architecture Heritage Foundation, 272
Art deco, 4, 85 (illus.)
Artesani, Charles, 25, 153
Atkins, Thomas, 59, 236
Atlantic Avenue, 83, 84, 193, 270–71, 291
Auerbach, Arnold ("Red"), 214
Automobiles, 14, 15, 79, 82, 112
AVCO, 19

Back Bay, 4, 16–17, 62, 68, 73, 99
    (illus.), 106, 121, 123, 141–42, 177,
    182, 192, 202–3, 213–14, 225,
    289, 295
Back Bay Center, 96, 101, 106, 107,
    120, 150
*Back Bay Ledger*, 73
Baltimore, Maryland, 74, 286
Barresi, Joseph, 171
Barry's Corner, 219, 220, 221, 222–23
    (illus.), 224, 324*n*29
Bartolo, Salvatore, 158
Bartolo's Ringside Café, 158, 318*n*24
Batson, Ruth, 57, 236, 237
Baxter, William L., 88
*Bay State Banner*, 238, 262
Beacon Construction Company, 203
Beacon Hill, 4, 57, 68–69, 87, 89,
    117–19, 125, 141, 168–72, 175,
    180, 186, 193, 204, 225, 235, 241,
    253, 259, 263, 267, 295; Architec-
    tural Commission, 204; Civic
    Association, 235
Beattie, Richard, 192
Beatty, Jack, 14
Becker, John, 257
Bell, Daniel, 234
Bellotti, Francis, 213, 241, 244
Belluschi, Pietro, 320*n*6
Berenson, Richard A., 48
Bethlehem Ship Yards, 19
Bicentennial, 275, 281, 282
Black community. *See* African-Ameri-
    can community
Blake, Harry J., 48
Blakely, Gerald, 147
Blaxton, Rev. William, 86
Blight, 66, 67, 76, 111, 177, 220
Bloomfield, Daniel, 97
Blue Hill Avenue, 60, 232, 255
Bolling, Royal, Sr., 224
Bonan, S. Pierre, 131, 132
Bond rating, 147
*Boston against Busing*, 297
Boston and Albany Railroad, 15, 98,

99, 100; yards, 98, 99 (illus.), 106,
    107, 122, 202
Boston Architectural Group, 185
Boston Assessing Department, 166–67
Boston Athenaeum, 4, 193
Boston Banks Urban Renewal Group
    (B-BURG), 232
Boston Board of Censorship, 95
Boston British Properties, Inc., 204
Boston Citizens' Council, 103, 104,
    119
Boston City Council, 22, 29, 41, 54–
    55, 61, 63, 84, 120, 126, 151–54,
    164, 195, 198, 211, 215, 220–
    21, 228–30, 274, 293
Boston City Hall (new), 185–86, 187
    (illus.), 188, 199–204, 206, 264–65,
    269, 270, 284, 289; competition,
    185; controversy, 187–88; Plaza,
    199, 201, 269
Boston City Hall (old), xiii, 22, 28, 42,
    53–54, 89, 99, 117, 148, 152, 160–
    61, 164–66, 171, 189, 195, 209,
    237, 240, 244, 247, 256, 259, 264,
    269, 272, 274, 290
Boston City Hospital, 11, 37, 52, 114,
    225
Boston City Planning Board, 51, 71,
    82–83, 124, 126, 142, 163, 177,
    189
Boston College, 26, 61–62, 92, 102–4,
    106–7, 110, 116, 189, 194, 217;
    Bureau of Business Research, 110;
    Bureau of Public Affairs, 110;
    Citizen Seminars, 104, 107, 109–11,
    116, 124, 146, 189, 194, 285;
    College of Business Administration,
    87; Law School, 171, 262
Boston Common, 4, 7, 10, 15, 38, 68,
    86, 87, 120, 141, 145, 178, 180,
    189, 289; underground garage, 87,
    123, 180, 182, 188, 189, 214
Boston Company, 204
Boston Coordinating Committee. *See*
    "Vault"

Boston Edison Electric Company, 47
Boston Elevated Railway, 226
Boston Five Cent Savings Bank, 47, 185
*Boston Globe*, 6, 21, 72, 95, 134, 196, 205, 247, 251, 263
Boston Harbor, xii, 285
*Boston Herald*, 6, 30, 72, 124, 134, 247
Boston Historic Conservation Committee, 193
Boston Home and School Association, 235
Boston Housing Authority (BHA), 75, 123, 126–27, 131–32, 157, 215
Boston Job Coalition, 236
*Boston Journal*, 72
Boston Latin School, 203
"Boston Medals," 213
Boston Metropolitian Authority, 71
Boston Municipal Research Bureau, 43, 90, 118–19, 171, 274
Boston-1915 movement, 69, 70, 71
Boston Pops, 214, 218
*Boston Post*, 6, 30, 72, 88, 120, 134, 143, 197
Boston Public Garden, 87, 189
Boston Public Library, xiv, 7, 11, 49, 93, 118; branch libraries, 11, 54
Boston Public School system, 57, 207
Boston Real Estate Board, 164
*Boston Record-American*, 72, 128, 134, 197, 247
Boston Redevelopment Authority (BRA), 127, 130, 135, 137–38, 145, 173, 177, 185, 191–96, 199–206, 212, 215–21, 224, 228–38, 258, 266, 272–76, 281, 289, 294, 298; Board, 185, 197, 274
Boston Retail Board, 97, 119, 192
Boston Safe Deposit and Trust Company, 47, 147, 192, 196, 204
Boston Sanitorium, 38
Boston School Committee, 29, 54–55, 61, 63–64, 151, 164, 236, 239, 240, 258, 261

Boston Society of Architects, 68, 71, 187, 194
*Boston Transcript*, 6, 72
Boston Transit Commission, 81
*Boston Traveler*, 6, 72, 247, 253
Boston University, 26, 71; Medical Center, 225
Boston Welfare Office, 254
Bourne, Philip, 185
Bowdoin Square, 140
Bowles, Chester, 258
Brace, Lloyd, 147, 192
Bradford, Robert F., 20, 21, 22, 78, 80, 83, 146
Bradford Hotel, 7
Bradley, R. M., Company, 99, 104, 127
Brady, George L., 120, 180, 319n67
Brandeis, Louis D., 69
Brandt, Willie, 148
Brattle Book Shop, 200
Breeden, Rev. James, 236
Breen, John, 122, 313n1
Brennan, Henry, 244
Brighton, 63, 92, 123, 235, 246
Bromley Heath housing project, 123
Brooke, Edward, 57, 241–43, 246, 247
Brown, John D. ("Handsome Jack"), 47
*Brown* v. *Board of Education of Topeka*, 60, 239
Bryant, Gridley, 38
Bulfinch, Charles, 68
Bunker Hill, 48, 216, 219; Monument, 216, 218
Burden's Drug Store, 208
Bureau of Public Information and Citizens' Relations, 163
Burke, "Jabber," 24
Burnham, Daniel H., 190, 320n18
Burns, Haydon, 98
Burns, Paul, 153, 171
Bush-Brown, Albert, 186
Busing, 297
Buxton, Frank W., 49

Bynoe, John, 30
Bynoe, Victor, 26, 30, 49, 57
Byrne, Garrett, 158

Cabot, Harriet Ropes, 193
Cabot, Cabot, and Forbes, 19, 120–
    21, 127, 147, 204
Callahan, William F., 81, 310*n*35
Cambridge, 245, 247, 271, 272
Cameron, Lawrence, 267
Cannam, Luella, 49
Campano, James, 316*n*65
Canton, 231
Cape Cod, 244, 245
Carens, Thomas H., 97
Carr, William, 62, 63
Casino Theater, 95
Cass, Melnea, 57, 237, 268 (illus.)
Castle Square housing project, 227,
    231
Cathedral housing project, 123
Cathedral of the Holy Cross, 93
Catholic Youth Organization (CYO),
    14
Catholics, 13, 42, 45, 92
Catlin, Ephron, 42, 44, 47, 97, 103,
    147
Center Plaza, 204, 321–22*n*51
Central Artery, 15, 82–84, 85 (illus.),
    86, 116, 119–20, 123, 182, 188,
    211, 293
Central Business District Committee,
    192
Chabrier, Yvonne, 178
Chamber of Commerce, 48, 49, 119,
    121, 164, 193
Champion, Hale, 267
Chandler, H. Darland, 141
Channel 4, 220
Chapman, Philip, 25, 146, 153
Chapter 121 A, 178, 191
Charles River, 69, 125
Charles River Park complex, 132–33,
    134, 135, 140 (illus.), 288
Charlesbank, 125

Charlestown, 29, 35, 67, 189–90, 196,
    216–19, 224, 230, 235
Chase, Perlie Dyar, 57, 61
Chelsea, 118, 169
Chestnut Hill, 97, 104, 111
Cheverus, Bishop Jean-Louis de, 13
Chicago, Illinois, 67, 73, 110, 250,
    286
Chicago Plan, 189, 320*n*18
Chicopee, 247
Chinatown, 84, 235, 293
Chinese Merchants Association, 84
Christian, Frank, 193
Christian Science Church, 203, 225
*Christian Science Monitor*, 30, 168,
    247
*Chronicle*, 58
Cintolo, Frannie, 279
Citizen Seminar. *See* Boston College
Citizens Action Committee (Balti-
    more), 74
Citizens' Committee for a Bostonian
    City Hall, 188
Citizens for Private Property, 220
*City Limits*, xiv
Civics Progress Committee, 143
Civil Rights Act, 1964, 236
Civil War, 68, 200, 212, 225
Clark, Paul, 147
Cleveland, Ohio, 67, 250
Clifford, Clark, 189, 286
Cloud, Royal, 227
Coalition politics, 235
Coard, Robert, 233
Codman, John, 204
Codman Square, 254
Coffey, Arthur, 153, 244
Coffey, James, 206
Colbert, James G., 128, 197
Collins, Frederick B., 152
Collins, John F., 25, 61, 72, 111, 139
    (illus.), 190–91, 212–14, 237–38,
    269–70, 280–81, 288–97, 322*nn*55,
    63, 328*n*31; and BRA neighborhood
    projects, 215–36; and business
    community, 191–94; campaign for

U.S. senate, 241–47; early life and career, 151–54; and Government Center project, 182–85; and Logue, 172–74 (illus.), 258–62; mayoral campaigns, 154–61, 162 (illus.), 205–8, 317*n*11, 318*n*24; mayoral papers, 316*n*75; mayoral terms, 161–68, 210–12, 252–58; and new City Hall, 185–88, 264–65; and Prudential Center, 175–78; and underground garage, 178–81; and the Vault, 166–68
Collins, Leo, 153
Collins, Margaret (Mellyn), 152
Collins, Mary Patricia (Cunniff), 152–54, 208
Collins, Patrick, 46
Collins, Paul, 153
Colonial Theater, 7
Columbia Point housing project, 123, 134
Columbia University School of Architecture, 186
Commercial Wharf, 271
Commission on Metropolitan Improvements, 69
Committee for North Harvard (CNH), 224
Committee to Save the North End, 84
Commonwealth Avenue, 16, 72, 92
Community Assembly for a United South End (CAUSE), 238
Community Councils, 157, 163
Community organizations, 157, 163
"Concept, The" (South End), 229
Concord, 48
Congress, United States, 240, 250
Congress Street, 101, 143
*Contested City*, xiv, 234
Coolidge, Charles, 19, 147, 166, 176, 192, 214
Cooper, Edward, 57, 237
Cooper, Gordon, 249
Copley Plaza Hotel, 6, 167
Copley Square, 7, 11, 68, 98, 110, 133, 142, 238

Copp's Hill Burying Ground, 48
Cornhill, 200
Cotting, Uriah, 200
Court Street, 102
Covell, Roy, 244
Craven, Catherine, 208, 211
Crawford House, 6, 141
Crite, Allan R., 226
Cunningham, Bill, 134
Curley, James Michael, 27 (illus.), 28, 77–78, 122, 152, 161, 171, 192, 286–88; early mayoral career, 9–11, 12, 14, 17–18, 20, 302–3*n*17, 305*n*57; and Hynes, 306*n*65; imprisonment, 20–22, 306*n*68; and New Boston Committee, 56, 62–63; 1949 mayoral campaign, 30–31, 32; 1951 mayoral campaign, 51–55; 1955 mayoral campaign, 113–14, 115
Curtis, Robert, 38
Cushing, Cardinal Richard J., 37, 49, 93, 95 (illus.), 106, 115, 116, 150, 161, 177, 209, 217, 287
Custom House, 4, 5 (illus.); tower, xi, 4, 105, 110
Cutler, Robert, 25, 156

Dacey, Kathleen Ryan, 62
*Daily Advertiser*, 6
Daley, Richard, 72, 73
Danbury Prison, 22, 23, 28
Davoren, John F. X., 263, 264
Day, William J., 261
Dazzi, Andy, 21, 26, 312*n*32
*De facto* segregation, 207, 261
De Mov and Morris, 315*n*48
De Rosa, Pete, 322*n*63
De Tocqueville, Alexis, 298
"Delaware Pilots," 322*n*59
Depression, Great, 8, 9, 10, 15, 19, 79, 83, 113, 147, 287
Desegregation, 297
Design Research, 272
Detroit, Michigan, 69, 238, 250

Development Administrator (BRA), 194

Dever, Paul A., 37, 80, 81, 87, 146

Devine, William, 153

Devonshire Street, 102

Dewey Square, 84

Dignan, Thomas, 47

Displacement of residents, 126, 135, 138

Dock Square, 277

Dolan, Chester, 114

Donahue, Frank J. ("Daisy"), 49

Dorchester, 35, 40, 41, 61, 62, 67, 72, 97, 119, 123, 164, 203, 212, 221, 231, 235, 246, 250, 254

Dorchester Heights, 53

Dow Jones industrials, 249

Doyle, Wilfred, 41

Dray, Richard, 260, 267

Driscoll, John T., 164

Dukakis, Michael, 317*n*13

Dumaine, Frederick C. ("Buck"), 84

Dwyer, Rev. William, 238

East Boston, 11, 29, 35, 52, 127, 151, 158, 190, 206, 215, 235, 291, 292; tunnel, 82, 106, 112

East Cambridge, 138

Eastern Gas and Fuel, 213

Eastman, Ralph, 48

*Economist* (London), 214

Ecumenism, 92, 94

Eisenhower, Dwight D., 21, 79, 80, 143–44, 156

Elam, Clarence, 57, 237

Elam, Harry, 57, 237, 238

Elections, mayoral: (1949), 24–32; (1951), 51–55; (1955), 113–15; (1959), 150–60; (1963), 205–8; (1967), 257–63; (1971), 272

Electronics industry, 73, 79, 288

Eliot, Byron, 49

Eliot, Charles W., 18

Eliot, Thomas Hopkinton, 18

Elizabeth II, Queen, 281, 282

Emancipation Proclamation, 60

Emergency Tenants' Council, 238

Eminent domain, 136

Emmanuel College, 26

Empire State Building, 5, 100

Empire State Plaza (Albany), 74

Employers Group Life Insurance Company, 204

Engineers' Group Incorporated, 305*n*58

Everett, 138

Fall River, 245

Family Assistance Plan, 296

Faneuil Hall, 48, 67, 140, 186, 187, 193, 201 (illus.), 266, 272, 273, 328*n*33; Marketplace, 271–74, 276–77, 278 (illus.), 279, 281, 282, 296

Farley, James, 287

Federal Housing Administration (FHA), 133

Federal Office Building (Government Center), 142

Federal Post Office and Courthouse, 4–5

Fenn, Daniel, 50, 57, 243

Fenton, John, 176

Fenway, the, 64

Fidelis Way housing project, 123

Fiedler, Arthur, 214, 281

Fifty-Year Plan, 9

Filene, Edward A., 69

Filene's, 6, 119, 134, 142, 185, 192; Basement, 6

Finance Commission (Fin Com), 43

Fingold, George, 152

Finn, Daniel J., 267

Fire (1872), 3, 68

Fire commissioner, 169

First Church of Christ Scientist. *See* Christian Science Church

First National Bank of Boston, 12, 42, 47, 97, 103, 147, 204

First Realty Corporation of Boston, 315*n*48, 49

Fish Pier, 8

Fitzgerald, John F. ("Honey Fitz"), xiv, 42, 46, 101
Fitzgerald, Mary K., 62, 63
Fitzpatrick, Connie, 158
Fitzpatrick, Bishop John B., 13, 212
Flanagan, James, 57
Fleming, Harry, 39
Floete, Franklin G., 142, 143, 182, 183, 184
Flynn, Raymond L., xiv
Foley, George, 208
Foley, Patrick, 63
Foley, William J., 62, 63, 195, 206, 207, 208, 211, 216, 230
Foley, William P., 206
Foote, Elmer, 24
Forbes, F. Murray, 52
Fore River Shipyards, 19
Formisano, Ronald, 235, 297
Fort Hill, 125
Fort Point Channel, 170
Forte, Felix, 212
Fourth of July concert, 281
Fox, Charles, 50
Fox, John, 88, 120
Framingham, 245
Frank, Barney, 267
Franklin, Benjamin, 38, 165
Franklin Field housing project, 123
Franklin Park, 53
Franklin Street, 166
Freed, Hirsh, 21, 24, 61, 158, 243
Freedom House, 57, 236, 237, 239
Freedom Trail, 48, 49, 280; Foundation, 48
Friedman, Lee M., 49, 61
Friedman, Robert, 49
Friedrich, Carl, 71
Furcolo, Foster, 122–23, 128, 142, 144, 146, 154–55, 169, 176, 197

G & G Delicatessen, 208
Galvin, John, 103, 104, 108
Gans, Herbert, 125, 128, 137
Garrison, William Lloyd, 200
General Court of Massachusetts, 28, 32, 43, 81, 89, 106, 117, 118, 120, 122, 144, 168, 176, 177, 220, 263, 264; House of Representatives, 90, 152, 171; Senate, 90, 113, 150, 151, 168, 171
General Electric Corporation, 19
General Neighborhood Renewal Plan, 215
General Services Administration, 142, 183
Gentrification, 291
G.I. Bill of Rights, 60, 67
Gilbert, Carl, 97, 110, 166, 190, 192
Gilchrist's, 6, 72
Gillette Company, 97, 110, 166, 190
Gilman, Arthur, 38
Ginn, Edwin, 125
Gleason, Herbert, 267, 317n13
Gleason, Timothy, 220
Glynn, William, 62
Goldberg, Arthur, 250
Golden Triangle (Pittsburgh), 74
Goldfine, Bernard, 120
Goldston, Eli, 213
Goo Goos. *See* Good Government Association
Good Government Association (GGA), 11, 43, 56, 69
Goodwin, Sammy, 24
Government Center, 96, 140–42, 145, 174, 181–85, 188, 197–98, 201 (illus.), 202–7, 211–14, 264, 270, 273, 277, 281, 284–85
Government Center Commission, 185
Graham, Donald, 189, 190, 224
Gray, Francis, 57
"Great Mayor," 68, 271, 277. *See also* Josiah Quincy
Great Society, 250, 256
Greater Boston Chamber of Commerce, 48, 49, 119, 121, 164, 167, 193
Greater Philadelphia Movement, 74
Greek community, 228
Greeley, William R., 67, 71
Green-Strip Plan, 229

Greenough, Richard, 38
Griffin, "Amby," 39
Griffin, Thomas, 153
Grove Hall, 232, 254, 255
Gruen, Victor, 132, 192
*Guardian*, 58
Guarino, John, 57

Hailer, Fred, 25, 62, 63
Hall of Flags, 7
Hannan, Robert, 247
Hanron, Robert, 134
Harbor Towers, 271
Harrison Gray Otis house, 137
Harvard University, 26, 71, 97, 116,
    127, 182, 194, 212, 213; Business
    School, 147, 219; Glee Club,
    214; Law School, 26, 171; Law
    School Forum, 26; School of Edua-
    tion, 64
Hatch, Francis W., 199
Hausserman, Oscar, 213
Haymarket Square, 6, 83, 140, 211
Haynes, Rev. Michael, 30
Hazard, Leland, 107, 108
Healey, Joseph A., 98, 107
Health facilities, neighborhood, 11
Healy, Robert, 207, 208, 210, 244,
    265
Henderson, Ernest, 257
Hennessy, Thomas, 127
Hennigan, James W., 151, 164
Herter, Christian, 80, 84, 103 (illus.),
    105, 109, 115, 116, 118, 146
Hester, Beula S., 49
Hester, Rev. William H., 49
Hicks, Louise Day, 207–8, 254, 257,
    260–63, 272, 328n24
Higgins, George, 252, 257, 280
Highway construction, 80
Hines, Paul, 47, 48
Hines, Peter, 206, 211, 239, 241, 253,
    322n59
Hispanic community, 230, 231, 235
Hodgkinson, Harold D., 46 (illus.),
    119, 120, 142, 185, 192

Hoover Commission, 50
"Hooverville," 8
Houghton and Dutton, 72
Hourihan, Michael, 91, 117
Housing, xiii, 55, 57, 76, 77, 123–24,
    215, 228, 230–31, 236, 239
Housing Act: of 1937, 66; of 1949, 75
Housing and Home Finance Agency,
    122, 133
Housing and Urban Development
    (HUD), 221, 224, 231, 238
Houston, Amanda, 58, 59, 226
Howard National Theater and Mu-
    seum Committee, 199
Howe, Louis, 287
Howells, Valentine, 100
Huntington Avenue, 101, 107, 120,
    145, 203
Hurley, Donald, 167
Hurley, William, 63
Huxtable, Ada Louise, 272
Hyde Park, 11, 208
Hynes, Anna (Healy), 39
Hynes, Barry, 40, 208, 211, 212, 253
Hynes, Bernard, 39
Hynes, John B., 23–24, 50–51, 76
    (illus.), 123–25, 159–61, 162
    (illus.), 165, 167, 170, 174–76,
    182–85, 188, 191–93, 202, 208,
    217, 227, 229, 253, 262, 269–70,
    280–81, 285–89, 293–95, 301n4,
    318n31, 319n45; and Back Bay
    center, 98–102; and central artery,
    84–86, 119–20; early life and
    career, 39–42; and Freedom Trail,
    47–49; and Government Center
    project, 139–43; as mayor, 33
    (illus.), 37–45, 46 (illus.), 144–49;
    1949 mayoral campaign, 25–32;
    1951 mayoral campaign, 51–55;
    1955 mayoral campaign, 113–15;
    and Prudential project, 121–23,
    311–12n17; and tax rates, 77–78;
    as temporary mayor, 20–22; and
    underground garage, 88–90, 120;
    and West End project, 125–39
    (illus.)

Hynes, John B., Jr. ("Jack"), 24, 37, 40
Hynes, Marie (Gallagher), 40, 41, 45
Hynes, Marion (Barry), 37, 40, 41
Hynes, Nancy, 40
Hynes, Richard, 40, 41, 144
Hynes, Tom, 39
Hynes Auditorium. *See* War Memorial
    Auditorium

Ianella, Christopher, 206, 211, 215,
    253
Iantosca, Richard, 259, 260
Iglesias, Carmelo, 238
India Wharf, 204, 271
Inflation (1960s), 250
Inquilinos Boricuas en Accion, 238
Internal Revenue Service, 158
Iovino, Tony, 57
Irish-American community, 26, 27,
    125, 215, 231, 243
Italian-American community, 26, 84,
    125, 215, 243

Jackson, Ellen, 236
Jackson, Ira, 273, 275
Jackson Square, 152
Jacksonville, Florida, 98–99
Jacobs, Jane, 124
Jamaica Plain, 11, 62, 117, 123, 152,
    154, 164, 190, 208, 212, 231, 291
Jewish-American community, 26,
    60, 94, 125, 232, 243, 255, 325n51
Joe and Nemo's, 6
John Hancock Building (1947), 98,
    110
John Hancock Life Insurance Com-
    pany, 49, 133, 147
Johnson, Claudia (Lady Bird), 208
Johnson, Lyndon Baines, 208, 250,
    256, 289, 322n63
Jones, Hubert, 238
Jordan Marsh, 6, 7, 119, 134, 192
Joyce, Francis, 62, 63
Joyce, Thomas, 104
Joyce, Rev. W. Seavey, 97, 102, 103
    (illus.), 105, 110, 111

Kallman, Gerhard M., 186
Kane, Katherine D., 267
Kargman, Max, 132, 315nn48, 49
Keblinsky, Joseph, 42, 151, 210, 247
Keenan, William, 25
Keesler, William F., 47
Keith, Sally, 6
Kelley, James, 25, 26
Kelly, Arthur, 97
Kelly, Francis E. (Frankie "Sweep-
    stakes"), 20
Kelly, John B., 20, 21
Kempner Realty Corporation, 132,
    315nn48, 49
Kennedy, Edward M., 242, 269, 270
Kennedy, John F., 25, 196, 205, 209,
    243, 256, 289, 305n57, 322n63
Kennedy, John F., Federal Building,
    201 (illus.)
Kennedy, John F., Library, 254
Kennedy, Joseph P., 305n57
Kennedy, Lawrence W., 125, 139, 148,
    185, 235
Kennedy-Nixon debates, 154–55
Kenney, Robert, 273, 274
Kern, Hap, 197
Kerr, William, 171
Kerrigan, John E., 18, 20, 37, 62, 63,
    207, 208, 216, 323n17
Kerrigan, John J. ("Bigga"), 323n17
Keyes, Langley, 233, 235
Kickham, Dr. Charles, 57
Kiernan, Connie, 118
King, Rev. Martin Luther, Jr., 49, 60,
    236, 294
King, Mel, 124, 225, 231, 236
King's Chapel, 48
Knowles, Edward F., 186
Kresge's, 72
Kruh, David, 199

L Street Bathhouse, 91
Lally, Rev. Francis, 128, 130–31, 197,
    216, 217, 220
Lally, Joseph P., 165–66
Lamson, Fred, 117

Langone, Frederick, 206, 211, 212, 215
Langone, Joseph, 212
Lasch, Christopher, 216
*Last Hurrah, The,* 24, 246, 261
*Late George Apley, The,* 261
Lawrence, David L., 73, 108, 109, 148
Lawrence, James, 185
Le Corbusier, 178, 186
Leather industry, 8, 84
Lee, Joseph, 63, 135, 315n49
Lee, Richard, 74, 173, 258
Leland, Timothy, 245, 252
Levenson, Barney, 24
Leventhal, Norman B., 203
Leventhal, Robert, 203
Levin, Murray, 160, 317n11
Lexington, 48
*Liberator, The,* 200
Lincoln Drugstore, 59
Lincoln House, 231
Lindsay, John, 262
Lippmann, Walter, 79
Little, Arthur D., 127
Little City Halls, 267
Liuzzi, Michael, 168
Lo Piccolo, Joseph, 316n35
Local Public Authority (LPA), 75
Loew's Orpheum Theater, 7
Logan International Airport, 80, 105, 112, 116, 158, 235
Logue, Edward J., 194–97, 202–3, 203–4, 270, 272, 275, 281, 289, 291, 293–94; and BRA, 216–36; and Government Center, 184–88, 197–201; invited to Boston, 173–74 (illus.), 175–77, 321n35; and Old Corner Book Store, 204–5; runs for mayor, 258–62; and South Boston, 215–16; and urban renewal, 188–90, 319n53
Lomasney, Martin, xiii
Long Island Hospital, 38, 53
Long Wharf, 5 (illus.), 271
Longshoremen, 217
Loop, the (Chicago), 73

Loughrea (Ireland), 95
Lowell, 118
Lowell, Ralph, 47, 147, 192
Lowell, Robert, 180
Luckman, Charles, 178, 319n61
Lund, Joseph, 104, 127, 197
Lupo, Alan, 156
Lydon, Christopher, 267
Lyons, Alice, 62, 63
Lyons, Louis, 17

McCloskey, Stephen E., 128, 197
McCord, David, 87
McCormack, Edward J., Jr., 61, 117, 175, 180, 247
McCormack, John W., 76 (illus.), 117, 183, 184
McCormack, Tom, 51
McCusker, Tom, 39
McDonald, Arch, 172
MacDonald, Norman, 103
McDonald, William J., 87
McDonough, Patrick J. ("Sonny"), 30, 31, 206, 207, 230, 322n57
McDonough, Tom, 51
McGovern, George, 272
McInerney, Timothy, 63
McKinnell, Noel M., 186
McLaughlin, Edward, 25, 57
McMorrow, John P., 151
McNamara, Edmund L., 256
Majestic Theater, 7
Malden, 117
Mansfield, Frederick, 37
Marblehead, 92
Marchand, Earl, 247
Marina Park, 279
Martin, Joseph, 183
Massachusetts Bay Transportation Authority (MBTA), 240, 254
Massachusetts Colored League, 59
Massachusetts Development Corporation, 103
Massachusetts Federation of Taxpayers, 103
Massachusetts 54th Negro Regiment, 180

Massachusetts General Court. *See* General Court of Massachusetts
Massachusetts General Hospital, 125
Massachusetts Institute of Technology (MIT), 71, 109, 116, 138, 186, 194, 203
Massachusetts Investors Trust, 98
Massachusetts League of Cities and Towns, 172
Massachusetts Parking Authority, 120, 180
Massachusetts Port Authority, 116, 191
Massachusetts Special Commission on Taxation, 98
Massachusetts State Crime Commission, 115
Massachusetts Supreme Judicial Court, 88, 102, 123, 175, 177, 191
Massachusetts Turnpike Authority (MTA), 81, 82, 122, 175, 191, 310*n*35
Massachusetts Turnpike Extension, 124
Massucco, Melvin J., 128, 197
Mattapan, 60, 208, 231, 232, 235, 246, 325*n*51
Mattapan Square, 60, 232; Board of Trade, 235
Matthews, Nathan, 323*n*8
Maverick Square, 158
Maxwell, Rev. Joseph R. N., 105
Mechanics Building, 123
Medford, 138, 199
Mellon, Richard King, 74, 107, 108, 109
Menzies, Ian, 250–51
Merchants National Bank, 146, 193
Merry, George, 247
Metropolitan Coal and Oil Company, 97
Metropolitan District Commission (MDC), 191
Metropolitan Planning Council, 110
Metropolitan Transit Authority (MTA), 106, 118
Metropolitan Transit District, 118
Michelson, A. A., 241

Milton, 231
Minnihan, Bishop Jeremiah, 161
Mission Hill, 63, 235, 293
Mission Hill housing project, 123, 134
Mitre Corporation, 19
Mitton, Edward R., 119, 192
Moakley, Joseph, 172
Mollenkopf, John, xiv, 131, 229, 234
Moloney, Francis, 50, 301*n*4
Moody's Investor Service, 147
Moore, Charlie, 21
Morgan, Robert, 47, 185, 270
Morse, C. R., 99 (illus.)
Morse, Wayne L., 158
Moses, Robert, 81, 127
Moskow brothers, 322*n*51
Mothers for Adequate Welfare, 254, 256
Motor Park, Inc., 87, 88, 120
Muchnick, Isidore, 62, 63
Mullins, William E., 87
Mumford, Lewis, 71, 109, 110
Municipal Research Bureau. *See* Boston Municipal Research Bureau
Murphy, Dr. Albert, 57
Murphy, "Spider," 24
Musco, Louis, 62
Museum of Fine Arts, 7, 186
Mystic River Bridge, 116

Nathanson, Louis N., 171
National Association for the Advancement of Colored People (NAACP), 57, 207, 237, 239, 261
National League of Cities, 172
National Municipal League, 50, 63
National Shawmut Bank, 204
Neighborhood schools, 262
Neighborhood Services Department, 257
Neighborhoods, 35, 266, 292, 293, 295
Neighbors of Government Center, 275
Netch, Walter, 320*n*6
New Bedford, 144, 245
"New Boston," 3, 34, 35, 66, 68, 111,

148, 149, 178, 203, 204, 208, 212,
    214, 237, 253, 256, 258, 264,
    266, 280–84, 289, 290–91, 292
    (illus.), 296
New Boston Committee (NBC), 52,
    54–57, 61–65, 77
*New Boston–1915*, 70
New Deal, 59, 131, 189, 287
New England Aquarium, 279
New England Merchants National
    Bank, 204
New England Mutual Hall, 56
New England Mutual Life Insurance
    Company, 47, 97, 186
New England Opera Company, 214
New England Patriots, 104
New England Telephone Company, 4,
    127, 147, 204
New Haven, Connecticut, 74, 173,
    188, 194, 196, 258, 260, 286, 289
New Haven Railroad, 15, 84, 115
New York, 110, 132, 195, 258, 262
New York Central Railroad, 15,
    98, 121
New York Streets section, 76 (illus.),
    106, 124, 125, 127, 145, 173, 225,
    231, 288
Newark, New Jersey, 100, 238, 250
Newspaper Row, 6
Newspapers, 172
Newton, 97
"Nigger Hill," 57
Ninety-Million Dollar Development
    Program for Boston, 190, 197, 214
Nixon, Richard M., 296
Nolan, Martin, 241–42
North Dorchester, 60, 231, 235, 237,
    255, 266
North End, 35, 53, 71, 84–86, 126,
    140, 151, 164, 206, 208, 211, 245,
    271, 279, 291, 293
North Harvard Street, 219
North Harvard Street Development
    Area, 224
North Shore, 82, 86

North Station, 48, 84, 125, 140
Norton, Clement, 62

Oakes, George F., 30, 47, 99, 100,
    312*n*19
O'Brien, Hugh, 42, 46
O'Brien, Thomas J., 51, 54
O'Brien, Walter A., 30
O'Connell, Cardinal William Henry,
    13, 14, 92, 93
O'Connor, Edwin, 24
O'Donnell, Kenneth, 241
O'Hare, Bill, 23
O'Hare, Jack, 23
O'Hare, Robert, 110
Old Colony housing project, 138, 218
Old Colony Line, 115
Old Corner Book Store, 204–5
Old Corner Committee, 205
Old Granary Burying Ground, 7, 48
Old Harbor Village housing project,
    218
Old Howard, 6, 95, 96, 141, 182, 199
Old Ironsides, 48
Old North Church, 47, 48
Old South Meetinghouse, 48, 195
Old State House, 48, 186, 201, 202
Old West Church, 137, 140 (illus.)
One, Two, Three Center Plaza, 204,
    321*n*51
O'Neill, Jack, 243
O'Neill, Thomas P. ("Tip"), 21, 22,
    24, 87
Open Housing Act (1968), 236
"Operation Revival," 162, 164, 240
O'Rourke, Kenny, 172
Otis, Harrison Gray, house, 137

Pappas, Tom, 26
Paramount Theater, 7
Parcel 8, 202, 204, 212
Park Street Church, 7
Parker, Stanley, 187
Parker House, 6, 164, 206, 267
Parkman, George F., 88
Parkman, Henry, 25, 31, 52

Parks, Paul, 236
Parks and recreation, 11, 57, 71, 163, 169
Parris, Alexander, 15, 16, 271, 277
Parrish, Ted, 238
Paul Revere house, 48
Peabody, Endicott ("Chub"), 110, 170, 210, 213, 241–47, 318n31
Pei, I. M., 185, 199, 201, 203, 204
Pemberton Square, 203
Peters, Andrew J., 40, 328n33
Peters, Malcolm, 37
Peterson, Paul, xiv
Philadelphia, 74, 186, 273, 282, 286
Piemonte, Gabriel, 57, 61, 63, 84, 151, 154, 155, 206, 208, 230, 322nn57, 61
*Pilot, The,* 217
Pittsburgh, 66, 74, 107–9, 148, 286
Pittsburgh Plate Glass Company, 107
Pittsburgh Renaissance, 74
Pittsfield, 91, 245
Plan A System, 28, 30, 51, 54, 55, 114, 214, 261
Plan E System, 28, 29, 50
Plymouth Theater, 7
Police commissioner, 169, 170
Polio, 117, 152, 154
Population, Boston, 35–36, 91, 147
Portuguese families, 231
"Power Politics," 157
Powers, John E., 87–88, 113–19, 144, 148, 150–51, 154–58, 159 (cartoon), 160, 164, 167–71, 176, 194, 206, 211, 217, 241, 244–46, 252, 288, 318n24
Progressive movement, 69
Protestants, 13, 42, 45, 92, 94
Provandie, Paul, 49
Prudential Center, 99, 100, 122, 123, 133, 145, 174–78, 182, 188, 203, 213–14, 225–27, 273, 281, 284, 288, 289, 319n56; tower, 178, 179 (illus.), 202
Prudential Insurance Company, 99–101, 121–23, 133, 150, 175–78, 191

Psychological reactions of displaced residents, 138–39
Public Garden. *See* Boston Public Garden
Public Works Department (state), 82, 84, 191
Puerto Rican community, 228, 231, 238, 295

Qua, Stanley E., 115
Quincy, 245
Quincy, Josiah, 3, 15, 16, 38, 68, 165, 271, 277
Quincy Market Building, 15, 16 (illus.), 272, 274, 277, 278 (illus.), 279, 280, 296
Quinn, Robert, 164, 170, 172, 263

RKO Keith's Theater, 7
Rabb, Sidney, 97, 186
Racial conflict, 197, 198, 261
Racial Imbalance Act, 1965, 239
Radcliffe Choral Society, 214
Railroads, 9, 15, 34, 69, 191
Rallies, political, 32, 52
Rand, Stuart, 25, 47, 52, 57
Randolph, 231
Rappaport, Jerome L., 26, 50–52, 56, 63–65, 122, 132–35, 141, 183, 184, 203, 293, 315nn48, 49
Rapson, Ralph, 320n6
Raymond's, 6, 72
Raymor-Playmor Ballroom, 59
Raytheon Corporation, 19, 74, 121
Redgate, Bernard, 324nn27, 29
Redgate, Marjorie, 324nn27, 29
Register of Probate, 154
Reilly, William A., 48
Reorganization Act of 1949, 50
*Report of a Thoroughfare Plan for Boston,* 82
Revere, 118, 169
Revere, Paul, house, 48
Rezendes, Michael, 264
Richardson, Elliott, 247
Ringside Café, 158

Ritz Carlton Hotel, 6, 267
Rockefeller, Nelson, 74, 258
Rockefeller Center, 100
Rogers, Chandler, 86
Rogers, Edith Nourse, 183
Rollins, Bryant, 236, 239
Roosevelt, Eleanor, 18
Roosevelt, Franklin Delano, 59, 154, 189, 287
Ropes and Gray, 19, 147
Roseland Ballroom, 59
Roslindale, 246
*Rough Road to Renaissance*, xiv
Rouse, James, 273–77, 279, 281, 297
Route 128, 19, 73, 81, 288
Roxbury, 9, 29, 59, 60, 62, 145, 152, 167, 190, 196, 212, 224, 231–39, 250, 255, 266, 291, 294
Roxbury Multi-Service Center, 238
Rubin, Morton, 233
Ryan, Robert, 103, 120, 127

Saint-Gaudens, Augustus, 180
Saint Anthony's Church, 200
Saint Brendan's Church, 40
Saint Catherine's Church, 217–18
Saint Coletta's School, 93
Saint Francis de Sales Church, 218
Saint Gregory's Church, 37
Saint John's Seminary, 217
Saint Joseph's Church, 128, 137
Saint Mary's Church, 218
Saint Matthew's Cathedral, 209
Saint Peter's Church, 96
Sales tax, 78, 144, 155, 156, 169, 170, 211
Saltonstall, Leverett, 48, 71, 211, 241
Sargent, Francis W., 247, 269
Saunders, Mary, 57
Save Boston Business Committee, 84
Save the West End Committee, 135, 136
Scagnoli, Henry, 153
Schabert, Tilo, 275
Schofield, William, 47, 48
School Street, 143

Scollay Square, xii, 6, 15, 72, 95, 96, 140–42, 164, 182–84, 198 (illus.), 199, 203, 214, 285, 289
Scott, Wilfred, 237
Sears, David, 199
Sears, John, 253, 259, 260
Sears Crescent, 199, 200, 201, 204
Sears, Roebuck Company, 64
Segregation, 207, 239, 261
Self-Help Organization–Charlestown (SHOC), 219
Senate, United States, 241, 243, 246
Shanks, Carroll, 100, 101, 121, 123
Shattuck, Henry, 25, 29, 52, 57, 156, 259
Shaw, Robert Gould, 180
Shawmut Bank, 204
Shawmut Peninsula, 86
Shea, Bob, 23
Sheehan, Frank, 23
Sheraton Corporation, 202, 257
Sheraton Plaza Hotel, 100, 121, 193, 252, 267
Shipping, xi, 8, 9, 15, 34, 69
Shoolman, Theodore, 131, 132
Shoolman and Bonan, 315*n*48
Shopping malls, 274, 281
Shubert Theater, 7
Simonian, Kane, 47, 127, 129, 134, 144, 192, 194, 196, 200, 314*n*34, 321*n*35
Sinnott, Richard, 243
Slade's Restaurant, 58
Slavet, Joseph F., 43, 90, 91, 118, 171, 173, 317*n*13
Slum clearance, 66, 111, 124, 131, 191
Smith, Edward, 317*n*13
Smith, Fred, 176
Snowden, Muriel, 57, 58 (illus.), 224, 235
Snowden, Otto, 57, 58 (illus.), 224, 235
Society of Military Engineers, 187
Soloway, Arnold, 194, 317*n*13
Somerville, 138, 199, 247

South Boston, 11, 29, 35, 40, 52, 62, 63, 67, 93, 94, 113, 123, 138, 151, 159, 167, 189, 206, 207, 215, 216, 218, 231, 235, 254, 261, 263, 291, 293

South End, 26, 49, 58–60, 76 (illus.), 93, 97, 106, 123–26, 134, 145, 173, 189, 196, 224–38, 266, 288, 291, 294, 296, 325n55; Businessmen's Association, 227; Neighborhood Conservation and Rehabilitation Committee, 227; Planning Council, 227; Tenants' Council, 238; Urban Renewal Committee (URC), 227, 229

South Shore, 82, 86

South Station, 84, 258, 279

Southeast Corridor, 235

Southeast Expressway, 119, 293

Special Development District, 215

Springfield, 91, 245

Stahl, Frederick A., 272

State Board of Education, 239

State House, xiii, 7, 68, 90, 171, 180, 186, 264, 285

State legislature. *See* General Court of Massachusetts

State Street, 72, 101, 201

State Street Bank and Trust, 4, 48, 204

State Supreme Judicial Court, 88, 102, 123, 175, 177, 191

Statler Hotel, 6

Stearn's, R. H., 6

Steel strike (1952), 83

Steele, Julian, 237

Stevens, Roger, 100, 101, 120, 121, 123

Stevenson, Adlai, 80

Stock market crash (1929), 8, 9

Stockton, Philip, 12

Stone, Edward Durell, 187

Stop & Shop, Inc., 97, 186

Storrow, James Jackson, 101

Straus, Nathan, 125

Students for Hynes, 277

*Style versus Substance*, 280

Suburbs, 35, 67, 79

Subways, 11

Sudbury Street, 143

Suffolk County, 118, 154, 169, 181, 244, 247; courthouse, 4, 203

Suffolk University, 26; Law School, 40, 152

Sullivan, Edward T., 267

Sullivan, Leo J., 169

Sullivan, Patrick, 61

Sullivan, William H., 97, 103

Sullivan Square, 189

"Summerthing," 268

Supreme Court of the United States, 60, 83, 239

Swampscott, 217

Symphony Hall, 4, 9, 37, 59, 115, 117, 161, 210, 266

Syrian community, 228

Tall Ships, 281, 282

Taunton, 245

Tavern Club, 141, 295

Tax abatements, 98, 101, 106, 121, 122, 145, 155, 175, 191, 287

Tax rate, 12, 37, 43, 77, 78, 107, 241, 251

Taylor, Balcom ("Bal"), 59

Taylor, John I., 21

Taylor, Ralph, 51

Taylor, Silas F. ("Shag"), 49, 59

Teaford, Jon, xiv, 72, 285, 317n82

Teamsters, 217

Teele, Stanley, 147

Television, 79, 154, 172

"Tent City," 238, 326n68

Textile industry, xi, 3, 8

Thompson, Benjamin, 272–74, 276, 281, 297

Thompson, John F., 170, 176

Tierney, John, 207, 243

Timilty, Joseph F., 51, 52, 54, 78

Tobin, Maurice, xiv, 17–22, 25, 26, 31, 39, 44, 61, 71, 78, 80, 87, 90, 303n17, 305n56

Tomasello, Joseph, 63

Touraine Hotel, 6
"Townies," 218, 219
Traffic, 14, 15, 37, 55, 69, 71, 83, 86, 112
Traffic commissioner, 169
Transportation system, 9, 14, 34
Troy, Jerome, 63
*True and Only Heaven*, 216
Truman, Harry S, 18, 22, 37, 50, 83, 305*n*56
Tufts New England Medical Center, 225
Tufts University, 26
Turley, Joseph H., 110, 313*n*41
Twelfth Baptist Church, 49

Umana, Mario, 25
Unemployment, 9, 10
United Community Construction Workers, 236
United Fruit, 15
United Shoe Machinery Building, 4, 85 (illus.)
United South End Settlements (USES), 227
United States Chamber of Commerce, 249
United States Conference of Mayors, 148
United States Fish and Wildlife Service, 110
University of California Architectural School, 187
University of California, Berkeley, 249
Urban Land Institute, 127
Urban League, 57, 236
Urban Renewal Administration, 195
*Urban Villagers, The*, 125, 128

Vahey, Edith, 183, 184
Van Arkel and Moss, 273
Vault, the, xiii, 147, 166, 167, 173, 192, 196, 197, 289
Vendôme Hotel, 6
Veterans Administration, 127
Vietnam War, 240, 243, 250, 256

Volpe, John, 84, 170, 213, 242, 244, 259
Voting Rights Act, 1965, 236

WEEI-Radio, 240
WGBH-TV, 110, 111
Walker, David, 195
Walpole State Prison, 93
Walsh, David I., 13
War Memorial Auditorium, 202, 213, 214, 244, 281, 289
Ward, Joseph, 144
Ward, Michael, 62, 63
Washington, D.C., 142, 143, 182, 183, 250
Washington Park, 231
Washington Street, 143
Waterfront area, 3, 5, 15, 34, 75, 193, 214, 270, 274, 291
Watts riots, 238, 250
Wayside Inn, 48
Weaver, Robert, 239
Webb, Roger S., 272, 274, 275, 276
Weems, Reginald, 60
Weinberg, Norman, 91
Welter, Becker, and Associates, 203
West End, xii, 11, 71, 86, 122–40, 183–84, 189, 199, 216, 226, 228, 316*n*65
West End Project, 126, 128, 129 (illus.), 133–34, 136 (illus.), 137, 139 (illus.), 140 (illus.), 141, 145, 174, 203, 227, 233, 235, 273, 284–85, 288, 315*nn*48, 49, 319*n*53
West Roxbury, 11, 291
West Stockbridge, 81
Westfield, 91
Weston, 81, 176
Weymouth, 245
White, Donald J., 111
White, Erskine, 147
White, Joseph, 61, 63
White, Kathryn, 266
White, Kevin H., 263 (illus.), 268 (illus.), 270–71, 296–98; and bicentennial celebrations, 282–83;

early life and career, 262; and
Faneuil Hall project, 271–79;
inauguration (first), 266–67; and
new City Hall, 269–70; 1967
mayoral candidacy and campaign,
235–36, 257, 259–61, 262–63
Whitehill, Walter Muir, 68, 139, 186,
193, 200, 204, 277
White's, R. H., 97
Whitney Street housing project, 145
Whitten, Robert, 82, 83
Wilbur Theater, 7
Wilkins, Raymond S., 161
Williams, Archbishop John J., 13
Williams College, 262
Winn, Robert, 47, 48

Winship, Thomas, 196
Winthrop, John, 118, 169
Worcester, 91, 245
Worcester County, 244
World Exposition (1915), 70
World Trade Center, 107, 112
World War I, 70
World War II, 3, 17, 18, 26, 34, 35,
41, 43, 44, 60, 62, 66, 72, 79, 80,
82, 92, 93, 104, 126, 127, 131, 138,
146, 152, 189, 196, 271, 275, 285
Wurster, William W., 187, 320*n*6

Young Democrats of Massachusetts, 63

Zerman Realty, 315*n*48